COMMUNICATION VIA SATELLITE: A VISION IN RETROSPECT

VIA SATELLITE:

POLICY ISSUES IN SATELLITE APPLICATIONS 1

A series of policy studies exploring the international legal, political and social aspects of satellite applications.

COMMUNICATION VIA SATELLITE

A Vision in Retrospect

DELBERT D. SMITH

A.W. SIJTHOFF – LEYDEN
A. W. SIJTHOFF – BOSTON, MASS.
1976

Library of Congress Cataloging in Publication Data

Smith, Delbert D
Communication via satellite

(Via satellite; 1)
Bibliography: p.
Includes index
1. Artificial satellites in telecommunications
I. Title. II Series
HE9719.S55 384.54'56 76-44905
ISBN 90-286-0296-8

ISBN 90 286 0296 8

Printed in The Netherlands.

For giving it meaning

. . . to my mother

. . . the memory of my father

. . . mary margaret, melissa and arianna

Every year if not every day
we wager our salvation
upon some prophecy
based upon imperfect knowledge.

Oliver Wendell Holmes

FOREWORD

One of the key themes of *Communication Via Satellite* is the role of visions and dreams in the development of satellite communication. To those of us who strived to realize the multifarious capabilities of communication satellites, the future at times seemed indeed to be more a dream than a reality. The technical and institutional barriers seemed occasionally to block the vision of a global communication satellite network. Sometimes the fate of the vision hung in the balance of a single person or a single decision. But communications satellites were born in an era in which innovation and risk-taking were recognized as necessary. The world had been shocked by Sputnik I and a Russian's first flight in space. The mood of the United States was positive toward reestablishing our image of technological superiority. Thus, even though these were obstacles, the general attitudes permitted a somewhat speculative development.

The implementation of operational communication satellite systems has been the fulfillment of one of our dreams. Several conclusions have been drawn from the technological achievement of communication by satellite. The capability of government, and in particular of NASA, to dramatically advance technology is past debate. That public benefit has been and can be a result of a government research and development program has also been established. What has not been identified in the historical sequence is the meaning of the developmental process for the role of government – both present and future – in regard to new technologies and the rise of technologies already developed.

Dr. Smith's study is eminently useful in this regard. *Communication Via Satellite* embodies his concern with the legal, social, and political implications of the development of satellite communication. The framework of technology integration, described in the Introduction and Conclusion, is uniquely appropriate for conceptualizing

NASA's part in the communication satellite story. Communication satellites are the product of a series of events which involve interrelated technical, political, and institutional factors. The book encompasses all of these in a unified picture to enhance public understanding of these events.

While *Communication Via Satellite* aims primarily at conceptual analysis, several conclusions of the analysis are worth enlarging. The study implies at the minimum that the federal role in technology development and applications must expand if technical innovation is to flourish. Particular attention must be given to the diffusion of technologies, and to the education of ultimate users of the technology. NASA, largely through its Office of Applications, has followed closely the histories of the integration of satellite technology into society. Future development of technology will require critical review of the patterns rehearsed in the implementation of commercial communication satellites.

Communication Via Satellite is a welcome addition to resources available to policymakers at the juncture of high technology and federal policy planning. Dr. Smith has served as a consultant to the Office of Applications in recent years, and has been a participant as well as an observer in social and commercial integration of satellite technology. The book reflects a practical concern with the issues as well as a scholar's ability to relate immediate problems to larger contexts. It is hoped that his work foreshadows a new attention to the problems raised by the social and commercial applications of communication satellites.

It is also hoped that the communications satellite story will in some way encourage us to reexamine our current overpreoccupation with the doctrines of relevance and costs and benefits where large technical innovation is possible, for where social change may result from such innovation sufficient experience rarely exists with which one can predict the future.

Leonard Jaffe
Deputy Associate Administrator for Applications
National Aeronautics and Space Administration
Washington, D.C.

PREFACE

The need and ability of people to communicate has been considered basic to the stability and development of societal structures. On the international level the "free flow of information" is argued to be a prerequisite to world peace and stability. Domestically, the effectiveness of a national communications system is said to shape social and political views, and to some the medium even becomes the message. Both mass communication systems and interpersonal systems are protected by laws and administrative regulations to ensure the validity of the process. The delivery systems for communication activities have undergone developmental changes over the years as new technologies have become operational. Huge industrial complexes have grown up as high technology has come to play a greater and greater role in the communications process. The developmental process is a continuing one where advances in technology impact the social and institutional concerns with communication. It has been argued that there will be a major communications crisis by the 1980s unless more is done to further technological innovation and application to meet the present and projected needs of the ever-increasing numbers of users. The paradox here is that to the user the technological system by which the process of communication is accomplished is immaterial; the technology is transparent. To the communications policy planner, however, the choice of the technology is paramount since it carries with it functional, cost-effective, political and social overtones. Thus it is that this volume focuses on a retrospective technology assessment of the communication satellite.

The satellite as a basic delivery system provides an example of a technological development that has done more than improve a given and existing means of communication. It has opened new realities which were evaluated during a relatively short time period of 1945 to 1976 and will continue on into the future. During this time period various public and private groups and individuals participated in a very sophisticated series of interactions. To the extent that these interactions, when looked at in retrospect, can be modeled and used prescriptively as determinative criteria for future policy choices regarding communication satellites, a benefit will have been provided. To the extent that other areas of satellite applications can be modeled, a double benefit will have been obtained.

Both the dreams of the past and the dreams of the future have made a contribution to the present reality of satellite communications. The fulfillment of these dreams, found in the application of technological innovation to the field of communications, has not ocurred in exactly the manner envisioned by the dreamers, however. The realities of federal communication policies, national security considerations, administrative agency creation and development, executive office policies, and the needs and concerns of user groups all condition and shape the development of communications via satellite. The problem is to understand the reality of this developmental process in order to optimize the interactions and facilitate the basic transfer from dream to reality and on to future dreams.

This is the basic idea of "a vision in retrospect" as used in the title of this book. It is an attempt to suggest the relationship between the visionary aspects of communication satellite development and the need for a retrospective analysis of the complex interactions that comprise the process. Given the relatively short thirty-year time frame for the first iteration of the vision-to-reality process, and the likelihood that the next iteration will be within an even shorter time frame, an understanding of the forces and counterforces that drive the system development process becomes increasingly desirable. Once an assessment of the general process and the extraction of a prescriptive model are accomplished it will be possible to reapply the model to the continuing process.

A study such as this, necessitating the analysis of primary documents and reports, together with an intensive interview schedule involving persons and organizations who are still actively engaged in the development and application of communication satellites, requires both a staff of knowledgable researchers and the cooperation of a large number of persons in responsible positions to provide the source material and personal insights.

The general encouragement of NASA and the specific support, advice and counsel of Charles W. Mathews, Associate Administrator, Office of Applications, who from the very outset, through his constant concern for my own freedom in planning and writing this book and by providing me the opportunity to experience the reality of NASA as an operational entity full of complexities and imperatives, has been of immeasurable assistance. In a real sense this volume is a product of a team research activity involving a major effort on the part of Patricia Kolb together with Christopher Swift, Kem Luther, Fred Beatty, and Sharon Strover. This volume grew out of research undertaken on behalf of the Office of Applications of NASA, a basic concern with an understanding of technology transfer in direct relation to communication satellites, and a realization that the domestic and international institutional legal problems of communication satellites may well hinder the application of the technology if not dealt with properly. The text of this book in no way reflects the official policy or positions of the National Aeronautics and Space Administration.

Major support and documentation as well as personal commentary were provided by Leonard Jaffe, Deputy Associate Administrator, NASA Office of Applications; S. Neil Hosenball, General Counsel, NASA; Arnold M. Frutkin, Assistant Administrator for International Affairs, NASA; Richard Marsten, Former Director of Communications Programs, NASA Office of Applications; Albert Christensen, Office of User Affairs, NASA Office of Applications; Robert Nunn, Former Special Assistant to the NASA Administrator; Walter Radius, Technical Coordinator for Communications, NASA Office of DOD and Interagency Affairs; and D.P. Rogers, NASA Office of Applications.

In addition, the following persons provided helpful critiques of initial drafts of some chapters of the manuscript: Stephen Doyle, Deputy Assistant Administrator, Office of International Affairs, NASA; Monte Wright, the Acting Director of the Historical Office, and Lee Saegesser, Archivist for the NASA Historical Archives, who made available special materials for background study; Robert Bernier, Manager of Special Projects, Comsat General; Richard Colino, Vice-President for International Relations and Corporate Planning; Comsat; John Briskman, Program Manager of Domestic Systems, Comsat General; and Daniel Fink, Vice-President and General Manager, Space Division, General Electric Company. The NASA Headquarters Library and its special staff were also helpful in finding needed documents.

For times past and continuing counsel I am indebted to Professor R.Y. Jennings, Whewell Professor of International Law, Jesus College, and President D.W. Bowett, Queens' College, Cambridge University, England.

I acknowledge with gratitude the competent assistance of Debra Simon who together with Vicky Metzel and Vicky Lucas dealt with the difficult secretarial tasks.

For their imagination and belief in this subject area I am indebted to the officers of A.W. Sijthoff Press; particularly I acknowledge my debt to Mr. J.H.Landwehr for his understanding and friendship and to Mr. Peter Dijkstra for his interest in the project. Once again special appreciation goes to F.B.C. of Cambridge.

Madison
December 21, 1975

D.D. Smith

CONTENTS

LIST OF ACRONYMS AND ABBREVATIONS

AAF	Army Air Force
ABC	American Broadcasting Company
AEC	Atomic Energy Commission
ARPA	Advanced Research Projects Agency
ASC	American Satellite Corporation
ASIL	American Society of International Law
ATS	Applications Technology Satellite
AT&T	American Telephone and Telegraph
BNSC	Broadcasters Non-Profit Satellite Corporation
BuAer	Navy Bureau of Aeronautics
CATV	Cable Television
CBS	Columbia Broadcasting System
CCB	Common Carrier Bureau
CEPT	Conference of Post and Telecommunications Administrations
Comsat	Communications Satellite Corporation
CPB	Corporation for Public Broadcasting
CPUOS	Committee on the Peaceful Uses of Outer Space
DOD	Department of Defense
EARC	Extraordinary Administrative Radio Conference
ECSC	European Conference on Satellite Communications
EIA	Electronics Industries Association
ESRO	European Space Research Organization
FCC	Federal Communications Commission
GE	General Electric
GTE	General Telephone and Electronics
HET	Health/Education Telecommunications
HATV	High-Altitude Test Vehicle
IARC	International Administrative Radio Conference
IBM	International Business Machines
ICBM	Intercontinental Ballistic Missile

ICSC	Interim Communications Satellite Committee
IFRB	International Frequency Registration Board
I.G.Y.	Internation Geophysical Year
Intelsat	International Telecommunications Satellite Organization
ITT	International Telephone and Telegraph
ITU	International Telecommunication Union
IWG	Intersessional Working Group
MTT	Message Toll Telephone
NACA	National Advisory Committee on Aeronautics
NASA	National Aeronautics and Space Administration
NBC	National Broadcasting Company
NET	National Educational Television
OSSA	Office of Space Science and Applications
OTP	Office of Telecommunications Policy
PSSC	Public Service Satellite Consortium
RCA	Radio Corporation of America
SITE	Satellite Instructional Television Experiment
STD	Satellite Technology Demonstration
STI	Space Technology Integration
TI	Technology Integration
UNESCO	United Nations Educational, Scientific and Cultural Organization
USAF	United States Air Force
WARC-ST	World Administrative Radio Conference for Space Telecommunications

INTRODUCTION

In this volume the strategy of communications satellite development is traced from its origins to the present. While the need exists for a study of this development per se, the purpose of this work goes beyond the activity of chronicling to an interpretational perspective. Studying the movement toward satellite communications in its institutional, legal and social context will, it is hoped, throw light on an emerging governmental role in technological society. The key term in this regard for the present study is *technology integration*. Events in the U.S. and Western Europe in the post-World War II era have precipitated a new social situation in the field of technology advancement. The term *technology integration* refers to a complex legal, economic and social process which is unique in the context of government-industry relationships.*

Defining Technology Integration

Although this study is concerned with one specific example of technology integration, it is the *prime* example since the parameters of the process have been defined by it. The course of this work has been dominated by the need to develop a theoretical framework around the developmental process of satellite communication which will put it in a functional perspective. This framework will be developed in more detail later in this chapter and in the Conclusion. At this point the immediate need is to acquaint the reader with the phenomenon of modern government participation in technology development and integration and to describe briefly the social forces which make it both a reality and a necessity.

Some of the social forces which have contributed to the emergence

* The concept and terminology have been created specifically for this study.

of technology integration as a distinct governmental process will shortly be examined. First, however, the phenomenon itself needs to be defined and described. As the term is used in this volume, *technology integration (TI)* will designate *the process whereby government manages the development, testing and application of new technologies such that the final result is an economically or socially useful application of technological innovation.*

This new role for the federal government has become apparent in the United States only in recent years. As the concept is used in this book, TI does not refer to every level of technology development. It refers to the large-scale, systematically developed technologies arising from the unique government/industry research relationships established during the last half-century. Space, defence, medicine, transportation and earth resources programs have been in the forefront of the movement. The culmination of this new governmental role is found, as was mentioned, in its clearest instance in the case of satellite communications. Modern government has found itself exceeding its traditional role as a passive regulator of technological innovation; it has become a manager of technology for the good of the public.

To describe TI adequately requires consideration of two recent and interrelated developments in the U.S. policy toward the growth of technology. The first is the emergence of government-sponsored research, and the second is the resultant practice of technology assessment. After considering these two developments, an attempt will be made to describe the parameters of TI in the context of the U.S. institutional framework.

Government Research

Scientific research has changed significantly in the last century. A hundred years ago the paradigm of scientific research was an economically self-sufficient scientist laboring with minimal laboratory facilities. For all their differences, the Englishman Charles Darwin in some ways bore more resemblance to the Greek Archimedes in his basic research procedures than to a modern American scientist in his well-equipped laboratory with access to sophisticated computers and multi-volume libraries. The key to the difference lies in modern government policies towards research and development. The government has made available vast amounts of public monies for basic research in the sciences, and in doing so has created its own technological establishment.

The portion of the U.S. federal budget devoted to research and development has increased tremendously since World War II. It is commonly estimated that two-thirds of all scientific research in this country is federally financed. The resultant use by an increasingly affluent society of the multitude of products and services resulting from current government-sponsored research has created the phenomenon commonly designated *technology transfer.* The process of technology transfer has been a recognized obligation of the U.S. government since the mid-sixties. The definition of technology transfer is now fairly well fixed. Technology transfer denotes "the process whereby technical information originating in one institutional setting is adopted for use in another institutional setting."[1] The term has been most often applied to the process of transferring government-funded research and development to private industry, to international groups, or to other federal agencies. The methods and mechanisms by which technology transfer is accomplished have been analyzed in some detail over the past decade.[2] This analysis has been more than an academic exercise; it has resulted in an improvement of the process of technology transfer. In some cases new government offices and programs have had significant input from the technology transfer discussions. The Office of Applications and the Technology Utilization Program of the National Aeronautics and Space Administration, for example, developed from the need to implement the transfer of technology.

The assumption by the U.S. government of the burden of supporting and conducting scientific research and the resulting transfer of research results has been a relatively recent phenomenon. The trend does not seem likely to reverse itself, given the present emphasis in the international arena on technological competition and the dependence of the private sector of the U.S. economy on the infusion of government-sponsored innovation for successful economic competition.

Technology Assessment

Growing out of government involvement in research is a second trend which both depends upon and has served as a check on the trend toward large government expenditures in research and development. *Technology assessment* and the more specific act of *technology forecasting* are the most well-known signals of this trend. In brief, technology assessment is the evaluation and control of technological advances. The need for technology assessment has occasioned in the U.S. Congress the introduction, over the last few years, of several bills calling for the establishment of an Office of Technology Assessment.[3] This action is the result of several factors. First, the unchecked expansion of technological innovations has been responsible for introducing to the public potentially deleterious items. By seeking to establish closer regulation of the flood of products resulting from newly-developed technologies, national governments have pursued implicitly, if not explicitly, the goals of preventative technology assessment. Second, the exponential growth of knowledge from open-ended scientific research has reached inundative proportions. The inability to index the vast accumulation of research data has contributed to directing scientific research into more user-oriented channels. The final instigating circumstance behind technology assessment, and the most tenuous of the three, is the generally-sensed need to gain some control over the potentially disruptive effects on the economy of unbridled technological innovation. Entire industries can find themselves outmoded within a year's time by a single technological advance. The response of technological assessment to this problem has been to develop methods of technological forecasting. Technological forecasting has been defined as "the probabilistic assessment, on a relatively high confidence level, of future technological transfer."[4] It seeks, within the confines of a general program of technology assessment, to gain some control over the unknown fact of human inventiveness. While the specific configuration and time frame of future technological developments is difficult to predict, technology forecasting has achieved some success in outlining probable advances in technology, and, as a consequence, has been able to exert some control over the possibility of surprise in technological advance.

Technology assessment is now a reality, even though it has not been centralized in the U.S. governmental structure. While some form of assessment has always accompanied technological innovation, the size and direction of assessment has lately been organized into unique modalities and has had a significant effect on the development of TI.

A Theory of Technology Integration

The trends toward greater investment in research and toward some kind of assessment of technological innovations combine in the process which is designated in this study *TI*. Although TI is a presently existing process, the theoretical framework for it remains largely undeveloped. Unfortunately, the theoretical framework created for the understanding and implementation of technology transfer is not totally relevant to technology integration. TI differs from technology transfer in its relationship to the act of technology assessment; technology transfer is a systematic response to large research efforts and, unlike TI, does not need a highly-developed notion of selective assessment to proceed. By way of example, the early efforts of NASA toward technology transfer were centered largely on information dissemination without specific selection procedures for determining user priority. TI, in contrast, depends upon a defined selection procedure being present in the transfer. TI stipulates that research done under government funding begin with select goals and end with the successful transferral of not only a theory, but also an identifiable procedure or a product to a predetermined user or group of users. In this regard the term *participatory technology* has also been employed, and shows even more clearly the divergence of the notion of TI from technology transfer. TI is concerned with the development and transfer of technology, to be sure, but it does this within a context of specific programs and goals. These goals in turn are specified from a perception of user needs, and the development of the technology involves user participation at several critical points along the developmental path. The participants in the technology integration process are the researchers, industries, and user groups who perceive the overall framework of user needs.

It is feasible to construct a model which is based on the recent experience of communication satellites and which would be applicable to future developments in other areas of technological advancement in the space sciences. While the detailed application of the model to other areas of government involvement in space science research is clearly beyond the scope of this book, it is part of the purpose of this volume to develop a rational model of the development of satellite communications. This model, which will be designated the *Space Technology Integration (STI) model,* will use the development of satellite communications as a case study. In the remainder of the Introduction a framework for the model and some of its more obvious ramifications will be briefly sketched. The framework will help to provide a generalized idea of what is meant by TI. In the Conclusion an effort will be made to define satellite communications as a paradigm case of the model, to develop the model, and to extend the implications of the model into future work on certain areas of satellite technology.

The Technology Integration Framework

Technology Flow

Selecting a framework for the space technology integration model is the most significant and at the same time the most difficult aspect of the model's development. TI, as it has been defined, is obviously a

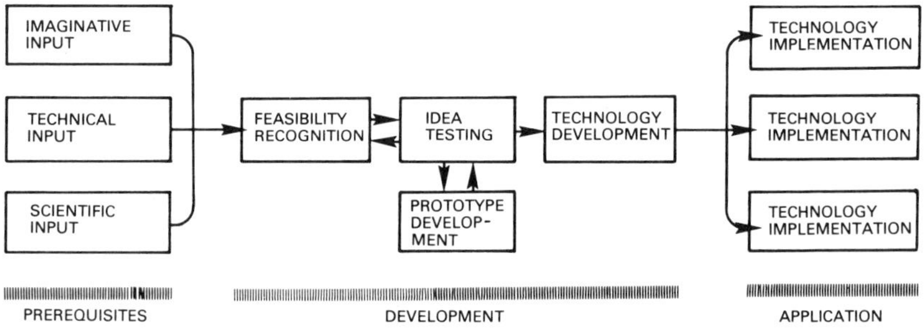

Figure # 1. Technology Flow in TI

complex procedure operating on many levels at once. The first prerequisite to developing a framework is to specify as broadly as possible the central technological flow of the TI process.

Figure 1 shows an abridged sketch of TI development in a logic flow chart. The chart indicates a few of the relationships which occur in TI. The first step, the recognition of feasibility, can have input from three major sources. The imaginative input can obviously come from several sectors of society. The influence of science fiction is a good example of how the literary sector of society can shape the course of technological innovation. The technical and scientific input comes from engineering and research sectors respectively.

Acknowledgment of the feasibility of a given technology is not necessarily a single, isolated step. It occurs in conjunction with and is corrected by a program of testing. If the tests and prototypes developed do in fact reinforce the original conception of feasibility, the developmental process moves into the actual production of the anticipated innovations. If the development encounters no unexpected difficulties it is then diffused into the general uses for which it was designed.

Government Management Spectrum

The framework in which technological movement occurs will be represented in the model by a two-dimensional axis. Vertical movement will signify an increase or decrease in government stimulation and regulation. It is labeled *government management spectrum* because the precise configuration of any stage of the technology flow depends upon its relationship to the stimulatory and regulatory modes of government interaction. Research and feasibility recognition in the TI process, for example, are more compatible with government protection and stimulation and are most likely to occur within the framework of government agencies or government-contracted research establishments, while the diffusion of a developed technology would probably be the province of a private agency under government regulation. Figure 2 shows some of the functions and modalities government might assume along the vertical spectrum.

Implementation Spectrum

The horizontal axis of the framework represents the general movement in TI from the recognition of a need which can be satisfied by technological innovation to the resultant use of that innovation to satisfy societal needs. The movement along the implementation spectrum is from abstract to concrete, from idea to hardware. The

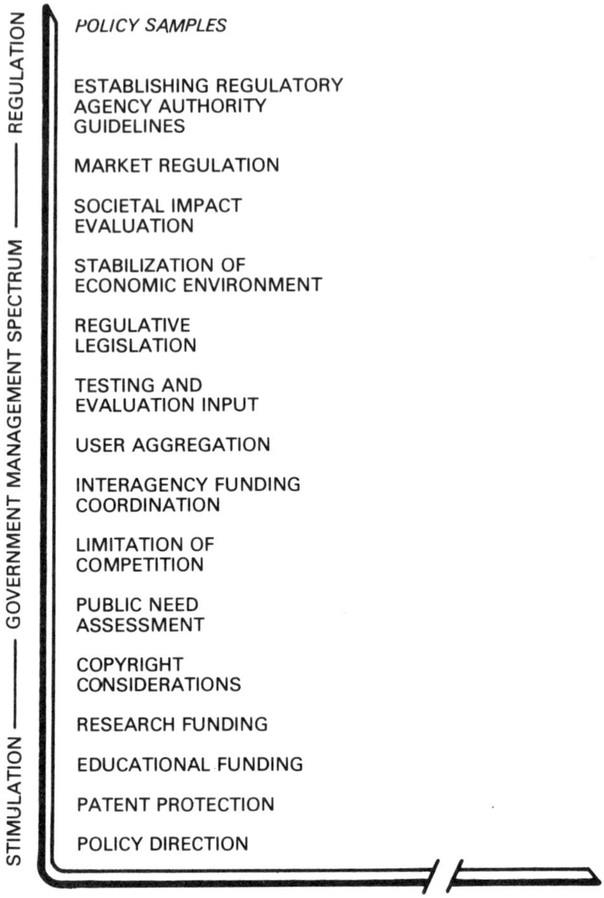

Figure # 2. Management Policy Scenario

stages of TI corresponding to the *need* are characterized by theories, projections and implementation plans, while the fulfillment of the need – the active use of the technology developed – is characterized by the embodiment of ideas in specific pieces of hardware.

In Figure 3 below, the horizontal axis of the framework is presented with examples of typical need-to-use functions.

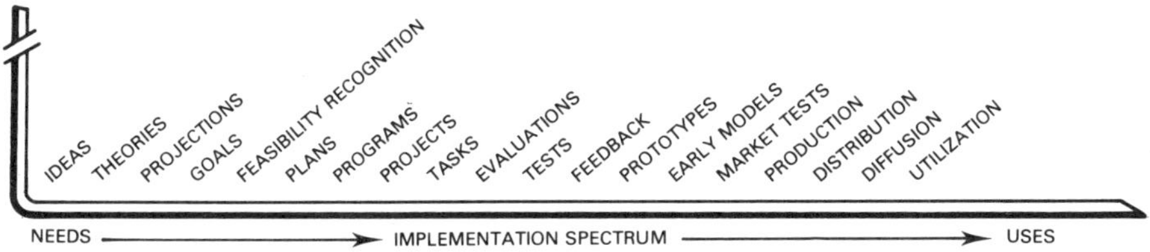

Figure # 3. Need-to-Use Scenario

A TI Framework

Once the framework is established it is possible to put the technological flow of TI together with the two-dimensional axes to produce a hypothetical framework of the generalized TI process. The integrated framework (Figure 4) is a visual representation of the modern process of TI. The technology flow has been placed within the two axes – government management and need-to-use – depicted in scenario form above. Even though not corresponding in detail to the scenario,

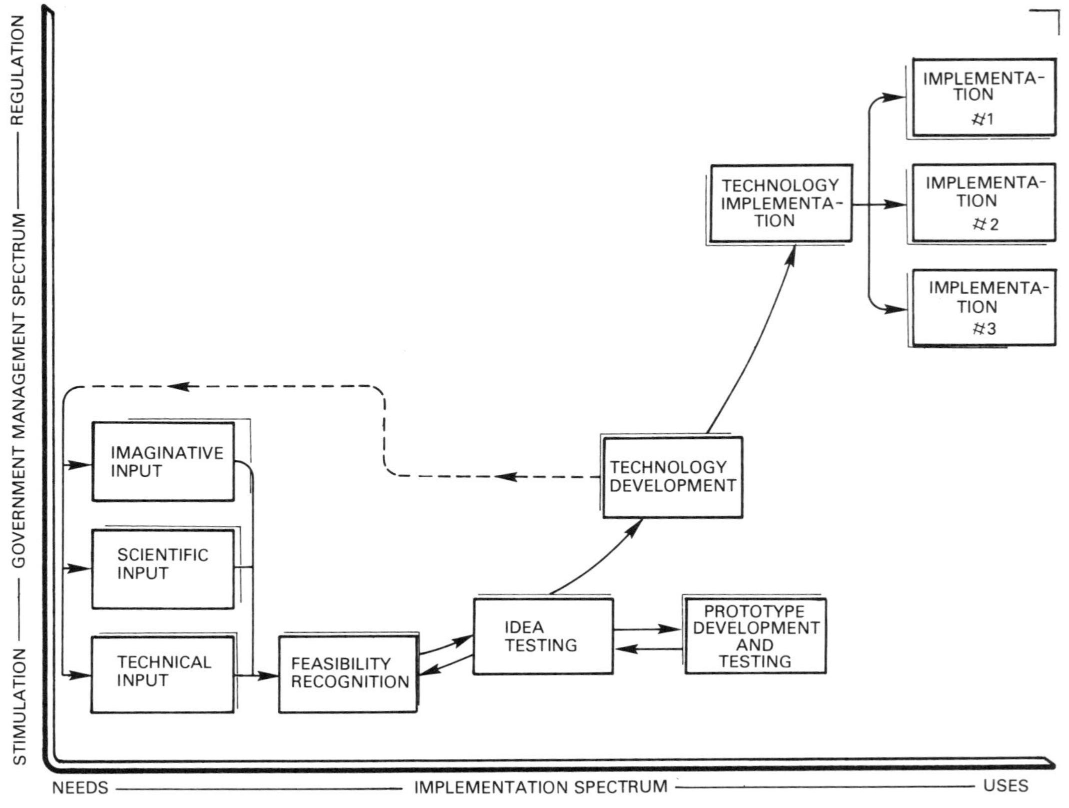

Figure # 4. TI Framework

movement along each axis is assumed to follow the general trends represented in Figures 2 and 3. This framework will be used in the Conclusion to develop a space technology integration model based on the development of satellite communications.

Notice that the regulation of the TI process is a function of the increasing diffusion of the technical hardware. Policy planning, accordingly, must take into account both the incompatibility of intense regulation with the stages of feasibility formulation and the conflict between research stimulation at the point of product diffusion. Examples of errors which might occur in this regard are (a) the introduction of a research breakthrough which antiquates the technical hardware at the point of the hardware's early economic struggles in the marketplace and (b) severe budgetary cutbacks on research and development without a corresponding adjustment of the completion time of the TI process.

The general flow of the TI process is away from government stimulation. This means that other motivational forces must be brought into play as the TI process proceeds. Policy planning needs to take this into account, and to aggregate economic and social forces which can assume the motivational burden at the appropriate points.

The dotted arrow on the framework notes the possibility of technology development instituting a new TI flow. Where funds are available for basic research and development, and where the scientific, technical and imaginative communities can combine to recognize the feasibility of a technological innovation, the process of TI is able to generate increasingly sophisticated stages of technological innovation.

These are only a few of the relationships suggested by the TI framework. In the Conclusion, a model will be elucidated for the specific instance of TI treated in this volume – the development of satellite communications – and a specific model of space TI will be formulated.

While the discussion of TI in this volume relies principally on the specific involvement of the U.S. federal government with aspects of the technology of satellite communications, the study of TI is not intended to be exclusively applicable to U.S. policy concerns. The concepts behind technology integration are international in their relevance; the interactions between governments and the process of technology development and application occur in the TI format wherever the development of a highly sophisticated technology is supported and controlled by a nation state. The conclusions of this study are also internationally applicable to the policy problems faced by modern nations in an increasingly technological world. Technology integration has indeed become a characteristic of modern government. The need for a more thorough understanding of it is vital to near- and far-term government planning. The ability to assess and manage technology for the public good will undoubtedly bear large returns to governments which are able to acquire the requisite capabilities.

Part I

STRATEGIES OF COMMUNICATION SATELLITE DEVELOPMENT

"The plan was this: If from the surface of the earth, by a gigantic pea-shooter, you could shoot a pea upward from Greenwich, aimed northward as well as upward; if you drove it so fast and far that when its power of ascent was exhausted, and it began to fall, it should clear the earth, and pass outside the North Pole; if you had given it sufficient power to get it half round the earth without touching, that pea would clear the earth forever. It would continue to rotate above the North Pole, above the Feejee Island place, above the South Pole and Greenwich, forever, with the impulse with which it had first cleared our atmosphere and attraction. . ."

"But a pea is so small!"

"Yes," said Q, "but we must make a large pea."

Edward Everett Hale
The Brick Moon, *1869*

1

PROLOGUE

The development of satellite communications is a rapidly changing reality connecting two sets of dreams. On the one side science fiction writers foresaw the possibility of using communication satellites for the improvement of modern communications. On the other side there is a current dream that satellite communications may lead to inexpensive and easily available modes of personal communications. Bridging these two sets of dreams is the present state of communications technology, where space systems are just beginning to remove the burden from overcrowded terrestrial communication networks.

The substance of the research contained in this volume lies in the region between the dreams. The present state of the art in satellite communications, however, is not unaffected by the pull of the future, just as the current level of technology responded in its turn to the subtle influences of past visions. In this chapter, accordingly, we will look at the two dreams in preparation for tracing the actual development of satellite communications.

Visions from the Past

The development of communication satellites began with individuals who first conceived and publicized the idea of using artificial bodies in space to relay communications. While the first fictional accounts of satellites and space communication bear little resemblance to technology as it exists today, they are not without significance since they represent the origins of the idea from which the technology eventually evolved. The earliest creative literary contributions tell us how the idea of satellite communications came into being and how it developed through varying degrees of technological sophistication.

The idea of an artificial satellite was first conceived in fiction by Boston clergyman, writer and editor, Edward Everett Hale. His notion of a "brick moon," a man-made body revolving around the earth, evolved from the "old chat and dreams, plans and jokes" of his college days at Cambridge in the 1830's.[1] The "Brick Moon" first appeared as a serial in the *Atlantic Monthly* in 1869 and 1870, and was later reprinted in an 1899 publication entitled *The Brick Moon and Other Stories.*

Hale's story concerned a group of scientific enthusiasts who planned to launch an artificial moon as a navigational aid to sailors. They built a moon large enough to be visible by telescope (200 feet in diameter), designed with a hollow center to reduce its weight and constructed of brick rather than iron in order to withstand the heat of friction during flight. The Brick Moon was to be launched into orbit by two gigantic water-powered flywheels. Shortly before the launch date, the moon was accidentally sent into orbit containing the thirty-seven workers, engineers, and their families, who had made their living quarters within the hollow chambers of the moon. It was two years before astronomers were able to calculate the Brick Moon's orbit and to observe it by telescope. Hale's storyteller, Captain Frederick Ingham, discovered that the inhabitants of the moon had survived the flight into space and were attempting to establish communications with earth. The first fictional account of communication via artificial satellite occurred when Ingham

> . . . counted on the edge [of the Brick Moon] thirty-seven specks arranged evidently in order, and, at one moment, as by one signal, all thirty-seven jumped into the air, – high jumps. Again they did it, and again. Then a low jump; then a high one. I caught the idea in a moment. They were telegraphing to our world in the hope of an observer. Long leaps and short leaps, – the long and short of Morse's Telegraph Alphabet, – were communicating ideas.[2]

Edward Everett Hale never intended the "Brick Moon" to be anything more than amusing fiction. When astronomer Asaph Hall discovered the two moons of Mars and referred to the smaller of the moons as "the veritable Brick Moon," Hale expressed pride in the recognition given by such a distinguished scientist to his "little parable."[3] He could never have anticipated that in the relatively short span of seventy-five years scientists would give the concept of an earth-orbiting communications satellite serious consideration; nor could he have conceived that in less than a century a commercial communications satellite system would relay voice and television signals across the globe via a network of technically sophisticated "brick moons."

In 1945, seventy-five years after Hale published the final installment of "Brick Moon," Arthur C. Clarke published an article in *Wireless World* proposing a worldwide communications satellite system. Clarke, a British electronics engineer, wrote his now historic paper in his spare time while serving as a Lieutenant in the British Royal Air Force. His paper, "Extraterrestrial Relays: Can Rocket Stations Give Worldwide Radio Coverage?", outlined the basic technical considerations involved in the concept of a communication satellite. Clarke proposed orbiting space stations which "could be provided with receiving and transmitting equipment and could act as a repeater to relay transmissions between any two points of the hemisphere beneath."[4] Calculating that at an altitude of 23,000 miles the station's orbit would coincide with the earth's rotation and remain fixed over one point on earth, he demonstrated that three such synchronous stations could provide worldwide communications coverage.

Others had hinted at the notion of a communication satellite prior to 1945. The noted German scientist and rocket expert, Hermann Oberth, proposed in 1923 that the crews of orbiting rockets could communicate with remote regions on earth by signaling with mirrors.[5] Between 1942 and 1943, *Astounding Science Fiction* published a series of articles by George O. Smith concerning an artificial planet, Venus Equilateral, which functioned as a relay station between Venus and Earth when direct communication was blocked by the sun. Clarke claims that his 1945 paper was not influenced by these earlier writings. He had not read Oberth's book, and although he admits to reading Smith's "Venus Equilateral" series, it did not consciously affect his work.[6] While claiming originality, Clarke also admits that, as is often the case with innovative ideas, if he had not proposed the idea in 1945 someone else would have done so by at least 1950: "The time was ripe and the concept inevitable; it was certainly bobbing around in the back of many ingenious minds."[7] In any case, with the exception of a Russian claim that Soviet scientists predated Clarke by theorizing in 1937 that television images could be relayed by bouncing them off of space vehicles, Arthur Clarke is generally credited with originating the modern concept of satellite communications.[8]

Other dreamers were also involved in early satellite communication plans. Clarke himself noted: "The people who deserve the real credit for communication satellites are those who converted my paper plans into hardware that will function flawlessly for months and years on end, thousand of miles above the Earth. I risked nothing except a few hours of my time, but others have risked their reputations."[9] The responsibility for developing the blueprints and hardware for communication satellites fell to other men. Prominent among them in the earliest days of satellite communications was John R. Pierce.

Pierce, as research director for Bell Laboratories, was a prime mover in the development of communication satellites. His first writings on the subject appeared in 1952, when, not yet willing to risk his reputation, he wrote under the pseudonym of J.J. Coupling in *Amazing Science Fiction* that communications with the moon and other planets were within reach of current technology. "The truth is," he wrote, "that you could order equipment for an Earth-Moon link from any of several manufacturers" and "granted a base on the moon, transatlantic television would be a snap rather than an almost insuperably difficult problem."[10]

By 1955, more confident that the scientific community was ready to accept his innovative ideas, Pierce dropped his pseudonym and began publishing persuasive technical articles under his own name. Among his most notable contributions to the early technical literature was a paper entitled "Orbital Radio Relays," which appeared in *Jet Propulsion* in April of 1955. This article proposed a detailed technical plan for passive communication satellites. It stated that "disregarding the feasibility of constructing and placing satellites" it would seem possible "to achieve broadband transoceanic communications with any one of three types of repeaters: spheres at low altitudes, a plane reflector, or an active repeater in a 24-hour orbit." [11] Pierce concluded his paper by urging other scientists to begin developing the technology necessary to construct rockets capable of launching communication satellites.

Pierce's initiative in promoting the idea of transoceanic satellite communication within the scientific and technical communities was an important factor in development of communication satellites. His career spanned the early developmental period; eventually he played a major role in the National Aeronautics and Space Administration's first passive communication satellite experiment, Project Echo. Together with Rudolf Kompfner, he invented the traveling wave tube, a wideband amplifier making the transmission of television signals via satellite feasible, and was instrumental in initiating American Telephone and Telegraph's (AT&T) Telstar satellite.

The technical development of communication satellites from

Clarke's first conception of the idea in 1945 to the first transatlantic transmission of television via Telstar did not occur in isolation. It coincided with and depended upon a series of parallel developments which merged to create a scientific and political atmosphere in which communication satellites could become a reality. One such parallel development was the emergence of related technologies. When Clarke proposed his plan in 1945, it was beyond the current technical state of the art. In the decade and a half following 1945, however, a number of technical breakthroughs made communication satellites feasible. In 1946, for example, researchers developed the transistor. Prior to its invention, electronics had depended upon bulky vacuum tubes. The transistor and miniaturized electronic components provided the light weight electrical systems vital to satellites. High-powered rockets with propulsion systems capable of delivering satellites into high-altitude orbits emerged from the U.S.-U.S.S.R. race to develop long-range intercontinental ballistic missiles. New high-speed computers solved the gigantic task of calculating and tracking orbits and the invention of solar cells provided a sustained energy source for the satellite. Such developments were the *sine qua non* of communication satellites.

The transformation of communication satellites from blueprint to hardware, however, depended on more than the mere emergence of technical know-how; it needed government support in the form of substantial financial commitments to research and development. By 1958, with the establishment of the National Aeronautics and Space Administration and the formulation of a national space program, such support was forthcoming. In the period from 1945 to 1958, however, the emerging U.S. rocketry and satellite programs on which the development of communication satellites hinged experienced a number of false starts and setbacks. Nevertheless, throughout the period gradual progress was made in both the military and scientific establishments. When the 1957 Soviet launch of Sputnik I finally shocked the U.S. into picking up the pieces of its fragmented space efforts, its scientists quickly made substantial progress in all facets of space activity including the communication satellite field.

Visions of the Future

In an area which has proved in the past to be responsive to imaginative dreaming it is not surprising to find that visions play a present role in determining the direction of technological innovations. No one can know exactly what technical or social configurations satellite communications may bring about in the future, but broad scenarios can be forecast which may approximate future developments.

It is possible to envision a future filled with a myriad of socially valuable services which could be provided via satellite. In the field of education the trend today is toward individualized learning made possible by technological developments such as computer-aided instruction and computer-managed instruction. Experiments are already underway to test the feasibility of using satellites for highly individualized and computerized educational programming. Other areas of future educational activity include the use of sophisticated information transfer systems to interconnect universities on regional, national and international base. Inter-library sharing offers capabilities for remote browsing, information retrieval and document delivery. An interconnected cable TV-satellite system could provide a means of creating home education utilities offering a wide choice of specified educational services, including computer-aided and -managed instruction, extension adult education courses, library access and continuing professional educational programming.

In the field of medicine and health care delivery, medical teleconferencing could expand the scope of existing medical schools, provide a means for continuing professional medical education, and provide paramedical personnel with the information necessary to undertake many services in the area of preventive medicine. Biomedical information networks could provide medical personnel with access to data banks with remote browsing, information retrieval and user response capabilites. In addition, the system could link hospitals, medical schools, clinics and medical libraries to provide services such as computer-assisted diagnoses, inventory control, patient record keeping with store-and-forward capabilities and instantaneous transmission of diagnostic tests and X-ray results. Satellite systems for remote monitoring and telediagnosis could enable physicians in central medical centers to monitor and diagnose patients in isolated areas.

Information transfer systems could also provide specialized business services. Satellite communication technology has many potential applications to corporate operations, banking and finance. In view of the trend toward merger, conglomeration and multinationalism in business, there is a need for sophisticated telecommunication systems to bring together widely scattered business operations with key decision makers. Future teleprocessing needs will lead to increased accessibility of teleprocessing services to small business organizations, the development of computer-to-computer links, the development of low-cost mini-computers and sophisticated input/output terminals including portable terminals, picture phones, light pens, and the improvement of data processing services and facilities.

In the field of banking and finance, future communication satellite applications include the creation of a "checkless society" through the development of an electronic payment system, the electronic transfer of stocks and securities, and the development of a sophisticated information transfer system providing services such as security quotations transfer, credit verification and automatic check clearance.

In addition to using advanced telecommunication and teleprocessing techniques to facilitate communication between widely-separated office and business centers, another area of satellite application lies in the substitution of communication for transportation to business. The use of home and neighborhood communication centers could possibly eliminate the need to travel to urban offices, and consequently help to eliminate traffic congestion in urban areas, and to control the energy drain and pollution problem resulting from auto travel.

Just as in private corporations, efficiency in government operations could increase as a result of the application of sophisticated information transfer systems. A satellite-based federal teleconferencing system could provide improved communication links and eliminate the need for routine government travel. Another area of government service which merits special attention is electronic mail delivery. As mail volume increases, the present antiquated methods of handling and delivery become less adequate. In the future, satellite transmission of mail and the use of cable television as the vehicle for bringing mail delivery into private homes may provide some solutions.

Prediction becomes even more uncertain as the time frame expands. One can imagine, if not foresee, a future where communication satellites are able to interconnect portable units which anyone could wear, giving instant access to any other person or groups on earth to those knowing the right coding sequences. Data banks might make available a vast amount of information to persons familiar with indexing formats. Business travel might be reduced nearly to the point of nonexistence by home office terminals.

Existing communications satellite technology is already capable of providing direct television signal transmission from a geosynchronous satellite to small, relatively inexpensive home or community receivers. Implementation of direct broadcast satellite systems will alter not only the traditional configuration of distribution systems, but also the character and content of the television programming.

Distribution of television signals via satellite has a number of technological advantages. A large number of countries, especially those in the Third World, have not been able to construct extensive terrestrial distribution networks because impassable terrain, remote or isolated populations and excessive costs have made traditional networks economically infeasible.

A direct consequence of this larger and more diverse audience will be a change in programming content and character. Different cultures will have different programming needs and expectations. Programming will have to be designed with specific target audiences in mind.

Direct broadcast technology could contribute to significant economic and social developments in the Third World, primarily through the use of educational programming. Formal academic training programs as well as adult education programs in agricultural and food production techniques, hygiene, disease prevention and birth control could be provided. Educational programming combined with the usual news and entertainment broadcasts will contribute to national, political and cultural integration by facilitating communication among various segments of society. Improved education will provide an important part of the foundation for national and international economic and social development.

It is hoped that the ability to receive any nation's programming will result in a profitable and beneficial information exchange. A greater exchange of information could generate two important sets of benefits. First, a freer flow of information could facilitate more rapid dissemination of technological and cultural advances, increasing the rate of social and economic development in every country. Second, the exchange of information could contribute to increased understanding among cultures, which in turn could result in reduced international tensions and perhaps even lead to the resolution of previously irreconcilable conflicts.

Technologically advanced modes of communication have the ability to transform our daily patterns of life more than any technology on the near horizon. This fact alone makes a study of the transfer of technology from research laboratories to the using public one of impressive significance.

2

U.S. ROCKETRY AND SATELLITE DEVELOPMENT (1945-1958): MILITARY RESPONSE TO THE TECHNOLOGIC IMPERATIVE

Since the first step in the transfer of technology is obviously the development of the technology to be transferred, it will be necessary to look in the next three chapters at the steps by which the U.S. government and the U.S.S.R. became the exclusive owners of satellite capabilities by the early 1960s. The pressures of international military rivalry were able to push technological research and development far faster than the new technology could be applied for peaceful purposes and gave rise to the need for large-scale transfer of space technology and applications to private and peaceful uses.

Military Rocketry

In the field of rocketry there was almost a direct correlation between the pace of technological advancement and the degree of international rivalry. World War II provided the first direct stimulus to the development of rockets as weapons of war. When the war ended in 1945, the Germans in particular had made significant strides in the development of military rocketry. Under the leadership of scientists such as Wernher von Braun they perfected the powerful liquid fuel V-2 rockets with a vertical range of 100 miles. Although Hitler had temporarily delayed funding for his *Wunderwaffen* after dreaming they would never reach England, by 1944 V-2s were being manufactured in quantity at Peenemünde, a vast underground military plant.[1]

Some German rocket experts were interested in the potential of rockets for space flight; in fact, the Gestapo once arrested von Braun on charges of placing interest in space flight ahead of weaponry development.[2] Since financial support for pure scientific research is too often lacking under any circumstances, German scientists found that the surest way to obtain funding for their rocket research was to accede to military goals. Von Braun has compared the position of his team of rocket specialists to that of the early "aviation pioneers when the airplane could only be developed because of its military value."[3] A parallel can be drawn here to satellite development as well. Just as the military requirements of World War I gave impetus to the development of the airplane and World War II produced the V-2 liquid fuel rockets, the long-range rockets that would ultimately carry satellites into space were a product of the cold war. Such high-powered rockets, along with the technology necessary to launch, guide and track them, developed out of the U.S.-U.S.S.R. race to produce long-range intercontinental ballistic missiles.

A prelude to the cold war arms race and ensuing U.S.-U.S.S.R. hostilities was evident in postwar attempts by both countries to lay claims to German rocket expertise. The American-Russian race for Berlin was paralleled by a similar "race for Peenemünde." The Peenemünde installation, located at Nordhausen, was well within the occupation zone assigned the U.S.S.R., but before the Russians could reach Peenemünde the American army, in an operation known as "Paperclip", managed to slip out the stock of nearly 100 V-2 rockets, together with Wernher von Braun and his team of 130 rocket experts.[4] Stalin was infuriated by the U.S. intrusion, but the Soviet Union did acquire the physical plant at Peenemünde.[5]

In 1945, when the Kremlin was still initiating its program of intercontinental rocket development, a United States Senate Special Committee on Atomic Energy heard testimony concerning U.S. development of rocketry from the director of wartime research efforts, Vannevar Bush:

> There has been a great deal said about a 3,000 mile high-angle rocket. . . . In my opinion, such a thing is impossible today and will be impossible for many years. . . . The people who have been writing these things that annoy me . . . have been talking about a 3,000 mile high-angle rocket, shot from one continent to another, carrying an atomic bomb and so directed as to be a precise weapon which could land on a certain target, such as a city. I say, technically, I don't think anybody in the world knows how to do such a thing, and I feel confident it will not be done for a very long period of time to come.[6]

Bush's negative attitude toward the development of long-range ballistic missiles was a reflection of the predominant attitude in the American political and military establishment at the time. A postwar military planning guide, *Towards New Horizons,* had also urged that the basis for future U.S. airpower supremacy be the development of jet aircraft capable of delivering nuclear weapons, rather than a costly long-range missile program.[7] Although the United States had acquired the world's top rocket design specialists in von Braun and his Peenemünde team, these researchers received little significant support for rocket development.

A chief reason for this lack of support was America's postwar sense of military security and complacency. The United States had emerged from World War II as the preeminent world power and sole possessor of the atomic bomb. U.S. supremacy was unchallenged, since her European allies, as well as Germany and Japan, were struggling to recover from the devastating effects of the war. The Soviet Union, too, faced a major rebuilding and recovery effort and thus did not constitute an immediate military threat in 1945. The United States returned to the business of peace and the maintenance of wartime productivity levels, secure in its position. Many American scientists continued to promote rocketry for scientific purposes, but, without the stimulus of international rivalry and military requirements, funding was minimal and the pace of development slow.

America's sense of military superiority and security, however, was short-lived. By the early 1950s cold war hostilities revitalized the development of military rocketry. In the interim the Soviet Union had achieved a headstart in rocketry development and, consequently, an initial advantage in the space race. A series of international events, beginning with the Berlin blockade of 1948, forced the United States to recognize the importance of ICBMs in the cold war arms race. In 1949 the Soviet Union succeeded in exploding an atom bomb, and in 1950 the Korean War intensified cold war hostilities and brought with it a new military urgency. By 1953 U.S. scientists had developed the hydrogen bomb, a thermonuclear weapon, which multiplied destructive powers.

In response to cold war hostilities, President Truman initiated American research and development of large liquid fuel rockets. The program, intensified under President Eisenhower, developed the Redstone, Navaho, Rascal, Snark and Matador rockets. In 1953 the United States for the first time spent in excess of one million dollars for rocketry research.[8] In 1954 an Air Force advisory committee under the leadership of John von Neumann recommended immediate development of ICBMs. The recommendation was approved by President Eisenhower, and a special Air Force task force began an urgent secret program to develop intercontinental missiles capable of delivering nuclear warheads. In military circles the project ranked in importance with the earlier Manhattan Project, which created the atomic bomb.[9] This crash program led quickly to the development of powerful intercontinental missiles, such as Atlas, Jupiter and Thor.

Early U.S. Satellite Proposals

The United States' initial lag in the development of rocketry was paralleled by a similar false start in early satellite programs. Soon after the end of World War II, the various military services undertook studies of the feasibility of an earth-orbiting satellite. The satellite programs were highly classified. The first public announcement of their existence was made in 1948, when Secretary of Defense James Forrestal reported to Congress in the "First Annual Report of the Secretary of Defense" that:

> The Earth Satellite Vehicle Program, which was being carried out independently by each military service, was assigned to the Committee on Guided Missiles for coordination. To provide an integrated program with resultant elimination of duplication, the committee recommended that current efforts in this field be limited to studies and component designs: well-defined areas of such research have been allocated to each of the three military departments.[10]

Even this guarded announcement met with a negative reaction both in the United States and abroad. The Soviet journal *New Times* referred to the "madman Forrestal's idea of an Earth Satellite" as an "instrument of blackmail."[11] In the United States personnel involved in the satellite program viewed the acknowledgment as an unwarranted disclosure of classified information. Consequently, no official reference in open literature was made to an American satellite effort until November 1954, when the Department of Defense, in a terse two-sentence comment, reported that studies continued to be made in the Earth Satellite Vehicle Program.[12]

These classified satellite efforts produced fairly extensive studies on the feasibility of satellite vehicles. Had they been given greater support, it is conceivable that the United States could have launched a satellite by 1951.[13] The programs, however, failed to go beyond the planning stage for two primary reasons: first, the various branches of the service involved in satellite development were unable to cooperate successfully in a joint effort, and second, the satellite program lacked a clear-cut military objective.

In October of 1945 the newly created Navy Committee for Evaluating the Feasibility of Space Rocketry submitted the first satellite proposal to the Navy Bureau of Aeronautics (BuAer) and recommended that: high priority be given to the development and launch of an earth satellite vehicle.[14] On the basis of this recommendation, BuAer placed contracts to investigate the technical feasibility of satellites which led to the design of a single stage satellite vehicle designated HATV (High-Altitude Test Vehicle). While the investigations yielded promising results, the cost for the preliminary phase of the program was estimated at anywhere from five to eight million dollars.[15] In view of these prohibitive cost projections, the Navy appealed to the Army Air Force (AAF) to join it in a joint satellite project. At an initial meeting held in March 1946, a tentative agreement was reached on a joint AAF-Navy experimental satellite program. A letter from BuAer to the commanding general of the AAF stated:

> It was agreed at the conference that the general advantages to be derived from pursuing the satellite development appear to be sufficient to justify a major program, in spite of the fact that the obvious military, or purely naval applications in themselves, may not appear at this time to warrant the expenditure.[16]

The joint effort, however, met with obstacles and delays. When the two services conferred for the second time, the AAF presented its own satellite proposal. The AAF had hoped to enhance its position in the joint project by demonstrating that it stood on an equal developmental level with the Navy. The result of the introduction of the second proposal was to halt all progress toward a joint project.[17] Each service afterwards pursued its satellite studies independently.

AAF satellite studies had begun 1946 when the AAF commissioned Project Rand, a semi-autonomous division of the Douglas Aircraft Company and forerunner of the Rand Corporation, to study the feasibility of earth orbiting satellites. The study, completed in time for the ill-fated AAF-Navy conference, reported that earth satellites were feasible and presented initial technical specifications for launching a 500-pound satellite in a 300-mile orbit within five years.[18] The Project Rand report, entitled "Preliminary Design of an Experimental World-Circling Spaceship," however, ruled out the use of satellites as military ballistic weapons. It was not technically possible at the time to launch a satellite vehicle capable of carrying the weight of an atomic bomb, and no other explosive could inflict enough damage to justify the cost of transporting it by satellite.[19] Consequently, a direct military objective for satellite development was still lacking.

The report attempted to salvage the satellite project by suggesting a number of other satellite applications including scientific research, weather forecasting and communications. A good deal of emphasis was placed on the potential of satellites as communication relay stations. While noting that the attempt in 1946 "to estimate the values to be derived from a development program aimed at the establishment of a satellite circling the earth above the atmosphere is as difficult as it would have been, some years before the Wright brothers flew at Kitty Hawk, to visualize the current uses of aviation in war and in peace,"[20] the Project Rand report nevertheless predicted that the potential for communications would significantly affect the future of satellites. The report not only suggested that satellite capability for communications could serve an indirect military purpose, but also pointed to its potential value as a commercial enterprise.[21]

Despite Rand's attempt to formulate a rationale for satellite development and further studies demonstrating its technical feasibility, the Department of Defense (DOD) in 1948 turned down both the Navy satellite proposal and the United States Air Force (USAF) Project Rand proposal.[22] The newly created DOD had assigned review of the satellite proposals to the Technical Evaluation Group of the Research and Development Board's Guided Missile Committee. Although the committee found that the feasibility of satellites was clearly established, it concluded that "neither the Navy nor the USAF has as yet established either a military or a scientific utility commensurate with the presently expected cost of a satellite vehicle."[23] In mid-1948 the Air Force rejected a second attempt at a joint effort.[24] The Navy program had advanced as far as it could on paper. Lacking funds to build flight vehicles to support their satellite program, BuAer abandoned the project. Since further satellite projects of any significance were not undertaken by the Army until 1954, when Wernher von Braun's Redstone rocket team proposed Project Orbiter, after 1949 only the Air Force continued to be active in the field, limiting its efforts primarily to Rand Corporation studies until the mid-1950s when a formal Air Force satellite program was authorized.[25]

Although the early satellite proposals failed because they could not demonstrate clear-cut military benefits, interest in the potential for satellites continued. In 1949 the Air Force commissioned the Rand

Corporation to resume its inquiry into military uses of satellite vehicles. Rand called a conference of consultants from both the social and physical sciences at Santa Monica in January to consider the topic of potential psychological effects of unconventional weapons—including satellites—upon the Soviet Union. The conference concluded that the "paramount utility of a satellite probably resides in its potentialities as an instrument for the achievement of political/psychological goals."[26] Its utility would lie in its psychological impact as a spectacle, as a useful instrument for both weather prediction and military reconnaissance, as an instrument of political strategy, and as a device for communication. The conference participants focused on communication satellites in terms of their potential psychological shock effect and their use for propaganda purposes. They concluded, however, that while "radio signals or voice messages from a satellite would probably have initial arresting and mystifying effects," the effects "would soon wear off and be adjusted to psychologically." Similarly, "signals or messages from a satellite could be used as attention getters, but other communications techniques . . . would probably prove more effective for disseminating propaganda."[27]

In 1953 a classified report on the status of the U.S. satellite program, commissioned by President Truman, again urged support for unmanned satellite experimentation. The report stressed the potential scientific, military and psychological value of satellites, noting particularly the military value of surveillance satellites and the psychological value of communication satellites as "a messenger of the free world."[28] Particular emphasis was placed on the importance of satellite development to America's position in the cold war. In a farsighted warning the report stated that "since the Soviet Union has been following us in the atomic and hydrogen bomb developments, it should not be excluded that the Politburo might like to take the *lead* in the development of a satellite," and that "if the Soviet Union should accomplish this ahead of us it would be a serious blow to the technical and engineering prestige of America the world over."[29] It was later documented that the Soviet Union was not only proceeding with the development of satellites, but according to one Soviet authority there had already been discussions among Soviet scientists in the early 1950s on the specific future possibilities of communication satellites.[30]

While the use of communication satellites as psychological and propaganda weapons was being considered and deemphasized, the military meanwhile was making some progress towards developing technologies related to the use of satellites for conventional communications. In 1945 the Army Signal Corp undertook Project Diana, an experiment aimed at testing the feasibility of using the moon, a natural satellite, as a passive reflector of radio signals. Within a year the engineers at Camp Evans Signal Laboratory in Belmar, New Jersey, transmitted and received the first radio echoes on an earth-moon path, proving that microwave signals could be transmitted through space with moderate power.[31] By 1948 a program was underway to determine the potential use of moon relays for communications.[32] In 1954 the Naval Research Laboratory successfully sent the first voice message from earth-to-earth using the moon to reflect radio signals. These experiments led to development of the Communication Moon Relay system, which was put to operational use for two-way transmission between Washington and Hawaii in 1959.[33] The principle of communication via moon relay developed by the Army Signal Corps and Naval Research Laboratory later became part of the background for NASA's first passive communication satellite, Echo I.

Scientific Interest in Space

The military potential of space was only one motivation for the U.S. space program. Scientific interest in space flight was also evident, although support for the development of rocketry and related technologies for purely scientific purposes was limited in comparison to the importance attached to military applications. In June 1946, a year after the German surrender, the U.S. Army began launch experimentation with its stock of captured German V-2s. Altogether, over sixty V-2 rockets were launched by the military between 1946 and 1952 from the White Sands Proving Grounds in New Mexico. Since the objective behind the launchings was primarily to gain experience, the Army invited scientists from military as well as academic research organizations to design a group of experiments utilizing the V-2 as a sounding device to probe the upper atmosphere and near space. In order to coordinate this research program, an informal Upper Atmospheric Rocket Research Panel was created which was comprised of representatives from the Army Signal Corps, the Army Air Force, the Naval Research Laboratory, Cal Tech and Johns Hopkins, Princeton, Harvard, and Michigan Universities.[34]

A number of researchers took advantage of this offer and utilized the V-2 as well as other launch vehicles to conduct scientific investigations. For instance, in a joint effort during February 1949 the Army along with the Jet Propulsion Laboratory of Cal Tech launched the two-stage Bumper WAC rocket to a record altitude of 244 miles and, in the process, obtained useful data about the nature of the ionosphere. The second stage of the rocket has the distinction of being the first man-made object to enter extraterrestrial space.[35] For this test, as well as for the others in the Bumper Project, a V-2 was used as the initial, booster stage and a WAC Corporal rocket as the second stage. Another research organization, the Air Force Aeromedical Laboratory, during the early 1950s tested the effects of high-altitude flight upon primates, mice, and other organisms. The V-2 rocket, however, offered limited opportunities for upper atmosphere research because the supply was shrinking, and also because it had not been designed primarily as a research vehicle. Consequently, the Applied Physics Laboratory of Johns Hopkins University, under contract with the Navy, began development of the Aeorbee research rocket. The Naval Research Laboratory sponsored the development of the aluminum Viking rocket, which embodied a number of significant technical innovations. Twelve of these Viking rockets were launched during the early 1950s, enabling scientists to obtain a considerable body of data on cosmic ray emissions and the nature of solar radiation. The overall success of the Viking program lent strong credence to the notion that it was possible to launch an artificial earth satellite within a few years' time.[36]

In addition, it was an activity of the scientific community which led directly to the first U.S. effort to launch a satellite. The motivation was provided by the International Geophysical Year (I.G.Y.), an international cooperative effort of scientists from sixty-seven nations, to study the earth's environment in a systematic and comprehensive fashion. The I.G.Y. took place during the eighteen months between 1 July 1957 and 31 December 1958. One of the recommendations for the I.G.Y. concerned the launching of a research satellite to collect measurements of geophysical phenomena in and beyond the upper atmosphere; during the summer and fall of 1954 a number of scientific organizations, such as the International Union of Geodesy and Geophysics and the Special Committee for the International Geophysical Year of the International Council of Scientific Unions, adopted resolutions urging the launch of an unmanned, orbiting spacecraft. Scientific groups in the United States expressed support for the proposal during 1955; in March of that year the National Academy of Sciences stated that such a project was indeed feasible and that it would be advantageous for the United States to launch an I.G.Y. research satellite. The Academy prevailed upon President Eisenhower to support the plan, and on 29 July 1955 the United States announced its intention to undertake a satellite project. The National Academy of Sciences and the National Science Foundation were vested with responsibility for the design and selection of the scientific experiments to be conducted aboard the satellite, and the Department of Defense was authorized to furnish the requisite launch vehicles.[37]

Although it was primarily the efforts of U.S. scientists and researchers, speaking through scientific bodies such as the National Academy of Sciences, which persuaded the government to commit itself to the development of an artificial satellite, the importance of cold war rivalries should not be overlooked, since during January 1955 Radio Moscow had, in fact, hinted that a Soviet satellite launch might be imminent. Had the United States been aware of the advanced state of Soviet rocketry, it might have urged a more expeditious development of an earth satellite and the required launch capabilities.

Project Vanguard

When it approved the idea of an I.G.Y. satellite, the White House did not specify which of the service branches – the Army, Navy or Air Force – was to have responsibility for launching the satellite. Each of the branches had offered different satellite proposals based on its own launch vehicle. As early as August 1954, the Army along with the Office of Naval Research had proposed the use of the Army's Redstone rocket for launching a small, research-oriented satellite. Referred to as Project Orbiter, the proposal received the support of Wernher von Braun; it was never implemented, however. The Air Force recommended the use of its Atlas rocket which was being developed for duty as an intercontinental ballistic missile. The Navy, finally, offered to adapt its Viking rocket for use in an I.G.Y. satellite project, arguing that its proposal could be unclassified since the development of the launch vehicle would proceed independently of the ICBM program. A special DOD Scientific Advisory Committee, appointed by Donald Quarles, assistant secretary of defense for research and development, reviewed the three proposals and selected the Navy's, which was eventually referred to as Project Vanguard.[38]

The decision was not without controversy: although the proposal of the Navy also received the recommendation of the DOD Committee on Special Capabilities, two members of the committee, including its chairman, Homer J. Stewart, were of the opinion that the Army's Redstone missile was the more suitable launch vehicle. Proponents of the Army's Project Orbiter later tried unsuccessfully to reverse the Vanguard decision. A major factor in the decision was that DOD did not want the I.G.Y. satellite project to interfere in any way with the development of a ballistic missile capability for national defense.[39]

In retrospect, policy analysts have called the selection of the Navy proposal a "notoriously bad decision."[40] The choice was difficult, however, because each of the proposals did have certain merits. The Navy, for example, was generally considered to be the leader in miniaturization, and furthermore, it had considerable experience with atmospheric phenomena, optics, radio astronomy and the use of upper atmospheric sounding rockets. The Army's Redstone rocket, on the other hand, was in a more advanced stage of development than the Navy's Viking and was capable of generating far greater thrust. The Scientific Advisory Committee did consider a plan for combining various features from each of the proposals but ruled out the idea after determining that interservice rivalries would inhibit an effective, cooperative effort. C. C. Furnas, successor to Donald Quarles as assistant secretary of defense for research and development, has noted with respect to the possibilities for interservice cooperation that:

> All of us [in the Scientific Advisory Committee] had had similar experiences with the military services. We were familiar with the rivalries and jealousies that would cause delay and frustration. We knew of the unwillingness of one branch of the service to contribute personnel, money or even information, at times, to a project for which some other branch would get much credit. We all felt a joint effort satellite would take a long time to get off the ground, much less reach outer space. We finally decided that breaking the space barrier would be an easier task than breaking the interservice barrier.[41]

Consequently, the Defense Department assigned responsibility for the I.G.Y. satellite to the Navy alone.

While the U.S. did stand to gain a certain degree of prestige from launching the first earth satellite during the I.G.Y., Vanguard's primary objectives were scientific. The importance of the prestige factor was tempered by "an aura of unwarranted, but nonetheless real, national complacency concerning the technical supremacy of the United States."[42] Consequently, Project Vanguard was a "comparatively low-level economical effort,"[43] designed specifically not to interfere with priorities assigned to the ballistic missile program. Like the earlier U.S. satellite programs, Vanguard lacked a full-fledged national commitment.

The Sputnik Challenge

The turning point in U.S. thinking regarding the importance of satellite development occurred in October of 1957, when the Soviet Union successfully launched Sputnik I. On 4 October 1957 the New York Times had a small, front page article telling of the astonishment of Western scientists on hearing a Russian colleague tell of the U.S.S.R.'s aggressive plans for an International Geophysical Year satellite. The next day's paper shocked Americans: the New York Times' headline read "SOVIET FIRES EARTH SATELLITE INTO SPACE: IT IS CIRCLING THE GLOBE AT 18,000 M.P.H." This was the world's introduction to artificial satellites. The Soviet "moon," as it was called, carried two radio transmitters and sent signals continuously at frequencies of 20.005 and 40.002 megacycles. At a weight of 184 pounds, travelling in an orbit 560 miles above the earth, this spacecraft was far more than a scientific or technical achievement; it had a tremendous psychological and political impact.

Against the cold war background of fear and suspicion, the satellite launch by the U.S.S.R. created a wave of reaction in the United States. Americans could not claim, as in the case of the A-bomb, that Russia had stolen their secrets. Had they surpassed American technology? Could the satellite be a weapon? Would the moon be their next conquest? Some U.S. scientists thought the satellite was sending coded information to the Russians from other countries; some feared it carried infrared cameras to detect military installations. Above all, the weight of the spacecraft and its high orbit suggested a critical difference in the military capabilities of the two super-powers: current American plans for satellites were considering a mere 21.5 pound satellite orbiting at 300 miles up; the Russians apparently possessed superior rockets whose thrust could send a heavier craft into a much higher orbit.[44] The U.S. scientific and military race against Russia reached a new level of concern.

U.S. scientific prestige soon plunged even lower. On 6 December 1957 a Vanguard rocket was barely off of the launch pad before it fell back and exploded.[45] The impact of these events shook American self-confidence. Wernher von Braun noted that:

> Overnight it became popular to question the bulwarks of our society, our public education system, our educational strength, international policy, defense strategy and forces, the capability of our science and technology. Even the moral fiber of our people came under searching examination.[46]

In an attempt to determine the cause of the U.S. satellite lag, military programs in particular came under investigation. The interservice rivalries and funding cuts which plagued the military effort came to light. Some critics blamed Defense Secretary Charles Wilson because he had favored slashing appropriations for the missile programs.[47] Others pointed to quarrels between branches of the military which led to duplication of effort. A House select committee distributed the blame more widely:

> Responsibility for the judgments which in retrospect were unwise, can hardly be confined to any administration or person. ... Much of the responsibility in our kind of society must rest with the people as a whole, who spurned what warnings there were of the evolving Soviet menace, until they could hear the radio beep or see the Soviet sputniks as they passed overhead. A clearer responsibility for our lag in missile development must rest upon those who knew better, but thought they could postpone facing these unpleasant facts. Some must rest upon those who had access to repeated intelligence warnings, but were, possibly by temperament, unable to believe that a "backward" Communist state could do scientific work of the order required to meet operational success in such an advanced field.... Anyone who would take Soviet claims at face value ran the risk of being labeled either a victim of their propaganda or an apologist for their system.[48]

The upshot of the Sputnik challenge was the establishment of a U.S. national space program. In the days following the momentous launch, the United States faced major questions of national security. The overwhelming response of the military and the Administration was to attempt to bolster the country's sense of strength and readiness. On 8 November 1957 President Eisenhower addressed the nation on science and security assuring that "earth satellites, in themselves, have no direct present effect upon the nation's security."[49] To end the much regretted delay of the U.S. I.G.Y. Vanguard project, he created the new office of Special Assistant to the President on Science and Technology, which would ensure that "such things as alleged interservice competition or insufficient use of overtime shall not be allowed to create even the suspicion of harm to our scientific and development program."[50] Eisenhower also gave the Army's Project Orbiter the approval as a back-up operation to Vanguard, and on 31 January 1958 the Army's Redstone rocket successfully launched the first U.S. earth satellite, Explorer I. The Explorer launch was the immediate response to the trauma of Sputnik and a forerunner of major space programs.

Despite Eisenhower's reassurance security fears dominated the early response. In 1957 the fantasy of atom bomb-equipped satellites circling the earth, ready to cover the U.S. with mushroom clouds, seemed not too far-fetched.[51] Although some officials disagreed with the significance attached to the Soviet achievement – calling it "a neat scientific trick" or a "ridiculous bauble" – the region of outer space now became the major battleground for rival U.S. and U.S.S.R. science programs.[52]

The U.S. response to Sputnik has been best described as a "political swing to science."[53] Sputnik toppled America's sense of complacency regarding its scientific and technical superiority; science began to exert a very real influence over national policy. President Eisenhower stressed to the American public the need for renewed commitment to scientific development within both government and educational institutions. Congress increased the appropriations for the National Science Foundation from $ 40 to $ 130 million,[54] and U.S. scientific organizations such as the Rocket and Satellite Research Panel called for a coordinated space program and a national space establishment independent from military programs.[55] These events marked the first steps toward the development of a comprehensive U.S. civilian space program designed to eliminate the obstacles to satellite development characteristic of the 1945-1958 period. The stage was set for a long-range program of scientific research and development no longer subject to the constraints of military requirements or interservice rivalries which plagued Project Vanguard and the early satellite proposals. Because of Sputnik U.S. prestige had become integrally tied to the success of an American space program. International rivalry, which had so often played a role in the development of military technology, again came into play in favor of scientific development. Subsequent government support and the commitment of substantial financial resources to a national space effort completed the backdrop against which the development of communication satellites could proceed.

3

THE CREATION OF A NATIONAL SPACE AGENCY (1957-1960): INSTITUTIONAL RESPONSE TO THE TECHNOLOGIC IMPERATIVE

After the Sputnik satellites shocked the country, a mood of popular and political anxiety caused a reexamination of national priorities and of U.S. technical and military structures. Congressional hearings probed; President Eisenhower spoke to the nation; scientific groups urged action; and the man on the street watched the skies, perhaps wondering when the Russian satellite would pass over his area.[1] A flurry of official actions began to define the U.S. space response to the Soviet Union's achievement.

National Space Objectives

On 7 November 1957 President Eisenhower created the post of Special Assistant to the President for Science and Technology, appointing James Killian as the first occupant. The president changed the Science Advisory Committee of the Office of Defense Mobilization to the President's Science Advisory Committee. This committee quickly undertook preparation of a report on a national space program for the president. The president summoned numerous officials to the White House, apparently in an effort to evaluate United States strengths and weaknesses compared to those of the Soviet Union. He also proposed a reorganization of Defense Department space efforts. Groups such as the National Science Foundation and the Atomic Energy Commission (AEC) began devising plans for a totally new agency charged with conducting space research and activities. Many different interest groups contributed input on what form the U.S. space program might assume.

Both branches of Congress examined missile capabilities in order to gauge U.S. preparedness and to investigate the potential for a space program. The Senate Preparedness Investigating Subcommittee of the Committee on Armed Services tried to determine "what can be done, what should be done, what must be done now and for the long pull."[2] The military space program came under close scrutiny.

The Russian satellite launch frightened Americans. Rockets capable of sending up a 200-pound spacecraft would allow the Soviet Union to send intercontinental missiles great distances. The military implications were obvious. Even though American scientists were uncertain about the accuracy of the Soviet guidance systems and therefore felt attack was not imminent, weaponry and national security apprehensions were paramount in the wake of Sputnik's trail across the skies. Congress brought up the possibilities of outer space military bases, discussed anti-satellite satellites, and considered the military potential of the moon under Russian or American flags. The Soviet Union's technological capability became an issue: if they could launch satellites, what else could they do? The investigation by the Senate Preparedness Subcommittee on military potentials led to a recommendation for a Special Committee on Space and Astronautics for the Senate in February 1958. The House of Representatives meanwhile established a comparable Select Committee on Astronautics and Space Exploration. Congress assigned to both new committees the task of framing legislation for a national program of space exploration and development.

The technology for satellite communications was still a matter of futuristic speculation. However, the hearings on a new space program gave a first major public airing to the possibilities for space communications. It is significant that consideration of the peaceful uses of space – weather and communication capabilities in particular – was possible only after the country made its initial response to Sputnik.[3] An emergency national space program for security and prestige reasons promised to advance associated technologies which were vital to the development of communications capabilities.

The federal government labored for one year to articulate totally new national space objectives. The President's Science Advisory Committee issued a statement on basic considerations for undertaking a national space effort which listed four factors important to a national space program:

(1) the compelling urge of man to explore the unknown,
(2) the military potential of outer space,
(3) the effect upon national prestige,
(4) the opportunities for scientific observation and experimentation.[4]

On 2 April the president sent to Congress his recommendations for a civilian space science and exploration program under a new agency, the National Aeronautics and Space Administration (NASA).[5] Congress passed laws to provide for (1) a reorganization and consolidation of the Defense Department's space effort and (2) the creation of an Advanced Research Projects Agency (ARPA) by the Secretary of Defense (Public Laws 85-325 and 85-322 respectively). The two special congressional committees on aeronautics began hearing extensive testimony on a national space program. Many different groups sent witnesses to testify before the two committees, including the Atomic Energy Commission, the National Advisory Committee on Aeronautics (NACA), the National Science Foundation, the Department of Defense, the State Department, and even private business. Numerous bills were submitted to Congress presenting different institutional arrangements for a national space agency. Among the pertinent issues were: (1) the question of at what level of authority this space agency might operate, (2) whether it would have a single or multi-headed administration, and most controversial of all, (3) whether this agency would be under civilian or military leadership.

The priorities adopted by the congressional committees provide a meaningful index to policy planning concerns operating with regard to space agency decisions of 1958. Space technology, like atomic energy technology, required legislative action which would eliminate the problem of multiple jurisdictions. Congress recognized in the case of both that a breakdown of the total areas of atomic energy or outer space into composite divisions would fragment jurisdictional claims of congressional committees. Hence the initial decision to establish centralized committees to carry out a national space effort was an attempt at streamlining the Congress' own operations, as well as an attempt to settle at an early stage the problem of potential confusion in federal agency responsibilities. When it later came to be seen that for communication satellites in particular multiple jurisdictions would still be the rule, the inadequacies of congressional planning came to light. As has been the case with many policy blueprints, the broad concerns of the 1958 Congress in creating a space program led to difficulty in dealing with specific problems growing out of communications space activities.

Toward a Space Agency

The House and Senate special committees considered five different types of organizations providing for:

(1) development of outer space by the Department of Defense;
(2) development of outer space by the Atomic Energy Commission;
(3) development of outer space by a new commission patterned essentially on the Atomic Energy Commission;
(4) coordination of a space program by the National Advisory Committee for Aeronautics and the National Science Foundation;
(5) development of outer space through a Department of Science at the Cabinet level.[6]

President Eisenhower had recommended a civilian agency to conduct space science activities except programs associated with military requirements. The President planned to absorb NACA into a new National Aeronautics and Space Administration headed by an appointed director. A National Aeronautics and Space Board composed of people from government agencies, DOD, and others eminent in science, education or public affairs, would advise the president and NASA's director.[7] Congress eventually adopted the basics of this plan.

NACA had begun planning for an expanded role in outer space in the aftermath of Sputnik. Congress in 1915 had created NACA, a civilian organization, as part of the pre-World War I preparedness campaign to supervise and direct the study of problems of flight and conduct research and experiments in aeronautics emphasizing practical solutions. World War II brought a change in NACA's direction; from the pursuit of fundamental research it moved into specialized research on immediate projects related to military applications. NACA was always known for its excellent relations with the military. Establishing research centers in many areas of the country, NACA engaged in relatively unpublicized research programs on aeronautics. At the time of Sputnik, NACA's space activities focused on advanced research and technical development rather than a hardware-using flight program. Fifty percent of its effort, or thirty-five million dollars worth, was space-related. Hugh Dryden, director of NACA, realized that "the future of the agency was possibly at stake. If NACA concentrated solely on aeronautical research, it would lose many of its best employees to whatever agency would emerge with the Nation's space program; on the other hand, if NACA were to take on the Nation's space program, it would face radical changes."[8]

Dryden planned to reorganize NACA for a space program, proposing expansion of staff and facilities, greater contract research, large-scale flight efforts with DOD, and cooperation among existing space-related organizations. In January of 1958 NACA leadership passed a resolution to implement the Dryden plan and sent a memo to President Eisenhower indicating it was ready to move. The Dryden plan recognized that the breadth of the nation's space program called for more than one agency, and that NACA had the best chance to integrate civilian-oriented space efforts with DOD interests.

However, the Administration wanted one agency with total authority and responsibility, and incorporated few of Dryden's suggestions into its final recommendations to Congress. President Eisenhower's decisions provided for a strengthened and redesigned NACA. He did not recommend DOD to head the space program because of the desire for civilian, scientific emphasis and DOD's deep involvement in a missile program. Lloyd Berkner, an eminent scientist and a leader in the I.G.Y. program, submitted relevant testimony on the matter of military space interests. He stated:

> In the present state of unstable military equilibrium, it is natural that we should be concerned for our military strength and effectiveness. With the gravest consequences at stake, no nation can afford to tip the balance adversely by weakening its military strength. But in facing the future of space technology with a biased emphasis on its military aspects, there is danger that we may fail to grasp the real opportunity for world leadership that space technology offers. Militarization of broad problems such as space technology that affect all elements of our national community suggest a considerable danger of our Nation succumbing too completely to a psychology of military direction and control. . . .[9]

The Atomic Energy Commission was rejected as a leadership organization because its program was not closely related to space technology and because a singleheaded agency was desired. NACA was an obvious and legitimate choice as the base for a new space agency.

Congress concurred and in July passed the National Aeronautics and Space Act of 1958, and on 29 July 1958, nearly one year after Sputnik, President Eisenhower signed the Act which provided that NASA absorb the old NACA. Program reviews by NASA and DOD got underway in order to divide up projects and facilities, with 1 October set as a deadline for all project transfers. NACA Director Dryden and Deputy Secretary of Defense Quarles met to assemble the new arrangements.

By late 1958, therefore, the new organization, NASA, and the military's ARPA were the two leading agencies for space activities. Up until this point the government had not concerned itself with the technology and development of communications satellites per se. This was to change rapidly as NASA and private industry progressed with their work in the area. Among the projects NASA inherited from other agencies were a number of satellite programs: the Navy transferred Project Vanguard responsibility to NASA although it continued at Naval Research Laboratories; it transferred the four remaining I.G.Y. vehicles to NASA, along with four lunar probes under military direction; also, communication satellite projects formerly assigned to another agency were now placed with NASA. One of the latter, a plan for aluminium, inflatable spheres, one with a 100-foot diameter which could reflect communications signals, became NASA's first communication satellite experiment. NASA called this program Echo.

The 1958 Space Act proved the necessary vehicle to stimulate exploration and development of communication satellites. NASA's establishment allowed a first concerted effort to examine and implement technology for satellite applications. NASA's charter, the product of much legislative thought, outlined its role in developing communications.

NASA's Charter with Regard to Communications

NASA's 1958 charter suggested a few important guidelines with regard to communication satellites. The arrangements relating to civilian versus military space activities are covered in broad terms:

> [Part b] The Congress declares that the general welfare and security of the United States require that adequate provision be made for aeronautical and space activities. The Congress further declares that such activities shall be the responsibility of, and shall be directed by, a civilian agency exercising control over aeronautical and space activities sponsored by the United States, except that *activities peculiar to or primarily associated with the development of weapons systems, military operations, or the defense of the United States* (including the research and development necessary to make effective provision for the defense of the United States) *shall be the responsibility of, and shall be directed by, the Department of Defense;* and that determination as to which such agency has responsibility for and direction of any such activity shall be made by the President in confirmity with section 201(e).[10]

The Civilian Military Liaison Committee, a joint NASA-DOD committee, was to work out the division of activities. In the applications field, however, it was obvious that both the military and the civilian sector would have communications needs, and that both would be interested in developing a level of expertise in communication satellites. Neither could assume all the work in communication satellites. Some felt, however, that the eventual NASA-DOD agreement on respective communication satellite programs did not reflect a formal decision on which sorts of satellites were militarily-oriented and which were not, but rather represented accommodation to the personnel and skill orientations of both organizations.[11] As will be seen, the division of responsibilities for communication satellites did fit military requirements very nicely. In any event, this section of the charter delineating peaceful versus military space activities had little direct impact on satellite communications.

The agency's objectives were very broad:

> [Part c] The aeronautical and space activities of the United States shall be conducted so as to contribute materially to one or more of the following objectives:
> (1) The expansion of human knowledge of phenomena in the atmosphere and space;
> (2) The improvement of the usefulness, performance, speed, safety, and efficiency of aeronautical and space vehicles;
> (3) The development and operation of vehicles capable of carrying instruments, equipment, supplies, and living organisms through space;
> (4) The establishment of long-range studies of the potential benefits to be gained from, the opportunities for, and the problems involved in the utilization of aeronautical and space activities for peaceful and scientific purposes;
> (5) The preservation of the role of the United States as a leader in aeronautical and space science and technology and in the application thereof to the conduct of peaceful activities within and outside the atmosphere;
> (6) The making available to agencies directly concerned with national defense of discoveries that have military value or significance, and the furnishing by such agencies, to the civilian agency established to direct and control nonmilitary aeronautical and space activities, of information as to discoveries which have value or significance to that agency;

(7) Cooperation by the United States with other nations and groups of nations in work done pursuant to this Act and in the peaceful application of the results thereof; and

(8) The most effective utilization of the scientific and engineering resources of the United States, with close cooperation among all interested agencies of the United States in order to avoid unnecessary duplication of effort, facilities, and equipment.[12]

This section from the charter summarizes the wide-ranging possibilities of NASA as a civilian agency. The peaceful development of space activities is one important emphasis. Another concerns the delineation of activities in the charter: the Congress allowed for private sector development of space interests by limiting aeronautical and space activities in the charter to a *research* orientation.[13] Congress restricted *operations* to the private sector or other government agencies.

This latter distinction reflected a traditional U.S. policy requiring operational or commercial activities to be conducted in the private sector, a policy quite different from that of many other countries. The U.S. government has "subsidized" in one way or another industries in the transportation, agriculture, and health, education and welfare areas with varying returns. The goal of such programs is frequently to keep as much economic activity as possible in nongovernment situations and to urge private entities to enter into provision of needed or useful services. The careful clarification between research and operations in the Space Act moreover serves to emphasize the conception of NASA as a highly advanced research organization, unique in the world. In addition, the field of communication manifests in particular the traditional trend in American policy which favors private enterprise development of new technology; over the past hundred years the federal government has assisted the development of the telegraph, undersea cable, and radio technology. Although the charter does not restrict government agencies from operating communication satellites, communications in the United States are traditionally controlled by the private sector. By implication, NASA would eventually transfer satellite communications technology, when developed to the proper point, to privately owned communications firms.

The charter omits any mention of regulatory or policymaking power for NASA. While Section (c) (8) of the charter gives the agency statutory responsibility for effecting the best utilization of U.S.

scientific and engineering resources, it does not set limits on NASA's role. Could NASA plan industry research efforts? Could it assume control of international negotiation efforts for space projects? Apropos to space communications, could it research satellite communications completely independent of industry efforts, keeping developmental research results from private enterprise? Or could it cooperate with *all* industries interested in, for example, satellite communications? Hypothetical problems reveal the breadth of the charter in providing only very general guidelines for NASA's policy planners.

By 1961 the charter's lack of specificity with regard to satellite communications was coming to light under the impetus of certain developments: (1) the highly successful demonstration of a passive communication satellite, Echo, in August 1960; (2) the intensified scrutiny of the technology by industry; (3) AT&T's announcement of plans to establish a satellite communications system; (4) a congressional report pointing out deficiencies and ambiguities in the government communications framework, not only with existing regulation matters (frequency allocation, rates, international communications responsibilities) but also with intragovernmental coordination, identification of a central federal authority for communications policy, and implications of various policies.[14] As NASA embarked upon its communication satellite program in 1959, with only vaguely defined charter responsibilities for space communications, especially with respect to the role of private communication concerns and international regulatory policies, these developments and their sensitivities were not envisioned.

Thus, while NASA's charter laid out basic organizational precepts, in the long run it would be shown far too general for situations involving NASA-private sector overlap. The establishment of NASA as an advanced space research organization served as the requisite impetus for communication satellite technology development. While the Defense Department undertook its own ambitious and highly classified communications program, the civilian agency, NASA, came to provide useful experimental data and carefully planned technological progress. As the space agency's proficiency was recognized, and as interest in communication satellites grew, other governmental entities moved to support NASA's experimentation and to consider imminent policy maneuvers associated with commercialization of the new communications tool. Key technology advances and NASA's solid relations with DOD and private industries brought the agency to a pivotal point in its own conception: how far could its research and development satellite program go before encountering political and economic issues? What role could NASA assume in dealing with those issues? What could be the relationship of a research arm of the government with commercial forces wishing to capitalize on a tax-supported development?

The years 1958 to 1961 were a time of key technological and political decisions which illuminated the variety of difficulties in formulating technological policy for the communication satellite area.

Technological Alternatives

By late 1958, when NASA was established, there were two recognized genres of communication satellite technology. Passive satellites, the first type, act simply as reflectors, allowing a beamed signal to bounce off of a mirror-like surface to a ground terminal. A passive satellite operates at low-altitudes and cannot amplify a signal, nor can it control that signal's direction. Anyone can make use of this sort of sphere reflector because it allows multiple and random access. There can be no earth-based control over a passive satellite's use. The passive satellite has the advantage of not requiring any electronic components which could fail or need repair; therefore it is very reliable. The main disadvantages of the early passive satellites were (1) a global system would require approximately twenty-four passive spheres which would be costly to launch, and (2) only large and expensive ground terminals could receive the reflected signals.

Active satellites, the second type, receive messages and retransmit (not reflect) them using a delayed or real-time electrical repeater and a terrestrial receiver. The active satellite contains a radio receiver to pick up a signal transmitted from earth, and a radio transmitter to retransmit the signal. It requires electronic amplifiers to increase the received signal strength. Two basic types of active satellites were envisioned in 1958: one, called a "store and forward" or delayed repeater type, accepts a signal while travelling around the earth, holds it until positioned over an appropriate ground station, and then retransmits it upon command; the other, called a "line of sight" repeater, operates at such high altitudes that it is able to reach the next station or another satellite without delay or movement of the satellite itself. A third variety of active satellite seemed in the very distant future in 1958. This was the synchronous satellite which was conceived of as operating at very high altitudes over one point of the earth, enabling the craft to broadcast to approximately one third of the globe. It later proved to be the case that this type of satellite was not as far from successful development as previously thought.

The advantages of active satellites are that they are directly controllable by their operators and that their ground systems require less costly and lower power equipment to receive the amplified and retransmitted signal. The disadvantages are that such satellites contain sensitive electrical equipment which might fail in space, making the entire satellite useless, and that they require larger, more powerful boosters to achieve orbit. The synchronous or high-altitude types of satellites offer the advantages of greater area coverage (theoretically only three synchronous satellites would be needed to cover the entire earth) and fixed coverage, obviating the need for extensive and complex tracking stations.

The Delegation of Satellite Responsibilities

Satellite communication systems came under intensive examination by government (NASA and DOD) and commercial entities during 1958. Actually, commercial interests in satellite communications predated the establishment of NASA. Besides the article by John Pierce mentioned earlier, the Radio Corporation of America (RCA) had also examined the concept of communications satellites in the early 50s[15] as had Lockheed Aircraft Corporation in 1954.[16] By the time U.S. booster technology demonstrated the capability to send satellites into orbit (1958), many corporations seemed convinced of an early and successful use of communication satellite technology, even though not one communication satellite had yet been launched. John Pierce, associated with Bell Laboratories, stated before Congress in early 1959 that four important advances in microwave art – better microwave antennas, broadband transistors, higher frequency transistors, and the development of a microwave amplifier called a maser – contributed to the increased commercial interest in satellite communications.[17] He indicated that Bell Laboratories were examining requirements for a passive satellite system.[18] International Telephone and Telegraph (ITT) selected the active satellite for its later studies because they were "somewhat afraid – for commercial use – of the large cost of the powerful transmitters necessary to establish the passive satellite connection" and they wanted "to try to take full advantage of this satellite to cover a large number of communication needs."[19] General Electric and Lockheed both indicated that they felt an operational system could be implemented soon.[20] By 1960 the major communications and aircraft businesses were actively pursuing NASA contracts for communication satellites as well as conducting their own research in the area.

American Telephone and Telegraph seemed to be moving most rapidly. It was working on a plan which envisioned the use of fifty active satellites weighing 150 pounds each, at random low-orbit around the earth. Random orbits sidestepped attitude control problems which at that time had not been solved. One commentator observed that "AT&T, with visibly the largest stake in the new business, pushed so aggressively that it raised fears in Washington that it was out to extend its already dominant position into commercial space communication. There was little doubt that AT&T, with assets of $ 22.6 billion, and able to make yearly capital outlays running around $ 2.5 billion, could take on the job."[21] As AT&T and other companies moved more and more quickly with their satellite plans, NASA as well as other government agencies were pressed to face many non-technical problems concerning legal, regulatory, international and economic implications associated with satellite technology.

NASA chose to embark upon its own communication satellite program and gave initial priority to a research and development plan over and above concern with policy matters. An orderly plan for national development in space required that NASA and the Department of Defense (the only government entities with space programs) jointly discuss their projects to try to avoid duplication and to coordinate their goals. In November of 1958 Killian and representatives of ARPA, NASA and the DOD met to decide on a policy for satellite-based communication systems.[22] It was decided that ARPA would continue to work in the active satellite field while NASA pursued passive systems. This decision reflected in part the DOD's programs with Score and Courier, both active satellites. The agreement did not imply that passive systems were intrinsically peaceful or that active systems had only military application. Rather, it seemed a logical division of responsibilities. Richard E. Horner, a former associate administrator of NASA, stated the following:

> We . . . decided on the basis of talents that happened to be in the various laboratories on either side, the inclinations, the relative utility in the military or the civil side and on the basis of this, we decided that . . . the active communications satellite [was] the responsibility of the Department of Defense.[23]

The personnel that NASA inherited from NACA and the various military programs had been working on the erectable structures required for passive communications, while individuals from the DOD had acquired electronics experience which would be valuable to active satellite experimentation. Additionally, NASA felt that the passive system had relatively early operational potential because it would not require as large a booster as an active system. A powerful booster was necessary to ensure the reliability of active satellite systems since it would enable the satellites to carry enough weight for precautionary equipment to forestall initial system failures.[24] There is also evidence that ARPA decided that an active satellite system had tactical advantages. The Defense Department considered that a communication satellite in a synchronous twenty-four-hour orbit would meet many military communication requirements. This interest probably influenced the NASA-DOD agreement regarding division of work on communication satellites. Therefore NASA and DOD agreed that the former should develop a passive satellite capability while DOD started on a program to develop certain forms of the active communication satellite.[25]

Early Active Satellite Experiments

Since its efforts with Vanguard, DOD had orbited one very successful experimental communication satellite called Score (Signal Communication by Orbiting Relay Equipment). This project showed that communications satellites might prove to be a much more realistic application of the technology than earlier studies of satellites as ballistic and psychological weapons had suggested; the military's need for an internal communication system to coordinate troops, aircraft, ships and missile installations around the world produced a concrete military requirement for communication satellites. Satellites were especially suited to the military's special communication needs of reliability, security, and resistance to interference or jamming. Both radio and cable communications, since cables were subject to sabotage or destruction by natural or accidental causes and high-frequency radio circuits had a low reliability and were subject to interception and jamming, lacked the perfection sought in a military communications system.[26]

In July of 1958 DOD assigned the communications portion of project Score to the U.S. Army Signal Research Laboratory, and within five months the Air Force successfully launched the satellite.[27]

Using simple off-the-shelf VHF equipment, Score broadcast a prerecorded Christmas message from President Eisenhower:

> This is the President of the United States speaking. Through the marvel of scientific advance, my voice is coming to you from a satellite circling in outer space. My message is a simple one. Through this unique means, I convey to you and to all mankind America's wish for peace on earth and good will towards men everywhere.[28]

This first voice communication via satellite dramatically demonstrated the potential of communication satellites.

The Score satellite design allowed for both delayed repeater and real-time active repeater operation. As a delayed repeater, the satellite would record information transmitted to it from a ground station and on command would transmit previously stored information back to earth. As a real time repeater, the satellite bypassed the recording mechanism and transmitted directly to ground stations located in California, Arizona, Texas and Georgia (although good contact with all was unusual). Both modes of operation were characteristic of an active satellite equipped with receiving and transmitting equipment, as opposed to the passive satellites which would be developed by NASA.

DOD did not plan Score as an operational prototype but rather as an experimental demonstration of the feasibility of satellite communication. During the twelve days that the batteries functioned, the experiment succeeded in achieving its goals. Among the Score achievements were "(1) the first successful relay of teletype signals through an orbiting station, (2) the first successful delayed repeater communication from earth to satellite to another point on earth at a later time, and (3) the first successful multi-channel teletype transmission by delayed repeater."[29]

Project Courier, a follow-up experiment to Score, demonstrated the feasibility and operational capabilities of a delayed repeater satellite communications system with potential military application.[30] The program had begun in September of 1958 when the Army Signal Research and Development Laboratory submitted the technical proposal for Courier to the Advanced Research and Development Agency of DOD. The Air Force launched Courier Ia on 18 August, but it failed to reach orbit due to a missile malfunction; subsequently, on 4 October 1960, they successfully launched Courier Ib into orbit. The Courier satellite was more sophisticated than Score:

the satellite payload was heavier; it was capable of transmitting twenty-two teletype channels and four voice channels instead of one voice or seven, sixty word-per-minute teletype channels; it operated at a higher speed; and it derived electrical power from solar cells rather than short-lived batteries.

Courier Ib experiments were designed to test communications performance, satellite performance, and system resistance to jamming. The satellite remained operational for only seventeen days before it inexplicably ceased to respond to ground control commands. The major contribution of the Courier experiment was its demonstration of the feasibility of delayed repeater high-capacity digital satellite communications. Nevertheless, the satellite's early failure keynoted the additional design and test procedures needed for eventual operational satellite applications.[31] The Score and Courier tests piqued interest in communication satellites rather than dramatically advancing the state of the art. Indeed, later Defense Department programs with communication spacecraft took a widely different turn, ultimately too ambitious for existing skills and equipment. Yet it was Score and Courier which until late 1962 remained as the only active communication satellite launches for the United States. Neither Score, primarily a demonstration satellite, nor Courier, a first step in engineering a space communications capability, were types of satellites particularly useful to military or commercial interests because of the two-hour delay involved in receiving a response to a given message. Most potential uses for satellite communications, including telephone transmissions (the major area of interest in the new technology) required simultaneous transmit/receive capabilities.

Passive Satellite Experimentation

NASA began its passive satellite experiments when it inherited two passive communication projects involving inflatable spheres. As early as 1956, W.J. O'Sullivan of NACA's Langley Aeronautical Laboratory began a program to design a twelve-foot diameter metal and plastic balloon, which would be launched during the I.G.Y. in a small container and then ejected and inflated when in space. Meanwhile, Pierce was working on the communication possibilities of radio mirrors as orbital relays.[32] Whereas O'Sullivan had designed his sphere to measure upper atmospheric densities, Pierce's idea emphasized communication possibilities of the sphere. Pierce promised O'Sullivan a cooperative experiment combining both uses of the inflatable sphere. By early 1959 NASA accepted the idea for Echo, a reflecting communications sphere, as its first communications satellite program.[33]

A predecessor of Echo, a small twelve-foot diameter inflatable sphere with little communications utility, was test-fired on 23 October 1958 by NASA with the Army as executive agent. The launch failed. This satellite, called Beacon, consisted of micro-thin plastic covered with very reflective aluminum foil. Four test launches of the balloon deployment system, called Shotput, were also conducted. The larger 100-foot diameter Echo was then in the design stages; planners hoped to launch it in late 1959 of 1960. Langley Research Center (formerly Langley Aeronautical Laboratory of NACA) built Echo from thin mylar plastic for light weight with a vapor deposit of aluminum for electrical conductivity. Its orbit was to be as high as possible to afford the largest possible time that two stations in the United States could observe it; altitude was also important to decrease the deterioration effects of the earth's own atmosphere upon the sphere.[34]

NASA made plans for a network of ground stations to watch and experiment with the satellite. Certain aspects of the Echo's tracking program grew out of arrangements made as part of the U.S. program with I.G.Y. The Jet Propulsion Laboratory of the California Institute of Technology in Goldstone, California, organized a station to transmit and receive satellite signals. The Naval Research Laboratory set up a similar station in Maryland. AT&T established a major complex at Holmdel, New Jersey, where it readied a sixty-foot diameter antenna to transmit and a horn reflector antenna to receive signals. This latter antenna was completely new and a great improvement over conventional dish antennas. The Holmdel station became a primary testing facility. Other testing stations which came to be involved with the Echo program were established in France, Great Britain, the U.S.S.R., Trinidad, and in the states of Texas, Iowa, New York and Ohio.[35] On 10 January 1959 NASA and DOD agreed on a "National Program to Meet Satellite and Space Vehicle Tracking and Surveillance Requirements for Fiscal Year 1959 and 1960" which delineated the departments' responsibilities, mutual use arrangements, and coordination mechanism; this was a necessary prerequisite to well-planned tracking of the Echo spacecraft.[36]

Echo I was built with seamed, tapered sections coming together at the top of the satellite, and was packed along with its inflating device into a small launch container. The inflating device was a stoppered bag of water that opened when the launch container reached space.

Low air pressures then vaporized the water, which unfolded and inflated the sphere. On 28 October 1958 the first test failed when the sphere burst apart. Scientists altered the inflation system and the folding pattern for packing the satellite.

On 13 May 1960 NASA launched the improved sphere with a new launch vehicle, the Delta I, but the guidance system malfunctioned and the satellite never reached orbit. The first Echo finally went into orbit on 12 August 1960. Stations all over the world observed the satellite and experimented with it. The system was tested, examined and declared a success. During Echo's first complete pass it transmitted a message by President Eisenhower from the Jet Propulsion Laboratory to Bell's Holmdel Laboratory. On 18 August Echo provided the first real-time satellite transmission of a transatlantic signal when the *Centre National d'Etudes de Telecommunication* in France received a signal sent by the Holmdel station.[37] Echo proved its multiple accessibility and was utilized by many participating terminals. Leonard Jaffe of NASA wrote "Echo I had more to do with the motivation of following communications satellite research than any other single event."[38]

The first passive satellite became a tremendous success and vindicated earlier speculations on space communications. NASA began an Echo II project in late 1960 to create a satellite more rigid than Echo I in order to resist the forces of drag in space and solar pressure. It launched Echo II on 25 January 1964. The second Echo satellite started the first international communications experiments between the United States and the Soviet Union under a bilateral space agreement between NASA and the Academy of Sciences of the Soviet Union.[39] The communications experiment consisted of signal transmissions between Jodrell Bank Radio Observatory of the University of Manchester, England, for NASA and the Zimenski Observatory of Gorki State University for the Soviet Union. Although the link performance was only marginal, NASA considered the experiment a diplomatic success.[40]

In responding to potential passive satellite operational requirements, NASA planned in its 1960-61 program to develop a multisphere payload capability aboard a single launch vehicle, reasoning that a worldwide satellite communications system would require several satellites simultaneously in orbit around earth. The purpose of this project, called Rebound, was to limit the cost of launching multiple satellites needed for a low-altitude system. The Douglas Aircraft Corporation performed an initial design study of a multilaunch spacecraft which would eject three or more Echo-type satellites at the proper intervals in a circular orbit.[41] Limited line of sight due to the earth's curvature meant that twenty-six satellites in a 3,000 to 4,000 mile orbit would be required to serve ninety-nine percent of ground stations. The logistic contrast with high-altitude, wide-area systems is obvious; however, such satellites were required to be geosynchronous, rotating through space at the same speed as the earth's surface below. Such synchronous satellites were thought hard to keep in position; hence NASA planned its program for a low-level system. The active/passive jurisdictional distinction with DOD also contributed to keeping NASA working only on passive designs.

Companies such as ITT, RCA, Bell Telephone Laboratories, General Electric, and others were all watching the Echo experiments to gauge commercial possibilities. Although Echo was highly successful, many people began to speculate that active satellites were the real hope of the future; they were far more reliable in terms of orbit than passive systems and a complete network required fewer of them than would a similar network based on passive spacecraft. Moreover, they were controllable and were not open to random use by any equipped station. Finally, ground terminals needed less power to receive their signals. Between Echo's 1958 inception and its August 1960 launch, industry research and government activity focused increasingly on active communication satellites.

A number of specific activities in addition to Echo fired this interest. They included: (a) problems with the satellite communications programs of the Department of Defense, (b) increased research and plans for commercial uses of communication satellites on the parts of Hughes Aircraft and AT&T, (c) international discussion of satellite communications and frequency requirements at the 1959 Geneva Administrative Radio Conference and U.S. preparations for the 1963 Extraordinary Administrative Radio Conference, and (d) NASA's realization of and response to emerging operational possibilities for satellites. When combined, these factors caused a rethinking of NASA's commitment to only passive satellite research, culminating in a reversal of that policy in August 1960. Each of the above four factors, from the DOD's satellite program difficulties to international frequency discussions, set the stage for the major decisions affecting the communication satellite technology on both the engineering and institutional levels. One predictive news article grasped the situation:

Officials of the National Aeronautics and Space Administration have recently realized that the pace of space developments is outstripping the Government plans, organization, and concepts.

The space agency, which had tended to view itself as primarily a scientific-engineering research group, now finds itself plunged, without preparation, into such broad public policy questions as subsidies, licensing, regulation, and private versus public development of space activities.

There is also a growing awareness that the present space organization and law – set up only two years ago – are not going to be adequate to deal with activities in space that cut across many areas of interest, both within the Government and without.[42]

Defense Department Satellites

The Defense Department's Project Score, the satellite Courier Ib, the initiation of a program called Notus, and the West Ford Project from 1958 to 1960 directly affected NASA's communication satellite program. The promise of the first two satellites and the disappointment of the West Ford Project influenced the willingness of NASA, as the only other government entity working on communication satellites, to pursue active satellite technology development.

Score was not technically innovative, although, as Dryden of NASA stated, Score showed in "dramatic fashion some of the potentialities of the commercial satellite. This first step is expected to lead to an economically sound, wideband, reliable worldwide communications system."[43] Courier, a refinement of the delayed repeater Score-type satellite, decisively demonstrated the concept of communication satellites' utility for military operations.[44] Both satellites added substance to arguments supporting active satellite development for operational commercial use.[45]

These successful experiments encouraged DOD to move toward more ambitious capabilities. Additionally, there were clear security imperatives that persuaded DOD to embark upon a large-scale program to develop a communication satellite, and the optimal spacecraft was identified as one in a synchronous twenty-four hour orbit. Such a satellite system stationed over the equator would fulfill major military global communication requirements for instantaneous message exchange. Designated Notus, this program was planned in three progressive projects: Steer, Decree, and Tackle. Steer was to use UHF in a polar orbit; Decree would be a synchronous satellite requiring a yet-to-be-developed launch vehicle; Tackle would be comparable to Decree but did not require a new launch vehicle. During the middle of 1958 ARPA reviewed studies and proposals for this sort of satellite system and in the fall issued a memorandum establishing the necessary requirements. However, the program proved overly optimistic and expensive. Technical problems associated with controlling the craft in orbit, the complex command coding, the heavy (1,000 pounds) weight of the craft, and the originally planned electrical system which quickly moved into obsolescence, overwhelmed ARPA.[46] Assistant Secretary of Defense John H. Rubel testified:

> It became evident... that each of these projects and hence the aggregate of projects, represented a considerably more difficult and more costly undertaking than had been contemplated at the start. It became apparent, too, that a number of projects... were aimed at near term objectives which could probably not be attained on schedule....
>
> Moreover, it became increasingly apparent that even if successful development demonstrations were accomplished, economical operations in space could not be accomplished on the schedules proposed....[47]

In September 1960 DOD reoriented the effort, calling it Advent.[48] However, Advent proved no more successful than Notus. The entire program was subsequently cancelled.

DOD had simultaneously become involved in a passive satellite program. Originally called Needles and later West Ford, this relay system grew out of a concept first introduced in 1958 by Lincoln Laboratories of the Massachusetts Institute of Technology. The West Ford plan called for a system of belts of small wire dipoles in orbit around the earth which could act as reflectors, each wire a small antenna for microwaves. This system was especially useful for military communications, although it would not be capable of good quality voice and television transmission. These dipole belts required little tracking, provided high reliability, and could support a very large number of independent circuits. The West Ford proposal caused a stir in the international scientific community which feared that the dipole belts would interfere with various astronomical experiments. However, U.S. National Space Board did give the Air Force research and development organization permission to undertake the project. Defense interest in the West Ford passive communications system served to undercut the distinct and functional division between NASA and DOD relative to space-based communications systems research on active versus passive relays.

The Defense Department's efforts with communication satellites, therefore, left a temporary gap in active satellite development. By late 1959 its energies were spread among five different projects – Steer, Decree, Tackle, Courier and West Ford. Even as Courier was proving itself in late 1960, work on Notus and later Advent was not going well, and the Defense Department's organizational and administrative requirements were evolving to meet modified pressures and needs. The original agreement with NASA regarding delegation of research on active and passive systems was not sufficient to allow DOD to meet tactical requirements (which encouraged the West Ford idea) as well as to develop the optimal active communication satellite it felt necessary. This gap was an invitation for a NASA-sponsored active satellite program.

Private Industry and Active Satellites

Meanwhile, private industry was urging more rapid development of space-based communication technology. Its target was logically NASA, the civilian space research organization, since it had statutory responsibilities to aid development of transferable technology. Both AT&T and Hughes Aircraft Company started a lobbying effort to persuade NASA to consider technology for active satellite systems. Ever since the Russian Sputnik focused attention on space, commercial communications carriers had begun to assess the satellite relay concept. Hughes Aircraft Company and AT&T had progressed the farthest on such studies.

Bell Telephone began its planning very early. During 1958 and 1959 Bell scientists investigated an operational passive satellite system and concluded that twenty-four spheres would be needed for nearly continuous transatlantic communications.[49] In discussing Bell Telephone's plans for communication satellites before Congress, John Pierce noted their activities at the Holmdel station. He also mentioned studies on components and structures for active satellite repeaters.[50] A Bell Telephone memorandum "Radio Communication by Means of Satellites" by C.C. Cutler was sent to Dryden of NASA in June of 1959 as a sample of what Bell was thinking about in the satellite field. This memorandum came to no conclusions as to which type of system (active or passive) was most desirable. The report aptly noted:

> Problems of propagation, modulation systems, noise and power efficiency are pertinent to all systems and can be considered in general terms. Other problems, such as susceptibility to jamming, secrecy, and portability apply particularly to military and tactical applications. Compatibility with existing systems, reliability, orbit stability and long life are particularly important to commercial (telephone system) use.[51]

The report suggested that passive systems might be most useful for commercial communications traffic while military requirements would best be met by active repeaters. AT&T's plans progressed to the point where by 1960 it publicly proposed a private low-altitude active satellite system to the Federal Communications Commission (FCC).[52] This was outlined to the FCC on 11 July and incorporated a service plan for fifty satellites in polar orbit at 3,000-mile altitude. Bell Telephone Laboratories had begun development during 1959 toward this end using their funds.

AT&T had also expressed sustained interest in FCC frequency allocations which would have some bearing on space communications. During 1957 when the FCC began proceedings on Docket 11866 concerning frequency allocations for microwave bandwidths, AT&T opposed allocations that would private microwave systems to use frequency slots possibly needed for space communications. AT&T and other communications firms prevailed upon the FCC to take no action on the matter even though the FCC had already decided to allow the licensing of microwave transmitters in the frequency under consideration. When in May 1960 the FCC reopened Docket 11866, AT&T gave testimony urging the commission to allocate or plan for frequencies useful for space relays. Although the fear was still prevalent that if private entities established microwave transmitters, in the near future there would later be a shortage of frequencies for satellites, the FCC nonetheless decided against the space interests of the common carriers. AT&T charged that the FCC decision was "shortsighted and favors only a small segment of the public."[53]

For its part Hughes Aircraft Company was interested in active satellite development exclusively. During 1959 Harold Rosen and Donald Williams, two engineers working at Hughes, came up with plans for a decidedly innovative satellite capable of attaining synchronous orbit. Along with Thomas Hudspeth, an electrical engineer, Rosen and Williams proposed a design for a satellite which could have a controlled spin once in orbit with antennas pointing at the earth at all times. By September of 1959 they were ready to present their ideas to Hughes' management for evaluation.[54] Evaluation was very favorable even though the project represented a sizable investment of capital and organizational maneuvering with NASA, the FCC and the Department of State.[55] The recommendation by the Hughes Communications System Division Director, S.G. Lutz, read:

> If another company gets into orbit first, much of the publicity and prestige value will be lost and we would have to compete for traffic. Furthermore, this must be a low-cost program and delays increase cost. Consequently, the program should be planned to start development now.[56]

Rosen figured the entire system of three satellites world cost five million dollars. Hughes management, however, was not certain enough of the plan to adopt it. Contacts were therefore made with NASA to assay its interest in this type of satellite. S.G. Lutz discussed in a 1959 study, "An Eventual Satellite Communication System," various parameters of the proposed synchronous system including economics, frequency sharing, multiple access, and jamming. A brochure called *Commercial Communication Satellite* was prepared by Rosen and Williams in January 1960 to describe the system.[57] Formal presentations were made to NASA in early 1960.[58] However, NASA was unsure of the Scout launch vehicle since it was still under development [59] and problems existed with respect to NASA working on active communication satellites, as well as with supplying a launch site. Pending resolution of these problems, NASA declined to implement the Hughes proposal.

Although there was no way Hughes could undertake sponsorship of boosters, launch site and the satellite, it decided to begin spacecraft development. During 1960 Hughes contacted the Department of Defense and the Space Science Panel of the President's Science Advisory Committee.[60] There was still not enough enthusiasm for any of these entities to act upon the synchronous satellite idea. Hughes' advanced concepts did nevertheless reinforce the validity of the active communication satellite as one of commercial promise. At least to some degree synchronous satellite salesmanship on the part of Hughes influenced NASA and DOD to reevaluate their division of communication satellite work into separate active and passive technologies. Rather than developing a fifth stage for the four-stage Scout launch vehicle, Leonard Jaffe of NASA proposed a change to a Delta rocket which was then being developed as a basic NASA launch vehicle. It was as a result of this change that DOD and NASA acceptance of the synchronous satellite project was ultimately assured.

4

COMMUNICATION SATELLITE POLICY PLANNING (1959-1964): NASA'S RESPONSE TO THE TECHNOLOGIC IMPERATIVE

The Communications Context

Possibilities for satellite communications were receiving increased attention during 1959 and 1960. Political and economic ramifications of the technology were beginning to surface and international frequency allocation for space telecommunications seemed necessary. These factors, among others, operated upon the policymaking levels of the U.S. government to force a detailed examination of communication satellite policy planning. Reviews of frequency allocation needs for space telecommunications were undertaken throughout 1959 and 1960, primarily by the State Department.[1]

The 1959 Geneva meeting of the International Telecommunication Union (ITU) took a first successful step in reserving some thirteen frequency bands for space communications. At that time interest in space communications frequency was expressed only by the United States, the United Kingdom and the U.S.S.R.[2] The meeting recognized the rapid progress in space research and the need for space telecommunications; hence, another ITU session was planned for 1963 to take up the matter of frequencies for space use. It was hoped by that time more experimental data would be available and national plans would be known.

Few foreign countries had expressed definite interest in satellite communications by 1960. The United Nations, however, established an ad hoc Committee on the Peaceful Uses of Outer Space in December of 1958 to extend the success of the I.G.Y. space experiments and to try to orient space activities toward peaceful ends. This became one early avenue for expression of international intentions regarding communication satellites.[3] By 1960 the U.N. committee was stressing the need for necessary frequency allocation as well as the potential of communication satellite technology.[4]

The effect of the early U.S. policy planning for the 1963 Extraordinary Administrative Radio Conference was to focus NASA's attention on the operational potential of communication satellites. In a letter of 12 July 1960, one NASA official stated the duty of NASA to lead in space communications research and development and its intentions to cooperate internationally:

> An operating worldwide communications satellite system is probably one of the first areas in which a practical use may be made of satellites. This practical use may be in either the form of active or passive communication relays for intercontinental or international communications. . . . Since communications transcend national boundaries, the exploitation of satellites for peaceful communications will require the closest possible active cooperative effort . . . greatest in the areas of ground terminals, the design and development of equipment, and frequency allocation and management.[5]

The renewed focus on active communication satellites occured within the context of this increasing awareness of international implications. AT&T had contacted France, Britain and Germany about low-altitude active satellite plans for transatlantic telephone and television.[6] If NASA were to plan adequately for its experimental frequency needs and its international responsibilities, it needed to consider active satellite technology. In short, the growing international context of satellite communications, as well as AT&T's rapid movement toward establishing an international private space telecommunications system, helped to influence NASA's changeover to active satellite work.[7]

NASA's recognition of communication satellite technology as an issue with important economic and political implications brought this question of active vs. passive satellite development to its decisive juncture. Although NASA publicly expressed enthusiasm for the technology throughout 1959 and early 1960, it was not until October 1960 that NASA Administrator Glennan in a public statement formally acknowledged the operational potential of communication satellite technology. This along with the decision to develop the active communication satellites constituted an early recognition of commercial opportunities in the field; it also foreshadowed what NASA would do when faced with pressures for technology development and eventual transfer to the private sector.

It is interesting to note that very early space program plans never emphasized the commercial applications of communication satellites. A program statement for NASA of January 1959 stated merely that "the NASA program in these areas [meteorological and communication satellites] is aimed at the solution of the scientific and technical problems inherent in each system and the demonstration of practical applications of the systems."[8] It was nevertheless understood in both industry and government circles that cooperation with each other was necessary in satellite communications, and that although definite commercial requirements or programs could not be established in 1959, "the Government must lead the way and that, later, commercial concerns [would be] prepared to invest large sums in proven techniques and hardware."[9]

NASA's initial communications program interests were represented by the Echo project and by the appointment of Leonard Jaffe of NASA to ARPA's Requirements and Technological Panel for Communications Satellites.[10] The latter group reviewed the programs of both agencies to eliminate duplication and to share information.[11] Both agencies pursued their separate programs until mid-1960, when NASA Administrator Glennan approached John Rubel, deputy director of Defense Research and Engineering, about the possibility of NASA developing an active, medium-altitude satellite.[12] Until this point NASA had given little thought to commercial applications of satellite technology. NASA's cautious attitude toward its future frequency needs is indicative of the priority level of this concern. Had the agency been interested in exploring commercially usable communication satellite technology, its frequency needs might have escalated earlier than they actually did. NASA noted, for example, in a response to a July 1960 congressional inquiry that

> the small space research bands allocated in the Geneva ITU Conference [1959], however, will be utilized to capacity and will give us some of the basic research frequencies needed. . . . Thus we may say that during this research phase of space operations, normal IRAC procedures will supply NASA with enough frequencies. Later, when widebands such as for a Weather Bureau meteorological satellite or for a commercial communications satellite become necessary, then the proposed 1963 ITU Conference should find and clear the bands needed.[13]

Even though NASA realized its statutory responsibilities in the securing of frequencies for space activities and the international nature of frequency allocation, as evidenced by its participation in the planning for the 1963 conferences, the space agency felt that no frequency increases would be needed between 1959 and 1963.

While NASA was not particularly aggressive in responding to industry interest in the technology, particularly on the part of AT&T, it must be remembered that the agency was still establishing its programs, and a great many other projects were demanding considerable attention. The marketing efforts undertaken by Hughes and AT&T met no direct response until late 1960,[14] although NASA met with AT&T as early as 29 June 1960 and with Hughes in August and with General Electric in September.[15] Undoubtedly NASA did feel a certain amount of pressure as a result of industry imperatives. One NASA internal memo commented in 1960:

> We should explain to Mr. Ford [then chairman of the FCC] the consequences of industrial activities upon our program. A number of interested firms, carriers, and broadcasters and electronic component manufacturers, have raised questions with NASA which indicates that they need to know immediately the attitude and approach of NASA toward the broader issues.[16]

NASA-industry contacts, therefore, were partly responsible for the agency considering policy problems involved in commercializing satellite communications.

Emerging Policy Concerns

The prospect of Echo's success was the immediate cause for undertaking policy considerations in communication satellites. Before Echo was launched, NASA Administrator Glennan spoke with President Eisenhower about his concern for impending commercialization and NASA-private sector relationships. President Eisenhower reportedly requested that the administrator begin to exploit the benefits of communication satellite technology. NASA, as a consequence, was given a lead role in communication satellite development focusing specifically on policy development, leaving technology development as a responsibility shared with private industry.[17]

Glennan proceeded to take two steps: first, he created a special office to conduct a full exploration of how to organize resources (financial and technical) to facilitate technology transfer; and second, he approached DOD to renegotiate the dichotomous active/passive satellite policy. Glennan's decisions in this matter constituted (1) a recognition of the technological possibilities and importance of low-altitude active repeaters for which DOD had no program; (2) a culmination of industry pressures for satellite communications; (3) a recognition of the problems of the Advent program, then the only active satellite program; and (4) a tacit realization of imminent international interest in or activity with the technology. On 9 August 1960 Glennan and the Deputy Secretary of Defense James H. Douglas agreed that NASA ought to begin development of active communication satellites;[18] in September Robert G. Nunn was appointed special assistant to NASA Administrator Glennan to work on policy problems concerning utilization of non-military communication satellite systems.[19] NASA, consequently, gained the jurisdictional mechanism allowing it to explore the promising active satellite field, and Nunn began to work with satellite policy resolution.

Even before his formal appointment as special assistant Nunn had formulated a series of major policy directives for government response to communication satellite issues:

(1) that operational satellite systems present issues that are international in scope;
(2) that many government agencies must be jurisdictionally involved in federal communication satellite R&D and utilization;
(3) that NASA has a dominant interest in the R&D phase although legislation is needed for definition of institutional arrangements for operational satellite systems;
(4) that commercial satellite applications still require much investment in R&D and that whether the government or private industry makes that investment is an issue; and
(5) that a national policy is requisite because of increasing commercial interest in the satellite.[20]

According to Nunn, these recommendations suggested that the government should not preempt any activity which could be undertaken by private enterprise, and that it should lead in developing commercial satellite applications and in maintaining distinctions between administrative (regulatory) and research and development responsibilities. Further, premature policy formulation should be avoided and some practical control over imminent commercial applications should be exercised by the executive branch.[20] The two basic issues precipitated in later discussions by these directives concerned the extent to which government should spend money in an area where there was industry interest and the propriety of allowing industrial organizations to launch satellites.[21] Nunn's appointment confirmed NASA's commitment to resolving these issues.

Nonetheless, policy considerations were relegated to a secondary status compared to technology development. The first priority was to get working communication satellites into the air. In September 1960, as policy problems began to mount around the impending commercialization and operational utilization of communication satellites, NASA's primary response still centered on technology research and development.

Dialogue with the Private Sector

By the time NASA made its decision to develop an active satellite capability, commercialization factors were gaining attention. A number of business and government studies were undertaken to explore both economic and institutional considerations: A "Business Planning Study for a Commercial Telecommunications Satellite" was prepared by Booz-Allen and Hamilton for Lockheed Aircraft Corporation;[22] the Rand Corporation was contracted by NASA for a number of research studies;[23] Jet Propulsion Laboratory in California completed "A Resumé of World Wide Commercial Communications";[24] United Research Incorporated prepared a policy study;[25] and a Senate *Policy Planning Report* outlined for Congress policy requirements current as of November 1960. Economic analysis indicated that communication demands were increasing:

> Whereas world population had expanded thirty percent in twenty years, the number of telephones had more than tripled to 133 million (over half of them in the U.S.), while overseas calls from and to the U.S. (some eighty percent of all international traffic) were increasing at a rate of almost twenty percent a year. The newer overseas telex or teletype service was growing even faster, at close to fifty percent a year.[26]

The Booz-Allen and Hamilton examination predicted that the projected demand would exceed the capacity of existing and presently planned cables within the near future.[27] Furthermore, it was indicated that development of a satellite system would be cost-effective in comparison to laying more cables to meet future demands. Rand Corporation studies estimated that a worldwide low-altitude system would provide 7,800 transoceanic channels, about twenty times the number now serving the United States, and that a single, high-altitude, twenty-four hour satellite would provide 4,800 channels.[28] In terms of cost per channel, Rand's figures indicated that a low-altitude system would cost approximately $ 8,500 a year per channel, compared with the cost of $ 27,000 a year per channel for a new underwater cable system.[29] It is apparent that the economic justification for communication satellites was an intensively studied factor in the early 1960's, whereas the institutional and political aspects of the technology's commercialization were assessed much more slowly.

NASA's role at this point can be viewed as one encompassing complex responsibilities. On the one hand, NASA was interested in facilitating satellite technology transfer to private industry; on the other, it had to develop satellite capability in the "public interest," a phrase not always synonymous with commercial interests. The space agency's responsibility was to preserve "the role of the United States as a leader in aeronautical and space science and technology and in the application thereof to the conduct of peaceful activities," a role exacerbated in the cold war context of rivalry with the Soviet Union.[30] A growing impetus to use the communication satellite as a tool to shape the U.S. image abroad forced the question of how soon communication satellites could be operational. The Senate *Policy Planning Report* observed:

> The fundamental question then arising is whether the United States should simply await the availability of such satellites in the normal course of space research, or whether the United States should identify particular programs, communication satellites among them, which it would deliberately accelerate in the interest of international cooperation and thus in the direct interest of national security.[31]

This policy question also coincided with a major economic consideration of private industry: to what extent and within what framework would NASA aid their developmental efforts in order to produce an early operational capability?

Special Assistant Nunn and Administrator Glennan agreed that conferences with industry would be useful to gather facts on development plans for communication satellites.[32] These conferences were planned for October of 1960. However, Glennan already had plans to field a public statement of NASA policy on communication satellites in early October. Apparently Glennan had proposed to

President Eisenhower that development of communication satellite technology was necessary, and that some entity should assume responsibility for this development. The president informally told Glennan that NASA should assume a lead role in the technology's development.[33] Thus, in a speech to the Oregon State Department of Planning and Development on 12 October 1960, Glennan, speaking of NASA's intended role, stated (1) that more research and development must be performed to bring satellite technology to an operational stage, (2) that a sound international policy was needed to implement an operational system and (3) that commercial services may involve nongovernmental activity in space.[34] He closed the speech by outlining NASA's plans for "early demonstration of the technical feasibility of very lightweight active-repeater satellites," and for support to private proposals on a cost-reimbursable basis for launch vehicles, tracking facilities, and technical services:

> Traditionally, communications services in this country have been provided by privately-financed carriers competing with one another to serve the public interest under Federal controls and regulations. There seems to be no reason to change that policy with the advent of communications satellites. It is clear, however, that such activities involving the launching of vehicles into outer space must be regulated in the public interest, even during the stages of developmental testing.[35]

Implying that NASA might decide to launch AT&T's satellite, the statement was the first public airing of several policies affecting NASA and private industry. The Oregon speech was an aggressive move for NASA; it touched off considerable interest in Congress and other governmental units.

Naturally many questions remained. The extent of NASA authority to provide launch facilities to private interests needed to be clearly determined; frequencies needed to be allocated, and appropriate licensing and international arrangements needed to be made. These were preconditions to the operation of any experimental commercial satellites. The prospect of institutionalized commercial systems raised even more complex issues: What type of system was best? Who would own the system? How would it be regulated? How could equal access be ensured and monopoly prevented? Would a monopoly or a licensing arrangement be advantageous? Who would negotiate arrangements for international participation in the system? These policy decisions were beyond the scope of exclusive NASA responsibility, but in late 1960 only the space agency was in the position to formulate policy.

The Congress moved to investigate the status of communication satellites with an inquiry led by Senator Lyndon Johnson and Representative Anfuso.[36] The Oregon speech was drafted with President Eisenhower's implicit approval but Congress had not been consulted.[37] As Congress and government agencies, primarily the FCC, geared up to face issues associated with industry involvement in the national communication satellite program, NASA continued on its own and outlined its policy of sponsorship for the low-altitude, active repeater Relay satellite project. Furthermore, a program philosophy was drawn up by the newly created Astronautics and Aeronautics Coordinating Board, composed of Army, Navy, Air Force, and NASA membership. The chairman of its Unmanned Spacecraft panel, Homer Newell, submitted to the panel a "NASA Program Philosophy on Communications Satellites."[38] The essentials of the document were that NASA would assist industry by supporting technically promising efforts on a cost-reimbursable basis and pricing vehicles, launches, and tracking facilities at NASA cost. Although the document describes NASA's Echo program and new, low-altitude, active repeater satellite plans, any mention of synchronous satellite plans was absent. The DOD's Advent program was supposedly adequate in that area.

Facilitating NASA's search for a program philosophy were the aforementioned industry conferences during the fall of 1960. Discussions arranged by Special Assistant Robert Nunn took place with various interested industries. These included international carriers such as American Telephone and Telegraph, International Telephone and Telegraph, and Radio Corporation of America. The following domestic carriers and equipment manufacturers were also represented: General Electric (GE), General Telephone and Electronics (GTE), Philco, and the Douglas Aircraft Company. The purpose of these conferences was to ascertain the extent of industry's then current involvement in the communication satellite field, to determine industry's intent to commit funds to the development of communication satellites, to discuss NASA's research and development program as a facilitator of an operational system, and to coordinate the roles of government and industry in developmental work and commercial applications.[39] The conferences were a clear indication of NASA's intent to promote the early establishment of an operational commercial communication system by formulating its research and development program in line with industry requirements and proposals.

Within the private sector AT&T had expressed the most interest in communication satellites. Hughes Aircraft Company had also begun exploring the possiblities for space communication, albeit on a lesser scale. Before September 1960 NASA had become aware of the satellite plans of both AT&T and Hughes Aircraft. By the 15th of that month AT&T was ready to request a NASA clarification of policies concerning aid to companies desirous of developing communication satellites. AT&T hoped that the space agency would be willing to launch its trial satellites on a reimbursable basis.[40] The Bell System was ready to commit thirty million dollars to the development of an active repeater, and up to three times that much if it proved feasible.[41] On 16 September 1960 representatives from AT&T met with NASA officials; in response to inquiries regarding the Bell System's plans and intent to commit funds to communication satellite development, George Best, vice president of AT&T, read a letter he had prepared for Glennan outlining AT&T's plans. The letter stated that "the Bell System now has underway the development of an active satellite and associated ground radio facilities and would like to proceed with an experimental trial of these facilities in intercontinental communications as soon as possible."[42] Best estimated that the first satellite could be ready for launch in eighteen to twenty months and noted that England, France and Germany had indicated a desire to participate in the experiment. Hughes Aircraft also had made contact with NASA regarding their ideas for communication satellites.

Moving quickly with its plans in the aftermath of Glennan's October speech, AT&T on 20 October 1960 presented NASA with a formal statement of the objectives and principle features of an experimental communications satellite. The document, "Proposed Bell System Experiment on Active Satellite Communications," stated that the first satellite could be launched within twelve months depending upon the assignment of necessary frequencies, the availability of launch vehicles, and agreements with foreign partners.[43] Another communiqué followed on 24 October 1960 which further outlined AT&T plans for communication satellite development beyond the experimental stage. This draft statement, which was submitted as a basis for discussions with NASA scheduled for 27 October, revealed that AT&T's communication satellite program would involve three phases. Phase I would consist of the launching of two experimental satellites within twelve months (the plan already submitted to

NASA). Phase II called for the launching in May 1962 of four additional satellites that would closely resemble the final commercial design, and Phase III involved the launching of twenty to forty satellites establishing a permanent overseas operation, the first scheduled for launch in May 1963.[44]

During the 27 October meeting it was made clear that NASA had serious reservation about AT&T plans for establishing an operational commercial network. Administrator Glennan opened the meeting by expressing several concerns. He noted first of all that the Bell plans did not take into account such requisite factors as vehicle availability, launch scheduling, and the need to mesh AT&T's anticipated satellite activities with NASA's research and development program. Further, Glennan noted that AT&T's form of publicizing its plans tended to create difficulties for NASA.[45] Glennan apparently had two fears: first, AT&T plans would proceed independently of NASA technical input and oversight, and NASA would not agree to provide launch vehicles on a first come—first serve basis, since it was responsible for coordinating the total developmental program. Second, Glennan was concerned that AT&T might aggrandize its public position by issuing misleading public announcements regarding NASA-AT&T cooperation.[46] At the conclusion of this meeting, an agreement was reached with AT&T to the effect that cooperative arrangements in the experimental research and development phase were appropriate and should be initiated. AT&T agreed that technical compatibility between Bell Laboratories' plans and NASA activities was desirable, and that preliminary conversations concerning the terms of a cooperative agreement which would consider the "so-called policy issues" should be initiated.[47] Although some observers felt that AT&T's early interest in communication satellites was part of a defensive maneuver and that its main commitment was actually with cable,[48] AT&T did manage with its own capital to get a satellite program moving.

The Eisenhower Policy

Discussions also opened among NASA, the FCC, and the executive branch. In early October 1960 Robert Nunn met with T.A.M. Craven of the FCC to discuss communication satellite policy. A memorandum of the meeting reports that "Mr. Craven stated that the FCC has no interest in getting into the space business. I [Nunn] ... reciprocated by saying that NASA has no interest in shaping national communications policy."[49] Nunn's concept of the issues revolved around the notion that communication satellite technology was not an essentially new instrument but merely extended a capability already existing and already under adequate regulation. NASA's primary role was then to launch satellites and to operationalize them as a system. The key concern of Nunn's office was how to organize money and resources to exploit the technology.[50] Yet during the next few months, as NASA decided how to enter active communication satellite development and how to facilitate the transfer of their discoveries and capabilities to the private sector, policy considerations and overlaps were unavoidable; even though the technical concerns of the space agency were not strictly issues of policy, they did have policy implications.

The executive branch was also considering policy matters. At a Cabinet meeting on 20 December 1960 NASA presented its recommendations for policy. A few days later President Eisenhower announced Administration decisions

> to achieve the early establishment of a communication satellite system which can be used on a commercial basis is a national objective which will require the concerted capabilities and funds of both Government and private enterprise and the cooperative participation of communications organizations in foreign countries. . . . With regard to communication satellites, I have directed the National Aeronautics and Space Administration to take the lead within the Executive Branch both to advance the needed research and development and to encourage private industry to apply its resources toward the earliest practicable utilization of space technology for commercial civil communications requirements. . . .[51]

This statement confirmed NASA's lead role in the communication satellite field and seemed even to mandate NASA's involvement beyond its research and development program. This opened the route to a cooperative agreement for AT&T's Telstar satellite demonstration and gave NASA a broader role in making arrangements for satellite experiments with private industry. With the nation now committed to early establishment of an operational communication satellite, NASA's role loomed large. This was the policy of a president soon to leave office; the decisions of President-elect John F. Kennedy would be much more critical for formulating NASA's role in satellite communications.

One of the space agency's first actions was to design specifications for an active, low-altitude repeater satellite project for its own program. This satellite, Relay, represented a government-sponsored alternative to AT&T's proposed low-altitude active satellite system. In October AT&T had requested authority from the FCC to operate an experimental satellite, following later (December 1960) with a submission to NASA of a detailed proposal for a joint undertaking.[52] The wider-based industry participation that would result from a competitive bid for NASA's Relay was obviously deemed more desirable than a single program of support for AT&T's Telstar in late 1960. One assessment noted that, whatever the government did through NASA to facilitate the development of the technology, it should avoid either creating a preferred position for AT&T or perpetuating one that already existed.[53] Later (January 1961) AT&T initiatives regarding negotiations with foreign nations for ground station facilities necessitated yet another top level AT&T-NASA meeting, at which AT&T indicated that it intended to submit a proposal in NASA's Relay contract competition in the hopes of avoiding NASA-AT&T duplication.[54] When discussion focused on AT&T's privately funded prototype satellite program, NASA indicated that, after a contractor had been chosen for the Relay contract, it would be possible for NASA to begin considering support of a privately-funded development program oriented toward operational prototypes.[55]

As government agencies became cognizant of imminent satellite commercialization, more interagency contact followed. Following the president's statement released 30 December 1960, NASA and the FCC began discussion of their responsibilities to facilitate rapid development of commercial communication satellite systems, and in February 1961 signed a memorandum of understanding outlining their respective roles and responsibilities. They agreed that NASA would promote commercial applications by directing its research and development toward that end, and that the FCC would continue to direct its activities toward the development and implementation of a commercial system through licensing and regulation of U.S. common carriers.[56] The memorandum was based on the assumption that the statutory authority of NASA and the FCC was adequate to enable those two agencies to guide the development of a commercial satellite system, but it also noted that "problems which may arise in connection with the regulation of a commercially operable system are being explored by both agencies and may result in legislative recommendations at a later date."[57]

As the year 1960 drew to a close, the course of events was leading towards AT&T's development and ownership of a commercial satellite system. Had those circumstances not changed, it is quite possible that by 1963 AT&T would have had its proposed worldwide communication satellite system licensed and regulated as a traditional common carrier by the FCC. Discussions had begun to coordinate NASA-AT&T research and development efforts and to work out policy issues such as patent and international arrangements. Subject to the award of the Relay contract, serious negotiations for launch facilities seemed imminent. AT&T had also entered into talks with the FCC to obtain authority to proceed with its plans.

The policy which took shape in late 1960 and early 1961 was developed out of expediency, its purpose simply being to proceed as quickly as possible with the development of an operational communication satellite system. In the absence of any congressional or executive policy directives to the contrary, NASA and the FCC moved along the lines of their own statutory authorities, with NASA developing technology and the FCC regulating commercial communications under traditional guidelines. Although it became clear by early 1961 that the policies developed by NASA and the FCC were not specifically designed to provide the easiest route for AT&T dominance in the communication satellite field, AT&T's preeminent position as the largest U.S. common carrier and sole international telephone carrier, together with its willingness and financial ability to commit large sums to the development of communication satellites, combined to give the image that commercial satellite utilization would very likely become AT&T utilization. Concern over the possibility of an AT&T monopoly was one factor that prompted a later reorientation of the direction that commercialization seemed to be following.

The Kennedy Policy

The year 1961 saw a rise in NASA's budget for communication satellite research and development and the finalizing of plans for Relay. A changeover in the administration from Eisenhower to Kennedy brought with it new direction and momentum in communication satellite policy and programs.

NASA's budget appropriations for 1961 reflected an increasing emphasis on satellite technology. Although the planned 1961 allocation for communication satellite programs was a considerable increase over that for 1960, newly elected President Kennedy sought an even larger increase, which by March elevated the budget request to nearly forty-five million dollars. This represented a ten million dollar increase over the Eisenhower Administration's request, which had been based on the assumption that industry would provide ten million dollars to NASA's developmental programs.[58] Kennedy's addition of that sum to the budget reflected a decision to postpone industry financing and provide full government financing of communication satellite research and developement.[59] Edward Welsh, once executive secretary of the National Aeronautics and Space Council, expressed the opinion that the ten million dollars previously designated as industry funding was in all probability intended to be AT&T funding, and that the Eisenhower Administration was prepared to let AT&T develop an operational communication satellite system.[60] If this is true, Kennedy's budgetary change marked a definite change in executive attitude regarding AT&T. It also indicated a desire to take another look at satellite technology and at the commercialization process.

In a press briefing on Kennedy's budget Glennan's successor as administrator of NASA, James E. Webb, was asked whether the budget change represented a basic change from the Eisenhower policy of government/industry partnership in the development of communication satellites, and whether this would hamper or preclude the possibility of NASA's launching a satellite for AT&T.[61] Webb replied that the basic change was simply to "postpone, until we know more than we know today, the real decision as to how this new result of space sciences and technology can be most usefully applied."[62] He noted that NASA now felt it was too early to start negotiations for industry to enter satellite operations, and that the budgetary change represented "a policy decision to have a good hard look at this before making commitments."[63] Webb repeated his interpretation of the budget addition before the House Committee on Science and Astronautics in April, adding a somewhat more direct reference to its implications for NASA-AT&T relations when he noted that postponing industry funding was made "pending . . . policy decisions as to the best means for *wider industry participation* and cooperation and coordination between American industry and the U.S. government. . . ."[64]

In the following year not only NASA, but the FCC, State, Justice and Defense Departments, the Executive Office of the President, the Space Council and a number of congressional commitees all examined the complex issues involved in establishing a commercial satellite system and gave an entirely new direction to American communication satellite policy. The addition of ten million dollars to NASA's budget for communication satellite development in March 1961 provided the first public indication that the government was not prepared to place the development of communication satellites in private hands until policy implications were carefully examined. Later events made it clear that the Kennedy Administration did not accept the procedures for implementing commercial operations outlined during the Eisenhower years.

The postponement of a final policy decision, however., did not deter the Bell System from going ahead with its privately funded experimental satellite program – an indication perhaps that AT&T still considered it possible to receive government sanction for establishing an operational system. In any case, AT&T determined that their satellite experiment was valuable enough to commit millions of dollar even without a final regulatory decision. In January 1961 the FCC granted AT&T a temporary license to conduct communication satellite experiments with England, France and Germany; in April the FCC informed NASA that since an experimental license had been issued, NASA need not wait for a final FCC ruling on frequency allocation for space communications in order to negotiate contracts with AT&T.[65] NASA delayed until after the announcement was made of the selection of RCA as the contractor for Project Relay in May of 1961, and then began negotiations to provide launch and tracking facilities for AT&T's Telstar experiment.

Within three months the details of the arrangement were worked out; on 28 July 1961 NASA announced that it had signed a cooperative agreement with AT&T "for the development and testing of two or possibly as many as four active communications satellites during 1962." Under the terms of the agreement AT&T would design and construct the satellite at its own expense and reimburse NASA for the cost of facilities and service provided. NASA would in turn provide Thor Delta launch vehicles, launching and tracking facilities and range and land crew services. AT&T agreed to report to NASA the results of its experiment and gave the government a royalty-free license and cross-licensing rights on any patentable inventions produced in the course of the AT&T experiment.[66]

Concomitant with budget changes the Kennedy Administration took a second look at communication satellite commercialization policies implicit in earlier mandates. Before taking office President-elect Kennedy had appointed an ad hoc advisory committee to examine and make recommendations concerning the national space program. Headed by Jerome Weisner, this group released a report on 21 January 1961 which was critical of both NASA and DOD. As far as communications were concerned, the committee's report stated that "the development investment required is so large that it is beyond the financial resources of even our largest private industry. Furthermore the use of commercial space satellites will require physical support of government installations as well as financial support."[67] The report recommended that the "Government, through NASA or the Department of Defense, should make available the required physical facilities as well as any extraordinary financial support required to make the undertakings successful,"[68] largely through an industry/government program. Recommending as well many new emphases in the space program, the Weisner Report, as it was called, still did not resolve debate concerning precise implementation of commercial communication satellite operation. Nonetheless, it was a positive effort in encouraging deeper examination of the nation's space program and satellite commercialization.

After Yuri Gagarin of the U.S.S.R. orbited the earth in April 1961, NASA came under even more scrutiny. That the Soviet Union was first to orbit a manned spacecraft was another blow to the sense of security of the United States. Five days after Gagarin's feat, the Bay of Pigs incident ocurred. American prestige and security were once again unsettled. One result of these events was President Kennedy's decision to expand the space program and to support a project for manned spacecraft landings on the moon. He also decided that space communications could be one area of early U.S. competence.

Kennedy personally took direct action toward formulating communication satellite policy, coordinating interagency relations, and safeguarding public interest, when in May 1961 he addressed a letter to NASA Administrator James Webb stating:

> I am most interested in having facilitated early development of communication satellites and will appreciate prompt determination by the Federal Communications Commission, the National Aeronautics and Space Administration, and other appropriate agencies of the conditions and safeguards under which that can go forward.[69]

Kennedy's letter further explained that he was hopeful public interest and private resources could be coordinated in the development of operational systems, but only "subject to establishing the necessary precautions," and requested that Webb keep him informed of activities and progress in that area.[70]

On 25 May 1961, in a special message to Congress, the president requested fifty million dollars more to be added to NASA's budget. The additional appropriations were directed to expedite public development of communication satellite systems in order to ensure that the requirements of government as well as commercial interests would be served.[71] NASA contended that the funds were necessary to materially facilitate the protection of the public interest in the operation of a commercial satellite system.[72] The space agency also noted that the public interest went beyond the avoidance of delay and included (1) the achievement of global communications coverage; (2) the stimulation of economic growth in other nations; (3) the realization of new and expanded communication services; (4) the assurance of equitable access to the system and non-discriminatory use of authorized channels; (5) strict regulation to obtain reduced rates wherever possible; and (6) the practical accommodation of both commercial and governmental needs for communications.[73]

In June and July of the same year the Executive Office furthered policy implementation by appointing Vice-President Lyndon B. Johnson, as chairman of the National Aeronautics and Space Council, to "undertake to make the necessary studies and government-wide policy recommendations for bringing into optimum use at the earliest practicable time operational communications satellites."[74] On 15 July E.C. Welsh, executive secretary of the Space Council, transmitted its "Communication Satellite Policy Recommendations" and a draft public release on the policy recommendations to the president. The letter of transmittal stated that the officials representing their respective departments and agencies on the Space Council, including Secretary Rusk (State), Deputy Secretary Gilpatrick (Defense), Administrator Webb (NASA), Chairman Seaborg (AEC), Attorney General Kennedy (Justice), Chairman Minow (FCC), and Deputy Director McDermott (Office of Civil and Defense Mobilization), had reached a unanimous decision on the recommendations.[75] With only minor revisions the president accepted the Council's recommendations intact and issued his official statement on communication satellite policy on 24 July 1961.

The president's statement outlined a coordinated national policy to guide the implementation of a communication satellite system. On the issue of ownership and operation, the president stated that:

> Private ownership and operation of the U.S. portion of the system is favored, provided that such ownership and operation meet the following policy requirements:
> 1. New and expanded international communications services be made available at the earliest practicable date;
> 2. Make the system global in coverage so as to provide efficient communication service throughout the whole world as soon as technically feasible, including service where individual portions of the coverage are not profitable;
> 3. Provide opportunities for foreign participation through ownership or otherwise, in the communications satellite system;
> 4. Non-discriminatory use of and equitable access to the system by present and future authorized communications carriers;
> 5. Effective competition, such as competitive bidding, in the acquisition of equipment used in the system;
> 6. Structure of ownership or control which will assure maximum possible competition;
> 7. Full compliance with antitrust legislation and with the regulatory controls of the government;
> 8. Development of an economical system, the benefits of which will be reflected in overseas communications rates.[76]

With respect to the role and responsibility of government, the president said that in addition to its regulatory responsibilities the government would:

> 1. Conduct and encourage research and development to advance the state of the art and to give maximum assurances of rapid and continuous scientific and technological progress;
> 2. Conduct or maintain supervision of international agreements and negotiations;
> 3. Control all launching of U.S. spacecraft;
> 4. Make use of the commercial system for general govermental purpose and establish separate communication satellite systems when required to meet unique government needs which cannot, in the national interest, be met by the commercial system;
> 5. Assure the effective use of the radio-frequency spectrum;
> 6. Assure the ability to discontinue the electronic functioning

of satellites when required in the interest of communication efficiency and effectiveness;

7. Provide technical assistance to newly developing countries in order to help attain an effective global system as soon as practicable;

8. Examine with other countries the most constructive role for the United Nations, including the ITU, in international space communications.[77]

Finally, Kennedy addressed the issue of interagency coordination, noting that he had asked the full cooperation of all government agencies in the implementation of his policies and had directed the National Aeronautics and Space Council to provide continuing policy coordination and to take responsibility for recommending any additional actions needed to achieve full compliance with his stated policies.

Under the stimuli of Gagarin's flight and early policy studies, the new Administration effectively accelerated the move toward commercialization of satellite communications with the president's policy statement. Mobilization of government entities, expansion of NASA's program, and the enunciation of Administration views led to the involvement of more government and public entities in the decision-making process. President Kennedy's actions removed some of the authority of NASA and the FCC, redirecting it to other government entities.

NASA's Experimental Communication Satellite Program

As a result of the policy initiatives in 1960 and 1961 and the general technologic imperative, NASA planned three active communication satellite experiments—Relay, Telstar and Syncom—to implement its research and development mandate.

Relay

After NASA decided to develop an active communication satellite, the agency contracted Space Technology Laboratories in November 1960 to determine technical requirements for an active low-altitude repeater. The objectives of this program were:

1. To demonstrate the feasibility of relaying wideband communication signals between ground stations via satellite relays in low altitude orbits;

2. To evaluate spacecraft performance and to test the life of communication satellite system components in the orbital environment; and

3. To measure the amount of radiation encountered, its effects on solar cells and diodes, and the effectiveness of various amounts of shielding.[78]

Out of seven bids, including one each from AT&T and Hughes Aircraft Company, RCA was selected in May 1961 to design and develop the Relay spacecraft under the direction of Goddard Space Flight Center.

The satellite was designed to transmit wideband television and telephone signals, to test performance in the Van Allen radiation belt, to measure radiation damage to electronic equipment, and to provide experience for an operational system.[79] One principal contribution was a new travelling wave tube. Relay's capabilities fulfilled certain of NASA's technological objectives in conducting advanced research in the areas of new communications packages, radiation effects, satellite stabilization and orientation, the testing of advanced components and variant satellite designs, and advanced research on such components as optical masers. These were the types of advances which were expected to lead to commercial operations.[80] At the time this low-altitude, active repeater program represented the most valuable choice and combinations of relevant technologies.

Relay was successfully launched on 13 December 1962. Carrying two sets of circuitry, the satellite became the first communication spacecraft to employ the principle of redundancy; that is, if one element of the communication system failed, a complete back-up system in the spacecraft was available for transmission. AT&T's Telstar satellite, which was actually launched earlier than Relay, had redundancy only in its command receiver and decoder elements. The redundancy capability was in fact a key to Relay's success because one transponder developed an operating problem, necessitating use of the alternate transponder. Relay was supposed to be electronically silenced after one year, but the circuit-breaking device which was to cause the silence failed. Relay therefore continued to operate, though deteriorating slowly, for two years more. Relay II, an only slightly modified version of Relay I, was launched on 21 July 1964. Improved solar cells, travelling wave tubes, radiation shielding, and power regulation mechanisms assured its long life. Relay II operated successfully until mid-1967.

Ground stations for Relay were located at Mojave, California; Andover, Maine (AT&T's complex); and Nutley, New Jersey (an ITT installation). Foreign stations were located at Goonhilly, England (for the British Post Office), Pleumeur-Bodou in France, and at Rio de Janeiro, Brazil. Relay transmitted telephone, television, and other electronic signals to Europe, South America and Japan.

Relay, a major technical success which contributed significantly to NASA's expertise in the active satellite field, also contributed to organizational/conceptual progress by:

(1) encouraging the development of global telecommunication networks;
(2) demonstrating that a global market for broadband communications already existed;
(3) providing a framework for international technical cooperation; and
(4) exporting U.S.-developed satellite technology to nations which would later join Intelsat, an international satellite consortium.[81]

Although perhaps overshadowed by publicity surrounding the Telstar satellite, Relay was the most advanced communication satellite on which NASA worked before adoption of the entirely new Syncom design.

Telstar

Officially the joint NASA/AT&T effort which produced Telstar had its genesis in the 1961 decision on government support of AT&T's private efforts with satellites. Since the hardware was actually developed earlier than that for the Relay satellite, Telstar was launched 10 July 1962, six months before Relay. Telstar was the nation's first active repeater satellite. Stations in New Jersey, Maine, Great Britain, France, Brazil and Italy were used for transmission via Telstar of voice, black/white and color television, facsimile, and high- and low-speed data. It was the first satellite developed and funded by private enterprise, setting a precedent in this type of government/industry arrangement.

Telstar's program objectives were to (1) demonstrate broadband transmission, (2) test operational communication satellite reliabilities, (3) obtain operational experience with ground terminals, (4) increase knowledge of tracking techniques and (5) provide space radiation measurements.[82] Telstar weighed as much as the later Relay

I but did not carry two transponders.

On the whole, Telstar made a tremendous impact on the nation by transmitting transatlantic live television, which demonstrated the possibilities for commercial satellite television and other services. The Telstar satellite was the first corroboration of performance predictions for tracking and orbiting an active low-altitude satellite. Bell Laboratories extended its ground station experience at Holmdel, New Jersey, by building its second station for Telstar at Andover, Maine. During one four month period over 400 transmissions were sent via Telstar.

The satellite performed according to predictions but for one factor: radiation in space caused by a U.S. high-altitude nuclear explosion on 9 July 1962. The higher levels of radiation damaged the satellite so that after four months Telstar began to ignore telemetered commands.[83] The damaged electrical elements were diagnosed and bypassed for a while, but by February 1963 the satellite ceased to respond.

Telstar II, with an improved version of Telstar I's command element, was launched on 7 May 1963. It continued experiments and demonstrations begun by the first Telstar. Providing necessary technical/operational knowledge for Bell Telephone Laboratories and NASA in the low-altitude active satellite field, the Telstar and Relay satellites proved that their design and construction could be easily adapted for commercial utilization. With attention focused on continuing commercialization plans, NASA nevertheless considered it necessary to test one more completely different communication satellite – a lightweight, spinning, high-altitude craft. It is significant that, without the favorable budget and policy mandates of 1961 allowing the agency to progress with an intensified experimental program, the testing of this new technology might have been indefinitely postponed.

Syncom

The year 1961, with a significant increase in NASA's budget, was critical to the final implementation of Harold Rosen's synchronous satellite concept, which was still struggling for acceptance after two years. Although during the 1962 NASA Authorization Hearings Administrator Webb said nothing about committing NASA to development of a synchronous satellite, he did state that he wanted "enough freedom to do whatever is in the government's interest, . . .

keeping this committee fully informed of what we are doing."[84] Bolstered by the president's statement of policy on 24 July, NASA, it appeared, could possibly expand into synchronous satellite development if it could make arrangements for nonduplication with DOD's Advent program. Advent was then the only synchronous satellite project in the national space program.

Falling victim to the same problems as the earlier Notus program, Advent was behind schedule; its electrical components were rapidly moving toward obsolescence, and the project was absorbing great quantities of money.[85] Hughes, with its new concept for a synchronous satellite, had contacted DOD during 1960 but did not obtain an affirmative response. However, during 1961 John Rubel, deputy director of Defense Research and Engineering and responsible for the Advent program, apparently concluded the Hughes' idea was more hopeful, at least in terms of technology development if not military applications, than the Advent project.[86] NASA recognized that there was a gap in active satellite technology for a synchronous orbiting spacecraft; however, before NASA could undertake synchronous satellite research, DOD would have to accede to NASA's plans. When Hughes' idea gained acceptance at NASA, some agency officials informally approached DOD about the possibility of adopting Hughes' proposal. The formal initiative had to come from DOD since it had the mandate to do research in this area. John Rubel of DOD became interested in the possibility of NASA accepting Hughes' proposal. Compared to the heavy and still developing Advent, the lightweight synchronous satellite of Hughes appeared very advantageous. This assessment of Advent eventually reached DOD's top-level policymakers, resulting in an endorsement of Hughes' synchronous satellite. In June Deputy Secretary of Defense Gilpatrick addressed a letter to James Webb supporting NASA's undertaking an interim communication satellite program:

> Mr. Rubel has told me about plans that he and Dr. Seamans [of NASA] are formulating for an interim synchronous satellite communication experiment with potential for an interim operational capability within the next 18 to 24 months. This plan involves the utilization of Project Advent resources for the installation of certain ground elements and the utilization of NASA funds and resources to provide the satellite vehicles. . . . You have my assurance of support in the event that, in your judgment, their proposals should be adopted.[87]

Without such an assurance NASA's assumption of synchronous satellite development would have constituted a breach in the earlier October 1960 NASA-DOD agreement, which provided that NASA would not work on the synchronous orbit satellites. As it turned out, the ground stations for Advent, mentioned in the Gilpatrick letter, were progressing well and were in fact the only salvageable portions of the $ 159 million Advent program, which was cancelled in May 1962.

Leonard Jaffe of NASA, who had been following Hughes' work, felt that NASA, because of its increased communication satellite budget, should accept Hughes' project.[88] Jaffe urged the agency to support the idea. Reinforced by DOD's sanction, the budget addition, and the mandate to develop as early as possible an operational communication satellite capability, Jaffe was able to persuade NASA to adopt the project in mid-1961.[89]

Goddard Space Flight Center was directed to draw up a preliminary project development plan prepared with the Army's Advent Management Agency.[90] Ground stations would be provided by the Army while NASA financed the spacecraft and launch. The project became a "sole source award," unlike Relay, since it was recognized that Hughes was far ahead of would-be competitors in its own research on the project.[91] Thus on 11 August 1961 NASA announced that Hughes Aircraft Company had been selected to build a synchronous satellite called Syncom.[92]

The high-altitude synchronous satellite, compared to the low-altitude active satellite, represents an important technological and economic breakthrough. A global communications system based on the low-altitude repeater requires substantially more spacecraft than a system utilizing synchronous satellites. Because the higher altitudes allow them to "see" a greater portion of the earth's surface, a system of synchronous satellites requires fewer vehicles, resulting in significant decreases in total system costs. Also, the higher altitude synchronous satellites are in sunlight for most of their orbits enabling solar energy to keep the satellites' solar power cells regenerated, whereas low-altitude satellites, which are out of the sun much of the time, have a more limited continuous power capability and operating time. Furthermore, the geostationary orbit of the synchronous satellite, enabling the satellite to remain stationary over one spot on the earth, obviates extensive tracking maneuvers, simplifying the ground operations and their physical requirements. For these reasons a higher altitude satellite was clearly more desirable for a global communication system. To develop and fly such a system so early in communication satellite technology's history was an important step in communication satellite progress.

Goddard and Hughes worked together to produce the completed spacecraft. Technical problems associated with hydrogen peroxide spacecraftcontrol and the decisiontoemploy a redundancy capability were solved. By late 1962 Syncom I was ready for launch via a Thor Delta vehicle from Cape Canaveral, although originally the Hughes' satellite had been designed to use a Scout launch vehicle and be launched from Jarvis Island, closer to the equator. On 14 February 1963 the satellite was launched; its equipment tested out on the ship Kingsport, which was acting as a mobile terminal during the craft's ascent. However, when the satellite's apogee motor was fired to bring it into a circular orbit coinciding with the earth's spin, the electrical equipment failed. Nonetheless, Syncom I did attain a synchronous orbit, the main objective of the experiment and indeed the most difficult technical problem.

Changes were made in Syncom II in response to problems diagnosed in the earlier satellite's failure. On 26 July 1963 Syncom II was successfully launched. It supported many communications experiments sponsored by NASA and DOD, the most famous of which was a transmission to the 1963 International Telecommunication Union conference in Geneva, where delegates were allocating frequencies for space communications. This demonstration resolved a technical question of time delay in synchronous transmissions; many people had expected that the time it took for a signal to travel to and from a high-altitude satellite would cause significant delays, resulting in garbled, overlapping conversation.

The final spacecraft of this series, Syncom III, was launched a year later into a virtually prefect geostationary orbit via a newer, more powerful launch vehicle called the Thrust Augmented Delta. Circling the earth at 22,300 miles altitude in its geosynchronous orbit, Syncom III fulfilled its mission objectives completely and added another proof of the usefulness of satellite technology to the private sector by televising the 1964 Olympic games live from Japan to the United States.[93] Syncom II was moved to a point above the Indian Ocean by 1965 for DOD operations, since NASA's own testing with the Syncom series was completed in 1964. Syncom III was also transferred to the military under NASA-DOD agreement.[94] Because the Advent program was not a success, DOD needed Syncom's communication capabilities. The Defense Department had been involved with the Syncom project since its inception and therefore was aware of the technology's unique ability to meet tactical communication requirements — that is, reaching remote mobile earth stations, maintaining transmission reliability, and providing quality transmissions. A simple, lightweight, spin-stabilized satellite was the significant communication satellite event of 1963.

Toward Commercialization

As NASA's research and development program began to mobilize around the objective of operationalizing satellite communications, the question of technology transfer became a major issue. The rapid development of the technology necessitated a policy in advance of actual satellite experiments and demonstrations. Significant factors involved in the implementation of a technology transfer policy were: (1) the certain existence of a commercial market for communication satellites, (2) the U.S. decision to be first with an operational system, especially with reference to U.S.-U.S.S.R. rivalries and competition, and (3) a traditional approach to government-sponsored research and development which results in eventual private sector control of most potentially revenue-bearing enterprises. NASA's energies and capabilities were thus oriented in two directions: developing its own experimental projects and providing input to the commercialization process. Aspects of NASA's Relay, Telstar and Syncom programs illustrate the intricacies of the agency's dual role in this respect. Various *technical* program decisions were integral to the shaping of national policy regarding the U.S. communication satellite effort, and each of these was made within the context of and at times parallel to *policy* decisions.

The interplay between technical and policy decisions is displayed in the relationships established between NASA, DOD and industry. First, the relationship between the Defense Department and NASA was an important factor. It is notable that for both Relay and Syncom the Department of Defense approved of NASA's plans. DOD in one sense actually helped to formulate those plans in issuing its opinions. Without such agreement it is doubtful the civilian space agency would have undertaken them. While DOD itself played a relatively minor developmental role in communication satellites (although its booster technology was critical), it had an important role in larger program directions. The relationship between program decisions and policy decisions must not be underestimated; the two are intricately related.

The fact that DOD's approval led NASA to work on Syncom had considerable impact on the establishment of a global commercial system in that the system came to use synchronous satellites only. In turn the progress of technology and its capabilities have led to renewed political concern centering on the benefits of satellites as well as on their potential for abuse.

Second, NASA's manner of handling relationships with industry is worth noting. Adoption of the Relay program offered the opportunity for industry participation in a satellite communications experiment; it also served to hold AT&T's pressure for NASA aid at arm's length since AT&T itself submitted an unaccepted proposal for Relay. Although the technical requirements for the project were primary, the decision did have policy implications. Relay effectively brought into the arena a company, RCA, which had not been as involved in communication satellites as had either AT&T or Hughes. It perhaps functioned as a publicly-sponsored alternative to AT&T's plans, about which NASA had been aware for some time. The adoption of the joint Telstar project came strategically *after* Relay was settled. Had the two programs been chronologically reversed it is likely that the agency would have been accused of giving away to a single private enterprise expertise developed at public expense. Still, the fact that NASA formally agreed to join the Telstar program may have had little actual effect on AT&T's research plans. Indeed, the company possessed funds enough to continue its own research pending governmental assistance.[95]

The case of Hughes Aircraft Company is opposite to that of AT&T. Hughes did not have an abundance of funds for communication satellite research, and until 1961 it was basically ineffective in convincing the government of the feasibility of its concepts. While AT&T confidently continued its research and development before the specific provisions for a reimbursable launch evolved, Hughes was ready to abandon its project in 1961 if NASA would not add its sponsorship. NASA's support had not been forthcoming primarily because of DOD jurisdiction in the synchronous satellite field, although certain design features in Hughes' idea also drew the agency's objections.

Although the final adoption of the Syncom project necessitated a sole source contract with Hughes, this was not in contrast with the agency's espoused "wider industry participation" policy for its communication satellite projects. NASA's Project Syncom represented a significantly different set of circumstances than would have a similar contract with AT&T for Telstar or Relay. Hughes presented no threat in terms of monopolizing satellite technology since it was only a builder of hardware. Also, the stepped-up mandate behind organizing and operating a satelite communications system, bolstered by reaction to Yuri Gagarin's flight, served to confirm Hughes' unique position.

NASA's development of communication satellite technology was characterized by contingencies derived from DOD and industry relationships. NASA acceptance of responsibility for technology development was compromised throughout these years by policy contingencies offered by the military and private sector. Executive decisions and priorities regarding U.S./U.S.S.R. space competition, the input of the military, and the interest of private industry were critical in the determination of a direction for government research and development. In sum, increasing governmental and private sector interest in communication satellites during the early 1960's set the stage for commercialization. The next few years were crucial to the implementation of an operational system; it is to those years that we now turn in order to identify emerging policy and institutional issues.

Part II

PATTERNS OF COMMUNICATION SATELLITE IMPLEMENTATION

It is with somewhat mixed feelings that I can claim to have originated one of the most commercially valuable ideas of the 20th century, and to have sold it for just $ 40.

Arthur C. Clarke
"A Short Pre-History of Comsats: or How I Lost a Billion Dollars in My Spare Time"

5

THE CREATION OF COMSAT: THE FIRST STAGE OF THE U.S. COMMUNICATION SATELLITE TECHNOLOGY TRANSFER

Although Arthur Clarke received only a small royalty from the publishers of his 1945 paper proposing communication satellites, the potential commercial value of his idea was soon recognized. As illustrated in the preceding chapter, commercial interest in communication satellites emerged in concert with the development of the U.S. space program and NASA's early communication satellite experiments. By 1961 a series of events, beginning with NASA Administrator Glennan's October 1960 statement sanctioning industry involvement in the development of communication satellites and culminating with President Kennedy's July 1961 policy pronouncement advocating private ownership and operation under appropriate public guidelines, made it apparent that the private sector would be involved in the communication satellite enterprise. What remained was the unprecedented task of organizing an effective framework for implementing the first nongovernmental activity in space in order to integrate the technology which had been developed. The issues involved were complex. Who would participate in the ownership of the system and under what arrangements? How could the enterprise be regulated to ensure against monopolistic abuse and to protect the interests of the public who had committed millions of tax dollars to developing the technology? This chapter chronicles the early public debate surrounding the transfer of communication satellites to the private sector. The initial outcome of that debate was the enactment of the Communications Satellite Act of 1962, which created a unique public/private corporation to own and operate the U.S. portion of a global communication satellite system. The establishment of the Communications Satellite Corporation, however, did not mean, as is often mistakenly assumed, that the government divested itself of interest in the development of communication satellites, nor did the Comsat Act completely resolve the complex issue of public vs. private roles in the field. While the creation of

Comsat concluded one phase of the policymaking process by establishing a corporate structure enabling the private sector to develop and operate commercial communication satellites, it also raised new policy questions. Among the most significant was the problem of determining the respective parameters of public vs. private responsibilities for further communication satellite research and development.

The Road to Comsat

The 1961 FCC Inquiry

In accordance with the 1961 Memorandum of Understanding between the Federal Communications Commission and the National Aeronautics and Space Administration, the FCC assumed responsibility for developing communication satellite policy and for implementing an operational system through licensing and regulation of U.S. common carriers.[1] Based on the assumption that it had sufficient statutory to direct policy, the commission began extensieve investigations to regulate the first nongovernmental venture in space.

In March 1961 the FCC opened an "Inquiry Into the Administrative and Regulatory Problems Relating to the Authorization of Commercially Operable Space Communications Systems, Docket No. 14024." The inquiry solicited views from all interested parties as to the best method of ensuring that international communications common carriers and others would participate in a satellite system on an equitable and nondiscriminatory basis. Between March and May, responses were filed by twelve parties.[2] The respondents, for economic reasons, generally agreed that a single or limited number of satellite systems were desirable. In the case of a joint venture, they favored shared ownership and operation of the system but disagreed as to its composition.[3] For their part, American Telephone and Telegraph and International Telephone and Telegraph wanted to limit ownership in the system to international common carriers with shares of ownership proportioned according to use of the system. General Telephone and Electronics favored a limited ownership plan that would include both international and domestic common carriers, while Lockheed Aircraft, General Electric and Western Union advocated broader-based ownership by common carriers, manufacturing companies, and possibly the public at large.[4]

The aerospace and communications equipment manufacturers

were adamant in their opposition to limiting ownership to international common carriers. In the belief that the limited ownership plan would ensure AT&T domination, they favored the establishment of a separate company to serve as a "carriers' carrier." Lockheed wanted to divide business into two distinct enterprises; they proposed an operating company, called Telesat, which would be owned jointly by communication carriers and also a separate joint service company formed by the equipment manufacturers. General Electric, on the other hand, had recently formed a new company, Communication Satellites, Inc., and suggested that it become the framework for a joint venture open to both carriers and manufacturers. The manufacturers argued that since many of the common carriers including AT&T, ITT, and RCA were themselves equipment manufacturers, it would be unfair for the government to exclude the non-carrier manufacturers. The Justice Department supported this opinion and stated that antitrust laws compelled that ownership be open to both carriers and manufacturers with equipment procured by competitive bidding.[5]

After considering the responses, the FCC issued its *First Report on Docket 14024* on 24 May 1961. The commission decided to explore a joint venture "composed only of existing common carriers engaged in international telephone and telegraph communication."[6] In essence this meant AT&T, the exclusive international telephone carrier, and ITT, RCA and Western Union, the three largest telegraph carriers.

The FCC report refrained from reaching any conclusions on the desirability or need for participation by domestic carriers in the joint venture, but opposed participation by equipment manufacturers and the public. In reference to ownership by equipment suppliers the commission stated definitively:

> We fail to see why ownership participation by the aerospace and communications equipment industries will be beneficial or necessary to the establishment of a satellite communication system to be used by the common carrier industry. On the other hand, such participation may well result in encumbering the system with complicated and costly corporate relationships, disrupting operational patterns that have been established in the international common carrier industry, and impeding effective regulation of the rates and services of the industry.[7]

In response to the antitrust issue, the commission offered assurances of its intention to require "adequate and effective provision, such as competitive bidding, to insure that there will be no favoritism in the procurement of communications equipment required for the construction, operation and maintenance of the satellite system."[8] The report concluded by issuing invitations to all U.S. international common carriers and interested government agencies to attend a conference to explore plans for organizing a joint venture by the international carriers.

The debate did not end with the FCC's *First Report.* Both General Electric and General Telephone and Electronics filed petitions for reconsideration, and the FCC was compelled to extend invitation to domestic carriers and equipment manufacturers to participate in the upcoming conference. On 25 July, however, just one day after President Kennedy issued his policy statement on communication satellites, the commission dismissed the GE and GTE petitions for reconsideration, upheld its original report, and issued a public notice calling solely upon international common carriers to organize an ad hoc committee to formulate a complete plan of organization for a joint venture in the development of a communication satellite system.[9] In addition to the four major carriers (AT&T, RCA, Western Union, and ITT represented by two subsidiaries), the FCC extended invitations to participate in the Ad Hoc Carrier Committee to five minor international carriers.[10] All except one accepted and participated in a total of seventy-five meetings held between August and October of 1961.

On 12 October the Ad Hoc Carrier Committee concluded its report. The most significant features of the committee's plan are summarized in the following organizational points:

> 1. The formation of a non-profit satellite corporation to develop, construct, operate, manage and promote the use of the satellite system. . . .
> 2. Ownership of the United States portion of the satellites would be in the participating carriers, and not in the satellite corporation. . . .
> 3. As at present, United States carriers would make their own arrangements with communications administrations, agencies and companies in foreign countries. . . .
> 4. The satellite corporation would be so structured that it should not be controlled by any one United States carrier. . . . [A plan was devised whereby each participant with a capital commitment of $500,000 would have two representatives on the

corporation's Board of Directors, and carriers not wishing to participate in ownership would be represented collectively by one director.]

5. To further reflect public interest and to broaden the bases of board representation, three public directors, one more than the representation of any single carrier, would be appointed by the President of the United States. . . .

6. Capital expenditures and expenses of operation of the satellite corporation, in the development, construction, operation, management and arrangement for the use of the satellites would be allocated among the participating owners in proportion to their respective capital commitments.

7. Each of the participating U.S. carriers would carry its investments upon its own books and in its own rate base [i.e. their investments would be included in their rate base for rate-making purposes]. . . .

8. Ownership would be open to any United States carriers authorized by the Commission (FCC) to furnish communication services via the satellites. . . .

9. Each United States carrier would be permitted to establish its own ground stations, participate in joint ownership of ground stations with other . . . carriers, or rent capacity in ground stations of other carriers – all as authorized by the Commission.[11]

In sum, the Ad Hoc Carrier Committee was proposing a nonprofit management corporation to develop and manage the satellite system on behalf of the carriers who would own both the satellites and ground stations.

The FCC's committee report met widespread opposition. Western Union dissented from the committee's recommendations and issued a minority report. According to the minority view, the committee's plan neither provided for the most economical arrangement nor adequately ensured that the venture would not be dominated by one company. Western Union advocated broadening the base of ownership by forming a public stock corporation which would own and operate both satellites and ground stations.[12] Opposition to the Ad Hoc Carrier Committee plan was also expressed in Congress through testimony given to the various House and Senate Committees investigating communication satellites. On 8-9 November 1961 the Senate Subcommittee on Monopoly held hearings to evaluate the ad hoc report and issued a negative opinion of the plan. The committee chairman, Senator Russell B. Long, took the view that the fact that the proposed corporation would manage but not own the system made it a screen for the interests of the common carriers.[13] In particular, Senator Long considered the plan too favorable to the interests of AT&T; in this regard he commented that "there may be a way of giving it directly to AT&T, but short of that, it seems to me you could not have made better recommendations to achieve the same result." [14]

The chief opponents of the FCC position were the Justice Department and those industries excluded from system ownership. For its part, the Justice Department repeatedly stated that implementation of the FCC's Ad Hoc Carrier Committee report would raise serious antitrust problems. Assistant Attorney General Lee Loevinger, before becoming an FCC commissioner, summarized the Department's position in testimony before the Senate Judiciary Committee. He stated that under the plan limiting ownership to international common carriers:

> The possibility would always exist that such ownership would result in limiting competition among the carriers in the furnishing of communication services, in the manufacture and sale of communication equipment, or in limiting competition in either of these areas of nonparticipating companies. Furthermore such limited ownership might well give de facto control to a single company, AT&T.[15]

Despite the opposition, the FCC remained convinced of the merits of limited ownership and defended its position both in the Space Council and before Congress during subsequent deliberations on an implementation plan. The plan eventually adopted for establishing the Communications Satellite Corporation, however, was substantially different from FCC recommendations. This difference is understandable in view of the fact that the commission developed its position from the parochial perspective of a single agency, while the Communications Satellite Act reflected government-wide input.

The FCC necessarily saw the development of communication satellites from the vantage point of an agency concerned primarily with licensing and rate regulation. In testimony before the Senate Judiciary Committee, FCC Chairman Newton Minow admitted that the commission looked at the problem of implementing commercial operations "purely in narrow regulatory terms."[16] In reference to the proposal for public stock ownership, Minow said:

> There is a broader question of social, economic policy here, which I think led to the idea of having public stock ownership. We [the FCC] are looking at that strictly in terms of how we are going to live with this day by day and regulate it.[17]

The new technology of satellite communications, however, raised important social, political, legal and international issues which were outside the FCC's immediate pragmatic concerns. The problem lay not with the commission for failing to adequately resolve these issues, but rather in the fact that the policy implications of transferring communication satellite technology to the private sector went beyond the scope of FCC jurisdiction.

The Administration Bill

When the FCC opened its inquiry in March of 1961, the Administration had not given through consideration to the policy implications of implementing commercial operations in space, much less to developing a new approach for organizing and regulating the commercial venture. President Eisenhower had issued a policy statement just prior to leaving office, but the Eisenhower statement simply said that industry should be encouraged to utilize communication satellites for commercial purposes. It did not specify any guidelines to deal with the policy ramifications of industry participation. Although Congress had begun to express concern and NASA had done extensive in-house analysis of the situation, the Eisenhower statement significantly lacked any mention of public interest considerations, such as achieving global coverage; stimulating new types of communication services as well as expanding existing services; assuring licensed carriers of equitable access and nondiscriminatory use of the system; imposing rate regulation; accommodating governmental as well as commercial requirements; and determining the multiple foreign policy implications.

Between March and October, when the FCC's Ad Hoc Carrier Committee completed its report, however, the Kennedy Administration took decisive actions toward coordinating communication satellite policy. As noted in Chapter Four, President Kennedy outlined a national policy in July 1961 favoring private ownership and operation of communication satellites provided appropriate conditions were met to safeguard the public interest. While the policy guidelines represented a significant step towards coordinating transfer of communication satellite technology to the private sector operations, substantial issues remained unresolved. Although Kennedy's policy was based on the unanimous recommendations of the National Aeronautics and Space Council, which represented the major government agencies interested in communication satellites, there was as yet no concurrence on how to implement the policy or on what organizational and regulatory arrangements were needed to provide adequate public safeguards. There was, as a consequence, some evidence of congressional concern over the president's policy. In August 1961 Senators Hubert Humphrey, Estes Kefauver, Wayne Morse, and thirty-two members of the House of Representatives sent a letter to the president urging him to avoid making quick decisions which might result in giving international carriers a monopoly in space communications.[18] The congressmen asked that the resolution of the ownership issue be delayed until the government had first developed an operational system. Nonetheless, after issuing his statement, the president took direct steps to implement his policy. He assigned E.C. Welsh, the executive secretary of the Space Council, the task of drafting a recommendation on the appropriate method for implementation.[19]

There were three options open. The policy could be implemented "(1) through administrative action on the strength of existing legislation," principally through amendment of the Space Act of 1958, "(2) by exercising executive authority, or (3) by new legislation." The decision was made in favor of new legislation. The principal disadvantage of this choice was expressed in the fear that lengthy congressional debates might seriously delay transfer to commercial operations. On the other hand, legislative action would allow Congress to express its views and avoid the possibility of delay over the issue of executive authority. A legislative mandate could also help protect the public interest by strengthening the FCC's control over powerful carriers such as AT&T.[20] Above all, a legislative proposal would provide Congress with a format for implementing communication satellite policy. The form of the statute itself was not considered as vital as the fact that the presentation of a bill would establish a framework for congressional action.[21]

In November 1961 Welsh was asked by President Kennedy to head an interdepartmental team that was to draft legislation for implementing an operational communication satellite system. Although the legislation proposed by the Welsh committee was not subject to approval by the Space Council, representatives from the agencies comprising the council, including the State and Justice Departments, the FCC and NASA, participated on Welsh's drafting team. The various agencies had different points of view on the fundamental issue facing the committee – the issue of system ownership.

There were three basic options open to the committee: (1) government ownership, (2) private ownership by carriers, and (3) broad-based private ownership. On the extremes, the Federal Communications Commission advocated ownership by existing common carriers, while the Department of Justice contended that antitrust laws prohibited limited ownership of a single satellite system by private enterprise. Although the FCC and NASA had previously taken a lead in directing communication satellite policy, the Justice Department exerted a disproportionate influence on the committee because of its close associations with the Kennedy Administration.[22] Moreover, the divergent points of view expressed in the executive branch were a microcosm of congressional attitudes. Consequently, the deliberations were conducted in a politically sensitive atmosphere which necessitated practical compromises. The political considerations effecting the drafting of the Administration bill are further illustrated in the following analysis of the Welsh committee proceedings:

> These options were not examined according to their technical and organizational consequences alone, but of necessity, were filtered through the political and psychological climate of opinion. This ethos concerned certain vague, but highly emotional issues such as "creeping socialism" and "predatory monopolies." Political as well as organizational feasibility had to be considered. If one agency considered that the system should be owned by the Government, it knew that the public airing of this view would incur the wrath of those who were ideologically committed to free, competitive private enterprise. If another agency favored ownership by the international carriers, it knew that proposing this alternative would meet the bitter attacks of those wedded to a firm construction of the antitrust laws. In short, the issue was political: it involved polemics and emotions as well as dispassionate consideration of the pros and cons.[23]

The Welsh committee reached a compromise on an expedient policy and proposed legislation advocating private industry operation of communications satellites but with a broad base of ownership. The Administration bill called for the formation of a new, privately owned, profit-making corporation to be financed by the sale of stock to both communications common carriers and the public at large, with restrictions on the percentage of stock which the carriers could control. Welsh outlined ten basic organizational principles which were incorporated into the Administration bill:

1. Private enterprise, operated for profit, with the anticipated benefits in efficiency which so often characterize private ownership and private initiative, including competitive procurement of equipment and services;
2. Protection of the public interest, through Government regulation and such policy and technical coordination as our national and international interests require;
3. Reasonable maximization of opportunity for private savings to nourish this great venture and to obtain returns from such investment through broad public sale of the voting and dividend-sharing stock;
4. Reasonable minimization of domination or control of this national asset on the part of any individual, company, or private concentration of economic power, by limitations on the amount of voting stock of directors subject to such control and by the broad-base ownership provision, which greatly lessens the opportunity for financial domination;
5. Increasing the availability of private investment, by not restricting the quantity of such investment to that amount which could be raised by a few chosen companies; thereby decreasing the likelihood of the need for Government subsidy of the operating company;
6. Speed of action, by authorization of a corporate structure for managing an operational system, prior to the completion of the initial tests and experiments as to the technology and equipment required, thus avoiding unnecessary delays, providing flexibility of funding, and instituting cooperation with the responsible agencies of the Government;
7. Delineation of authority and responsibility, rather than leaving uncertain who is responsible for what, in the Corporation and in the Government;
8. Coordinated action through legislation, so as to make doubly clear to the world that the United States is committed to success in this field, on the basis of private enterprise, nondiscriminatory access, freedom of investment, and broad public benefit;

9. Foreign participation, through investment in the Corporation up to the maximum permitted by law, through ownership and management of ground facilities abroad, and through nondiscriminatory access to the system's use;
10. Recognition of the rate-base practices of regulated companies in the communications field by providing a class of nonvoting stock for authorized carriers, which investment would be subject to the regular rate-base treatment, similar to that accorded other capital investments by the FCC.[24]

Legislative Debate

Including the original Administration bill and its amended version, there were a total of sixteen legislative proposals submitted to Congress for implementing communication satellite operations – thirteen in the House and three in the Senate. The numerous bills submitted in the House of Representatives stemmed from the fact that House rules preclude multiple sponsorship of legislation. Actually, there were only six distinct pieces of legislation introduced in the House, and they basically reflected the same three concepts embodied in the three Senate bills.[25] Similarly, the hearings on communication satellite legislation conducted by the House Committee on Interstate and Foreign Commerce raised no significant issues that were not repeated in the Senate hearings. For purposes of clarity, then, the issues surrounding the enactment of the Communications Satellite Act of 1962 are best illustrated by focusing on activities in the Senate where the most important debate occurred.

In addition to the Administration bill (S 2814), which was introduced to the Senate on 7 February 1962, Senator Robert Kerr, chairman of the Senate Committee on Aeronautical and Space Science, introduced a proposal for communication satellite legislation (S 2650) on 11 January 1962; Senator Estes Kefauver submitted Senate bill (S 2890) on 26 February. The major feature distinguishing the three bills was their approach to the ownership question. The three proposals reflected the same three options that had been considered by the Welsh drafting committee: the Administration bill proposed broad-based private ownership; the Kerr bill favored private ownership by existing carriers; and the Kefauver bill advocated government ownership.

Kerr's bill proposed the formation of a corporation financed by the sale of 5,000 shares of stock valued at $ 100,000 each. Only U.S. common carriers authorized by the FCC and willing to purchase a minimum of five shares would be allowed to purchase stock. With the major exception that the corporation would be a profit-making carriers's carrier, rather than a nonprofit management corporation, the Kerr bill reflected the preference of the international common carriers as expressed in their ad hoc report to the FCC. The Kerr bill has also been characterized as basically corresponding to the approach to communication satellite policy developed previously under the Eisenhower Administration.[26] It is doubtful that Senator Kerr was committed in principle to his legislation. In fact, less than a month after submitting his bill, Kerr agreed to cosponsor the Administration bill, raising some speculation as to his motives for introducing Senate bill 2650. One theory holds that the Kerr bill was a political maneuver to push Welsh's drafting committee into action. Fearing that the interests of the participating agencies would conflict and prohibit agreement, Kerr may have introduced his legislation first in order to prompt quick resolution of differences within the executive branch.[27] Another possible motive might have been to provide a cushion against congressional reaction to the Administration bill. In comparison to Kerr's bill, which was extremely favorable to the interest of industry, the Administration's support of broad-based private ownership and modified private enterprise appeared much more representative of the public interest.

Unlike Kerr, Senator Kefauver was ideologically committed to his bill advocating government ownership. Kefauver and the cosponsors represented a liberal Democratic faction in Congress that strongly opposed monopolistic tendencies of corporate enterprise. They felt that government ownership of operational communication satellites, at least initially, was the only method to ensure against monopolistic abuse. Senate bill 2890 called for the formation of a corporation which would be owned and operated by the U.S. government and financed by the sale of stock to the public in an amount not to exceed $ 500,000. The concept of government ownership had little chance for success in a Congress firmly commited to the American tradition of private enterprise, but the small faction favoring the proposal were extremely vocal, active and influential. They formed a well-organized opposition to the Administration bill.

The proposals for communication satellite legislation were referred to the Senate Aeronautical and Space Science Committee in February and to the Commerce Committee in April 1962. Proponents of the

Kerr bill argued before the committees that communications had traditionally been provided by private enterprise and that the existing carriers were most experienced and capable of establishing an operational system in the shortest period of time. Moreover, they contended that the Administration's proposal for internal control over corporate operations through broad-based representation on the board of directors and strict external regulatory control by the president and the State Department would create a bureaucratic structure and would confuse the lines of decision-making authority, thereby delaying system operations. In general, the opposition argued that the Kerr bill would strengthen already powerful companies, particularly AT&T, and increase the tendency toward monopoly despite the proposed safeguards included in the bill. Doubt was cast on the ability of the FCC to effectively regulate a consortium, and concern was expressed that existing carriers might delay the development of communication satellite technology in order to guard against the obsolescence of their existing communications equipment.[28] Given the weight of these arguments and strong Administrative opposition to the Kerr bill, both Senate committees made some modifications but reported on the Administration bill favorably.

In response to the testimony received in their hearings, however, the space and commerce committees did amend the Administration bill. Among the most significant changes were (1) a reduction of the purchase prices of stock from $ 1,000 to $ 100 per share, (2) an enlargement of the board of directors to include three directors appointed by the president, (3) authorization of ground station ownership by communications carriers as well as the corporation, (4) an alteration of the president's role in planning a communication satellite system, (5) an increase in government supervision over corporation buying practices to ensure competitive procurement, and (6) a revamping of the State Department's function to an advisory role by deleting a provision authorizing the State Department to conduct foreign negotiations for the corporation.[29]

Although certain of these amendments were made in response to the liberal demand for protection of the public interest against monopolistic abuses, the modifications failed to satisfy the Kefauver opposition. In order to voice their views in favor of government ownership and postpone passage of the Comsat Act, the opposition pushed for further debate on the Administration bill. The Subcommittee on Antitrust and Monopoly of the Judiciary Committee, chaired by Senator Kefauver, opened hearings on communication satellite legislation despite the fact that no bills were referred to it. Then, in August 1962, employing the tactic of a filibuster, the opposition succeeded in having the Administration bill referred back for consideration by the Foreign Relations Committee of the Senate.[30]

The proponents of government ownership based their position on four arguments. First, they argued that private ownership could not be reconciled with antitrust laws. They contended that the Administration bill could not ensure competitive procurement because the largest carriers were also the largest equipment manufacturers.

> Vertical integration of international communications carriers and the manufacturers of the equipment they use, moreover, inhibits a free competitive system. The choice which is before us is between Government ownership of a taxpayer-financed resource, with operation for the benefit of all the American people, or ownership by a Government-created private monopoly.[31]

Advocates of the Administration bill countered this argument by contending that their bill established adequate safeguards to ensure competitive bidding by limiting any one company's ownership percentage, by delegating sufficient regulatory authority to the FCC, and by providing for broad representation on the corporation's board of directors.[32]

Second, the advocates of government ownership argued that an early transfer of communication satellite operations to the private sector could result in the development of a mediocre system and prohibit future development. Kefauver claimed that the government could initiate operational systems as rapidly as industry, and that the carriers might actually impede the development of an operable satellite system to protect their investment in existing communications equipment.[33] Moreover, he argued that communication satellite technology was not far enough advanced to be turned over to private development and that control for profit by private industry might lead to the establishment of a low-altitude system which would soon be made obsolete by synchronous satellites.[34]

The thrust of their third argument centered on the contention that since communication satellites were developed at government expense, the benefits belonged to the public taxpayers and should not be given away to private enterprise. This argument was summarized in the minority report of the Commerce Committee which stated:

> All the elements necessary for the very existence of an operational satellite communications system have been financed by all the taxpayers of the United States. It is our belief that all these same taxpayers should receive the benefits of the system when it becomes operational. There can be no justification for giving this vast resource that has been financed by the taxpayers away to a small group of stockholders for their private gain. The taxpayers have already paid for their right to share in the returns.[35]

While proponents of this argument strengthened their case by quoting such figures as "'25 billion in government research and development' without sources to back them up,"[36] the argument was essentially vulnerable. There was little support for the contention that a non profit government system would cost less, since private operation would save the public the expense of operating the system. Furthermore, there was ample precedent, particularly in the case of the aviation industry, to justify transfer of government-developed technology to private industry.

The final argument in support of government ownership focused on the issue of international relations. Since the foreign counterparts of the Comsat Corporation would be government agencies, the corporation would be dealing directly with foreign governments. On the other hand, the Administration bill, particularly with the amendment restricting the State Department to an advisory role, would place the corporation in a position to establish foreign policy. Senator Kefauver claimed that this bill would virtually turn over the "power of the State Department in negotiating an important international matter . . . and delegate our sovereignty to a private corporation."[37] On the strength of this argument, those opposing the Administration succeeded in referring it back to the Foreign Relations Committee. However, the committee, by a vote of thirteen to four, reported the Administration bill favorably to the Senate without amendments, stating that "the committee majority is satisfied that the bill makes adequate provision for the protection and preservation of the authority of the President to conduct the foreign relations of the United States."[38]

After the Administration bill was sanctioned by the Foreign Relations Committee, it became the pending business on the Senate floor on 10 August 1962. When opponents began a filibuster to block passage of the bill, the Senate leadership filed a petition for cloture to end debate on the bill. Influenced by proponents urging enactment of the Administration bill and Democrats desiring to enhance the poor legislative record of the Eighty-Seventh Congress, the Senate on 14 August 1962, for the first time since 1927, voted to invoke cloture by a majority of sixty-three to twenty-seven. On 17 August the Communications Satellite Act of 1962 passed the Senate by a vote of sixty-six to eleven, and ten days later was passed by the House of Representatives. Finally, on 31 August, President Kennedy signed the bill into law.[39]

The Comsat Charter

While there was nothing particularly novel in the policymaking process leading to the enactment of the Communications Satellite Act, the product of that process, the creation of a public/private corporation, was unique. Although the concept of statutory-created corporations was not new, the dual public/private nature of the Communications Satellite Corporation was unparalled in scope. The Communications Satellite Act created a private corporation and granted it a monopoly in the business of intercontinental satellite communications for the expressed purpose of facilitating the public goal of developing a global communication satellite system. The corporation would serve both private and public interests. The Comsat Act established an elaborate system of checks and balances to ensure the public/private character of the enterprise.

Basic Provisions

The Communications Satellite Act states specifically that the Comsat Corporation would "not be an agency or establishment of the United States government."[40] The government would neither own any portion of the corporation nor guarantee investments to ensure the profitability of the venture. Yet the Comsat Act protected the public interest by establishing a structure of internal and external controls over corporation management. Internal controls are provided through a broad base of ownership and through government representation on the corporation's board of directors. External controls are established through legislative provision which specify the federal government's range of authority to coordinate, plan and regulate Comsat activities.

Section 304 of the Communications Satellite Act contains the provision concerning the financing of the corporation. It gives the corporation the authority to issue capital stock which carries voting rights and is eligible for dividends. Subject to certain limitations, the stock can be held by anyone. The price per share of the initial stock offering was not to exceed $100 in order to encourage wide distribution to the American public. Communications common carriers specifically authorized by the Federal Communications Commission were eligible to buy shares, and fifty percent of the stock was initially reserved for purchase by the carriers. To ensure that the carriers would not dominate ownership, however, the act stipulates that at no time after the initial stock issue could the aggregate of shares of voting stock owned by carriers exceed fifty percent. Section 304 (c) enables the corporation to issue additional securities exclusively to authorized carriers, who could then modify the rate base in order to reflect these investments. However, this class of stock carries no voting rights. In effect, these financing provision established an internal control over business operations by limiting carriers to a percentage of controlling interest, and encouraging wide public distribution of the stock.

A second internal control which marks the public character of the corporation is established in Section 303(a). This provision outlines the composition of the corporate board of directors. Six board members are elected annually by stockholders who are communications carriers, with no individual carrier eligible to vote for more than three candidates; six directors are elected by other stockholders. In addition, three board members are appointed by the president of the United States with the advice and consent of the Senate. This provision is not entirely without precedent. When Congress established the Union Pacific Railroad in 1863, the incorporating legislation provided for presidential appointments to the company's board of directors. In the Union Pacific case, however, the government had a financial interest at stake in the corporation. The practice of appointing public representatives to the board of the private Comsat Corporation in which the government had no financial commitment was unprecedented.[41]

The Comsat Act establishes external controls over the corporation's activities and policies in Section 201. This provision outlines the jurisdiction of the federal government in regard to communication satellite activities and delineates government powers to coordinate, plan and regulate activities of the Comsat Corporation. While government regulation of private enterprise is commonplace, the extent of public involvement provided for in the Comsat Act, particularly with respect to the government's authority to plan and coordinate Comsat Corporation activities, is unique. The president, the FCC, NASA, and the State Department are all given certain areas of authority.

The president's authority is delineated in Section 201(a). Seven executive functions are prescribed. The president would:

> (1) aid in the planning and development and foster the execution of a national program for the establishment and operation ... of a commercial communications satellite system; (2) provide for continuous review of all phases of the development and operation of such a system, including the activities of a communications satellite corporation ...; (3) coordinate the activities of governmental agencies ... to insure ... compliance at all times with the policies set forth ...; (4) exercise such supervision over relationships of the corporation with foreign governments ... as may be appropriate to assure that such relationships shall be consistent with the national interest and foreign policy of the United States; (5) insure ... foreign participation in the establishment and use of a communications satellite system; (6) ... insure the availability and appropriate utilization of the communications satellite system for general governmental purposes ... and ... (7) help attain coordinated and efficient use of the electromagnetic spectrum and the technical compatibility ... with existing communications facilities. ...[42]

The Federal Communications Commission is given extensive regulatory power over the Comsat Corporation. The FCC has authority to ensure competition, including competitive bidding in the procurement of equipment and services required for establishing the space system and ground stations; to ensure nondiscriminatory use of and equitable access to the satellite system and ground stations at reasonable cost; to regulate the allocation of facilities to users; to ensure technical compatibility between satellites and ground stations, and between the satellite system and existing communication facilities; to prescribe accounting and rate-making procedures; and to approve technical characteristics of the system. The commission could also institute proceedings to require the corporation to establish communications with a particular country in any case where the secretary of state advised that such communication was in the national interest. The FCC is further directed to grant authorization for construction and operation of ground stations to both the corporation and authorized common carriers. Other commission functions include the authority to authorize the corporation to issue shares of stock or borrow money; to ensure that no substantial additions are made to the system unless required by the public interest; to require additions to the system when necessary to serve the public interest; and to make rules and regulations as required to carry out the provisions of the Comsat Act.[43]

The role of the State Department in regard to the conduct of international Comsat negotiations is strictly limited by amendments to the original Administration bill. Yet, while the Communications Satellite Act specifies that the corporation rather than the State Department would conduct relevant foreign negotiations, it did require notification to the State Department of such activities. The State Department is also authorized to advise the corporation of relevant foreign policy considerations and to assist in negotiations upon request of the corporation.[44]

Ramifications for NASA

NASA's responsibilities, as defined in the Communications Satellite Act, involve close relationships with the State Department, the FCC and the Communications Satellite Corporation. In addition to Section 201(c) (3), which directs the State Department to consult NASA on technical feasibility before it advised the FCC to require Comsat to provide communications services to a particular foreign country, the Comsat Act assigns six statutory responsibilities to NASA. Section 201(b) directs NASA to "advise the Commission [FCC] on technical characteristics of the system." This provision is particularly important since the FCC does not possess in-house technical expertise in the communication satellite field. The commission did establish an Office of Satellite Communications, but did not build a large technical staff.[45] Consequently, the FCC relies heavily on NASA for technical guidance in exercising its regulatory responsibilities over Comsat.

The remaining provisions specify NASA responsibilities to the Communications Satellite Corporation. The space agency is obligated to:

. . .

(2) cooperate with the corporation in research and development to the extent deemed appropriate by the Administration in the public interest;

(3) assist the corporation in the conduct of its research and development program by furnishing to the corporation, when requested on a reimbursable basis, such satellite launching and associated services as the Administration deems necessary for the most expeditious and economical development of the communications satellite system;

(4) consult with the corporation with respect to the technical characteristics of the communications satellite system;

(5) furnish to the corporation, on request and on a reimbursable basis, satellite launching and associated services required for the establishment, operation, and maintenance of the communications satellite system approved by the Commission; and

(6) to the extent feasible, furnish other services, on a reimbursable basis, to the corporation in connection with the establishment and operation of the system.[46]

The language of the last four provisions is quite clear. NASA is required to furnish support services for certain Comsat activities but has some leverage to decide when or whether such services should be provided. NASA is further obliged to furnish launching and associated services to Comsat upon request for the establishment and maintenance of actual systems operations. This requires that NASA use its facilities to meet the corporation's schedules and to coordinate its own launch requirements with Comsat's schedule. With the exception of technical consultation, the costs of all NASA services must be paid for by the corporation. Although the law does not establish the principles to be applied in calculating reimbursement and does not state whether Comsat is obliged to reimburse NASA for unsuccessful launch attempts, a firm policy was established in subsequent NASA-Comsat negotiations specifying the terms of reimbursement and dictating that the corporation would assume financial liability for launch failures.[47]

The language of the second provision dealing with NASA's cooperative research and development responsibilities with Comsat, however, is extremely vague. NASA is directed to cooperate with Comsat in research and development to the extent it deems "appropriate in the public interest." Determination of how much or what types of research and development is in the national interest becomes a policy issue. Further, the provision does not require that Comsat reimburse NASA for research and development.

The Communications Satellite Act does not clearly delineate the respective roles and responsibilities of Comsat and NASA in the area of research and development. On one hand, the expressed purpose of the act is to create a private, profit-making corporation to develop and operate a communication satellite system; it also specifies that Comsat is to "conduct or contract for research and development related to its mission."[48] On the other hand, NASA is given both a vague mandate to cooperate in research and development and a number of specific technical and advisory functions which necessitate the maintenance of an ongoing expertise in the communication satellite field. Moreover, NASA has other statutory responsibilities in addition to those delineated in the Comsat Act. The National Aeronautics and Space Act of 1958 prescribes a role for NASA in the communication satellite field in its general mandate to ensure U.S. leadership in space technology and its application. The Comsat Act neither confirms nor preempts this mandate. In the absence of clear-cut definitions, the transfer of communication satellite technology to the private sector in 1962 raised a new policy issue – the issue of public vs. private responsibility for further communication satellite research and development.

Comsat Research and NASA Funds

The inevitable question facing Congress and the space agency after a tremendous investment of funds and expertise in satellite communications was what happens after the technology is transferred to the private sector? Could private industry adequately develop and sustain an optimal communication satellite system? Could or would industry be able to perform its own research and development and contribute to advancing the technology? To what extent should the government support private enterprise? Should NASA continue communication satellite research and development?

NASA Budget Controversy

As early as 1963, within a year after Comsat was established, Congress began to express concern that continuation of federal support for communication satellite research and development would, in effect, directly subsidize the development Comsat had been expressly created to do. This concern focused mainly on NASA since the space agency has a statutory responsibility to assist the corporation. Many congressmen had assumed in 1962 that the establishment of Comsat would relieve the government of the costly burden of communication satellite research and development.[49] On the contrary, NASA's budget request for communication satellites increased after 1962. NASA requested $35.5 million for satellite communications in 1962, $49 million in 1963, and $55.8 million in 1964.[50] At the same time, Comsat was slow in getting started. After passing the Comsat Act, Congress adjourned before acting on the nomination of incorporators, although President Kennedy made recess appointments in October 1962. It was April 1963 before the Senate finally confirmed their nominations and another year elapsed before Comsat began to issue public stock. Some congressmen interpreted the situation as evidence of "foot dragging by the corporation and an intent to 'get a free ride' on continued high-level Government expenditures."[51]

When the Senate Subcommittee on Communications convened hearings on satellite communications in February 1963, Senator John Pastore, the committee chairman, responded negatively to NASA plans for continuing communication satellite work. Although Pastore had actively supported the Comsat Act – in fact, he had cosponsored the Administration bill in the Senate – he did not think the taxpayers, who had already given Comsat the basic technology, should continue to finance development. Pastore argued that the decision to commit public funds to further communication satellite research and development was a high-level policy matter. He summarized his objections in his questioning of NASA officials:

> It strikes me that the administration . . . made a very important decision, when it decided this would be a private corporation, and they should be in the field of operating this commercial venture. Now the big question is . . . why shouldn't all of the research and development . . . be done by the private corporation. Why is it necessary to use taxpayers' dollars in order to do it, and then make a contribution to this private corporation?[52]

Many of the arguments in support of the Communication Satellite Act had been based on the premise that private industry would have more initiative and take greater risks to develop and operate a communication satellite system faster and more efficiently than the government would.[53] Pastore said that recent claims that government support was needed in order to prevent delays in the establishment of an operational system gave credence to the opponents of the Comsat Act, who had argued that the legislation was premature.[54]

The questions Senator Pastore raised were repeated in March when the Senate Commerce and Space Committees held confirmation hearings on the nominations of Comsat's incorporators and again in the course of the 1964 NASA authorization hearings. Opponents of continued public expenditures saw little reason why Comsat should not assume the financial burden for research and development. They pointed to the fact that ninety to ninety-five percent of NASA's work was contracted out to private industry and questioned why the government should continue to subsidize Comsat, particularly in view of the fact that many of the contractors would themselves be major stockholders in the corporation.[55]

The controversy climaxed during the 1964 NASA authorization hearings when the space agency submitted its 55.8 million dollar budget for communication satellites with the stated objectives of the program being to ensure "the full development and realization of communications satellite potentials through continued research, development and flight test" and to assist "in the early establishment of operational communications satellite systems."[56] In the opinion of a Subcommittee of the House Science and Astronautics Committee, the budget request posed three major policy questions:

(1) Should taxpayers, through NASA, undertake any research benefitting the stockholders of this profit-making corporation, or should the corporation itself finance the research?
(2) If there is justification for public expenditures on research and development, how are the responsibilities and objectives of NASA and the Communication Satellite Corporation to be demarcated?
(3) Have any provisions been made to reimburse the Government?[57]

These issues became the focus of questions directed to NASA during the course of the hearings.

Throughout the hearings NASA maintained that its statutory responsibilities necessitated continuing communication satellite research and development. NASA had a definite mandate in the Space Act of 1958 to ensure U.S. leadership in space technology, including satellite communications. Further, as stated above, the space agency had responsibilities under the Communications Satellite Act of 1962 to advise and consult the FCC, Comsat and the State Department. NASA argued that it had to "maintain its technical proficiency by a substantial research and development program" in order to discharge these functions.[58] Referring to NASA's role in relation to Comsat, Leonard Jaffe, then NASA director of communication systems, explained:

> The Corporation [Comsat] can be expected to carry on applied research and development, at their own expense, directed toward the components of this initial system, and eventually toward second and third generation operational systems. But the Corporation cannot be expected to engage in research and development for applications of communication satellites to other than common carrier use. Nor can they be expected to assume the full burden, immediately for advancing the technology on a broad front, for to do so would demand a disproportionate share of available resources and possibly preclude a fair return to the Corporation's investors.
>
> At present, then, and in fact for an indefinite period into the future, NASA's role is to carry on experimental activities directed toward future systems, in much the same fashion as government agencies now perform exploratory R&D for civilian aircraft and power industries.[59]

NASA pointed to a number of precedents for supportive government research and development. Both NASA and its predecessor, the National Advisory Committee on Aeronautics, had "traditionally carried out ... research which ... advanced aeronautics in this country, and supported a variety of industries, namely, the aircraft companies and the airlines."[60] The work of the National Experimental Center of the Federal Aviation Administration and the Atomic Energy Commission provided other precedents. The space agency contended that such support was necessary, particularly during Comsat's formative years, to ensure that the United States would remain dominant in the communication satellite industry. Continued leadership was deemed important to both national prestige and the national economy. Jaffe pointed out that economic benefits would be derived not only from the revenues produced from the use of communication satellites but also from the capture of the potential foreign market for equipment.[61] NASA officials further noted that the benefits of continuing research and development would not accrue to Comsat alone: many of NASA's proposed communication satellite program objectives, such as increased satellite reliability and the development of station-keeping systems, were common to meteorological satellites and to "other flight systems of interest to several government agencies."[62] Also, Comsat as well as the electronics industries would benefit from NASA's program.[63] Finally, NASA pointed to the stipulation in the Comsat Act which directed the space agency to cooperate with Comsat in research and development to the extent deemed appropriate in the national interest. It noted that the national interest includes "service to less developed areas, and techniques for improving the spectrum economy."[64] In addition, there were areas of communication satellite research and development which were "not within the purview of the corporation" and "which must obviously be done by the Government."[65] Examples included:

> exploring use of higher frequencies to extend the frontiers of the frequency spectrum; investigation of high-powered satellites which would permit use of very small ground facilities which might be carried on ships, emergency mobile land units, and aircraft (this capability could result in an application of communications satellites to air and sea traffic control procedures); incorporation into stationary communications satellites equipments to provide for other observations in the national interest such as scientific experiments or meteorological sensors; and investigation of high-powered broadcasting satellites which could broadcast radio or television programs directly to all the home receivers in a very large area on the Earth.[66]

While the arguments for an independent government communications program were strong, the problem of demarcating the respective responsibilities of NASA and Comsat raised some difficulties. NASA emphasized that its research and development would be directed toward advanced systems while Comsat's research and development would be aimed at establishing initial operating systems. The agency insisted that it had attempted to formulate a program that would not conflict with Comsat's research and development: NASA's work would be directed toward advancing the technology beyond what the corporation would be willing to undertake.[67] NASA spokesmen told Congress that they would not undertake "in any way, to develop spacecraft that might exist in the immediate future," since this was the corporation's responsibility.[68] Although the rationale was sound, the space agency actually had been forced to develop its fiscal year 1964 program in advance of consultation with the corporation.[69] NASA's budget was necessarily drawn up early in the fiscal year before Comsat was formally organized and the program was based on conjecture of what Comsat would need or be willing to develop on its own.[70] The space agency, however, assured Congress that every effort was being made to establish liaison with Comsat at the earliest possible date and to coordinate their respective programs. NASA Administrator James Webb on 27 March 1963 had addressed a letter to Comsat's president, Joseph Charyk, in which he offered to brief Comsat on NASA's program and to establish a basis for "continuous consultation and coordination."[71] Furthermore, seventy-four percent (i.e., $41.1 million) of NASA's 1964 budget for satellite communications was designated for an Advanced Syncom project, which was designed to develop a more sophisticated version of the earlier Syncom satellites.[72] The heavy emphasis on synchronous satellite experimentation appeared justified at the time, since Comsat was initially expected to develop and operate a medium-altitude system.[73]

The subject of reimbursement provided the final point of contention in the 1964 authorization proceedings. Although NASA assured Congress that Comsat would be required to reimburse the government for launchings and any other identifiable services as stipulated in the Comsat Act, some congressmen felt that the corporation should also reimburse NASA for supportive research and development. The House Subcommittee on Applications and Tracking and Data Acquisition considered a proposal to include language in the NASA Authorization Act which would require Comsat "to pay, compensate or reimburse NASA for expenditures in research and development for the benefit of the Communications Satellite Corporation."[74] In response, NASA maintained that Congress had already carefully defined the categories for reimbursable services in the Comsat Act and that "no further legislation to broaden these categories" was needed.[75] Since the space agency, as a matter of policy, did not intend to undertake near-term research and development for Comsat's benefit, further legislation in this matter was unnecessary. In general, NASA believed that an encumbering reimbursement requirement could hinder the agency's long-range communication satellite research and development. On behalf of Comsat, Leo D. Welch, chairman of the board, issued a detailed statement in rebuttal to the House proposal, in which he argued that such an arrangement would be "exceedingly difficult, if not impossible to administer."[76] Welch pointed to the difficulty of arriving at equitable monetary settlement since benefits to Comsat could not be calculated accurately for years after a NASA research and development project was initiated. Moreover, he maintained that it was untenable to ask Comsat to contribute to the cost of research and development which it had not specifically requested and which was directed toward broad applications rather than specific corporate interests. Finally, Comsat claimed that the proposal would be inequitable unless all of the communications and aerospace companies that derived benefits from NASA programs were also required to contribute to financing NASA research and development.[77]

The language proposing reimbursement for research and development was not written into the House version of the 1964 NASA Authorization bill. However, when the bill was sent to the Senate, Estes Kefauver, who had originally opposed the Comsat Act by claiming that it constituted a relinquishment of tax-supported research and development to a private monopoly, proposed an amendment to the Authorization Act which stated:

> That no part of any funds authorized to be appropriated by this Act may be obligated or expended for the conduct of any scientific or technological research or development activity for or on behalf of any person providing satellite communications services other than an agency of the United States Government, or for the furnishing to or on behalf of any such person of any scientific or technological advice or information, unless such person has been obligated by contract approved by the Comptroller General to make reimbursement to the Administration for a proportionate share of all costs incurred for or in connection with the conduct of such activity or the furnishing of such advice or information.[78]

Under the provisions of this amendment, Comsat would have been required to reimburse NASA for providing advisory services and for a proportionate share of the cost of continued communication satellite research and development.

Although the Kefauver amendment was rejected, the Senate did ratify a substitute amendment introduced by Clinton P. Anderson, the chairman of the Senate Space Committee. The enacted amendment read:

> That no part of any funds authorized to be appropriated by this Act may be obligated or expended for the furnishing of any

> scientific or technological services for the *exclusive benefit* of any person providing satellite communications services other than an agency of the United States Government, except at the request of such person on a reimbursable basis.[79]

According to this language, Comsat was required to reimburse NASA only for research and development activities designed exclusively for the corporation's benefit. The amendment did not, in effect, create any new categories for reimbursement beyond those already established in the Communications Satellite Act. Moreover, since none of NASA's 1964 appropriations were specifically designated to support Comsat, no reimbursement was required in fiscal year 1964. The amendment was subsequently dropped from the 1965 NASA authorization bill based on NASA's recommendation. The space agency contended that the so-called "Comsat Provision" was unnecessary since, in the absence of the provision, it had always been NASA policy to require reimbursement for services provided for the exclusive benefit of any non-governmental entity.[80] Thus the attempt to legislate a more precise formula for reimbursement proved inconsequential. However, it did indicate the intent of Congress to set definite boundaries around the domain of public-supported communication satellite research and development.

6

THE INITIATION OF INTELSAT: SATELLITES FOR GLOBAL COMMUNICATIONS

The two major objectives of the United States foreign policy on satellite communications have been to further international cooperation and to protect the national interest. These policy objectives were incorporated into the 1958 National Aeronautics and Space Act, NASA's charter.[1] The Congress specified in this act, which is the foundation of U.S. space policy, that peace and international cooperation would govern the exploration and utilization of space by the United States:

> The aeronautical and space activities of the United States shall be conducted so as to contribute materially to one or more of the following objectives:
>
> . . .
>
> (7) Cooperation by the United States with other nations and groups of nations in work done pursuant to this chapter and in the peaceful application of the results thereof; . . .[2]

In order to carry out this mandate, Congress authorized NASA to engage in a program of international cooperation:

> The Administration, under the foreign policy guidance of the President, may engage in a program of international cooperation in work done pursuant to this Act, and in the peaceful application of the results thereof, pursuant to agreements made by the President with the advice and consent of the Senate.[3]

The development of rocket, satellite, and other aerospace technologies was also influenced by national security considerations and by the atmosphere of international suspicion that characterized the cold war period. Security as well as commercial considerations were the primary impetus for Section 102 (c) (5) of the NASA charter, which states that the nation's space program is to contribute to "the preservation of the role of the United States as a leader in aeronautical and space science technology and in the application thereof to the conduct of peaceful activities within and outside the atmosphere." These concerns helped to shape space policy even though NASA, a civilian agency, was given the major role in the development of the technology. Furthermore, according to the NASA charter, discoveries of military value are to be made available to agencies concerned with national defense. The charter also defines the research roles of NASA and the Department of Defense:

> The Congress declares that [aeronautical and space activities] shall be the responsibility of, and shall be directed by, a civilian agency . . . except that activities peculiar to or primarily associated with the development of weapons systems, military operations, or the defense of the United States (including the research and development necessary to make effective provision for the defense of the United States) shall be the responsibility of, and shall be directed by, the Department of Defense; . . .[4]

Therefore, in order to preserve U.S. technological leadership, NASA was required to consider the policy implications of its cooperative experiments and to channel them into areas with minimal political and military ramifications. This was the case when NASA examined possibilities for international experimentation with communication satellites.

Early International Space Cooperation

Within the National Aeronautics and Space Administration, the Office of International Affairs has responsibility for the negotiation, implementation and monitoring of the cooperative programs mandated by the NASA charter. As of 1975, nearly sixty nations have entered into agreements with NASA for the purpose of joint experimentation and scientific inquiry. The categories of experimentation have included ground-based use of data acquired via earth resources survey satellites, lunar sample analyses, cooperative flight projects, reimbursable launchings, and tracking and data acquisition. Over ninety countries and international organizations have engaged in at least some form of aerospace activity with NASA since the inception of the agency. The spectrum of activities has ranged from the joint U.S.-Great Britain Ariel satellite program for ionospheric investigation to international participation in the Apollo manned space flights. NASA's ongoing cooperative ventures follow guidelines which recognize the interests of the United States as well as those of foreign countries. Specifically, these project guidelines provide for:

1. Designation by each participating government of a central civilian agency for the negotiation and supervision of joint efforts,
2. Agreement upon specific projects rather than generalized programs,
3. Acceptance of financial responsibility by each participating country for its own contributions to joint projects,
4. Projects of scientific validity and mutual interest,
5. General publication of scientific results.[5]

The Echo program was NASA's first cooperative effort involving communication satellites. In 1959 one NASA official noted that the Echo program was especially attractive to scientists and engineers working outside the agency: "Project Echo is an . . . appropriate opportunity for participation by independent research facilities since it involves a passive satellite which will travel over every portion of the United States and over parts of Canada and Europe."[6] Potential experimenters from the federal government as well as from U.S. corporations and universities met during March 1960 in order to discuss their roles in the Echo communications experiment. Project Echo became a multinational endeavor when NASA received notice from various foreign scientists of their willingness to participate in the program.[7] The scientists represented a number of countries, including Canada, Great Britain, France and the Netherlands. Interested organizations ranged from the University College at Aberystwyth, Wales, to the French Meteorological Service. The fact that several agencies from the same country were involved in Project Echo posed difficulties for future cooperative experimentation. NASA would have to choose among foreign agencies for participants in the experiments since it would not always be possible to select every group that indicated an interest. In connection with this early period of international cooperation, Arnold W. Frutkin, director of the Office of International Affairs, noted that "NASA was soon forced to establish criteria for the recognition of foreign agencies with which to deal in cooperative space projects," and that "it became quickly apparent that internal struggles were underway in most interested countries to determine which agencies would obtain control of space planning and operations."[8]

The international interest in Echo I was encouraging to those from the United States involved in the space program. When the Echo satellite was placed in orbit on 12 August 1960, President Eisenhower renewed the invitation for international participation by stating that Echo could be used by any nation for experimental purposes.[9] Shortly after the launch of the satellite, a group of NASA officials, meeting at Goddard Space Flight Center, discussed the possibilities for continuing foreign involvement. They agreed that "every effort should be made to ensure maximum foreign participation in experimentation," particularly if Echo II were launched within a few years' time.[10]

The Beginnings of Formal International Arrangements

While NASA was engaged in its Echo satellite program, the U.S. private sector, particularly AT&T, was involved in discussions with various European nations regarding the development of communication satellite systems. In time AT&T was able to interest the telecommunication entities of Germany, Britain and France in a commercial system. As envisioned by AT&T, the system would have utilized active repeater satellites at an approximate orbital altitude of 2,200 miles for the transmission of telephone and television signals across the Atlantic Ocean. After a period of experimentation with telephone transmissions, AT&T planned to develop an operational system capable of handling several hundred transatlantic telephone conversations simultaneously. The channel capacity of the system would also have been used for the transmission of television programming between the European and North American continents.[11]

Concurrent with the AT&T initiative, NASA was moving into a more formal relationship with foreign agencies so as to facilitate the testing of its series of active repeater satellites. Experimentation with Relay I and II required overseas ground stations and also greater coordination and data exchange than did the Echo program. Initially, it was proposed that NASA build and operate the European ground stations, but an alternative was developed at the insistence of Arnold Frutkin, with the approval of T. Keith Glennan, administrator of NASA at that time.[12] Accordingly, NASA decided to interest the governments of foreign nations in the construction and operation of these stations. Taking representatives from AT&T and ITT along in order to avoid any appearance of division, NASA first approached England and France because these countries seemed the most likely to contribute the necessary stations. After several days of negotiating by NASA's Arnold Frutkin and Leonard Jaffe, both England and France decided to join the effort and build the ground stations. In February 1961 the NASA negotiators signed a memorandum of understanding with the United Kingdom; the agreement was confirmed in March by an official exchange of diplomatic notes.[13] During that same month, a similar agreement was reached with France, and once again the agreement was confirmed by an exchange of notes.[14] These two memoranda marked the inauguration of formalized cooperation between the United States and other nations in the experimental use of communication satellites. By the end of 1961 cooperative agreements had been reached with West Germany and Brazil; within three years, memoranda of understanding had also been signed with Italy, Japan, Canada, India, Spain and the Scandinavian Committee for Satellite Telecommunications. All of these memoranda were essentially the same: the telecommunication agencies of the foreign nations agreed to provide ground stations for the reception and transmission of voice or television signals while NASA furnished the satellite radiation characteristics and orbital parameters needed for the operation of the terminals. The memoranda also dealt with radio frequency selection, operating schedules, temporary interconnection with terrestrial telecommunication networks, and the dissemination of data obtained from the satellite experiments to the scientific community. In addition, there was to be neither exchanging of funds nor commercial exploitation by any participant of the joint satellite research.[15]

It is significant to note that these international agreements were promulgated between technical agencies (NASA and foreign telecommunications entities) as opposed to more political organizations. Although formally agreed upon by the diplomatic corps of the respective governments, the memoranda of understanding were drafted on a purely technical/professional level and proved to be a satisfactory method of advancing the utilization of the technology.[16]

After signing the agreements with England and France, NASA during July 1961 established an international working body to coordinate experimentation with the Relay and Telstar satellites. The organization was initially referred to as the Communication Satellite Working Group and later renamed the Ground Station Committee. The Ground Station Committee joined project and assistant managers of the Echo, Relay and Telstar programs with representatives from the foreign ground stations and from private sector communications carriers. Under the chairmanship of NASA's Leonard Jaffe, the committee met nine times during the period between its first meeting held in Paris during July 1961 and its final meeting of this particular series held at Cape Kennedy in December 1964. The diverse character of the committee provided an "expert forum for the selection of suitable radio frequencies, the definition and scheduling of transmissions tests and consideration of the interests of each and all the participants."[17] The work of the committee helped to demonstrate both the technical promise of communication satellites and "the sincerity of U.S. advocacy of global cooperation in the establishment of a commercial system of communications founded on satellites."[18] Finally, it was this group of ground stations that provided the foundation for a global system and facilitated the early commercialization of the technology.

As early as 1960, when the Senate Committee on Aeronautical and Space Sciences analyzed the present and planned uses of the radio frequency spectrum for space telecommunications, it became apparent that the United States lacked a comprehensive policy on communication satellites. A report issued by the committee on 4 December 1960 referred to the absence of a satellite policy and noted that no single federal agency had been delegated the responsibility to develop one.[19] The report also asserted that greater worldwide interest in space communications would be necessary in order to advance a United States position on frequency allocation at the 1963 Extraordinary Administrative Radio Conference of the International Telecommunication Union. The report suggested that the United States delegation to the ITU conference adopt a position favoring a frequency allocation for a commercial system.[20]

The inchoate space communications policy was discussed in other sectors of government during the early 1960s. In a memorandum dated August 1960, Robert Nunn, then special assistant to the administrator of NASA, suggested that the government develop a communication satellite policy that reflected the necessarily international scope of any commercial system. He further stated that the relevant policy issues "are not purely domestic and cannot be resolved solely on the basis of principles which tend to control the resolution of domestic issues."[21] In addition, the growing interest of the private sector in the commercial potential of communication satellites necessitated long-range policy formulation by the government.[22]

In a statement released during January 1961, President Eisenhower called for the early establishment of a revenue-producing communication satellite system and noted that a global enterprise would require the capabilities and funds of government and private organizations as well as the participation of telecommunication entities from foreign countries. Eisenhower also acknowledged the success of NASA's international program and the rapid advance of communication satellite technology.[23]

At the interdepartmental level, officials from the State Department and NASA met during early 1961 in order to study international policy questions.[24] In February NASA and the Federal Communications Commission promulgated a memorandum of understanding giving both organizations the responsibility to facilitate international space communication activities within the framework of U.S. international obligations and objectives.[25] This memorandum, prompted by the AT&T Telstar project, allocated the respective jurisdictions of NASA and the FCC over communication satellites.

During the following summer President Kennedy decided to organize these intra- and interdepartmental discussions into an overall policy position. On 24 July 1961 he issued a statement inviting all nations to participate in a global satellite system. The president declared that the federal government would play an active role in the development of the system, and that international message carriers such as AT&T and ITT would not be granted complete responsibility for its establishment and operation.[26] He also indicated that the international satellite communication policies of his Administration were to be more aggressive and far reaching than those of the previous one. Indeed, the rapid development and implementation of a global system was emerging as the primary objective of United States communication satellite policy. The initial cooperative ventures of NASA, according to NASA Administrator Webb, had already established a firm pattern of mutual assistance upon which an operational system could be based:

> We have sought to make arrangements which provide interested countries the greatest possible opportunity for participation in experimentation. This should pave the way for further cooperative agreements that may be necessary, particularly when operational systems become technically and economically feasible.[27]

As indicated in Chapter Four, the Kennedy policy statement was an expression of the operational imperative; the actual implementation of the technology, however, depended upon finding workable solutions to such policy questions as the extent of foreign participation and the amount of service to the developing nations. The instrument that the government selected to represent the United States in a global system would determine the degree to which these considerations influenced policymaking and international relations. Comsat was that instrument.

The question of ownership, with its obvious international implications, was one of the more divisive issues in the drafting of the Comsat legislation. The three basic approaches – government, carrier, and broad-based private ownership – were considered in a global context during meetings of the Interdepartmental Drafting Committee held in autumn 1961. As one of the agencies participating in the discussions, the State Department itself was divided on the issue. The Offices of International Organization Affairs and the Legal Advisor favored federal government ownership of the communications entity representing the United States in a global system, while the Bureau of Economic Affairs and the Office of International Scientific Affairs argued that the U.S. portion of the system should be owned and managed by a private corporation.[28] However, the entire department was united in the view that a communication satellite system should benefit all nations, including the developing areas of the world, and that it should be organized on a multinational basis and not as a "domestic corporation seeking profits."[29] Eventually, the State Department along with the Justice Department and the Federal Communications Commission endorsed the private enterprise approach in the belief that a corporation under close government supervision would best be able to meet the policy requirements enumerated by President Kennedy. According to the statement of Under Secretary of State McGhee to the Senate Committee on Aeronautical and Space Sciences, private ownership of the U.S. portion was not a significant foreign policy issue and would not affect U.S. foreign relations.[30]

By late 1961, the Interdepartmental Drafting Committee had sent a draft bill to President Kennedy. As mentioned in Chapter Five, the legislation proposed by the committee was characterized by operational considerations and by the external regulatory measures holding the corporation accountable to the government. According to Section 201 of the draft legislation, the president would supervise the corporation's relationships with foreign governments and other international bodies to ensure that its activities were consistent with the U.S. national interest and foreign policy. The same section also required the president to make arrangements for foreign participation in the establishment and use of a commercial satellite system. Section 402 prohibited the corporation from entering into negotiations with any international agency or foreign government. Instead, the corporation was to notify the State Department and the latter would conduct the necessary negotiations and approve all international agreements and arrangements. In addition, special attention was to be given to the provision of satellite telecommunication services to the developing nations.

After the proposal was approved by President Kennedy and submitted to the Congress,[31] business interests expressed concern that an excessively large government bureaucracy would hinder the corporation's operation and management. At a meeting of the Senate Aeronautical and Space Sciences Committee, the executive vice president of AT&T, James Dingman, stated that the "proliferation of governmental supervision . . . could result in conflict and confusion which might smother the initiative and leadership which are essential to the accomplishment of the national purpose involved."[32] Eventually, corporate concerns prevailed, and the enacted version of Section 402 limited the role of the State Department to that of an advisory capacity:

> Whenever the corporation shall enter into business negotiations with respect to facilities, operations, or services authorized by this Act with any international or foreign entity, it shall notify the Department of State of the negotiations, and the Department of State shall advise the corporation of relevant foreign policy considerations. Throughout such negotiations the corporation shall keep the Department of State informed with respect to such considerations. The corporation may request the Department of State to assist in the negotiations, and that Department shall render such assistance as may be appropriate.[33]

Regarding the timetable for State Department involvement, Secretary of State Dean Rusk indicated to the Senate Foreign Relations Committee in February 1962 that the department would be involved in the negotiating process during the early organizational phase of the international system. Rusk also observed that a number of issues, mostly technical in nature, would remain unresolved until after the initial phase of negotiations had been completed.[34] However, he hoped that the discussion of such issues would not require substantial participation of the department because it did not have the available staff.[35] In other testimony Secretary Rusk stated that private ownership of the United States portion of an international system would not pose a problem when dealing with foreign governments.[36] Rusk also said that the bill provided the United States government with adequate authority for the protection and furtherance of its foreign policy objectives. Moreover, he believed that its passage would bring the United States closer to the establishment of a global satellite system and that this would be advantageous for the nation's foreign policy.[37]

The deputy administrator of NASA, Hugh L. Dryden, indicated to the Senate Foreign Relations Committee that there was an immediate foreign policy objective in addition to those already outlined by Secretary Rusk. Dryden told the committee that passage of the Communications Satellite Act would place the United States in a favorable negotiating position at the upcoming ITU conference, which was to assign frequencies for communication satellites.[38] The United States would be able to obtain favorable reaction to its proposals from other nations if it appeared to be moving in the direction of an operational system. Agreement on frequency allocation was a critical step in the process of achieving a viable global communications satellite system.

As approved by Congress, the Communications Satellite Act of 1962 did make the United States dependent upon a uniquely structured public/private corporation for the implementation of its communication satellite policy goals. Congress established the Communications Satellite Corporation as the chosen instrument of U.S. policy in the belief that private enterprise, with its acknowledged managerial skills, would be able to develop the global system in an efficient and expeditious manner. The actual development of the system, however, would depend upon the interest and involvement of foreign nations. Consequently, policymakers from the United States conducted exploratory talks with the United Kingdom and Canada as early as October 1962 in order to discuss their interest in an international venture. In December of the same year, U.S. representatives attended the European Conference of Post and Telecommunications Administrations (CEPT) held in Cologne, West Germany, at which time additional European nations expressed their willingness to participate in a commercial system.[39]

The United States needed to formulate specific proposals in order to negotiate effectively with the European nations. At the outset of this policymaking process, officials from Comsat and from various sectors of government expressed differing opinions as to the role of the federal government in the actual negotiations. The friction between Comsat and the government became evident shortly after President Kennedy appointed incorporators for Comsat in October of 1962. Philip L. Graham, publisher of the Washington Post and the first chairman of the Comsat Corporation, objected to what he claimed was the interference of the State Department in Comsat's international policy planning.[40] Graham's successor, Leo D. Welch, also viewed the State Department as an impediment to successful negotiations. In addition, he charged the Federal Communications Commission with an "invasion of the managerial functions of the corporation."[41] Such antipathy was partially the result of the elusive public/private character of the corporation: the government believed that Comsat, as a creation of Congress and the chosen instrument of U.S. satellite policy, should be held accountable to governmental processes; whereas the individuals from private industry directing Comsat perceived it primarily as a profit-oriented organization.

The conflict between Comsat and the State Department was manifested in other ways. For example, Comsat originally expected a series of bilateral agreements with the major telecommunication countries (Britain, France, Germany, Italy and Japan) to be the most advantageous method of operating in the formative stage of the international enterprise.[42] It was assumed that other nations would follow suit after these initials agreements had been reached. This negotiating strategy had already been utilized by NASA for its ground station agreements with foreign communications authorities. In addition, the early history of AT&T's transoceanic cable negotiations led Comsat to believe that the bilateral approach would be successful in the satellite discussions. However, after a series of talks with European representatives in autumn 1963, Comsat returned home with noncommittal responses "both on the bilateral format and on the level of negotiation."[43]

In contrast with Comsat's bilateral stretegy, the State Department argued for a multilateral negotiation approach with special allowances for flexibility. This approach was defended in 1963 by the deputy assistant secretary of the department's International Organization Affairs Bureau: "In seeking solutions to problems involving an international satellite communications system, we need an approach that is not doctrinaire but functional; these problems may require different kinds of arrangements—bilateral, regional and multilateral."[44] According to the department, the European nations would not negotiate individual arrangements with Comsat similar to AT&T's bilateral cable agreements with its foreign partners. Furthermore, the State Department did not think it likely that the European nations—the major users of the global system besides the United States—would permit their telecommunications administrations, rather than their foreign policy agencies, to negotiate arrangements with Comsat.[45] Thus the State Department favored international contact among the governments of all of the prospective users of the system in addition to agreements between private, commercial entities. This position had been advocated as early as autumn of 1962 by William Carter of the State Department's Bureau of Economic Affairs.[46]

In June 1963 President Kennedy organized an ad hoc Communications Satellite Group in order to coordinate government efforts in the field of commercial satellite communications.[47] This committee was composed of representatives from the Department of Defense, State Department, NASA, FCC and other interested agencies.[48] A major responsibility of the Communications Satellite Group was the examination of Comsat's draft principles for international cooperation. In particular, Comsat and the members of the group addressed the question of ownership of the global system. The State Department "advocated a truly multilateral international organization that would own and operate the system,"[49] whereas Comsat wanted to own and manage the system itself. Moreover, Comsat continued to insist that it, and not the government, negotiate the necessary agreements with foreign nations.[50] The negotiating principles of Comsat were not finalized until the latter half of 1963, after the ITU's Extraordinary Administrative Radio Conference and a meeting of the European Conference on Satellite Communications.

Frequency Allocation Discussions

Although passage of the Communications Satellite Act and the subsequent attempts at policy clarification brought the United States closer to the establishment of a global system, a number of other problems remained unresolved. One such problem, appropriate frequency allocations, was often the subject of congressional questioning on the Comsat Act. At that time NASA's Dryden asserted that utter confusion would occur unless the international community reached a satisfactory agreement on frequency assignments for communication satellites.[51] Even as early as 1959, long before the passage of the Comsat Act, the government was considering the question of frequency allocation for communication via satellite. At the 1959 International Administrative Radio Conference (IARC) of the ITU, the United States delegation argued for a comprehensive frequency allocation. But a majority of the conference participants decided to assign only thirteen narrow bands for satellite experimentation. The IARC participants did agree to convene an Extraordinary Administrative Radio Conference (EARC) sometime before 1965 in order to assign frequencies for operational satellite communications. Shortly after the IARC, the Department of State, NASA, FCC, and the Interdepartmental Radio Advisory Committee began preparations for the anticipated EARC. NASA was especially instrumental in the development of United States policy for the conference.[52]

The ITU eventually convened its Extraordinary Administrative Radio Conference in Geneva, Switzerland, during October 1963. The conference was held in order to allocate radio frequency bands for various space activities including satellite telecommunications.[53] Specifically, the EARC delegates would have to determine the amount of frequency bandwidth necessary for the operation of a commercial global system. In addition, the delegates needed to ascertain whether the frequency assignments should be reserved exclusively for satellites or whether they should be shared with terrestrial telecommunication systems.

For its part, the United States was able to formulate specific proposals relating to frequency assignments and to present them to other delegations by the opening of the conference. As a result, the United States had a major impact on the agenda of the preconference discussions.[54] In general, the members of the U.S. delegation along with Canada, France, and the United Kingdom favored a comprehensive frequency allocation.[55] On the other hand, the Soviet Union recommended a limited allocation,[56] perhaps an indication of its opposition to a private, commercial system and the fact that its satellite program was in an earlier developmental state than that of the United States. Furthermore, the Soviet Union did not want any portion of the radio spectrum to be reserved for the exclusive use of communications satellites.[57] By the close of the EARC, the delegates had negotiated a satisfactory compromise of the divergent positions and had allocated sufficient bandwith to meet the anticipated requirements of communication satellites for the coming decade.[58]

To a great extent, the frequency allocation policy of the United States was an expression of its technological and operational imperatives. The debate on the issue of whether frequencies should be assigned on a provisional or on a permanent basis was especially revealing in this regard. Both the Soviet Union and Israel argued for provisional frequency assignments. The delegation from Israel stated that space communication "was both the privilege and the exclusive possibility of the great countries only."[59] Advocates of this position believed that a permanent or definitive allocation would benefit those nations that were the first to utilize outer space for telecommunication; any nation wishing to establish its own system at a later date would be hampered by the absence of available frequencies. In contrast, the United States wanted such a definitive allocation in order to guarantee the commercial viability of the global system. The U.S. delegation believed that private corporations and national governments required assurance that their substantial investments in a satellite system would not be threatened by repeated changes in allocation policy. Once again the EARC participants voted in favor of the policy recommendations of the United States and chose to consider the allocations as definitive.[60]

Regarding the ITU's ongoing regulatory responsibilities, the Soviet Union wanted the ITU to coordinate all space communication activities. Such a role might have enabled the ITU to halt any plan for utilization of outer space that was in violation of its rules and regulations. The delegation from France also favored the assignment of coordinating functions to the ITU, and suggested that all nations notify the International Frequency Registration Board (IFRB) of frequency allocations to terrestrial systems which might interfere with satellite telecommunications. As the nation with the most advanced satellite technology, the United States strongly objected to the French and Soviet proposals, primarily because they were potential obstacles to the development of an operational satellite system. In addition, the United States opposed the imposition of a greater administrative burden upon the ITU. As a compromise, the EARC participants delegated an informal coordinating role to the IFRB and requested that any nation intending to launch a space object inform the ITU as to the likelihood of signal interference or other harmful effects resulting from the project.[61]

In sum, the resolution of the frequency allocation issues at the 1963

EARC enabled interested nations to proceed with the development of a global communication satellite system.

Early Intelsat Negotiations

The European nations began to formulate the principles that would govern their negotiating activities while the United States was engaged in its own policy clarification process. As early as December 1962, the European Conference of Post and Telecommunications Administrations, referred to previously, established a committee that (1) examined the various problems associated with European participation in a global satellite system; (2) recommended a basis for discussion between CEPT and the United States; and (3) studied the management possibilities for the system. Following CEPT, an intergovernmental meeting was held in London during July 1963 in order to establish the European Conference on Satellite Communications (ECSC). Since the initial criterion for membership in ECSC was participation in CEPT, its origins were technical in nature. ECSC subsequently evolved into an organization composed of political and technical advisors when governmental departments other than telecommunications administrations became interested in communication satellites. By November 1963 ECSC had been established as the negotiating counterpart to Comsat.[62] This allowed the Europeans to form a bloc for negotiations with Comsat,[63] and eliminated the possibility of negotiating a series of bilateral agreements, as had been proposed by Comsat earlier in 1963.

European solidarity served as a catalyst to bring about agreement between Comsat and members of the ad hoc Satellite Group regarding the basic negotiating principles of the United States. Essentially, Comsat and the government policymakers decided to press for international ownership, multilateral negotiations and representation at the upcoming Rome discussions by a U.S. team composed equally of government and Comsat officials.[64] Furthermore, Comsat and the State Department decided that any agreements reached at Rome should encourage foreign nations to participate in the use and ownership of the system. It was assumed that the technical and operational development of the system would be delayed by protracted discussions and by the adoption of any international agreement which minimized foreign participation.[65]

Although the United States was prepared to begin the talks, it was still necessary to persuade Europe and other nations to enter into formal discussion. Insofar as the immediate launching of the system was concerned, Great Britain had apparently been taking an obstructionist role by suggesting that cable or at least the next generation of cable technology could best serve international communication needs.[66] Furthermore, according to NASA's Leonard Jaffe, many nations were "footdragging" because they feared that the United States, represented by Comsat, would dominate the system.[67] Apparently, the European nations were delaying the commencement of negotiation in order to gain a more effective bargaining position.

During this period of time the U.S. international telephone and telegraph carriers were evaluating their communications requirements for the remainder of the decade. In order to plan effectively for growth, especially in the North Atlantic corridor, these carriers needed to know when a satellite system would become operational. For its part, AT&T hoped to use a mix of cable and satellite technology—if a satellite system were available by 1966 or 1967—rather than simply laying additional undersea cable in the North Atlantic area. This preference was indicated in a letter, dated 12 December 1963, from AT&T's James Dingman to Leo Welch, chairman of Comsat.[68] The overall effect of this growing private sector concern was to place increased pressure on the Europeans to join in the development of the international system. By the end of January 1964 Great Britain and other European nations had expressed definite interest in beginning the negotiations.[69]

A new phase in the history of space communication began in February 1964 when the United States and the European nations met formally in Rome to negotiate the arrangements leading to the creation of the International Telecommunications Satellite Consortium (Intelsat). Held at the invitation of the ECSC, this important meeting was attended by representatives of the Western European nations, Canada, the United States, Japan and Australia.[70] The fact that there were no Third World nations in attendance reflected a "pragmatic approach," since more than eighty percent of the world's international telephone traffic was controlled by the Western industrialized countries. The rationale was that inclusion of the developing nations in the negotiating process would have made it even more difficult to reach a satisfactory agreement.[71]

Prior to the Rome conference the U.S. delegation had made it clear that the United States was prepared to establish a global system regardless of any conditions that might be imposed on Comsat by other nations during the course of the negotiations.[72] Nevertheless, the general atmosphere at the opening of the conference was conducive to friendly negotiation. Such matters as draft agreements and treaty language were not discussed at the Rome conference; instead, the negotiations were exploratory in nature with the majority of discussion centering on basic organizational principles and on potential obstacles to the establishment of an operational system. The participants did agree that responsibility for management of the satellite system should be delegated to Comsat, at least on an interim basis.

Ownership percentages, voting procedures and the duration of the interim arrangements were the primary issues that remained unresolved at the close of the Rome meetings. The United States and the ECSC held differing positions on all of these questions. Regarding the last issue, the ECSC favored a relatively short, three-year period for the interim arrangements in the belief that a longer duration would unduly support the continuance of U.S. leadership in world satellite communications. Furthermore, the European nations anticipated an early increase in their technical capability, which would enable them to assume a more equal footing with the United States in the operation of the satellite system. The U.S. delegation advocated a longer interim period so as to accumulate more practical experience in the use of the technology before attempting to negotiate the definitive arrangements.

Regarding the issue of ownership, the delegates at the Rome conference generally agreed that multilateral financial participation was a reasonable approach. The crucial question, however, was the size of the capital contribution of the Western European nations. Wishing to supply a considerable portion of the capital outlay, these nations supported a plan which would base ownership percentages upon the investment of each signatory in relation to the total amount required to capitalize the satellite system – roughly $ 200 million. The United States asserted that the $ 200 million figure was misleading because it represented only a small fraction of the total U.S. expenditure since the 1950s for satellite research and development. The delegation from the United States believed that this vast financial outlay as well as the overall technological superiority of the United States justified granting majority ownership of the consortium to Comsat, regardless of the size of the European investment in relation to the $ 200 million figure.[73]

The next series of meetings was held in London during April 1964. At these sessions the U.S. delegation suggested that negotiations be conducted between the governments of the interested parties and also between their respective telecommunications agencies. Comsat was to represent the United States in the latter discussions. As explained by William Carter of the State Department, the purpose of this suggestion was to meet the anticipated European insistence upon an intergovernmental agreement and to delineate Comsat's management concerns. By the close of these discussions a consensus was reached that was essentially favorable to the U.S. position.[74]

Two other major problems resolved at the London meetings were ownership percentages and the duration of the interim arrangements. Regarding the first issue, the delegates decided to allocate investment and ownership shares according to the proportional use of the system by each participant. The anticipated use of the global system by each signatory in 1968 for relaying its long-distance telephone traffic was the criterion for the apportionment; data for the estimates were furnished by an ITU Plan Committee Meeting of the International Telegraph and Telephone Consultative Committee and the International Radio Consultative Committee, convened in Rome in late 1963, and by a meeting of telephone traffic experts held in Montreal, Canada, during April 1964.[75] Comsat's ownership quota was set at 61 percent; the combined European share was 30.5 percent; and the total Canadian, Japanese and Australian share was 8.5 percent. Those in attendance also agreed on a procedure for the allocation of ownership shares for future participants: a *pro rata* portion would be taken from those nations that had already invested in the system. In the event that every nation in the world joined the organization, the U.S. share would decline to 50.6 percent of the total investment.[76] The European delegates had wanted these new allocations to be taken almost exclusively from Comsat's ownership percentage.[77]

The delegates to the London meetings also resolved the dispute over the duration of the interim arrangements. A multilateral body, the Interim Communications Satellite Committee (ICSC), was given the responsibility for the design, development, construction, maintenance and operation of the space segment. This committee was to issue a report either one year after the initial system became operational or by 1 January, 1969.[78] The committee report would recommend either a continuation of the interim arrangements or appropriate organizational and administrative changes; an international conference would be convened within three months in order to consider the recommendations.[79] Irrespective of any changes proposed by the ICSC in its report, the Intelsat signatories were to formulate definitive arrangements at the earliest possible date, with a tentative goal of 1 January 1970.[80]

The negotiations were resumed in Washington, D.C., during July 1964 in order to resolve the remaining outstanding issue, that of voting procedures. At this meeting it was necessary for the delegates to agree upon a voting formula for decisions involving basic system choices, contract awards and other important matters. A simple majority rule formula was not adequate because Comsat had already been awarded sixty-one percent ownership during the negotiations of the previous spring. If adopted, a majority rule arrangement would have given Comsat absolute veto power. Instead, on 23 July 1964, the delegates agreed upon a complex decision making formula: a decisive vote on any major substantive issue required the concurrence of Comsat, with its sixty-one percent quota, as well as those of other ICSC members, the combined voting strength of which totalled at least 12.5 percent. This figure automatically dropped to 8.5 percent if the ICSC were unable to reach a decision within sixty days.[81]

On 23 July, the last day of the conference, negotiators from thirteen nations and the Vatican City initialed the Agreement Establishing Interim Arrangements for a Global Commercial Communications Satellite System and the related Special Agreement. The initialing of the documents signified the conclusion of the treaty drafting process; the remaining option for interested nations was one of either approval or disapproval.[82] Less than a month later, on 20 August 1969, at the Treaty Division of the U.S. State Department, the interrelated agreements[83] constituting the interim arrangements were opened for signature.[84] The agreements also entered into force on that day and the International Telecommunication Satellite Consortium was a reality.

Although Comsat and the State Department differed on negotiating strategy prior to the Rome and London conferences, they agreed upon the two fundamental objectives of United States communication satellite policy: (1) to develop a global system as quickly as possible and (2) to realize the economic and technological benefits resulting from the operation of the system. The State Department also perceived two other important aspects of U.S. policy: (1) to enhance national prestige and (2) to strengthen U.S. political relations with the developing nations by means of a global system linking both low and high traffic areas.[85] While the latter policy goal could have become a major point of contention between Comsat and the State Department, disagreement did not occur along this line. Instead, the two organizations disagreed over the extent of State Department influence in the policymaking process and the nature of the department's role at the negotiating sessions. As it turned out, the government and Comsat eventually assumed complementary roles during the formulation of the interim agreements.[86] Officials from Comsat negotiated the technical and financial arrangements for the satellite system while the State Department took the lead on matters relating to organizational structure and U.S. foreign policy interests. Nonetheless, the negotiating posture of the United States was determined significantly by Comsat and by the imperative to establish a global system as quickly as practicable.

Several factors contributed to the operational imperative; the most important of these was the fact that the technology for the system was developing rapidly—if not already in existence—at the time of the 1963 Extraordinary Administrative Radio Conference. NASA was the most advanced and sophisticated satellite research and development organization in the world, and the Department of Defense was releasing previously classified information relating to space communications. The communication satellite technology transfer process was underway, and these resources were becoming available to private industry in the United States for utilization. The majority of the economic and technological "spin-off" benefits would certainly accrue to U.S. domestic private enterprise and, indirectly, to the general public as a result of an early commercialization of the technology.

A question arises as to why the Western European and other nations would enter into an agreement that had been shaped primarily by the interests of the United States. First, the European signatories did not have sufficient technological expertise to develop a satellite system unilaterally; second, U.S. private enterprise was actively pressing for negotiations and an expeditious implementation of the system. The various European telecommunications administrations were well aware that the United States operated the majority of the international message circuits, and that AT&T, the exclusive international U.S. voice carrier, owned twenty-nine percent of Comsat. These two carriers, in fact, were able to exert considerable leverage upon the European nations, which could either commit themselves to the use of satellite technology and be assured of an ownership share and a management voice in a global system, or avoid such a commitment and risk obsolescence of the transoceanic cable network, representing a substantial European investment. There was little choice in the matter according to the British postmaster general: "... the government's view is that the only way of preventing an American monopoly in this sphere [global communications] is to join a partnership with the United States and other countries and so secure the right to influence the course of events."[87]

The strong negotiating position of the United States induced the European nations to enter into formal discussion. However, the formulation of organization arrangements and launch of a space segment did not require the participation of the developing nations; consequently, they did not attend the 1963-64 negotiating sessions, even though many subsequently joined the organization. At that time it was assumed that a relatively small forum of Western nations—those supplying the initial capital and technology for the system—would be able to draft an international agreement in an orderly and expeditious fashion without lengthy delays and political disagreements. Convening a large representative body comparable in size to the U.N. General Assembly or an ITU Plenipotentiary Conference would probably have hindered the operational development of the global system.

Intelsat Definitive Arrangements

Comsat and its foreign partners quarreled frequently during the years following the negotiation of the interim arrangements, despite the fact that space and ground segments of the Intelsat system were performing smoothly. Under the direction of Comsat, the consortium was launching a third generation of satellites and the entire system was producing substantial revenues, and yet many of the areas of disagreement that characterized the 1964 discussions began to reappear during the second half of the 1960s. Moreover, the relationship between Comsat and the State Department continued to be less than optimal even though Comsat had been virtually guaranteed freedom of operational management by the federal government.

The Years Before the Definitive Arrangements

During the mid-1960s the United States was confronted with increasing economic challenges from Japan and the Western European nations. Often, these nations had been able to utilize advanced technologies more inexpensively and efficiently than the United States, which had developed and financed them. In order to ensure that the U.S. aerospace industry remained the leader in technology development, the federal government placed controls on the exportation of technology likely to be applied to communication satellites.[88] The controls were enforced by the U.S. Office of Munitions Control, an office of the State Department. Although it delayed nearly ninety-five percent of foreign request for technical information, the Office of Munitions Control ultimately refused only two to three percent of these requests. Nevertheless, the imposition of these trade restrictions created some problems between the United States and its allies across the Atlantic, many of which questioned the national security justifications for the restrictions. In a number of cases European industry chose to develop the relevant electronic and aerospace technologies on its own, rather than waiting for the State Department to release the restricted information.[89]

The European signatories also expressed dissatisfaction over the distribution of hardware contracts. During the development of the third generation of satellites (Intelsat III), Europe received only four percent of the total hardware contracts while providing twenty-five percent of the capital for the system. The position of the European nations was that contracts should be allocated in proportion to the capital outlay from each country,[90] whereas Comsat insisted on adherence to Article X of the Agreement, which stated that contracts were to be awarded to the manufacturer capable of providing the best combination of price, quality and delivery time. In 1967, as a result of this contract situation, a consortium of the European aerospace industries, EUROSPACE, advocated the establishment of a separate European satellite system. This development and other indications of growing support for a regional system had an impact: thirty-seven percent of the initial contracts for the Intelsat IV series were awarded to non-American firms.[91] However, there were long delays in delivery and other problems relating to the European contractors, and thus the share of contracts awarded to non-American industries decreased to ten percent for the remainder of the Intelsat IV development program.[92] The increased costs of hardware manufactured in Europe caused the developing nations to express dissatisfaction and to complain that Intelsat, in effect, was subsidizing European industry. A spokesman for the Arab-Latin American bloc stated: "Ironically, we [the developing nations] are partially paying for all this education and abetment of already industralized nations."[93]

The United States attitude toward regional systems was another source of concern for the Europeans during this period. Policymakers in the United States believed that the existence of separate or regional systems would undermine the global efforts of Intelsat. Additional problems concerning frequency assignments, unwanted noise and the distribution of orbital slots might occur as a result of these smaller systems. For their part, the European nations grew more insistent that provisions be made for regional networks independent from Intelsat. France was already exploring the feasibility of using geostationary satellites for communication with French-speaking parts of the world.[94]

There were two major reasons for launching a regional or domestic satellite system: (1) nations large enough to support such a system wanted to retain control over their domestic communications, and (2) these nations wanted to gain competence in the development of communications and aerospace technologies. Indeed, Eurospace, as stated above, had been advocating the establishment of a regional network in order to improve the overall capabilities of Western European industry.[95] For a time the United States, especially Comsat, remained intransigent on the regional issue. But the fact that the United States had proposed its own domestic system as early as 1965 made it difficult to maintain opposition to a separate European system. The State Department, in fact, reasoned that the development of these systems within Europe was preferable to the growth of another international system, which could operate in direct competition with Intelsat.[96] Therefore, a regional satellite system serving the Western European nations would be justifiable and similar to the establishment of a domestic system within the United States. Comsat countered with the argument that the European nations were too small to launch communication satellites either individually or cooperatively.[97] President Johnson took a somewhat more flexible position on the issue of regional systems in a 1967 policy statement before Congress:

> Intelsat members should adhere to Intelsat supervision in any use of domestic or regional systems. Such supervision shall include coordination of design so that all communication is compatible with the global system.... Technical regulation is also necessary so that positions in orbit can be assigned, frequencies can be allocated and energy from satellites does not interfere with other communications systems.[98]

The president also stated that "adequate provisions must be made so that any international traffic which is diverted will not jeopardize the economic efficiency of the Intelsat system.'[99]

The growing dissatisfaction of the European nations also resulted in sharp criticism of Comsat's dominant position in the consortium. At an international conference in 1967 it was stated that the United States could maintain control "only at excessive political cost."[100] The existing formula for allocating votes according to national use of the Intelsat system was the primary cause of the growing pressure for independent systems. In an attempt to demonstrate the inadequacy of the allocation formula, one U.S. advisor pointed out that if the Soviet Union chose to join the organization, it would be entitled to minimal representation on the ICSC due to the fact that it used only a small fraction of the total number of international message circuits.[101]

Within this milieu of discontent the United States and the Western European countries formulated their positions for the upcoming negotiations on definitive arrangements. The European nations began this process at the European Space Telecommunications Conference in early 1967. Although the initial national views were widely divergent, the participants generally agreed that they would have to challenge the technical and economic dominance of the consortium by the United States. Unofficially, France advocated United Nations management of the global system because it believed that this would prevent the emergence of two competing systems, one controlled by the U.S.S.R. and the other by the United States.[102] The French view was significant because some members of the ICSC advocated the formation of a new international governmental organization to replace the existing Intelsat administration. As stated by the Scandinavian representative serving as the ICSC vice chairman, "We want an organization in which all countries of the world – all users of telecommunications – can take part and in which it will be in their own interest to take part."[103] Nonetheless, the European nations were unable to reach a consensus on communication satellite policy; nations like Spain and Portugal did not have the economic motivation to overcome the "technology gap" as did the more industrialized nations.[104] Despite their various levels of technological development, the European nations did manage to concur on the desirability of removing Comsat as the system manager, restricting its voting power and developing separate, regional systems.

As early as November 1967, at the twenty-ninth meeting of the

ICSC, the United States called upon the committee to begin formulation of definitive arrangements. The Interim Agreement specified that the ICSC was to compile a report by 1 January 1969 which contained proposals for these arrangements. Along with its request the United States submitted a list of proposals and advocated their inclusion in the 1969 report. As a concession to the European partners, the United States proposed the negotiation of a contract in which management activities and authority would be more clearly delineated than they had been in the previous arrangements. It also advised the establishment of a new organ, the Assembly of Members. Composed of all signatories, the major functions of the Assembly would be to consider the annual report of the governing body, to approve changes relating to management, and to advise the governing body on the operation of the satellite system. Decisions were to be made on a simple majority vote basis, provided at least two-thirds of the signatories were present. The United States did not foresee an important role for the Assembly in view of this quorum provision and the fact that it would meet on an annual basis only. The Assembly proposal, in effect, was an attempt to placate nations that felt excluded from decision making during the period of the interim arrangements. In general, however, the proposals of the United States were similar to the provisions of the 1964 arrangements; for example, ownership percentages would be correlated to usage of the system, and the composition of the governing body would reflect this apportionment, with none of its members controlling more than fifty percent of the vote. An affirmative vote by at least two-thirds of those governors present would constitute a majority for substantive decisions.[105]

In 1968 the United States created an internal policy group which consisted of representatives from the State Department, the Federal Communications Commission, Comsat, and the Director of Telecommunications Management. Occasionally, officials from NASA and the Department of Defense also participated. Unlike policy-making for the interim arrangements, there were only two significant areas of disagreement within the group: division of responsibilities for the system manager and the advisability of regional satellite systems. For its part, Comsat wanted to maintain its position as management body and to restrict the proliferation of these regional systems. Eventually, after yielding to pressure from the State Department and the FCC, Comsat agreed to internationalize management functions relating to administrative and financial matters while retaining technical and operational responsibilities. The policy group also favored the implementation of a single, global satellite network but did not rule out regional systems so long as they were "technically and economically compatible with Intelsat."[106] As a result of the group's unification of its satellite policy, Comsat was able to present its position paper to the ICSC before the commencement of negociations for definitive arrangements, thereby influencing the parameters of discussion.

After examining the proposals and recommendations that had been submitted to the committee throughout the year, the ICSC completed a draft report at its thirty-sixth meeting in December 1968.[107] As expected, the ICSC report contained a wide range of national positions regarding definitive arrangements. The fact that not all of its recommendations were unanimous did not surprise many of the signatories, because the primary areas of disagreement had remained controversial since the 1964 negotiations. The recurring problems of organizational structure, voting and ownership percentages, contract award procedures, regional and domestic systems, and the delegation of management authority were again the major topics of debate. Nonetheless, those responsible for the ICSC report agreed on the advisability of (1) replacing Comsat with a management entity accountable to the governing body of Intelsat; (2) giving the consortium a legal personality; (3) negotiating a voting formula that reduced the influence of the United States and the other major users of the system; and (4) drafting two agreements, one between participating nations and the other between their authorized telecommunications agencies.[108]

Definitive Arrangements

In accordance with Article IX of the Interim Agreement,[109] the government of the United States convened the Plenipotentiary Conference to Establish Definitive Arrangements for the International Telecommunications Satellite Consortium in Washington, D.C., on 24 February 1969. A total of sixty-seven Intelsat signatories as well as observers from twenty-nine non-member nations, the International Telecommunications Union, and the United Nations attended the Plenipotentiary Conference. Member and observer delegations discussed the ICSC report and other matters relating to the future of Intelsat in a series of plenary sessions and in four working committees.[110] Predictably, the conflicts revealed in the ICSC report emerged as the primary areas of contention at the 1969 conference. For example, the United States and the developing nations favored a "best price" provision as the basis for letting hardware contracts, whereas Great Britain, France, Germany, Italy and Japan asserted that the contract awards should be in proportion to ownership percentages.[111] Although the delegates were unable to resolve all of the outstanding issues, the 1969 Plenipotentiary Conference was "an important prelude to progress at the later sessions" and also "provided the first forum for a fruitful exchange of views among all Intelsat members so that it was possible to gauge the likelihood for success and to commence a process of mutual education."[112]

The delegates in Washington, D.C., also established a body known as the Preparatory Committee in order to continue the work that had begun at the Plenipotentiary Conference. The major responsibilities of the Preparatory Committee were to review the reports and summary records of the four working committees; to consolidate the numerous proposals that had been submitted to the plenary sessions, thereby reducing them to a manageable level; and to prepare alternative draft agreements for the consideration of the Resumed 1970 Plenipotentiary Conference.[113] In order to achieve these objectives, the committee convened three separate sessions during 1969. At one of these sessions the United States delegation and its supporters presented a synoptic compromise package for the consideration of the full Preparatory Committee.[114] In this document the United States offered to diminish the management powers of Comsat and to reduce the U.S. voting strength on the Board of Governors. The United States and the other sponsors of the document also proposed that the Intelsat organization be vested with a legal and juridical personality. Another compromise proposal included the establishment of a Secretariat under the supervision of the Board of Governors. The Secretariat would perform the financial, public information, legal and procedural functions of Intelsat management.[115]

The United States had hoped that these compromise proposals would be generally acceptable to the Intelsat membership and result in an early resolution of the negotiations. But the Western European signatories and a number of developing nations refused to endorse the American draft proposals. Consequently, a third meeting of the Preparatory Committee was convened in November 1969, at which time Algeria, Canada, India, Japan, Mexico, the United Arab Republic, and the Western European countries presented their alternative draft proposals.[116] An important and controversial recommendation of this group was that the Assembly of Parties be designated the principal administrative organ of Intelsat. This proposal, of course, was in direct contrast to the position of the United States. These nations also sought to establish a Directorate General which would be responsible to the Board of Governors and would carry out duties relating to the development and operation of the satellite system. Approval of this measure by the Plenary Session would have virtually eliminated Comsat as system manager within five years of the date that the final arrangements entered into force. Both the United States government and Comsat opposed this provision and claimed that its adoption would lead to inefficient management of the global system.[117]

Those nations supporting either set of draft proposals comprised only half of the total number of Intelsat signatories, which by that time had reached seventy-five. In order for one group or the other to predominate, it would have to attract additional support from the ranks of the uncommitted signatories. Another possibility for a resolution of the conflict involved the formulation of an effective and mutually acceptable compromise. This was accomplished at the Resumed Plenipotentiary Conference.

Held from 16 February to 20 March 1970, the Resumed Plenipotentiary Conference was attended by sixty-seven signatories and by representatives of eighteen observer nations, the ITU, and the United Nations. The Australian and Japanese delegations, in an attempt to reconcile the opposing delegate blocs, submitted an outline of a compromise package focusing primarily on the management issue.[118] The major elements of the proposal have been summarized by one analyst in the following manner:

> 1. They [Australia and Japan] proposed that the agreements should accept the principle of full internationalization of management responsibilities after a transitional period.
> 2. During the transitional period, there would be a Secretary-General with an independent staff, as well as a contract between the Board of Governors and Comsat for continuing technical and operational management of the Intelsat space segment for a period of six years from entry into force of the Definitive Arrangements.
> 3. At the end of this transitional period, all managerial functions would be placed under a Director-General as the chief executive officer of Intelsat although technical and operational

functions would be contracted out to competent entities to the maximum extent practical.[119]

The delegates from Australia and Japan also proposed that any one signatory's voting strength be limited to forty percent, that investment be in proportion to use of the system, and that the consortium have a four-level organizational structure – namely, an Assembly of Parties, a Meeting of Signatories, a Board of Governors, and a management body.[120]

The response to the compromise document was generally favorable even though it failed to resolve all of the outstanding issues. A member of the United States delegation observed that the suggested compromises were "constructive suggestions and... may offer avenues toward resolution of the issue of management."[121] Due to time considerations, however, the participants of the 1970 conference were not able to formulate treaty draft articles incorporating the principles set forth in the compromise document. As a result, the conferees decided to recess and to transfer the work of preparing the recommended texts of draft agreements to an Intersessional Working Group (IWG).

During the remainder of 1970, the IWG held three extended drafting sessions in order to consider policy questions and to prepare treaty language for the definitive arrangements. One of the more controversial outstanding issues was whether the Assembly of Parties should be authorized to formulate general policy for the guidance of the Board of Governors. The United States asserted that this course of action would lead to disruption, political disagreements and inefficient decision making. As stated by one member of the United States delegation, "Every time a member nation disliked an action of the Governing Board, that nation could claim it was contrary to the guidance principles and demand a meeting of the Assembly."[122] The vote on this matter went against the United States during the spring session of the IWG.

After the bulk of the work had been completed by the IWG, the seventy-eight national delegations at the final Plenipotentiary Conference, held from 14 April to 21 May 1971, were able to finalize the texts of the definitive arrangements. This was accomplished by splitting the plenary session into two committees, one of which was responsible for approving the text of the Intergovernmental Agreement[123] and the other for approving a text of the Operating Agreement.[124] In each committee finalization of draft articles and treaty language amendments required an affirmative vote by at least two-thirds of those present. A similar voting procedure was followed when the two agreements were submitted to the plenary session for consideration and approval. Although the delegates engaged in few debates, a draft article relating to capitalization limits for the consortium did receive attention. The issue was decided when the voting delegates set the upper limit on investment at $ 500 million.[125] The Board of Governors is allowed to increase this amount by as much as ten percent, but further increases must be approved by the Meeting of Signatories. After resolution of this and all other issues, the final drafts of the definitive arrangements were ready to be voted upon by the assembled Intelsat membership. On 21 May 1971 seventy-three national delegations voted in favor of the final draft; no negative votes were cast. France, the Malagasy Republic, Mexico and Monaco chose to abstain.[126]

In contrast to the 1964 agreements, the definitive arrangements marked an important shift from technical and operational considerations to a mixture of these plus political and institutional concerns. In order to meet the demand of smaller user nations for a greater voice in the decision making process, the consortium was restructured into four distinct organs, two of which – the Assembly of Parties and the Meeting of Signatories – offer general membership and decision-making powers on a one-nation-one-vote basis. A simple majority is decisive on procedural questions and an affirmative vote by two-thirds of the participants is required for a decision on substantive matters.[127] A third administrative organ, the Board of Governors, is responsible for the "design, development, construction, establishment, operation, and maintenance of the Intelsat space segment" and for the adoption of plans and programs "in connection with any other activities which Intelsat is authorized to undertake."[128] As such, the Board of Governors is the successor of the ICSC. The board is composed of approximately twenty signatories; the voting strength of each individual member is in proportion to its use of the satellite system. As a concession to the concern over the dominant position of the United States within the consortium, Article IX of the Agreement stipulates that an individual governor cannot "cast more than forty percent of the total voting participation of all Signatories and groups of Signatories represented on the Board of Governors."[129] The same article encourages the board to reach unanimous decisions. When this is not possible, an affirmative vote by at least four governors with two-thirds of the weighted vote or "an affirmative vote cast by at least the total number constituting the Board of Governors minus three" is decisive on substantive questions.[130] Procedural questions are decided by an affirmative vote of a simple majority of those governors present and voting.[131]

Concerning management activities, the fourth organizational level, the program approved at the 1971 conference provides for the eventual replacement of Comsat as system manager. Under this two-stage program, which began with the entry into force of the definitive arrangements, an executive organ was established in order to acquire management functions and responsibilities over a six-year period. This organ will be headed by a Secretary General until 31 December 1976, by which time a Director General must be appointed by the Board of Governors and confirmed by the Assembly of Parties.[132] During the first stage Comsat performs administrative and financial services for Intelsat until the Board of Governors determines that the Secretary General is prepared to assume these duties. At the same time, Comsat is accountable directly to the Board of Governors for the performance of technical and operational management services until 31 December 1976. After that date and until the expiration of its six-year contract, Comsat provides these services under the supervision of the Director General, rather than the Board of Governors. The executive organ is to acquire a permanent structure no later than six years after entry into force of the definitive arrangements.[133]

The Intelsat Global Communications System

The years of multilateral negotiations climaxed on 20 August 1971 when the definitive arrangements were finally offered for signature. Entering into force on 12 February 1973, the definitive arrangements inaugurated a new administrative era for Intelsat, now known officially as the International Telecommunications Satellite Organization.[134] Although the various negotiations were often frustrating, the seven-year history of Intelsat – from the 1964 discussions in Rome to the final 1971 Plenipotentiary Conference – was not always characterized by disagreements among the U.S. State Department's Munitions Control Board, foreign aerospace contractors, Comsat Corporation and the European Conference on Satellite Communications. With the operational imperative supplying the major impetus, the organization gradually accomplished the purpose for which it had been created – namely, establishment of a global commercial communication satellite system. During the ten-year period that began with the interim arrangements, the Intelsat system grew from the single transatlantic link, Early Bird, to the global network of high capacity Intelsat IV satellites positioned over the Atlantic, Pacific and Indian Oceans. The 240 voice circuit capacity of the Early Bird spacecraft is miniscule in comparison to the channel capacity of the Intelsat IV satellites, which range from 3,000 to 9,000 circuits depending upon the technical configuration. Nevertheless, even Early Bird's 240 voice channels were competitive with AT&T's high-performance TAT-4 cable which had been equipped with 408 telephone channels. The TAT-4 was the most advanced transoceanic cable operating at the time of the Early Bird launch.[135]

Since the commencement of full-scale commercial operations on 1 May 1967, the Intelsat system has continued to improve general signal quality, to introduce new telecommunication services and to increase the number of message pathways. As of May 1975, Intelsat was providing 325 regular communications pathways among nations scattered across three oceans and five continents.[136] The expansion to global coverage has been accompanied by the growth in the total volume of message traffic relayed via satellite. Through 1967 satellite users leased the equivalent of 1,049 half-circuits on a full-time basis. By 1972 this figure had reached 7,527, of which 4,760 were utilized for message transmission across the Atlantic Ocean.[137] And by 1975 telecommunication users had leased over 10,000 half-circuits for full-time voice and record service. [138] Although telephone signals constitute the major portion of satellite message traffic, the Intelsat system also handles data, telex, teletype, facsimile and television relay transmissions.

The global satellite network realized its first net operating profit during the last quarter of 1967. The profit figures and the total amount of revenues continued to rise through 1973, during which time the net worth of the organization surpassed $ 235 million.[139] At an April 1974 meeting in Acapulco, Mexico, a report was issued to the signatories in attendance which stated that Intelsat had "achieved a rate of return for the use of capital" during the period from 12 February to 31 December 1973 which "resulted in the distribution of approximately $ 37,500,000 to the signatories."[140] The annual growth rates for satellite traffic in the Atlantic, Pacific and Indian Ocean regions are expected to remain above fifteen percent throughout the second half of the 1970s, and thus the financial success of Intelsat should continue well beyond 1980.

The remarkable technical, operational and financial success of the global system has prompted many developing nations to join Intelsat. The interim arrangements of 1964 were initialled by only fourteen different countries and telecommunications entities; within eleven years the total number of signatories had reached eighty-nine. By 1975 sixty-four signatories were operating a total of 111 antennas at eighty-eight separate ground locations.[141]

As of 1974, Intelsat had launched four series of increasingly powerful satellites in order to meet the growing demand for telecommunication services. The organization introduced transatlantic satellite service in June 1965 with the Early Bird (Intelsat I) spacecraft, launched in April of that year as the first operational communication satellite. The first of the Intelsat II satellites was launched on 26 October 1966; however, the apogee motor malfunctioned and the synchronous orbit was not attained. During 1967 three Intelsat II satellites were successfully placed in geostationary orbit, one over the Atlantic and two over the Pacific. The spacecraft launched on 11 January 1967 provided the first full-time satellite service over the Pacific Ocean.[142] Although Intelsat II satellites had a channel capacity equal to that of Early Bird (240 circuits or one television channel), they were capable of multipoint operation and far greater geographic coverage.[143]

The goal of a global communication satellite system became a reality during the summer of 1969 when a Intelsat III satellite was positioned over the Indian Ocean after a short period of commercial service in the Pacific region. Until the completion of this maneuver the Indian Ocean area had been without commercial satellite coverage. From 1968 to 1970 five Intelsat III spacecraft were launched into synchronous orbit and used on a regular commercial basis. All of these satellites had a capacity of 1,200 voice quality circuits and a design lifetime of five years; the average orbital weight of each spacecraft was 332 pounds.[144]

The transmission of television programming around the world has been one of the most dramatic applications of satellite technology. The volume of global television traffic soared during the period of Intelsat III service: half-channel hours for television transmission and reception increased from 1,372 in 1968 to 6,792 in 1972. The Intelsat system has provided live worldwide coverage of the winter and summer Olympics, the first Apollo lunar landing mission, the U.S. president's visits to China and the Soviet Union, and many other events of international interest.[145]

The combined channel capacity of the global system was increased substantially by the successful launch of seven Intelsat IV satellites between January 1971 and May 1975. Launched aboard Atlas Centaur boosters, three of these high-capacity satellites have been placed above the Atlantic Ocean to handle the especially heavy communications traffic between Europe and North America. With two spacecraft operating over the Pacific Ocean and another two over the Indian Ocean, the organization has achieved global coverage with its fourth series of satellites.[146] Nonetheless, traffic carried via the Intelsat IV network is expected to approach the saturation point in the transatlantic corridor during 1975. Consequently, Intelsat is preparing a new generation of satellites to meet traffic requirements in the latter half of the 1970's. The first spacecraft of this series, Intelsat IV-A, was successfully launched from Cape Canaveral on 25 September 1975. Each of the six Intelsat IV-A's will be equipped with twenty transponders and will have almost double the channel capacity of the Intelsat IV satellites. Finally, Intelsat has announced procurement plans for yet another series of satellites, Intelsat V. Spacecraft of this series are to be equipped with the equivalent of 25,000 channels. Approximately one-third of this capacity will be reserved for transmissions in the eleven to fourteen GHz frequency bands. It is expected that the first Intelsat V satellite will be launched either in 1979 or in early 1980.[147]

The implementation of satellite technology for routine, point-to-point international transmissions proceeded rapidly despite the numerous political disagreements among the nations that negotiated the organizational arrangements. The Intelsat system extended communication possibilities to the developing areas of the world, which otherwise would have had to have waited years for land line or undersea cable links. In the final analysis, the justification of U.S. international satellite policy has been the financial and operational success of the Intelsat system itself. Regarding satellite usage for domestic communications within the United States, commercialization has come more slowly because an extensive terrestrial telecommunications network was already in place when satellite technology emerged. A complex institutional controversy also prolonged the policymaking process. In fact, this country did not introduce domestic satellite systems and services until after the Federal Communications Commission announced its multiple-entry policy decision in the summer of 1972. The operational imperative that fostered the establishment and growth of Intelsat simply did not exist domestically in the United States. Where it did exist, in large countries with available resources, such as the Soviet Union and Canada, domestic systems were implemented relatively early in the history of satellite communications.

7

THE EMERGENCE OF THE DOMSATS: THE SECOND STAGE OF THE U.S. COMMUNICATION SATELLITE TECHNOLOGY TRANSFER

The passage of the Communications Satellite Act of 1962 and the subsequent promulgation of international arrangements for operating a commercial system concluded a major phase in the history of satellite communications. The intent of the 1962 act was to promote the development of a global satellite system; Congress created the Communications Satellite Corporation and gave it exclusive rights to operate the U.S. segment of the system. However, the act did not define the place of Comsat or any other entity in the establishment and operation of domestic satellite (domsat) systems; it simply acknowledged that such systems were a possibility:

> It is not the intent of Congress by this Act to preclude the use of communications satellite systems for domestic communications services where consistent with the provisions of this Act nor to preclude the creation of additional communications satellite systems, if required to meet unique governmental needs or if otherwise required by the national interest.[1]

When a market for domsats developed sooner than anticipated, the loose wording of the Comsat Act gave rise to new policy questions which were not resolved until the early 1970s.

The fact that the Comsat legislation did not deal more specifically with the question of domestic satellites is understandable, because in 1962 the commercial value of satellites was seen almost entirely in their potential for global communications. The act was drafted on the assumption that at least for the near future, operational systems would employ low or medium altitude spacecraft modeled after Bell Laboratory's Telstar satellite. Since nearly fifty satellites of this design would have been required for an operational global system, it was believed that an international consortium was the most economical way to absorb the high costs of such a system.[2] Moreover, the medium altitude satellite was not considered suitable for domestic use because, when launched into orbit, it would be in line of sight with ground terminals located within the territorial landmass for only a small fraction of its orbital period.

The key to opening the domestic market was the development of the geostationary satellite. As late as 1962, scientists at Bell Laboratories insisted that geostationary capability was still ten years away.[3] The cancellation of the Department of Defense's synchronous Advent satellite program after an expenditure of $ 170 million lent strong support to Bell's prediction. The situation changed in February 1963 when NASA began to launch the Syncom series of satellites. The success of Syncom II, III, and the Early Bird spacecraft demonstrated the technical feasibility of geostationary satellites.[4] Comsat quickly adopted the new technology and chose to utilize geostationary satellites for the global system. But even more important, the achievement of geostationary capability and the concomitant decrease in space segment capital costs enormously expanded the range of applications on the domestic front. A myriad of legal and organizational problems, however, delayed the introduction of commercial domestic services within the United States until the launch of Western Union's Westar I in April 1974. For almost eight years a variety of government agencies and a dozen major American corporations struggled over the complex question of domestic satellite ownership. The entire structure of the new industry remained uncertain until 1972 when the Federal Communications Commission issued its multiple-entry decision enabling any qualified entity, subject to certain conditions, to own and operate a domestic satellite system.[5]

The Participants

The long domsat controversy began on 21 September 1965 when the American Broadcasting Company (ABC) applied to the Federal Communications Commission for authority to launch and operate a synchronous satellite for transmission of its domestic television programming from New York and Los Angeles to 268 network affiliates throughout the continental United States, Alaska, Hawaii, Puerto Rico, and the Virgin Islands. Each of the affiliates would have been equipped with a special ground receiving terminal. ABC also planned to provide satellite facilities without charge to the National Educational Television network for the distribution of noncommercial programming to educational stations in those areas. It was estimated by ABC that intercity satellite relay would result in annual cost savings of approximately five million dollars over a five-year period. At that time ABC was paying AT&T nearly twelve million dollars annually for long-distance, television distribution services.[6] The application was formulated in conjunction with Hughes Aircraft Company, which not only provided technical assistance for the proposal but also planned to construct the satellite and to experiment on its own in special program networking. Approval of the application by the FCC would have given Hughes Aircraft another customer for its satellites, since at that time Comsat and NASA were the only satellite operators.

Even though the FCC eventually rejected the application, it was the ABC proposal that precipitated the FCC inquiry into alternative domsat institutional arrangements. Thus on 2 March 1966 the commission issued a *Notice of Inquiry* inviting any interested party to respond to the ABC proposal in writing and to submit general comments relating to the operation of domestic communication satellites and to the authority of the FCC to regulate and license such activities.[7] Specifically, the FCC solicited comments as to whether it "may promulgate policies and regulations, looking toward the authorization of nongovernmental entities to construct and operate communications satellite facilities for the purpose of meeting their private or specialized domestic communications requirements."[8] In all, nineteen parties responded to the FCC invitation on or before the deadline of 1 August 1966.[9] The submissions of the Ford Foundation, Comsat, and AT&T were the most significant. Each of these organizations also submitted a detailed proposal for a satellite system before the end of that year.

In its comments the Ford Foundation argued that the FCC did have the power under existing legislation to authorize entities other than common carriers to launch and operate domestic satellite systems.[10] Moreover, the Ford Foundation proposed the establishment of a Broadcasters Non-Profit Satellite Corporation (BNSC). Organized as either a private cooperative or a common carrier, the BNSC would have owned and operated a synchronous satellite system for the distribution of commercial and educational television programs across the United States. The revenues from relaying the commercial programs to local affiliates would have been used to subsidize the nation's educational television networks. This arrangement would have attracted the three major commercial networks by offering them improved and expanded transmission services at tariff rates slightly lower than those charged by AT&T at that time for land-line distribution. The relatively low operating costs of the nonprofit satellite corporation, according to the Ford Foundation, would have resulted in savings of more than thirty million dollars annually. A major portion of these savings would have been used as a "social dividend" to subsidize the development of noncommercial educational television stations around the country and to finance the creation of instructional programming for schools and colleges. This subsidy, in effect, would have been composed of the unrecovered expenditures of the federal government in developing the technology and the monopoly profits exacted from the commercial networks for transmitting their programming.[11] With FCC approval the nonprofit corporation could have begun operation by the late 1960s with satellites stationed over each of the four continental United States time zones.[12] According to McGeorge Bundy, then president of the Ford Foundation, the people of America were to be the direct beneficiaries of this innovative proposal, at last receiving a valuable social return on the millions of dollars in public funds long invested in the space program.[13]

Empowered by its enabling legislation to develop an international system, Comsat was also interested in finding a variety of domestic applications for communication satellites. The market potential for domestic services was unquestionable since the United States alone owned approximately fifty percent of the world's telephones and forty percent of all television receivers. Furthermore, Comsat found itself at that time in the enviable position of being overcapitalized for its original mission of developing a global communication system. The $ 196 million stock offering of 1964 represented the estimated cost of establishing a satellite system based on the medium-altitude satellite then available.[14] The development of the synchronous satellite drastically reduced these costs and left Comsat with a surplus of funds available for domestic investment. Since it had a legislative mandate in the communication satellite field and the only practical experience in the operation of a commercial system (Intelsat), Comsat claimed exclusive right to the domestic market in its legal brief before the FCC. Comsat, in fact, argued that the 1962 legislation gave it a monpoly over both international and domestic satellite communications, and that the FCC was without authority to license any other entity in the ownership and operation of a domestic system.[15]

During December 1966 Comsat again asserted that the FCC did not have the power under existing legislation to authorize a noncarrier entity, such as Ford's BNSC, to launch a domestic system.[16] Comsat filed these comments with the FCC in response to a *Supplemental Notice of Inquiry,* which the commission had issued during October in order to expand the scope of its inquiry.[17] Along with its remarks on the Ford plan, Comsat submitted its own proposal for a comprehensive, multipurpose satellite system that would have commenced operation in 1969 with a single satellite, a large transmitting facility on both the Atlantic and Pacific coasts, and nearly sixty smaller receive antennas scattered across the country. The capacity of the system and the range of applications would have been augmented in three successive phases over a nine-year period. By 1978 the system would have included four high-capacity satellites capable of operating in the frequency bands above ten GHz and over two hundred ground terminals. As envisioned by Comsat, the system would have transmitted television, telephone, data, and other types of message signals[18] – unlike the systems that had been proposed by ABC and the Ford Foundation, both of which were essentially for domestic television distribution.

During the middle 1960s AT&T operated approximately eighty-five percent of the long lines and interconnections for television distribution and direct distance dialing telephone services within the United States.[19] Access to satellite facilities provided organizations such as ABC and the other network broadcasters with an opportunity to distribute their programming in a cost-effective manner without relying upon AT&T's terrestrial network. Thus the advent of the geostationary satellite constituted a special challenge to AT&T and its virtual monopoly of domestic telecommunications. Accordingly, AT&T's strategy in its 1966 comments before the FCC, as it was throughout the entire domsat controversy, was to protect its substantial investment in terrestrial technology and at the same time to develop its own share of the new domsat market. In its reply comments on the ABC application during August 1966, AT&T questioned the economic and technical feasibility of authorizing non-carriers to own and operate satellite systems. AT&T's preferred institutional arrangement was a multipurpose system operated by a single common carrier. This also was essentially the position of Comsat, the Hawaiian Telephone Company, ITT World Communications, and the Western Union Telegraph Company.[20]

Responding to the FCC *Supplemental Notice of Inquiry,* AT&T asserted that Ford's BNSC, despite its proposed nonprofit status, would actually operate as a communications common carrier and, therefore, would be within the purview of the Communications Act of 1934. As a consequence, Sections 201 and 202 of that act would preclude the BNSC from offering free service to the educational broadcasters. Approval of a discriminatory rate structure, AT&T stated, would require additional legislation, not simply an FCC policy decision.[21] Moreover, AT&T objected to the idea of using the overall cost savings attributable to advancing communications technology in order to finance one particular application, television program distribution. Rather, according to AT&T, "the most equitable and readily available method of making an even-handed dispersion of any such savings is through the rates charged the general public for common carrier services."[22] Furthermore, in its view, the development of a number of low-capacity special purpose systems would lead to orbital overcrowding and inefficient usage of the radio frequency spectrum.[23]

In addition to comments on the Ford plan, AT&T submitted a proposal for a comprehensive, multipurpose satellite system that would have been thoroughly integrated into its existing cable and microwave networks. AT&T contemplated introducing domsat services in 1969 with two synchronous spacecraft, each operating in the four to six GHz region of the spectrum and with a capacity of twelve television channels or 9,600 voice-grade circuits. For its initial phase of operation, AT&T planned to construct seventy-three receive-only terminals and two large transmit/receive terminals, one near New York City and the other near Los Angeles. The second phase of the domestic system would have begun in 1972 and continued through the second half in the 1970s. During this period AT&T would have built twenty-six additional ground stations and launched four high-capacity spacecraft. The cost of the entire system was estimated at $ 450 million. AT&T also anticipated that its proposed system would meet domestic communication requirements through 1980.[24]

The space segment for the AT&T system would have been owned and managed by Comsat. AT&T had first proposed such an arrangement in a letter, dated 23 March 1966, from L.F. Wingert to James McCormack, Comsat's chairman of the board.[25] AT&T's preference in this matter was not surprising because at that time it owned twenty-nine percent of Comsat's outstanding stock. Moreover, AT&T expected to retain control of the ground facilities, which represented nearly fifty-five percent of the capital costs for the system and possibly a similar percentage of the profits. The ground segment ownership pattern, in fact, was the major difference between AT&T's proposed system and that of Comsat.

The validity of Comsat's claim to a monopoly of the domestic market was still highly uncertain during this period.[26] This was partially the result of its satellite proposal of December 1966 which had not specified the relationship between the domestic system and Comsat's role as manager of the Intelsat consortium. Thus it was unclear whether Comsat intended to operate the domestic system entirely independent of the global network or to incorporate it into the Intelsat framework. Either course presupposed that Comsat possessed sufficient resources to develop both systems and that such a course of action would not involve Comsat in a conflict of interest.[27] Furthermore, it is arguable that if Comsat were given a monopoly of all satellite activities, then revenues from the domestic system would have had to have been shared with Comsat's partners in the global consortium. Even worse, as it was argued by some parties, the Intelsat membership also might have been entitled to a voice in the domestic telecommunications policy of the United States. This, of course, was forbidden under the Communications Act of 1934. One method for averting such a prospect would have been to exclude Comsat from the domestic market altogether.

The majority of the participants were in agreement regarding the potential of satellite technology to contribute to the overall efficiency and capacity of the nation's telecommunications systems; they disagreed as to the type and number of systems which would best realize the service potential of the technology. By early 1967 two parties had urged the FCC to authorize a pilot or demonstration program in order to acquire practical experience upon which to base a definitive policy decision. One of them, the Ford Foudation, advised that a satellite demonstration program be carried out by NASA in cooperation with other federal agencies and with interested parties from the private sector. In the view of the Ford Foundation, the space agency was the logical candidate for such a coordinating role because it was essentially a disinterested party and did not have a stake in the development of the market for domsat services. The foundation recommended that spacecraft of the Applications Technology Satellite series, with which NASA at that time had begun experimentation, be utilized for interference testing and for interim transmission of both commercial and educational television programming.[28]

Comsat also attempted to reconcile the various opinions about domsat institutional arrangements, and on 31 March 1967 it proposed an ambitious fifty-seven million dollar pilot program featuring two high-capacity satellites, each capable of transmitting message signals to any point on the North American continent. Like Comsat's system proposal of the previous year, the pilot program was to have been multipurpose in scope: Comsat planned to experiment with voice, record, and television transmission as well as to assess the economic advantages of relaying these types of communications via satellite as opposed to conventional, terrestrial distribution methods. Comsat also stated that it would investigate the feasibility of using satellite technology to interconnect the nation's educational radio and television stations. According to the program's technical configuration, large earth terminals with eighty-five to one-hundred-foot antennas would have been constructed near New York City and Los Angeles for the transmission of television signals and general telecommunications to the Western mountain and Pacific coast regions. Thirty small, receive-only stations also would have been installed at locations in the western time zones in order to demonstrate the unique distribution capabilities of satellites. Comsat intended to supply the necessary capital itself and operate the pilot system under government supervision. Joint ownership of the ground segment and access to channel capacity would have been open to any authorized common carrier. Finally, the plan incorporated the major point of the Ford Foundation proposals by making color television circuits available to noncommercial broadcasters without charge.[29] The implementation of this program could have divided the domestic communications market between Comsat and AT&T, with Comsat supplying satellite services, at least on an interim basis, and AT&T continuing to provide terrestrial facilities and services.[30]

In order to assure careful consideration of the relevant policy issues, the FCC invited all interested parties to respond to the Comsat recommendation on or before 18 September 1967.[31] Of the twelve respondents to the commission's request, the Hawaiian Telephone Company, General Telephone and Electronics, and AT&T came out most strongly in favor of the pilot program. For its part, AT&T advocated common carrier ownership of the necessary ground stations. This was essentially the position that AT&T had assumed during the earlier controversy involving the ownership of the Intelsat stations located within the United States.[32] Other organizations, including the Columbia Broacasting System (CBS), National Broadcasting Company (NBC), and Western Union, gave qualified support to the idea of a pilot program but warned against the possibility of Comsat obtaining an undue advantage in the struggle to develop the domestic market for satellite services. On the other hand, ABC and, not suprisingly, the Ford Foundation opposed the Comsat plan and suggested instead that a government agency like NASA conduct the demonstration. Furthermore, the Ford Foudation argued that the pilot system as envisioned by Comsat would not provide adequate interconnection services for the nation's educational television stations.[33]

The most attractive feature of Comsat's pilot recommendation and also of its system proposal of the previous year was that they both emphasized domestic telecommunications in general and not simply the provision of noncommercial broadcast services. Indeed, these proposals placed the company in a competitive position in relation to other potential applicants despite the fact that the FCC at that time had not determined whether Comsat was legally qualified to operate a domestic system in view of its commitment to Intelsat. Within a year, however, Comsat's pilot program would receive the recommendation of the President's Task Force on Communications Policy. During this same period of time a number of other major companies had begun to evaluate their own resources, to draft blueprints for satellite systems, and to explore the possibilities for alliance with other interested parties.

The FCC's Domsat Decision

The responsibility for regulation of electronic communications within the United States has always been divided among Congress, the Federal Communications Commission, the White House, and the marketplace. In general this pluralistic approach has resulted in a balanced regulatory program. In the case of communication satellites, however, the unique nature of the technology and the continuing process of technology transfer from the government to the private sector as well as the controversy within the private sector itself over control of the market all threatened to delay the launch of an operational domestic system for an indefinite period of time.

The Rostow Report

Shortly after Comsat had submitted its pilot proposal, it was decided that a comprehensive examination of the entire communications industry was needed as a basis for a definitive FCC decision on the domestic system ownership question. With this in mind President Lyndon B. Johnson, appearing before a joint session of Congress on 17 August 1967, announced the creation of a special communications task force headed by Eugene V. Rostow and stipulated that any domestic satellite network established within the United States would have to be compatible with the U.S. commitment to the global Intelsat system.[34]

In his policy statement the president ordered the new task force to examine the economic and service advantages of alternative institutional arrangements for domsat ownership. Ultimately, it was the responsibility of the FCC to announce a definitive decision regarding the organization of the domestic satellite industry. One possibility would have been to confine Comsat to the international satellite arena and to grant a monopoly of both ground and space facilities to AT&T or to any other terrestrial carrier. Another prospect would have been to award control of the space segment to Comsat or to a corporate entity created specifically by Congress for this purpose. In either case the satellite operator would have been authorized to sell its services to only established common carriers. The FCC also might have chosen open entry as its policy; the market place would have then determined the manner and the rate at which satellite technology was made available to the public, with one option being the creation of a number of competing specialized systems. Finally, the commission could have adopted a variant of the Ford Foundation proposal and retained the space segment for public ownership. In any event the government's objective was to ensure the efficient, economical , and orderly development of a national satellite system.

The task force studied the situation for a year and published its findings on 7 December 1968. The Rostow Report, as it is commonly called, concluded that initial cost estimates did not indicate that substantial savings would result "in the very near term from the substitution of satellite facilities for the terrestrial equivalent. . . ."[35] A mutually advantageous blending of the new technology into the old was perceived as the most prudent course. The members of the task force also doubted that a domsat would be able to generate sufficient funds to subsidize noncommercial programming on the scale envisioned by the Ford Foundation.[36] While Rostow and his associates acknowledged that much of the relevant data was still incomplete, they did endorse the multipurpose concept in the belief that a system capable of many applications would not be more expensive than one reserved exclusively for television distribution. Because operational satellite experience was needed before a domestic system could be fixed into a particular institutional pattern, the task force proposed a "modest operational pilot domestic program, with Comsat playing the leading role."[37] As trustee of the space segment, Comsat was advised to employ advanced hardware, including sophisticated electronic systems, high-gain directional antennas, and large solar panel arrays. It was also directed to experiment with television distribution and to implement a pricing system that reflected the decreased costs of providing this service with satellites. Furthermore, free circuits for educational television were to be offered on a temporary basis at least until more complete cost data became available.[38]

Since it was likely that a pilot program would exert a "shaping influence on the future regulatory pattern" for the domsat industry, the task force recommended that satellite carriers be prevented from obtaining a preemptive position in the struggle for control of the market. Specifically, the Rostow Report stated that the choice of Comsat as trustee of the program did "not reflect a judgement that it is entitled to such ownership as a matter of 'right' under the 1962 Communications Satellite Act."[39] Instead, the task force proposed the division of ground terminal ownership among Comsat, the common carriers, and users in order to ensure the orderly development of the pilot system.[40]

Relying on Comsat's pilot proposal of 1967, the demonstration program outlined in the Rostow Report was an ambitious attempt to reconcile a number of differing points of view. It is significant, however, that the pilot program was never undertaken even though it was one of the Rostow Report's major recommendations.

An Interim Domestic Communications Policy

January of 1969 brought a new president to the White House, and the Federal Communications Commission was still wrestling with the domestic satellite problem, as it had for the past four years. In an attempt to resolve the controversy, the White House announced that it would soon issue a major policy recommendation to the FCC. The Nixon Administration intended to formulate guidelines which defined the public interest because, in its view, the commission had been unable to find a workable solution. Administration aides asserted that the FCC had depended too heavily on adversary hearings between the competing industrial parties and then had attempted unwieldy compromises of the divergent positions without ever giving the public interest due consideration. The Administration also observed that such basic questions as space segment and ground terminal ownership had yet to be resolved.[41]

On 23 January 1970 the Nixon Administration urged the FCC to adopt an interim domsat policy allowing any entity with the requisite financial and technical resources to launch and operate a satellite system. The policy recommendation, which was submitted to FCC Chairman Dean Burch in the form of a memorandum, also stated that it would be ill-advised for the commission to attempt to limit the "number or classes of potential offerers of satellite services" or to establish an outright monopoly with a single entity chosen as the instrument of domsat communications policy.[42] Rather, it was believed that open entry and competition promised the greatest benefits to the economy and to the general public:

> Subject to appropriate conditions to preclude harmful interference and anticompetitive practices, any financially qualified public or private entity, including Government corporations, should be permitted to establish and operate domestic satellite facilities for its own needs; join with related entities in common-user, cooperative facilities; establish facilities for lease to prospective users; or establish facilities to be used in providing specialized carrier services on a competitive basis.[43]

Furthermore, the Administration wanted a flexible regulatory policy that would permit competitive pressures, and not arbitrary constraints, to determine the tariff rates for specialized satellite services. Even under conditions of unrestricted entry, orbital slot overcrowding was not expected to be a problem because financial and managerial considerations would tend to limit the number of domsats actually launched. At a White House news conference on the day that the policy statement was released, Administration advisor Clay T. Whitehead surmised that it would be possible to accommodate from fifteen to twenty satellites within the available orbital arc for geosynchronous spacecraft.[44]

The immediate response of private industry to the White House "open skies" recommendations was generally favorable. The commercial networks expressed unqualified support in the belief that open entry would enable the private sector to proceed with the development of specialized television distribution systems. Comsat, anxious to implement its own proposal, announced that it would apply for authority to launch a system and that, subject to FCC approval, it would offer a full range of communication services.[45]

The only major recommendation of the Rostow Report that eventually was implemented turned out to be the one concerning the establishment within the executive branch of a permanent office for the development and coordination of national communication policy. During early 1970 President Nixon asked Clay T. Whitehead to reorganize the Office of Telecommunications Management, previously a part of the Office of Emergency Planning. On 20 April 1970 the Office of Telecommunications Policy (OTP) was established under Whitehead's direction.[46] As defined by an executive order, the primary responsibility of OTP was to formulate "the executive branch policies and programs pertaining to communication matters and seek to implement them through various means, including proposals of legislation."[47] OTP did not intend to transgress upon the independent regulatory functions assigned to the FCC by the Communications Act of 1934; rather, it would present the point of view of the White House on issues relating to telecommunications policy. Throughout the domsat controversy OTP, speaking for the Nixon Administration, argued for an "open skies" policy and favored the establishment of multiple, competing systems over a single, comprehensive satellite network. The fact that the commission eventually announced a decision authorizing any qualified entity to operate a satellite system was partially a result of OTP influence. Although critics charged that OTP had encroached upon the legal authority of the FCC throughout the domsat affair, the eventual FCC decision was in fact definitive and set the stage for a series of industry responses.[48]

New Private Industry Proposals

On 24 March 1970, concurrent with Administration decisions leading to the creation of OTP, the four-year-old domsat dispute entered a new phase when the FCC invited all interested parties to apply for permission to construct and operate a communication satellite system. In its, *Report and Order* released on that date, the FCC stated that it was not prepared to authorize either a pilot program or any other specific proposal and that, furthermore, it had been unable to determine whether specialized systems, multipurpose systems, or an "open skies" policy would most fully realize the domestic potential of communication satellites.[49] Instead of attempting to prescribe an overall institutional arrangement for the domsat industry, the FCC requested interest parties to draft concrete proposals and to submit them to the commission for consideration:

> Thus, we [FCC] will consider applications by all legally, technically and financially qualified entities proposing the establishment and operation of domestic communications satellite systems designed to provide the capability for multiple or specialized communications services. Applicants may propose the rendition of such services directly to the public on a common carrier basis or by the lease of facilities to other common carriers, or any combination of such arrangements. Applicants may also propose private ownership and use or the joint cooperative use of the system by the several owners thereof. Applicants may further propose the shared use of some facilities by different systems, or a division in the ownership of various system components (e.g., user ownership of earth stations to afford direct access to the space segment of a common carrier or cooperative system).[50]

Authorization by the commission of each application would proceed in a manner consistent with the provisions of the Communications Act of 1934 and other pertinent statutes as well as with the interests of the general public.[51] Finally, in a memorandum attached to the *Report and Order,* the FCC concluded that it did possess the legal power under both the 1934 act and the Communications Satellite Act of 1962 to authorize "any entity, either common carrier — including Comsat — or non-carrier" to own and operate a domestic satellite system.[52]

In response to the FCC request eight companies drafted domsat proposals and submitted them to the commission by the deadline of 15 March 1971. One of these companies, Hughes Aircraft, applied for permission to launch two twelve-transponder satellites and to construct two large ground transmission stations and seven receive-only terminals. The proposal was formulated in association with General Telephone and Electronics Corporation. GTE expected to use the Hughes space segment to interconnect its areas of local telephone service in Pennsylvania, Florida, Indiana, and California. At each of these locations GTE planned to construct and operate large transmit/receive terminals. According to the terms of their arrangements, Hughes would lease eight noninterruptable transponders to GTE while reserving the remaining capacity for the transmission of cable television programming.[53]

Another of the applicants, Western Tele-Communications, proposed to launch two satellites, each equipped with twelve transponders, for the purpose of extending its common carrier operations to all fifty states. Anticipated areas of service included data, computer, CATV, and broadcast television transmissions. The company chose North American Rockwell as the contractor for the spacecraft.[54] The MCI Lockheed Satellite Corporation, formed by Lockheed Aircraft and MCI Communications, also filed an application for a multipurpose satellite system. Fifteen earth stations operating in the twelve to thirteen GHz bands and five in the four to six GHz bands were to have provided services to the forty-eight contiguous states. The categories of domestic service included network television and CATV program distribution, electronic mail delivery, carrier trunk service, and private line voice and record services. Lockheed was named the contractor for the system's three forty-eight transponder satellites.[55]

Fairchild Industries also intended to use the higher bands of the radio spectrum for its proposed multipurpose satellite system. With FCC approval of its application, Fairchild would have launched two 120-transponder satellites and erected six large earth stations, two smaller transmit/receive stations, and over 100 receive-only terminals. These large 120-transponder satellites were to have been modifications of the ATS-6 design. Fairchild hoped to utilize the majority of the satellite transponders for the transmission of AT&T's public telephone message traffic. At that time Fairchild had been attempting to persuade AT&T to lease point-to-point channels aboard the 120-transponder spacecraft rather than purchasing them from Comsat.[56]

The Western Union Telegraph Company applied for authority to install and operate a multipurpose system featuring three twelve-transponder geostationary satellites, seven transmit/receive earth stations, and six receive-only terminals. According to the Western Union application, a portion of the company's total volume of record traffic, which had been relayed through terrestrial networks, would be rerouted and transmitted via the satellite system. Western Union also planned to introduce message service to Alaska and Hawaii and to distribute television programming to all of the fifty states.[57] Another private sector organization filing a domsat application was RCA under its Global Communications (Globcom) and Alaska Communications (Alascom) subsidiaries. RCA proposed to launch three satellites and to construct a system of thirteen ground stations for the initial period of commercial operation. The ground segment would be expanded by an additional twenty-three transmit/receive stations and 370 receive-only stations as the demand for telecommunication services increased. RCA also stated that it would provide a wide range of services to users in the continental United States and Hawaii. The focus of the RCA proposal, however, was on the development of Alaska's internal communications networks, which the company had purchased from the U.S. Air Force in 1969. In order to improve communications in Alaska, RCA stated that it was prepared to offer leased line and public toll telephone message services to both civilian and military users. RCA also planned to distribute television and radio programs to remote Alaskan communities.[58]

As indicated in its 1966 proposal, AT&T preferred to lease a space segment from another carrier, Comsat, and let it assume the financial risks of satellite launch and operation. In 1970 the two companies again entered into negotiation for the purpose of developing a joint domestic system. According to the March 1971 application, Comsat would procure, launch, and operate three geosynchronous spacecraft for AT&T as well as provide tracking and control services. Comsat would receive $ 262 million over a seven-year period for these services. The entire capacity of the space segment would be leased to AT&T, which in turn intended to provide public and private-line telephone, Picture phone®, digital data, and television services, as well as to wholesale channels to other carriers. AT&T planned to construct and operate major ground stations at five locations.[59]

Finally, Comsat filed an application with the FCC for a multipurpose system, designed to serve all users and carriers except AT&T. The company intended to launch three twenty-four transponder satellites, manufactured by Hughes Aircraft and of the same design as those specified in the lease arrangement with AT&T. The initial ground segment would consist of four transmit/receive stations and a receive-only installation located near Talkeetna, Alaska. Comsat planned to distribute network television and CATV programming, to offer public broadcasting and other educational services, and to improve overall message service to and within Alaska.[60]

Each domsat applicant had also been encouraged by the 1970 *Report and Order* to suggest appropriate regulations and guidelines for the new industry. In particular, the commission solicited comments regarding the initial role of AT&T, user access and hardware procurement policies, and the desirability of instituting procedures for the resolution of technical or economic conflicts between applications.[61] However, the participation of AT&T in the domsat industry presented the commission with special problems. For instance, there was the question whether AT&T would subsidize its entry into the specialized service markets with the guaranteed revenues from its public toll telephone monopoly. It was believed that such an activity, referred to as cross-subsidization, would either discourage or foreclose entry by rival carriers into these specialized markets. Furthermore, AT&T's size and economic strength alone would prevent other applicants from approaching "the problems and possibilities of domestic satellite applications from a reasonably equal competitive opportunity position."[62] Accordingly, nearly all of the applicants suggested that the commission impose special restrictions on AT&T. Hughes Aircraft, for example, urged that AT&T be confined to providing public telephone service only; MCI Lockheed recommended that it be excluded from the domestic satellite industry altogether, at least on an interim basis.[63]

Two of the applicants, Comsat and Fairchild, used the occasion to argue against the open entry option: each company urged the FCC to organize the entire industry as an outright monopoly and select it as the only purveyor of domestic satellite services. On the other hand, Western Union and MCI Lockheed argued in favor of multiple, competing systems and suggested that Comsat be prohibited from engaging in any domestic communications activity.[64]

New Government Agency Proposals

It was at this juncture that the Justice Department entered the arena. In comments submitted to the FCC, the Justice Department endorsed the entry of AT&T into the domsat industry but noted that special conditions would have to be attached to AT&T participation in order to prevent it from engaging in anticompetitive or monopolistic practices. First, the department recommended that the commission void AT&T's tentative lease arrangement with Comsat and re-open the contract to competitive bidding. Second, the applicant eventually authorized to carry the Bell system traffic should be prohibited from leasing satellite capacity to the commercial network broadcasters. This last restriction would have prevented Comsat from both serving AT&T and launching its proposed multipurpose system because the latter would not have been profitable without the support of the network broadcasters. Furthermore, the Justice Department rejected Comsat's argument that applicants with manufacturing (Hughes Aircraft, Fairchild) or carrier (RCA, Western Union) interests should be barred from owning and operating a domestic satellite system. The department contended that the entry of such companies would not create a competitive danger. Indeed, the development of several multipurpose systems, in the opinion of the Justice Department, would ensure a vigorous and competitive market for satellite services. In another matter the department expressed conditional support for the Fairchild system proposal and noted that a major portion of AT&T's public telephone message traffic would have to be rerouted from ground cable to satellite carriage in order to realize the economies of scale inherent in the 120-transponder satellite. The department, however, questioned the reliability of the proposal's technical design.[65]

The addition of a new voice from government, that of the Justice Department, threatened to complicate and prolong the policymaking process even though the department itself advocated early resolution of the controversy. Already, the inability of the FCC to conclude the dispute, then entering its sixth year, and to release a definitive policy decision was becoming a source of aggravation for the Nixon Administration. During October 1971, in fact, the White House again pressured the FCC to adopt its "open skies" recommendation. In a letter to the FCC, OTP Director Clay Whitehead advised the commission to issue construction permits to all of the applicants. According to Whitehead, the demand for domsat services was sufficient to support several of the proposed systems, and that although the total proposed transponder capacity far exceeded the then current needs, market forces would determine which systems became operational. Whitehead also noted that only FCC indecisiveness was forestalling the advent of domestic commercial satellites: "There are customers waiting for satellite services and prospective suppliers with the capital and the will to offer them on a commercial basis. . . . We see no reason for the government to continue keeping these groups apart."[66] Finally, the expeditious resolution of the domsat controversy would stimulate approximately $ 450 million in investments and create employment in the aerospace and electronic industries.[67]

The focus of attention returned to the FCC during the latter half of 1971 and early 1972 as it evaluated overall organizational schemes for the domsat industry, the eight applications from the private sector, and the recommendations of the Justice Department and OTP. For nearly a year industry and government alike waited for the FCC to conclude the controversy with the issuance of a definitive policy statement. On 17 March 1972 the commission finally released the staff report of its Common Carrier Bureau (CCB).[68] The CCB findings, however, were presented in the form of a proposed policy order; the document simply contained the recommendations of the bureau, not the final views of the entire commission.

The CCB document enumerated the reasons for not attempting to select either one kind of space segment or a few of the applications on the basis of their comparative merits. Either approach, in the CCB's opinion, would mean continued FCC hearings. Moreover, either alternative would be "inconsistent with the policy objectives of encouraging diverse entities to exploit the potential advantages of this technology [satellite] to achieve new communications services, as well as expansion of the scope and flexibility of existing services."[69] The CCB also argued against OTP's "open skies" recommendation. Authorization of all of the proposed systems – the combined transponder capacity of which was in excess of near-term demand for satellite services – would lead to hasty corporate mergers regardless of the public interest. Satellite carriers that were unable either to recover their investment cost or to merge with other carriers would have been gradually eliminated from competition. The result, according to the CCB, would be increased fragmentation of the market for satellite services.[70] Instead of unrestricted open entry, the bureau suggested that applicants with similar technologies be required or at least encouraged to share in the ownership and operation of a common space segment. In defense of this policy recommendation, referred to as "Open Entry Option II," the bureau asserted that shared use of space segments would lower the total investment and overhead costs for the participants.[71] Furthermore, the development of these shared systems would tend to insulate the tariff rate structure for terrestrial telecommunications from any severe financial losses that might be incurred by one or more of the satellite carriers.

In order to illustrate this approach, the Common Carrier Bureau grouped the eight domsat applicants into four major systems according to the number of transponders proposed per satellite. The first of these major systems could have included Hughes Aircraft, Western Union, RCA, and Western Tele-Communications because each had originally proposed systems utilizing twelve-transponder satellites. RCA and Western Tele-Communications were given options of participating in joint ventures or developing independent systems; the latter alternative would have required that the applicant file a public interest justification.[72] For its second system the CCB suggested that AT&T and Comsat share in the ownership of a space segment based on the twenty-four-transponder satellite.[73] MCI Lockheed and Fairchild would have been allowed to pursue their original plans due to the unique nature of their forty-eight-transponder and 120-transponder satellite proposals.[74] Under the CCB plan participants in a joint system would have financed implementation and management expenditures on a cost-sharing basis and would have been free to sell their shares at any time, subject to FCC approval. Individual ownership of the ground terminals also would have been permitted, with joint ownership reserved for stations in close proximity. Finally, the modification or expansion in overall message capacity of any of the space segments would have been contingent upon FCC approval.[75]

In addition to its plan to divide the entire domestic satellite industry into four major systems, the policy recommendations of the CCB differed from those of OTP in another important respect. In autumn 1971 it was the position of OTP that: "Any measure necessary to prevent anticompetitive behavior can be taken if and when such practices appear; to establish them at the outset without firm assurance that they are necessary would have the effect of precluding rather than fostering competition in this new field."[76] In contract the CCB suggested a number of regulations designed to protect smaller companies, especially those offering specialized services, from the consequences of unrestricted entry. The first of these was directed at AT&T and had been proposed by the Justice Department during the previous summer:

> In view of all of the foregoing, it is our [CCB's] judgment that realization of the potential public benefits from satellite technology can best be achieved by limiting AT&T, at least in its initial system proposal for the use of satellites, to those of its services that are essentially monopoly services, such as message toll and wide area telephone services.[77]

Regarding GTE's satellite application, the bureau was of the view that GTE should submit evidence to the FCC that its plan to interconnect areas of local service via satellite would not adversely affect interstate telephone message service.[78] It was also stated that Comsat and satellite hardware suppliers like Hughes Aircraft, Lockheed, and Fairchild should be required to form separate corporate subsidiaries for their domestic carrier operations.[79] In order to give the applicants an opportunity to respond to these and other CCB recommendations, the commission announced that it would hear oral arguments during the following May.[80]

Within a month OTP's Clay Whitehead responded to the CCB's *Proposed Report and Order* during a news conference at the National Association of Broadcasters convention in Chicago, Illinois. Threatening a direct confrontation with the commission, Whitehead stated that his office was prepared to go to Congress to obtain legislation in support of its open entry recommendation.[81] In written comments filed with the commission on 22 April 1972, OTP again urged the commission to authorize any entity with adequate financial and technical resources to launch a domestic satellite system.[82] Another interested party, the Justice Department, stated that the existence of multiple, competing systems would encourage technological innovation, and thus it argued against CCB's "Open Entry Option II," the plan requiring applicants with similar technologies to share common space segments.[83]

During the oral discussions held before the FCC on 1 and 2 May, those applicants that would have been required to form coalitions argued against the CCB staff report. Western Union, for example, stated that it would not be able to maintain cost control or provide diverse services under a consortium arrangement. Both Hughes Aircraft and GTE declared that their own joint system proposal of 1971 offered more technical and economic advantages than did the CCB arrangement. AT&T and Comsat also expressed dissatisfaction with the staff report. On the other hand, Fairchild and MCI Lockheed supported the consortium approach. Under the CCB plan both would have been allowed to develop their own systems. MCI Lockheed also encouraged the commission to prohibit AT&T from using satellites to offer private-line telephone and other specialized services. A CCB recommendation that did receive general approval, however, was the one encouraging satellite carriers to offer free or reduced rates to public broadcasters for television distribution services.[84]

Final FCC Decision

A new era in the history of communication satellites began on 16 June 1972 when the Federal Communications Commission announced its decision authorizing any qualified entity, subject only to specific technical and antitrust considerations, to launch and operate a domestic satellite system.[85] The choice of multiple entry as the pattern for the new industry concluded the seven-year controversy. On the basis of available evidence, the FCC decided that it would have been unwise to select one type of system as the optimal configuration or to choose "one or more systems through comparative hearings."[86] Instead, the commission opened the market to numerous, competing satellite carriers and announced that each of the domsat proposals would be processed individually to determine the financial and technical credibility of the respective applicants. The eight applicants were requested to inform the commission by 25 July 1972 whether they intended to pursue their pending proposals or modify them in light of the June decision.[87]

Although the commissioners incorporated many of the CCB's rule suggestions into the June policy statement, they did reject the staff's most controversial recommendation and decided not to impose consolidations and sharing arrangements upon any of the applicants. It was the FCC's belief that the management expertise of each system applicant could best determine whether specific joint operations such as "launch risk pools" were to be undertaken. However, the multiple-entry decision did not mean quite the same as unlimited open entry – the policy postion that had been advocated by OTP for over two years. The White House office had urged the commission to issue construction permits to any applicant with suitable financial credentials and, in essence, to let the marketplace dictate survival. But under this approach the economic strength of certain carriers would have given them an unfair advantage in the development of the specialized satellite service markets. Consequently, the FCC adopted a variety of rules and regulations, many of which had been suggested by both the Justice Department and the Common Carrier Bureau, in order to provide substantial incentive for new satellite entrepreneurs to compete in the emerging industry.

Two of the FCC's regulatory measures were directed at AT&T. The first of these limited AT&T's use of satellite facilities to the provision of its two basic switched services: message toll telephone and WATS (Wide Area Telephone Service). AT&T was also free to use satellites for the AUTOVON system it operated for the Department of Defense and for emergency restoration of communications in the event of temporary outage of terrestrial facilities.[88] These provisions were designed to give other satellite entrepreneurs an opportunity to implement their proposals and to develop the market for specialized services before having to compete with AT&T. The prohibition on AT&T's entry into these markets, however, would be reevaluated by the commission when the specialized carriers achieved a substantial fill of their satellite capacity or three years after the commencement of AT&T's satellite operations.[89]

In the other major ruling involving AT&T, the commission determined that the joint proposal of Comsat and AT&T was contrary to the public interest and to the overall multiple-entry policy objective.[90] As a consequence of this decision, AT&T was left with two options for domestic service: AT&T could choose either to own and operate a space segment itself or to lease channel capacity "under tariff from Comsat or any other carrier who elects to proceed solely as a carrier's carrier. . . ."[91] This ruling was influenced by the fact that AT&T still owned twenty-nine percent of Comsat's stock, whereas the other international carriers had already disposed of their interests.[92]

Comsat also faced a difficult decision as a result of the commission's disallowal of the lease arrangement with AT&T, as proposed in their joint application of March 1971. In essence, Comsat was required to choose between pursuing its application for a separate multipurpose system or providing a space segment for AT&T. If Comsat chose to launch the multipurpose system, it was free to offer services to end-users and also to wholesale channel capacity to any common carrier with the exception of AT&T. If, on the other hand, Comsat chose the second option, it would have to "operate exclusively as a carrier's carrier—not engaged in retailing communications services to the public—and provide such service under a tariff offering which would afford an opportunity for other carriers to have non-discriminatory access to the same system."[93] Authorization of both of Comsat's system applications, in the view of the commission, would have given the company "an extraordinary advantage and head start over all other potential domestic satellite entrants seeking to develop specialized services in competition with Comsat as well as with AT&T's terrestrial services."[94] Finally, Comsat was required to form an independent corporate subsidiary regardless of which proposal that it chose to implement.[95]

The June policy statement also included an endorsement of GTE's plan to provide long-distance toll telephone services. A major advantage of the proposal, the commission stated, was that it "would introduce . . . the perspective and expertise of another responsible entity into the planning and operation of the interstate MTT (Message Toll Telephone) network, which heretofore has been the sole responsibility of AT&T."[96] Final authorization was contingent upon a showing by GTE that its system would serve the public interest. Specifically, the commission was concerned about the effects of the system upon the efficiency and economy of the existing interstate public telephone network. The FCC also required GTE to submit a plan for rerouting telephone traffic in the event of a temporary outage or mechanical failure of the satellite facilities.[97] Finally, GTE was required to establish a separate subsidiary for its domestic satellite activities and, like AT&T, was prohibited from entering the specialized service markets at least for the initial period of commercial operation.[98]

The FCC also ruled on several matters involving other system applicants. The commission stated that Hughes Aircraft would not be issued a construction permit until it afforded prospective CATV customers "the option of owning receive-only earth stations to obtain the Hughes program offering and that of any other CATV program distributor offered by means of the Hughes system facilities."[99] In another matter satellite equipment manufacturers were required to form separate subsidiaries before implementing their system proposals.[100] The commission also requested satellite carriers to revise the tariff rate structure for service to Alaska, Hawaii and Puerto Rico in view of the distance-insensitive capabilities of satellites.[101] Before the FCC decision the charges for services to the outlying states and territories followed the international rather than the domestic pattern. With the advent of the domsats it was considered practicable to lower the rates for service to these areas because the surface distance between sender and receiver would not be a critical factor in determining the costs of message transmission via satellite.

Another significant FCC ruling gave special purpose users like noncommercial broadcasters and local carriers the opportunity to own and operate receive-only ground stations.[102] Finally, in accordance with its CCB staff conclusion, the commission decided simply to encourage, and not to require, satellite carriers to offer preferential rates to public broadcasters and other educational interests.[103]

The FCC's policy decision of 16 June 1972 passed by a four to three vote. The fact that the FCC barely attained a majority was an indication of the complexity of the issues and the deep divisions within government concerning the optimal configuration for domsat ownership. In particular, the commissioners in the minority objected to the restrictions attached to the participation of AT&T and Comsat in the industry. One of the dissenters, Dean Burch, criticized the commission's rejection of the Comsat-AT&T lease arrangement and charged that it had taken off "into the blue sky of academic abstraction" by not building upon the guaranteed traffic of the Bell system.[104] The prohibition against AT&T entrance into the competitive specialized markets would also mean that the "consumer will have to pay artificially inflated prices for specialized services during an initial three year developmental period...."[105] For their part, Comsat and AT&T protested the FCC's disallowal of their proposed lease arrangement and, along with four other parties, filed petitions for reconsideration or clarification of the *Report and Order* by the deadline of 25 July 1972.[106]

For the remainder of the year the FCC evaluated the six petitions, a Memorandum of Understanding and Supplementary Agreement submitted by Comsat and MCI Lockheed, and reply comments of other interested parties. On 22 December 1972 the commission issued an amended policy decision.[107] This time the vote was unanimous. The FCC's major new action was to endorse a plan according to which Comsat, MCI Communications, and Lockheed Aircraft would jointly own and operate a multipurpose, domestic satellite system. The organizational relationship for the enterprise, named CML Satellite Corporation, would preclude dominance by any of the three partners and would minimize the possibility of a conflict of interest resulting either from Comsat's business arrangement with AT&T or its participation in the Intelsat consortium.

The CML proposal replaced Comsat's original application for a multipurpose system. The commission reappraised its 16 June rejection of the Comsat-AT&T lease arrangement in light of the minority role of Comsat within CML and concluded that a domsat reserved for the exclusive use of AT&T would no longer be inconsistent with the multiple-entry policy decision.[108] Furthermore, the commission decided to drop the June election provision, which required Comsat to choose between launching its own multipurpose system or providing a space segment for AT&T.[109] As a result, Comsat was free to pursue its contractual arrangement with AT&T and to implement the multipurpose CML system. In making this decision, the commission noted that the total channel capacity of the prospective domsats was sufficient to accommodate all retail message carriers in the immediate future; thus the public interest did not require that "other carriers have access to the system used by AT&T...."[110] Final acceptance of the Comsat-AT&T application was conditioned upon the removal from Comsat's board of directors of any person affiliated with

AT&T.[111] However, the FCC did continue the prohibition on AT&T entry into the specialized service markets until three years after the commencement of its satellite operations.

Aftermath of the Multiple-Entry Decision

The FCC multiple-entry decision established the policy guidelines and overall regulatory framework for the domsat industry and signaled the end of the second stage of the U.S. communication satellite technology transfer. Nonetheless, it is interesting to notice what has transpired in the wake of the decision. As of late 1975, the number of prospective satellite operators has been cut in half: Western Tele-Communications, Hughes Aircraft, Fairchild, and MCI Lockheed have decided to forego the implementation of their own systems, at least for the near future, primarily because of economic pressures. An analogous development has been the tendency of some companies to consolidate their separate resources and to begin planning joint systems. In addition, a number of new policy issues involving, for example, service to Alaska and the entry of the International Business Machines Corporation into the domsat arena have been brought before the FCC. Accordingly, what follows is a brief review of the upcoming domsat systems and a few of the significant policy controversies that emerged during the 1973-75 time frame.

In early 1973, shortly after the release of the amended ruling, Western Union became the first domsat applicant to receive an FCC construction permit. And on 13 April 1974 Western Union's Westar I satellite was launched from Cape Kennedy and then successfully positioned into a synchronous orbital slot 22,300 miles above the equator at 99° west longitude, south of Dallas, Texas, and west of the Galapagos Islands.[112] Westar I, the first United States domestic communication satellite, has been equipped with a total communications capacity of 7,200 two-way voice grade circuits or twelve simultaneous color television channels. Western Union actually commenced commercial operations with Westar I on 16 July 1974. The second spacecraft, Westar II, in the Western Union series, was launched into synchronous orbit during October 1974. The ground segment for the Western Union system consists of large transmit/receive stations located near New York City, Chicago, Atlanta, Dallas, and Los Angeles. In addition to its traditional data and record services, Western Union intends to provide various private-line telephone services to business and institutional users around the country.[113]

The American Satellite Corporation (ASC), a fully-owned subsidiary of Fairchild Industries, has leased three noninterruptable transponders aboard Westar II for its communications network serving government and commercial users. Fairchild abandoned the 1971 satellite proposal when AT&T decided to continue its contractual arrangement with Comsat for a leased space segment. The ASC government system has been targeted to the Department of Defense's Advanced Research Projects Agency and the Air Force Defense Meteorological Satellite Program. The ground complex includes five terminals, each of which is located at a military installation and equipped with a small, portable dish antenna for sending and receiving high-speed digital communications. ASC has also established a network of three large, fixed ground terminals serving business organizations in the New York City, Dallas and Los Angeles metropolitan areas. Interconnection with the facilities of other carriers has enabled ASC to extend its commercial operation into San Francisco, Pittsburgh, Chicago and Washington, D.C.[114]

RCA Globcom and Alascom are expected to launch the first of three high-capacity satellites for their system in late 1975 or early 1976. The three-axis stabilized, twenty-four transponder satellites for the system are being developed by RCA's Astro-Electronics Division. Even though Westar I was the nation's first domestic satellite, it was RCA that actually introduced domsat services into the United States. On 5 April 1973 RCA signed an agreement with Telesat Canada to lease two transponders aboard the Anik II satellite. With these leased circuits along with an initial ground segment of four earth stations, RCA has been providing communication services between New York and San Francisco and between both cities and Alaska.[115]

Throughout the second half of 1974 RCA Alascom and Western Union were engaged in a debate concerning satellite service between the contiguous states and Alaska. Although Western Union had not been authorized to serve Alaska, it questioned RCA's utilization of the Canadian Telesat system in view of the fact that a U.S. domsat, Westar, was already operational. Western Union claimed that its system could handle Alaska's present communication requirements. While awaiting an FCC ruling in the matter, RCA Alascom continued to use the Anik space segment on a month-by-month basis after the September expiration date of the lease arrangement with Telesat. Eventually, the FCC ruled in favor of Western Union by ordering

RCA to transfer all domsat traffic, including traffic between the forty-eight contiguous states, to the Westar space segment until the scheduled launch of its own satellite in December 1975. In addition, RCA's plan to supply intrastate message services to Alaska appears to be in jeopardy since both the state of Alaska and AT&T have raised substantive objections. At least until these issues are resolved, RCA will be limited to the provision of services to the lower forty-eight states, according to the FCC policy order of 6 November 1975. The company was also required by this order to form a subsidiary for its domsat operations.[116]

AT&T has been proceeding with the construction of the ground segment for its joint system with Comsat. The first of the Comstar satellites for the system will be delivered in late 1975 and launched into a geosynchronous orbit in March 1976. When fully operational, the system's three satellites, each equipped with 14,400 voice circuits, will provide a variety of communication services to Alaska, Hawaii, Puerto Rico, and the continental United States.

Until early 1974 GTE Satellite Corporation, the wholly owned subsidiary of General Telephone and Electronics, had intended to lease channel capacity from Hughes Aircraft. After this agreement lapsed, however, officials from AT&T and GTE Satellite announced plans to utilize a single space segment rather than developing separate system. According to the proposal filed with the FCC on 18 April 1974, the joint system would include seven ground stations compared to the total of ten if the two companies had proceeded independently. Further, it was expected that the plan would reduce their total investment costs by nearly forty million dollars.[117] On 7 February 1975, however, the Common Carrier Bureau urged the full commission to reject the proposal because GTE Satellite had not demonstrated that joint ownership "of earth stations in the AT&T system would provide public benefits that would not be achieved by AT&T ownership alone."[118] As of fall 1975, the commission had not issued a definitive ruling on the matter.

In compliance with the FCC order, Comsat established a separate corporate subsidiary in 1973 for all of its non-Intelsat activities. At the present time Comsat General is developing the space segment for the AT&T system. Comsat General has also begun to construct a maritime communication satellite network, Marisat. Beginning in late 1975, synchronous satellites stationed over the Atlantic and Pacific Oceans will transmit high-quality voice, data, and telex signals to U.S. Naval and Merchant Marine vessels at sea. The ground segment includes a shore terminal near Southbury, Connecticut, on the Atlantic coast and another near Santa Paula, California, on the Pacific coast, Comsat General owns eighty percent of the enterprise, with the minority share divided among Western Union International, RCA Globcom, and ITT Worldcom.[119]

On 6 September 1974 Comsat General was named the U.S. participant in Aerosat, an aeronautical satellite program being developed in a joint effort by the United States, Canada and the ten member nations of the European Space Research Organization (ESRO). Comsat General and ESRO will each own forty-seven percent of the venture; the remaining six percent will be controlled by Canada. The purpose of the Aerosat system is to provide improved air traffic communications to aircraft flying across the North Atlantic Ocean. The first synchronous satellite of the program is expected to be launched by late 1977, with a second satellite launch following at a later date. Air traffic services to U.S. aircraft will be provided by the Federal Aviation Administration, which will lease the satellite circuits from Comsat.[120]

Finally, Comsat General along with the International Business Machines Corporation (IBM) recently began a controversial realignment of the CML Satellite Corporation. On 12 July 1974 IBM made known its intention to purchase the majority ownership share of the CML Satellite Corporation, at that time owned by Comsat General, MCI Communications, and Lockheed Aircraft. According to the application submitted to the FCC on that date, IBM and Comsat General would reorganize CML Satellite into a new joint enterprise fifty-five percent owned by IBM and forty-five percent owned by Comsat.[121] Lockheed and MCI would each receive $ 2.5 million for their CML ownership shares. The two companies decided to forego participation because neither was able to make the necessary capital investment for a satellite system. Subject to FCC approval, IBM and Comsat General expected to launch a satellite system specializing in data and record transmission by the late 1970s.

The IBM-Comsat plan was considered by some observers to be a positive development because "it would establish a joint venture between the nation's leading computer maker and its only experienced satellite carrier.[122] However, many specialized carriers feared that IBM, with its vast financial and technological resources, would eventually dominate the data transmission markets. It was noted that implementation of the plan would lead to a situation in which Comsat General owned and operated space segments for both

IBM and AT&T; the final outcome would be the formation of an "interlocking arrangement" among the companies whereby voice communication was reserved for AT&T and data communication for IBM.[123] Some of the carriers opposing the reorganization plan included Western Union, American Satellite Corporation, Data Transmission Corporation, RCA, and ITT.

Throughout the remaining months of 1974 the FCC examined the joint proposal and the many objections that had been raised by interested parties. On 23 January 1975 the commission announced a decision permitting the two companies to proceed with their restructuring plans. Two conditions would have to be met, however, before the FCC granted final approval: (1) the entry of at least one more partner into the reorganization plan, and (2) the allocation of ownership percentages in such a manner that none of the individual partners controlled more than forty-nine percent or less than ten percent of the enterprise. The FCC also required IBM to establish a separate corporate subsidiary for its satellite activities. According to commissioner Abbott M. Washburn, these restrictions would minimize the risk of IBM and Comsat General engaging in anticompetitive practices in the data transmission markets.[124] In September 1975 it was announced that Aetna Life and Casualty Company would join IBM and Comsat General as the third partner in the enterprise and own fifteen percent of the stock, and that the company would be named Satellite Business Systems, Inc.[125]

8

THE DIRECT BROADCAST CONTROVERSY: UNITED NATIONS RESPONSE TO THE TECHNOLOGIC IMPERATIVE

The Technologic Imperative and Direct Broadcast Satellites

Every major technological advance generates demands by diverse elements of society for an institutional response to channel further experimental and operational development of the innovation so as to maximize its benefits and minimize the social and economic costs. The precise response demanded depends on the interaction of several social, political and technical factors. The development of satellite communications considered in this volume has examined several of these forces. The advent of communication satellite technology has created a series of conflicting demands on the national and international levels to maximize the benefits of any advance to various states, while minimizing the concomitant adverse side effects or the advantages of another state's technological advance.

The trend toward benefit and cost tradeoffs can be seen at each strategic point of the implementation process for communication satellites. When the Soviet Union launched Sputnik in 1957, political, scientific, military and popular pressure focused on the need to deter abusive application of the technology by matching or surpassing the Soviet missile capability. As a direct consequence, NASA was established to lead the American space effort.[1] Out of the same milieu came pressures for the development of satellite communications technology and somewhat later for transfer of that technology to the private sector of the American economy which resulted in Comsat.[2] Successful experimentation with communications satellites by the United States, both alone and in cooperation with other nations, opened the possibility that satellites could bridge important gaps in the increasingly important global communications network. The preliminary structures and the later definitive arrangements of Intelsat were established to maximize the benefits to be derived on an international plane from rapid technological development.[3] The same technological developments made possible tentative plans for designing direct broadcast satellites capable of transmitting program-carrying signals directly to ground receivers, bypassing the complex terrestrial redistribution networks employed by the members of the Intelsat system.

The controversy over direct satellite broadcasting displays the tension between benefits and costs in sharp focus. Direct broadcasting from satellites carries with it the promise of a number of benefits, including more efficient and extensive program dissemination on a national level both for educational and entertainment purposes and for increased interchange of ideas and information between cultures. Perhaps the most important of these is the potential for improving the quality of education. In all of the developing countries, and even in some of those considered developed, a shortage of well-qualified teachers has hindered national development, setting in motion a search for means to overcome the shortage. Educational television has been used successfully in many parts of the world to distribute over a wide area resources previously available only in isolated special teaching facilities. In a large number of countries, however, the absence of a well-developed, in-place terrestrial distribution system for educational programming, compounded by the difficulty of installation due to high costs, difficult terrain or a widely dispersed population, has prevented full realization of television's educational potential. Direct satellite broadcasting technology is capable of overcoming these barriers, provided that certain economic and technical obstacles are overcome.

Along with its promise of increased interchange among peoples, direct broadcasting has also created concern among potential "receiving states" that the new technology will be exploited for purposes of propaganda or for cultural or economic imperialism. As early as 1963 that concern generated demands that a restrictive international legal regime be imposed on the use of direct broadcasting to prevent potential misuses. The significant initiatives in that regard have centered in the United Nations, taking place in a variety of agencies, including the ITU, UNESCO and the General Assembly's Committee on the Peaceful Uses of Outer Space (CPUOS).

During the United Nations debate, three main positions have emerged. After a short initial period at the opposite pole, the Soviet Union has led Argentina, Brazil, Egypt, France and the Eastern European bloc in expressing concern over the potential for satellite transmission of politically subversive or culturally disruptive broadcasts across national boundaries without the prior consent of the receiving state. A number of less developed states have echoed the Soviet concern over propaganda. Morocco, Iran, Sierra Leone, and India, among other Third World states, have been especially concerned about cultural imperialism and the possibility that commercial advertising by the industrial powers would disrupt the social fabric of developing nations. Some Third World nations have suggested that any television program displaying consumer-oriented societies in a favorable light would create a demand for consumer goods among their own citizens which could delay or perhaps even thwart national plans for social and economic development.[4] The key elements upon which these states would ultimately base an international institutional response are the principles of national sovereignty and the need to protect established cultures against intrusion from abroad.

Opposition to the restrictive regulatory approach taken by the Soviet Union has been led by the United States, which has argued, first, that any regulation was premature, since no one could determine with any degree of certainty either the configuration of future direct broadcast systems or the nature of the political, economic and legal problems likely to arise when such systems finally become operational, and second, that an excessively restrictive policy could stifle the initiatives necessary to develop and implement direct broadcast technology. The third tenet of the United States' position has been the contention that a regime of prior consent and program control would violate both the First Amendment and the principle of the free flow of information contained in the Declaration of Human Rights, and would, therefore, be unacceptable as a matter of constitutional policy.

Sweden and Canada have taken an intermediate position, recognizing the need to incorporate both the free flow of information and the protection of national sovereignty and cultural diversity into any viable regulatory scheme. To achieve that goal, the two states have advocated a regime based on international cooperation expressed in a prior agreement between the broadcasting and receiving states. Under the Swedish-Canadian proposal, program content would be determined by a bilateral prior consent agreement rather than by a global agreement as proposed by the Soviets.

The United Nations Debate

The 1963 ITU Conference

Direct broadcast satellites first appeared as an issue before an international body at the 1963 Extraordinary Administrative Radio Conference held in Geneva by the International Telecommunication Union. In 1959 at the World Administrative Radio Conference the ITU had allocated thirteen narrow frequency bands for experimental use by space services. Recognizing the temporary adequacy of that allocation, the Union convened the 1963 conference for further consideration of the underlying issues.[5]

At the 1963 ITU conference, France and a number of less developed states proposed a complete ban on radio and television broadcasts from space, pending definitive international agreements on a regulatory structure for direct broadcasting.[6] The United States countered with the suggestion that experimentation of all kinds be permitted in the bands allocated in 1959, pending further study by the International Radio Consultative Committee, a technical study committee of the ITU.[7] With Soviet support, the American position prevailed. Although the Soviet Union had taken a protectionist position during the 1950s regarding radio broadcasts beamed into its territory, its delegates joined with the American position because Soviet communications research had emphasized direct broadcast technology and the Soviets did not want its potential limited by restrictive international agreements.[8]

The Outer Space Committee

The United Nations Committee on the Peaceful Uses of Outer Space was the next international body to address the question of direct broadcast satellites. Originally created in 1958 as an ad hoc committee to promote outer space research,[9] CPUOS was established on a permanent basis a year later.[10] The direct broadcast issue was raised again in 1966 when the United Arab Republic proposed a prohibition of direct broadcasts, pending an international agreement, during CPUOS discussions of the draft *Treaty on Principles Governing the Activities of States in the Exploration and Use of Outer Space, Including the Moon and Other Celestial Bodies.*[11] The Outer Space Treaty was unanimously approved by the General Assembly in December 1966 and after signature by the required number of states, entered into force on 10 October 1967.[12] While the treaty did not include a ban on direct broadcasting, it did contain several provisions likely to affect developments in that area. Article I, paragraph 1, provides:

> The exploration and use of outer space, including the moon and other celestial bodies, shall be carried out for the benefit and in the interests of all countries, irrespective of their degree of economic or scientific development, and shall be the province of all mankind.

In the context of direct broadcasting, this provision raises the question to what extent space powers are required to distribute the benefits of space technology to those states technologically or economically incapable of maintaining their own direct broadcast systems. Less-developed states argue that benefits from space exploration should be regarded as the common property of mankind and distributed equitably.[13] However, since the provision is stated in broad terms and is not limited to parties to the treaty, the soundest construction is that the "free use" provision is a general statement of principle and does not, for example, impose on the space powers the obligation to provide other nations with sufficient assistance to enable them to exercise the right of equal access to space guaranteed them by paragraphs 2 and 3 of Article I.[14]

Article II provided: "Outer Space . . . is not subject to national appropriation by claim of sovereignty, by means of use or occupation, or by any other means." The first implication of this provision is that no state may prevent the passage or stationing of a satellite in space vertically above its territory. Two main considerations support the policy of Article II. First, international law, recognizing that certain areas play such an important role in world affairs, has by custom or treaty defeated all claims to sovereignty over such areas. The most prominent examples are the high seas, with their importance for international commerce, and Antarctica, because of its value as an area for scientific research.[15] Second, since the earth is continuously rotating on its axis, as well as revolving in orbit around the sun, patterns of sovereign domain determined by the vertical projections of national boundaries would become tangled and, therefore, unmanageable.[16]

Article II carries with it a second consequence which affects primarily the broadcasting state. Direct broadcast satellites are usually geosynchronous, occupying a stationary position with respect to the earth's surface. Since certain portions of the geosynchronous orbit are most useful for certain states, those states have an interest in retaining control of the corresponding orbital slots. The United States, for example, has an interest in the segment of the geosynchronous orbit corresponding to the arc between 60° and 135° West longitude.[17] Roughly the same segment would be most advantageous for Canada and the countries of Hispanoamerica. However, by defeating all claims to a particular area of outer space based on use or occupation the treaty theoretically prevents any claim of preemption based on the fact that the claimant state had previously stationed a satellite in a particular orbital slot.

Article III requires all states which are parties to the treaty to conduct space activities in accordance with international law, including the United Nations Charter, in order to maintain international peace and to promote international cooperation and understanding.

Finally, Article VI imposes international responsibility for activities carried out in space by a state or its nationals. When activities are conducted by non-governmental entities, governmental authorization and continuing supervision are required. Foreshadowing future developments, Article VI also provides that when activities in space are carried out by an international organization, responsibility for compliance with the provisions of the Outer Space Treaty is borne jointly by the organization and by the individual state members of the organization.

The Working Group on Direct Broadcast Satellites

After passage of the Outer Space Treaty, the Outer Space Committee resumed its discussion of the direct broadcast issue during the spring of 1967. At that time both Egypt and the Soviet Union reiterated opposition to unregulated transmissions from orbiting spacecraft. The French delegation recommended a general compromise between the principles of national sovereignty and free flow of information which would permit the receiving state to exercise control between the satellite and the private receiver. Sweden warned the committee that a direct broadcast system could have an especial impact on the developing nations unless guidelines were drafted to protect them from undue foreign intrusion.[18]

The intensity of the conflict made necessary a formal examination of the direct broadcasting issue. As a result, the General Assembly passed Resolution 2260 (XXII) requesting the Committee on the

Peaceful Uses of Outer Space "to study the technical feasibility of communication by direct broadcasts from satellites and the current and foreseeable developments in this field, as well as the implications of such developments."[19] At the June 1968 meeting of the CPUOS Legal Sub-Committee, Sweden and Canada proposed to implement Resolution 2260 by establishing a special working group within CPUOS to study direct broadcasting. The proposal was incorporated into the report of the Committee on the Peaceful Uses of Outer Space, and placed on the agenda for the twenty-third session of the General Assembly. The suggestion was accepted, and on 20 December 1968, the General Assembly created the Working Group on Direct Broadcast Satellites.[20]

With a mandate from the General Assembly, the Working Group became the center for discussion of the broadcast issue for the next five years. The group convened for three separate two-week sessions prior to 1 June 1970, when it temporarily ceased functioning. During the interregnum following the third session, three events sharpened the direct broadcast debate. The ITU World Administrative Radio Conference for Space Telecommunications met during the summer of 1971 to set aside certain frequency bands for exclusive use by satellite systems, and a year later the Soviet Union submitted to the General Assembly a highly restrictive draft convention covering direct broadcast satellites. Later in 1972 the UNESCO General Conference, despite its traditionally favorable attitude toward direct broadcast satellites because of their potential educational value, adopted an important declaration calling for a moderately restrictive legal regime for direct broadcast satellites. Concurrent with the passage of the UNESCO document, the Outer Space Committee and the General Assembly called on the Working Group to resume debate on the broadcast controversy. As a result, the Working Group convened for a fourth session in June 1973 and a fifth during March 1974.

The Working Group met for the first time in New York on 11-20 February 1969 to consider the technical and economic feasibility of direct broadcast satellites. In its report, the Working Group concluded that operational transmission via satellite directly to community receivers could be close at hand and that transmission to augmented home receivers could become technologically feasible as soon as 1975.[21]

Having considered the technical characteristics of direct broadcast satellites during its first session, the Working Group held a second meeting in Geneva between 28 July and 7 August 1969 to consider the social, cultural and legal implications. Several delegations presented working papers which identified possible categories of offensive programming. With the exception of the United States, all the participants agreed that some type of regulation was needed to guarantee respect for internal state affairs. There was, however, little agreement regarding specific restrictions. The French adopted a narrowly legalistic position, arguing that there should be a code of conduct for all direct broadcasting which would ban certain types of programming including propaganda likely to impair international or national peace, broadcasts detrimental to the dignity of the individual, and commercial advertising.[22] Most Third World nations, with their fears of the power of the television medium and of American or Soviet domination, supported the French position. The Swedish and Canadian delegations issued a joint working paper urging adoption of a broader, more moderate set of international controls with details of regulation to be handled by the ITU and by regional broadcasting organizations.[23] The United States took the position that while states could feel legitimate concern about direct broadcasting, imposition of international regulations should be deferred until a greater understanding of the implications of direct broadcast technology could be gained through further experimentation.[24]

Another area of disagreement at the second session of the Working Group centered around the interpretation of the "free use" principle contained in Article I(1) of the Outer Space Treaty, which provides that the exploration and use of space shall be conducted for the benefit of all countries, regardless of economic and scientific development.[25] The working paper submitted by the French delegation proposed that Article I(1) be implemented by granting all states whose territory is affected by direct broadcasts the right to use the radio transmitters installed in the satellites on a fair and reasonable basis.[26] That proposal introduced the issue of equal access in the specific context of direct broadcast satellites into the debate.

In its report of the second session the Working Group took no position on any of the questions discussed. Instead the Working Group noted the paradoxical potential of direct broadcasting both for increasing the level of international understanding and cooperation through increased information, and for increasing international tension through programming which ridiculed cultural or religious beliefs or emphasized inequalities of standards of living.[27] Reiterating the need for international cooperation, the Working Group urged continued study of the international legal questions related to direct broadcasting, including prior consent, program content and spill-over.[28]

In September 1969 the parent CPUOS met again. The Soviets, who had become increasingly alarmed by the American position, argued that the issue of direct broadcast satellites should be referred to CPUOS' Legal Sub-Committee and an international code of conduct drafted.[29] Fearing that the Legal Sub-Committee would approve a narrow, restrictive code of conduct along the lines proposed by the Soviet Union, the American delegation proposed instead that the Working Group be reconvened after the next ITU conference which had been scheduled for 1971 to allocate space frequencies. The Outer Space Committee compromised, delaying referral of the broadcast issue to the Legal Sub-Committee, while calling for the Working Group to meet in the summer of 1970, a year prior to the ITU session.[30]

When the Working Group resumed its investigation of the social, cultural, and legal implications of direct satellite broadcasting at its third session, held in New York, 11-12 May 1970, the formulation of concrete governing principles proved impossible because of the broad differences of opinion existing among the Working Group membership. However, by the end of the third session, a clear picture of each delegation's position had emerged, providing a basis for subsequent, more concrete discussions of the Working Group.

France and the Soviet Union each submitted a draft declaration of principles to the third session expressing a strong legalistic approach to the regulation of direct satellite broadcasting. The Soviet delegation's "Model General Principles" included a prohibition against racist and militaristic propaganda and a strict prior consent provision requiring broadcasters to secure agreement from the recipient state.[31] In case of delinquency in this regard the aggrieved nations would have been entitled to counteract unwanted broadcasts by "any available means,"[32] leaving open the question whether the proposed remedy included destruction of the offending spacecraft.

Even more restrictive than the Soviet draft was the declaration proposed by the French delegation, which contained a very detailed code of international conduct which would have both placed strict limits on commercial advertising and prohibited a broad range of potentially offensive programs.[33] The remedial provisions of the French proposal would have authorized the receiving state to require prior screening of all programs except those of an "informative nature," and in that case the draft provided for a posteriori control.[34]

The final report of the third session did not pass on the merits of either draft declaration; instead, the report recognized that, although further exploration of all alternatives was desirable, cooperation at the regional level appeared to be the most practical means of employing the developing technology to best advantage.[35] Consequently, the report urged member states, regional organizations, the ITU and UNESCO to take the necessary steps to facilitate regional arrangements for the future use of direct broadcast systems.[36]

At the close of the meeting, the Working Group did not request an extension of its mandate from CPUOS, since constructive resolution of the direct broadcast question did not seem likely in light of the polemical tone of the first three sessions.[37] Throughout the remainder of 1970 there were no major discussions on direct broadcasting within the United Nations, and the issue remained dormant until the summer of 1971 when the ITU convened a conference on space telecommunications.

The 1971 International Telecommunication Union Conference

The ITU held its World Administrative Radio Conference for Space Telecommunications (WARC-ST) at Geneva from 5 June to 17 July 1971. The conference broadened the competence of the ITU to encompass all space transmissions, including international broadcasts to augmented home television receivers, and approved several measures of importance to the future of direct broadcast satellites.[38] Perhaps most importantly, the ITU allocated a number of frequencies for satellite telecasts, subject to various conditions and sharing agreements. Most of the frequencies assigned are several times higher than those currently used by standard home receivers.[39] Because such receivers would require extensive modifications to enable them to receive signals in the frequency ranges assigned to broadcast satellites, the ITU limits eliminate, as a practical matter, most of the potential dangers which have motivated many delegations to the Working Group to advocate a restrictive regime for direct satellite broadcasting.

Other rulings of the 1971 WARC-ST conference affect the conditions under which direct broadcasting systems may come into existence. Article 9A of the Radio Regulations was amended to require any government intending to orbit a direct broadcast satellite to publish relevant technical information prior to launch in order to permit accommodation and coordination with other direct broadcast systems.[40] In addition, Resolution Spa 2-3 § 428A amended Article 7 to limit "spillover":

> In devising the characteristics of a space station in the Broadcasting-Satellite Service, all technical means available shall be used to reduce, to the maximum extent practicable, the radiation over the territory of other countries unless an agreement has been previously reached with such countries.[41]

The precise impact of this section on the issue of prior consent, among others, remains unclear. United States experts, for example, have argued that § 428A applies only to design characteristics and is irrelevant to the question of prior consent.[42] Under that construction, the complainant state would not be compelled to demonstrate unacceptable interference, but it would have to support the broader, but nonetheless technical, objection that the broadcasting state had not reduced spillover as much as technically possible. Hence, the regulation appears to proscribe any transnational broadcast which is not technically unavoidable, unless the receiving state has given its consent.[43] Thus, § 428A arguably represents an international consensus favoring the establishment of a regime for direct broadcasting based on the prior consent of the receiving state.

By imposing frequency limits within which broadcast satellites would be permitted to operate, and arguably by imposing a prior consent regime, the 1971 ITU conference could have quieted the demand for protective regulation of direct broadcast satellites, making early compromise possible and removing unnecessary constraints on technical development. Present production-line television receivers—those most likely to be available in countries concerned about abuse of direct broadcast technology—are incapable of receiving signals transmitted from satellites without expensive and technically complex augmentation. With the potential for abuse eliminated for all practical purposes, states at all levels of development could have initiated on a broad scale the type of bilateral and regional cooperation necessary before the undisputed benefits of direct broadcasting can be realized. Despite the existence of circumstances favorable to compromise, those states advocating a restrictive regime for direct broadcasting continued to press their demands.

The 1972 Soviet Draft Convention

Concerned about the American progress with communications satellite technology, the Soviet Union unexpectedly introduced its restrictive "Draft Convention on Principles Governing the Use by States of Artificial Earth Satellites for Direct Television Broadcasting" to the General Assembly on 8 August 1972.[44] In a letter addressed to the Secretary-General, Soviet Foreign Minister Andrei Gromyko requested that the twenty-seventh session of the General Assembly examine the feasibility of an international agreement for satellite broadcast regulation and that the Soviet proposal be included on the agenda.[45] The Soviet Union intended its draft to provide the foundation for a universally binding treaty approved by the CPUOS Legal Sub-Committee.

As submitted, the Soviet draft contained nearly all of the restrictive principles proposed during the previous meetings of the Working Group, including a strict provision permitting direct satellite broadcasting to foreign states "only with the express consent of the latter."[46] Article IV provided that any party to the proposed convention would undertake to exclude from programming transmitted via satellite "any material publicizing ideas of war, militarism, nazism, national and racial hatred and enmity between peoples, as well as material which is immoral or instigating in nature or is otherwise aimed at interfering in the domestic affairs or foreign policy of other states." Article VI elaborated the general statements of Article IV, listing specific categories of satellite broadcasting which would be illegal:

> (a) Broadcasts detrimental to the maintenance of international peace and security;
> (b) Broadcasts representing interference in intrastate conflicts of any kind;
> (c) Broadcasts involving an encroachment on fundamental human rights, on the dignity and worth of the human person and on the fundamental freedoms for all without distinction as to race, sex, language or religion;
> (d) Broadcasts propagandizing violence, horrors, pornography, and the use of narcotics;
> (e) Broadcasts undermining the foundations of the local civilization, culture, way of life, traditions or language;
> (f) Broadcasts which misinform the public in these or other matters.

The ban on specific categories of program content was supported by Article XII, which would have denied any party to the convention the right to enter into any subsequent international agreement which conflicted with the convention. Thus, the proposed program content limitations were apparently intended to apply even if the broadcasting and receiving states had agreed to waive one or more of the limitations. Consequently, under the Soviet draft, any third state which considered the programming exchanged between the broadcasting and receiving state – even if pursuant to an agreement between the two – to fall within the proscribed categories, could invoke the remedial procedures foreseen in the Soviet draft, even if there were no possibility that the third state's citizens would receive the allegedly objectionable transmissions. In addition, the proposal also forbade advertising, except "on the basis of specific agreements specially concluded between those states concerned."[47]

The foundation for the remedial process was laid by Article VI, which imposed international liability of states against a broadcasting state where programming contained proscribed materials. Article VII extended the liability of the broadcasting state to include any act of illegal broadcasting by one of its nationals, whether or not the broadcast was actually transmitted by a government agency. The imposition of international liability presumably made available to the objecting state all of the normal remedial procedures provided by international law. Article IX, however, also permitted the target state to "employ the means at its disposal" to counteract the illegal irradiation of its territory by a foreign state.[48] This particular provision had been included in the Soviet list of model general principles, annexed to the report of the Third Working Group.[49] The 1972 draft convention did not state explicitly whether retaliatory military action against the satellite would be permissible in such cases. However, that interpretation was given credence by language contained in Foreign Minister Gromyko's letter conveying the draft convention to the Secretary-General:

> States may utilize the means at their disposal to counteract illegal direct broadcasting of which they are the object, not only in their own territory but also in outer space and other areas beyond the limits of national jurisdiction of any state.[50]

Gromyko's statement leaves open a number of undesirable responses by the target state, including the destruction of the satellite in space. Eventually, however, the Soviets indicated that only "lawful" measures would be authorized under the convention.[51]

The Secretary-General referred the Soviet draft to the Committee on the Peaceful Uses of Outer Space, where further consideration of direct broadcast issues by the Working Group was proposed. The General Assembly accepted the recommendations, passing Resolution 2916 requesting the Outer Space Committe to "elaborate principles governing the use by States of artificial earth satellites for direct television broadcasting with a view to concluding an international agreement or agreements."[52]

The 1972 UNESCO Declaration

At approximately the same time the General Assembly voiced its approval of regulation of direct broadcasting by passing Resolution 2916, the states favoring minimal regulation, among them the United States, suffered a second setback at the seventeenth General Conference of UNESCO. On 15 November 1972, despite its traditional support of freedom of information, UNESCO adopted the restrictive *Declaration of Guiding Principles on the Use of Space Broadcasting for the Free Flow of Information, the Spread of Education and Greater Cultural Exchange.*[53] Three main articles established the declaration's restrictive framework. Although urging states to take into account the principle of freedom of information, Article IX (1) recognized the necessity that states "reach or promote prior agreements concerning direct satellite broadcasting to the population of countries other than the country of origin of the transmission." Concurring, Article VI (2) affirmed the right of each state to determine the content of educational programs broadcast by satellite to its people. The same paragraph supported the right of the receiving state, where programming is produced in co-operation with other countries, to take part in the planning and production on an equal footing with those other states. This equal access provision did not propose any specific arrangements. Within that framework, Article VIII of the UNESCO declaration called for broadcasters and their national, regional and international associations to cooperate in both the production and exchange of programs and the training of technical and program personnel.

The provisions of the UNESCO declaration were not legally binding upon the space powers; rather, they represented the consensus of opinion within UNESCO regarding satellite broadcast regulation. As such, the document served as a general framework for the discussions on direct broadcast control that were conducted during subsequent sessions of the Working Group and the CPUOS Legal Subcommittee.

Renewal of the Working Group's Mandate: The Fourth Session

At the end of its third session, the Working Group had not recommended renewal of its mandate, and consequently had ceased functioning because of the lack of progress and the polemical tone of the debates during the first three sessions. However, the 1971 ITU Convention, the Soviet draft convention and preparations for the UNESCO declaration added new fuel to the debate. When the General Assembly instructed CPUOS to begin work on the elaboration of principles to govern direct broadcasting, it also authorized the Working Group to convene for a fourth time to consider the new initiatives.[54]

When the fourth session convened in New York in June 1973 the Working Group had no clear mandate. Ordinarily the full Outer Space Committee would have met prior to the Working Group session to formulate assignments for the Working Group. When the Working Group opened its meetings, however, CPUOS had not met since the adoption of the resolution calling upon CPUOS to elaborate principles governing direct broadcasting. After some debate, the Working Group accepted the suggestion of its chairman, Olof Rydbeck, to offer advice to the Outer Space Committee regarding the elaboration of such principles.[55] In this context, the Working Group considered the presentations before it.

Perhaps the most important contribution made at the Working Group was the alternative draft declaration proposed jointly by the Swedish and Canadian delegations. Known officially as "The Draft Principles Governing Direct Television Broadcasting by Satellite,"[56] the Swedish-Canadian proposal attempted to reconcile the free flow of information with national sovereignty through the application of the basic principles of cooperation and participation. Like the Soviet draft convention, the joint Swedish-Canadian proposal would have required the broadcaster to secure the consent of the recipient state:

> Direct television broadcasting by satellite to any foreign State shall be undertaken only with the consent of that State. The consenting State shall have the right to participate in activities which involve coverage of territory under its jurisdiction and

control. This participation shall be governed by appropriate international arrangements between the States involved. . . .[57]

The draft declaration did not, however, include an explicit program code. Instead, Article VIII would have mandated participation of the recipient state in "the scheduling, content, production and exchange of programmes and all other aspects, including if appropriate, the training of technical and programme personnel."[58] The combination of prior consent and participation provisions would have nullified the potential for offensive program content, while permitting the participatory states to tailor programming to their respective needs. Although the prior consent provision was comparable to that proposed in the Soviet draft, the Swedish-Canadian draft would have permitted interested states to consent to any type of programming, while the Soviets advocated the establishment of prohibitions against specific categories of content.[59]

The Swedish-Canadian draft declaration also would have distinguished between technically unavoidable spillover and the intentional transmission of television signals to a foreign country. While the prior consent clause would not have operated in the case of unavoidable spillover, the draft declaration specified that the consent and participation provisions were to be applicable in situations:

(a) where coverage of the territory of a foreign State entails radiation of the satellite signal beyond the limits considered technically unavoidable under the Radio Regulations of the International Telecommunication Union; or
(b) where notwithstanding the technical unavoidability of spillover to the territory of a foreign State, the satellite broadcast is aimed specifically at an audience in that State within the area of spillover.[60]

If any state concluded that another was violating the principles set forth above, the joint document would have authorized the former to call upon the latter to enter into consultations regarding the alleged violations. If the consultations did not reach a mutually acceptable settlement, the aggrieved state would have been entitled to seek a settlement through the established procedures for the resolution of disputes "such as conciliation, mediation, arbitration or judicial settlement."[61]

The Swedish-Canadian draft appears to be a useful compromise between the Soviet and American positions. The proposal contains an explicit prior consent provision, similar to that sought by the Soviets, but it omits the controls on program content so vehemently opposed by the American delegation. Nonetheless, the omission is potentially compatible with the Soviet position, since the shared control of specific programming could serve as an effective substitute. The joint proposal also assures American broadcasters that they would not be forbidden to transmit commercial programming to other nations on the basis of objections based on content, provided they were able to persuade the receiving state to consent to receive direct broadcasting. In addition, a state irradiated by spillover resulting from consented transmission between two other states could not interfere with the transmissions on the ground that it had not also consented, if the spillover were technically unavoidable and not specifically directed at the complaining state. Finally, the fact that the document did not authorize censorship or contain a list of proscribed programs would seem to ease the American constitutional objections to international broadcast regulation.

Because the fourth session of the Working Group had no clear mandate, its report took no position on any of the materials presented. Instead, it merely stated in general terms the main positions in each issue, without specifying details of any position or even noting which countries took a particular position. The Working Group recommended that it be convened again prior to the thirteenth session of the Legal Sub-Committee scheduled for May 1974, and that it be empowered to make specific recommendations to the sub-committee.[62]

The Fifth Session of the Working Group

Both CPUOS and the General Assembly accepted the recommendations of the fourth Working Group that a fifth session be convened to develop specific recommendations designed to assist the Legal Sub-Committee in its efforts to elaborate principles governing direct satellite broadcasting.[63]

The participants in the fifth session extended the progress made by the fourth Working Group away from the hostility that characterized previous debate on the issue. Both the Soviet Union and the United States assumed more moderate positions at this session of the Working Group. Implicitly conceding that the elaboration of guiding principles might facilitate development of the technology, the United

States introduced its own draft declaration of principles to the Working Group. Framed in general terms, the American "Draft Principles on Direct Broadcast Satellites"[64] did not attempt to enumerate illegal broadcast applications. In contrast to the Soviet document, the American proposal took a positive approach, encouraging rather than limiting the use of direct broadcast satellites. The draft recognized the need for direct broadcasting to develop within the limits imposed the ITU technical parameters and procedures, as well as by international law, including the United Nations Charter and the *Outer Space Treaty*.[65] In its proposal the United States also included the principle that direct broadcasting should be carried out in a manner both compatible with the maintenance of international peace and sensitive to the differences among cultures.[66] Within that framework the American delegation proposed that the evolving technology be applied so as to "encourage and expand the free and open exchange of information and ideas."[67] Implementation of the fundamental principle of the free flow of information was to be achieved by promoting access of every state to both transmitting and receiving facilities insofar as technical obstacles could be overcome.[68] The organizational and programming barriers were to be overcome through cooperative efforts of international organizations and regional broadcasting associations,[69] with any disputes to be resolved by established procedures.[70] Finally, the draft principles introduced by the United States delegation called upon the United Nations and its member states to "review the questions of the use of satellites for international direct television broadcasting if practical experience indicates the need for such a review."[71]

From the beginning of the direct broadcast debate, the basic tenets of the American position had been the free flow of information, deferral of regulation until concrete problems have arisen, and application of the evolving technology through regional cooperation. Thus, in one sense, the proposed principles simply formalized the previously established position. Nonetheless, the American draft represented an important step toward compromise. Until the Working Group's fifth session, the United States had opposed any attempt to establish limitations, whether binding or not, on direct broadcasting. By introducing its own set of draft principles, the United States accepted the proposition that the establishment of such nonbinding principles would facilitate the development of the technology. The American proposal also recognized for the first time the need to include a provision for broad access in order to ensure the two-way flow envisioned in the principle of free flow of information. Although conditioned upon the ability to overcome unspecified "practical difficulties," the shared access principle represented another step toward resolution of the direct broadcast controversy.

At the fifth session of the Working Group, the Soviet Union also took a more moderate position, presenting its own draft declaration of principles.[72] The substantive provisions were essentially identical to those of the 1972 draft convention, with two exceptions. The first exception was the draft declaration's omission of the listing of proscribed categories of program content in Article VI of the draft convention.[73] Although the specific listing is omitted, the general proscriptions of programs promoting militarism, racial hatred and cultural subversion contained in Article IV of the convention are retained in Article IV of the draft declaration, leaving the scope or effect of the limits on program content substantially unaffected.

A second difference between the two drafts relates to the issue of spillover. Under Article VIII (2) of the 1972 draft convention, any state believing itself subjected to unintentional radiation would have been entitled only to request consultations with the broadcasting state. The draft declaration would have authorized the offended state to compel immediate consultations regarding program content if the unintentional spillover were receivable in its territory by ordinary receivers or receivers augmented by simple devices.[74] Both drafts would have proscribed any intentional broadcast unless authorized by prior agreement between the broadcasting and receiving states.[75]

The final difference between the two Soviet drafts is found in the remedial provisions. Article IX (1) of the 1972 draft convention would have permitted any party to the convention to

> employ the means at its disposal to counteract illegal television broadcasting of which it is the object, not only in its own territory but also in outer space and other areas beyond the limits of the national jurisdiction of any State,

leaving open the possibility that an offended state might consider itself entitled to destroy the satellite relaying allegedly unlawful programming.[76] The counterpart to Article IX (1) in the draft declaration limits the response of the complainant state to those "measures which are recognized as legal under international law."[77]

Despite the near identity between the operative provisions of the 1972 draft convention and the 1974 draft declaration, the former represents a moderation of the Soviet position. By accepting a non-binding declaration, rather than a treaty, as the appropriate mode for expressing an international consensus, the Soviets moved toward compromise with the American and Swedish-Canadian positions.

In contrast to earlier reports, the Working Group's fifth session reported some progress toward resolution of the direct broadcast controversy, with the announcement of a general consensus on the issue of the general goals of direct broadcasting, the applicability of international law, the rights and benefits of states, the principle of international cooperation, and the issue of state responsibility.[78] On the remaining major issues the Working Group was unable to report a consensus. Consequently, its fifth session report merely restated the main positions taken on those issues during the debate. When the fifth session ended, the sharpest division remaining was over the question of prior consent. The delegations remained divided into three main factions on the issue of prior consent, with the largest group favoring a legal regime granting the receiving state the right to deny its consent. That group argued that prior consent is consistent with the recognized right of each state to regulate its own communications system, and that a prior consent regime would avoid contravention of national broadcasting legislation.[79] The same faction also noted that the international community had already adopted the principle of prior consent when it adopted Article 7, § 428A of the ITU Radio Regulations at the 1971 WARC-ST Conference.[80]

The second major group maintained that a clear distinction must be drawn between direct broadcasts intentionally transmitted to a foreign state and those received there as a result of unavoidable spillover. In the first case, it was argued, prior consent should be required, because the principle of sovereignty gives each state the right to determine the form of its own political, economic and social systems, and therefore, the flow of information in its territory. Further, the inequality of opportunity to use direct broadcast technology strengthens the need for the protection which would be provided in a regime based on the concept of prior consent.[81]

The third major faction rejected the principle of prior consent altogether. These delegations argued that the right of prior consent would give the receiving state the authority to veto the transmission of any given program, thereby progressively undermining the principle of the free flow of information set forth in Article 19 of the Universal Declaration of Human Rights.[82] Also, the imposition of a regime based on prior consent would inhibit full realization of the benefits of direct broadcast technology, particularly for domestic systems, if the principle were applied to spillover.[83]

Despite its inability to resolve this discord on the question of prior consent, the delegations to the Working Group were able to agree that participation and access of receiving states to direct broadcast systems might ease many of the concerns expressed.[84]

On the spillover issue, two main positions remained at the end of the Working Group's fifth session. The first group argued that since some spillover would be unavoidable, international principles should be elaborated to minimize international conflict. The other faction responded that technical developments might eliminate most problems created by spillover before individual reception in spillover areas will have become posssible, thus obviating the need for a legal framework to resolve spillover disputes, particularly when technical procedures are already available under the auspices of the ITU.[85]

The last key issue upon which the delegations were unable to establish a consensus was the question whether a set of international principles governing direct broadcasting should proscribe certain categories of program content. One group of delegations argued that any such legal regime should combine a prior consent provision with an obligation to exclude from direct broadcasts programs which would threaten international peace, or which would promote war, militarism or social hatred, or which would undermine the foundation of the local civilization in any way.[86] The listing of programs to be banned resembled those contained in both the Soviet Union's 1972 draft convention and its 1974 draft declaration of principles.[87]

The second main position was similar to that advanced by the Swedish and Canadian delegations in previous sessions. The report of the fifth Working Group noted that some delegations had espoused the view that because of political, economic, social and cultural differences among states, the establishment of general principles or objective criteria for applying those principles would be very difficult, if not impossible. Further, it was argued that the inclusion of a principle of prior consent in a legal regime governing direct broadcasting would render restrictions on program content unnecessary, particularly if prior consent were complemented by a principle providing for participation of the receiving state. [88] The related view was expressed that, if the conduct of direct broadcasting was to be governed by the key principle of international cooperation, the inclusion of limitations effectively dictating program content would be inappropriate.[89]

During the debates regarding program content the question of the permissibility of commercial programming or advertising arose. One faction supported the view that to the extent direct broadcast advertising created a demand in the receiving state for a particular product or in any other way generated conditions unfavorable to local industry, such programming would be undesirable and should be permitted only when expressly permitted by the receiving state.[90] Other states argued that no distinction should be drawn between advertising or commercial programming and any other category of program content.[91]

The Deliberations of the CPUOS Legal Sub-Committee

Under General Assembly Resolution 3182 (XXVIII), the fifth session of the Working Group was authorized to submit specific recommendations to the CPUOS Legal Sub-Committee prior to its thirteenth session in order to facilitate the sub-committee's efforts to elaborate principles governing the use of direct broadcast satellites.[92] Burdened with other work when it opened its thirteenth session in Geneva on 6 May 1974, the Legal Sub-Committee established a working group of the whole to consider the fifth report of the Working Group on Direct Broadcast Satellites.[93] Limiting its consideration to those issues upon which the Working Group had obtained a general consensus, the sub-committee's working group formulated five principles in the same subject areas, but was unable to reach complete agreement on any of them.[94]

The CPUOS Legal Sub-Committee met again in February and March 1975 for further consideration of principles to govern direct broadcast satellites. When the fourteenth session ended, a working group of the Legal Sub-Committee issued a report[95] considering all of the major issues related to direct broadcasting rather than limiting itself to those debated during the thirteenth session of the Legal Sub-Committee.[96] Representing the latest stage of the direct broadcast debate, the fourteenth session report presents a series of draft principles, some of which demonstrate general agreement while others are as yet officially in dispute. Among those issues upon which agreement was reached were the applicability of international law, the rights and benefits of states with respect to direct broadcast technology, international cooperation and state responsibility. Despite preliminary accord in these areas, formal disagreement continued in the key areas of prior consent, program content, participation and spillover.

On the question of the purposes and objectives of direct broadcasting, the evolution of the debate toward agreement suffered a setback. The Working Group had reached a consensus at its fifth session that direct broadcasting should serve the purposes of maintaining international peace, facilitating economic and social development, and promoting intercultural understanding.[97] It concluded that states "should carry out direct television broadcasting by satellite exclusively in a manner comparable with these objectives."[98] However, the Legal Sub-Committee's draft presented two alternatives, one making the policy objective mandatory, while the other diminished the specificity of the obligation by deleting the express requirement that direct broadcasting be conducted in a manner exclusively compatible with the stated goals.[99]

The consensus established at both the fifth session of the Working Group and the thirteenth session of the Legal Sub-Committee regarding the applicability of international law was not jeopardized by further discussion. The report of the fourteenth session of the subcommittee recognized that the United Nations Charter, the Outer Space Treaty, and the International Telecommunication Convention with its Radio Regulations had established general limits within which direct broadcasting would have to evolve.[100] There was, however, some dispute whether the principle should state that direct broadcasting "shall be" or "should be" conducted within those limits. Since all of the proposals under consideration would, if approved, become non-binding declarations of principle, the conflict is not insurmountable.

The third issue upon which a consensus was achieved at the fifth meeting of the Working Group was the question of the distribution of rights and benefits of direct broadcasting. The delegations agreed that all states have an equal right to conduct or authorize direct broadcasting, and that all states are entitled to share in the benefits of the new technology, regardless of their degree of economic or scientific development.[101] The sharing of benefits thus foreseen was to include increasing opportunities for access to direct broadcast systems, based on specific agreements between the states concerned.[102] The basic consensus was not disturbed at the fourteenth session of the Legal Sub-Committee. Two sub-issues were, however, left unresolved.[103] First, some delegations advocated inclusion of a provision limiting direct broadcast activities to either governmental agencies or entities under government supervision. The inclusion of such a provision would be important to the imposition of the international liability of states, and would therefore be an essential part of any regime designed to impose enforceable restrictions on program content. In all of its proposals, the Soviet Union has consistently sought to restrict direct broadcast activities to those entities controlled by their respective governments.[104] The United States has resisted such attempts, because it supports the use of direct broadcast satellites for commercial programming. A second sub-issue arose regarding whether the right of equitable sharing in the benefits of direct broadcasting should be stated in obligatory or normative terms.[105]

Strong recognition was given to the principle of international cooperation in the report of the fifth Working Group which described cooperation as a "touchstone for the development and use of direct television broadcasting by satellite," and called upon states and international organizations, both governmental and non-governmental, to make every effort to enhance the capabilities of interested states to take advantage of direct broadcast technology.[106] Disagreement surfaced, however, in Legal Sub-Committee discussions regarding the application of the principle. Some delegations argued that direct broadcasting should be "based on" international cooperation, while others advocated a regime in which direct broadcasting would "encourage" international cooperation.[107] The former position was consistent with the Swedish-Canadian position that international cooperation is essential to the realization of the educational potential of direct broadcasting, and that any set of governing principles should include a general prior consent provision. The position that direct broadcasting should "encourage" international cooperation expressed optimism regarding the educational value of direct broadcasting, but did not mention – and presumably implicitly rejected – the principle of prior consent.

The final area in which consensus was obtained by the fourteenth session of the Legal Sub-Committee was the issue of state responsibility. The delegations at the fifth Working Group had agreed that states should bear international responsibility for direct broadcast activities as described in Article VI of the Outer Space Treaty.[108] Beyond that point disagreement on the issue surfaced. Some delegations argued that a state should bear international responsibility for all activities carried out by its nationals, regardless of whether the government had any authority under its constitution and laws. Other delegations rejected that argument, contending that such a principle would have made states internationally liable for the content of programming, a result which would have been unacceptable, especially for those states whose broadcasting entities were not subject to state control.[109]

The Legal Sub-Committee's drafting group resolved the disagreement and achieved a complete consensus regarding the question of state responsibility for direct broadcasting. Building on the foundation laid in the Outer Space Treaty, the draft principle accepted by the drafting group would impose responsibility on a state to ensure that all activities carried out by the state or under its jurisdiction are conducted in conformity with the whole set of draft principles.[110] Where direct broadcasting is carried out by an international organization, international responsibility would be borne both by the organization and by individual member states.[111]

Despite agreement on a number of questions, the Legal Sub-Committee failed to achieve a consensus on several key issues. The issues of prior consent and participation proved insoluble for the Legal Sub-Committee as it had for the fifth Working Group.[112] After the sub-committee's fourteenth session, two main positions remained. Proponents of the first position would prohibit direct broadcasts to any state unless that state had consented. If consent were given, the consenting state would have the right to participate in activities related to coverage of its territory. These consent and participation principles would not apply, however, where coverage of the foreign state resulted from technically unavoidable spillover as defined in the ITU's Radio Regulations.[113] This position appears to correspond to the principles proposed by the Swedish and Canadian delegations to the fourth session of the Working Group.[114]

The second faction rejected the principle of prior consent, preferring instead a legal regime based on an undefined foundation of participation and cooperation.[115] The sole concrete element of cooperation approved by the second faction called upon the broadcasting state to consult with any receiving state on the request of the latter; however, the principle proposed would call for such consultations only with respect to restrictions imposed by the broadcasting state.[116]

A similar division was reported on the issue of spillover. One position would require the broadcasting state to use "all technical means available to reduce, to the maximum extent practicable, the radiation over the territory of other countries" unless a prior agreement has been reached between the broadcasting and receiving states.[117] The other position imposes no requirement, but merely states that "all reasonable means should be used to reduce to a minimum any unintended radiation of the territory of other countries."[118] The latter position is consistent with the unlimited regime advocated by the United States, while the former would be an integral part of the prior consent regime proposed in the Swedish-Canadian drafts.

On the issue of program content, the American position merged with the Swedish-Canadian positions despite the conflict between the two on the question of prior consent. They proposed a principle calling for cooperation between states with respect to programming, program content, production and exchange of programs.[119] The Legal Sub-Committee draft also reports a position, like that advocated consistently throughout the debates by the Soviet delegation, which would require states to exclude, regardless of other agreements, programming material which: (1) is detrimental to the maintenance of international peace; (2) publicizes war, militarism, nazism or racial hatred; (3) is aimed at interfering in the domestic affairs of other states; or (4) undermines local culture in any way.[120] A third disputed paragraph relating to program content would permit commercial advertising only on the basis of prior agreements.[121]

Closely related to the questions of prior consent and program content is a draft principle defining unlawful or inadmissible broadcasts. The first clause of the draft principle reported by the sub-committee is taken verbatim from Article VI of the draft principles presented to the fifth session of the Working Group by the Soviet delegation.[122] It provides that the international liability of states arises when either broadcasts are conducted without the express consent of the receiving state, or the broadcasts contain proscribed material, or when unintentional spillover is compounded by the broadcasting state's failure to enter into appropriate consultations with the receiving state.[123] The draft principle again drew from the Soviet proposals to the fifth Working Group when it authorized the receiving state to take any remedial measures recognized as legal under international law, without placing any priority upon negotiation, conciliation, arbitration or any of the other conflict resolution techniques preferred in the United Nations framework.[124] The states which opposed a direct broadcast regime based on program content limitations or prior consent, and consequently opposed outlawing any broadcast, rejected the draft principle in toto.

Prospects for Resolution of the Direct Broadcast Controversy

When the direct broadcast debates began in 1963, they were not characterized by any special sense of urgency, since direct satellite broadcasting was neither technologically nor economically feasible in the foreseeable future. Since then the pressure to impose international controls to prevent potential abusive applications of the technology has increased sharply, primarily because of rapid, highly visible technological progress. NASA's experimental communication satellite programs, especially those using Application Technology Satellites (ATS) 1, 3, 5 and 6, and the operational successes of the Intelsat system have been particularly instrumental in overcoming technological barriers to direct broadcasting.[125] These experiments, combined with ambitious plans for more advanced experimentation, including the Indian-American SITE experiment and the Canadian-American CTS projects,[126] have motivated other countries to develop their own experimental or operational direct broadcast programs. At the Panel Meeting on Satellite Broadcast Systems for Education convened by CPUOS in Tokyo in April 1974, Japan announced that it would launch an experimental direct broadcast satellite in 1976,[127] and the Canadian and Brazilian delegations outlined plans to launch new domestic satellites to facilitate communications with their vast, remote hinterlands.[128] The French delegation offered free time on its Symphonie satellite to French-speaking African nations for educational programming,[129] and the European Space Research Organization announced plans to establish an operational regional broadcast system by 1980.[130] Indonesia and Iran announced long-range preparations for educational television broadcasting via satellite, and Malaysia discussed its program to install 5,500 television and radio receivers and 2,000 electric generators in rural locations in order to improve its national educational system.[131] Although the Malaysians plan to rely on terrestrial distribution, they could become users of the Japanese satellite if costs prove to be sufficiently low. Just before the Tokyo meeting, the Soviet Union sent Statsionar I satellite into synchronous orbit over the Indian Ocean in March of 1974, probably indicating that the Soviets have begun to operationalize the long-awaited Intersputnik satellite system through which the Soviet Union proposes to provide broadcast service to developing nations.[132]

Although the technological developments justify some increase in an international institutional response, the magnitude of the increase seems disproportionately large in comparison to the imminence of potentially abusive applications. Examination of the United Nations debates in direct broadcasting indicate the presence of three factors which have disrupted the processes which normally operate to establish an equilibrium between the forces which motivate technological development and those which support the creation of a regulatory institution to control abuses of the evolving technology.

The first of these is the failure to gauge accurately the relationship between specific experimental developments and the final technical configuration of a direct broadcast system which could be used for the purposes cited by proponents of a restrictive international legal regime. For example, the report of the first Working Group concluded that satellite transmission of television signals direct to unaugmented home receivers was "not foreseen for the period 1970-1985," because present technology did not possess the means to transmit sufficiently powerful signals from satellites.[133] A number of governments erroneously interpreted this statement at future meetings of the Working Group to mean that telecasting directly to home installations would begin in 1985. Actually, the Working Group concluded that it would not be economically practical at any time before 1985, and perhaps not for some time after that.[134] National position papers submitted to later sessions of the Working Group based their analyses of the direct broadcast issues on the figures established during the first session. Not always accurate, the initial findings alarmed those nations concerned about propaganda and cultural imperialism, and may have added a note of urgency to their draft recommendations for the Working Group.

The second factor which has upset the normal equilibrium between technological and regulatory interests is the failure to assess realistically the limitations imposed on operational direct broadcasting by economic factors. In those more developed countries which have equipped themselves at great cost with an extensive terrestrial network for the distribution of television programming, transition to operational use of direct broadcast satellites would entail a radical realignment of the existing distribution patterns. In the United States, for example, transmission to home receivers would eliminate the need for local television stations, the common carrier land lines connecting the local stations with the central program production facilities of the major television network organizations and cable television companies. Understandably, therefore, special interest groups have opposed the use of direct satellite broadcasting for national programming. Until a reliable economic analysis balancing the cost of the necessary realignment against the benefits of a direct broadcast network has been made, countries already possessing extensive television distribution networks are not likely to make a rapid transition to direct broadcasting.

For those reasons, the newly evolved technology will probably be most beneficial to the less developed countries. Such states generally have television broadcast facilities which serve only a few major cities. The construction of a comprehensive national network using conventional ground facilities is often economically unfeasible due to the present cost of hardware. The broadcast satellite can dramatically reduce these costs, especially when serving a large geographic area, difficult terrain, or a widely dispersed population.[135] In addition, a direct broadcast television network could become operational in a fraction of the time needed to construct a terrestrial system based on cable and microwave. Both of these factors recommend direct broadcasting to such nations as Brazil, India and Indonesia, where topographical features prevent the construction of truly national television systems. Once operational, a direct broadcast system could contribute significantly to national development by facilitating national integration and improving the quality of the country's educational system.[136] In addition, users of direct broadcasting would probably reap other less direct benefits, including national economic development and access to foreign and international information resources.

Despite the relatively large range of advantages to be derived from direct broadcasting by those countries which do not yet have an extensive investment in terrestrial distribution systems, two main economic impediments still delay operational use by those countries. First, the cost of operating a direct broadcasting satellite system will still remain prohibitively expensive for individual less developed countries. At the United Nations Panel Meeting on Satellite Broadcasting Systems for Education, sponsored by CPUOS in Tokyo during February and March, 1974, the UNESCO representative presented an analysis of the financial requirements for satellite broadcasting, concluding that a viable system dedicated exclusively to educational television would require a population base of 100 million, assuming a gross national product of $ 200 per capita.[137] He further noted that other combinations of population and income could lead to viability, and that Iran, for example, could support a viable direct broadcast educational network with a population of thirty million, but $ 1,000 per capita income.[138] By the same formula, if the annual per capita income were $ 100 – the prevailing income level of many African and Asian nations – it would take a population of 200 million to support the satellite system. In these cases, therefore, the introduction of satellite television will depend upon cooperative arrangements on a regional basis,[139] on the use of multipurpose satellites capable of telephone and data switching, as well as television broadcasting, and on international financial and technical assistance.

The second impediment is the shortage and high cost of ground receivers. At present, few Third World states have an adequate number of receivers to make any form of television broadcasting useful. In Asia, for example, only Japan and Singapore have enough television sets per capita to meet the minimum standard established by UNESCO as necessary if television is to serve as a useful educational tool.[140] The shortage of standard receivers is compounded by the fact that, at the current state-of-the-art, standard ground receivers require extensive augmentation to pick up the relatively weak signals transmitted by the satellites now in orbit. Augmentation increases the price of both individual receivers and the entire receiver network.

The report of the first Working Group estimated the cost of modifications to standard television receivers which would be utilized as community receivers at 150 dollars, while the cost for modification of home receivers was estimated to fall between 40 and 270 dollars.[141] The high cost of the receivers places them beyond the reach of the vast majority of individuals in nearly every country. Hence, in the absence of substantial governmental assistance, economic factors will prevent the establishment of a network of receivers which is both capable of receiving signals broadcast directly from outer space and large enough to justify the enormous investment needed to establish the space segment of a direct broadcast network. The necessity of governmental assistance in establishing the receiver network facilitates governmental control and hence provides added protection against potentially abusive applications.

The third factor disturbing the balance between technological and regulatory pressures is the failure of direct broadcasting antagonists to understand the extent to which existing technical regulations perform the functions of the proposed international legal principles. The most important examples are the ITU regulations which restrict satellite telecasting to frequencies several times higher than those normally used by standard television receivers,[142] and those which require the broadcaster to use all means technically available to reduce as much as possible the signal radiation over the territory of other countries in the absence of an agreement to the contrary.[143] The first group of regulations increases the complexity and, therefore, the cost of the necessary receivers, thus reinforcing the economic factors limiting the application of direct broadcast technology. The second group is arguably identical in effect to the prior consent regime supported by advocates of a restrictive approach to the technology.

The ideal international institutional response must strike an effective balance between the interests motivating technological progress and those advocating a restrictive regulatory response. At present an imbalance exists in favor of regulation, with the consequences, first, that the implementation of the technology is likely to be deterred, and second, that agreement in the international arena is unlikely until an equilibrium is established. While policy considerations may dictate some regulation at this time, any regulatory scheme should reflect a realistic assessment of the impediments to technology applications already established by technical and economic factors and existing regulation. Although the delegates to the fourteenth session of the Legal Sub-Committee were unable to reach a consensus on the key issues of prior consent, program content and spillover, the foundation for compromise seems to be present, and an effective accomodation of the competing interests upon that foundation should bring to fruition attempts to establish preliminary international regulatory structures to further the development of direct broadcast technology.

The Utility of a Draft Declaration

A major breakthrough in the direct broadcast debate occurred at the fifth session of the Working Group when both the United States and the Soviet Union submitted draft declarations of principles. By doing so the Soviet Union relinquished—at least for the moment—its demand that the community of nations establish a binding international legal regime restricting the use of direct broadcast satellites. At the same time the American delegation implicitly conceded for the first time that a non-binding statement of general principles would not interfere with development of the technology.

The establishment of an international consensus on a nonbinding declaration of principles seems a sound foundation upon which to build experimental and operational experience. First, the potential abuses which have caused the demand for limitations on the applications of direct broadcast technology are not yet imminent in any practical sense, thereby mitigating any need for immediate resort to a formal convention, rather than a declaration of principles. For similar reasons, the structuring of a definitive international regime which will effectively control possible abuse while providing the optimum conditions for procuring the benefits of direct broadcasting is at present impossible, because the actual problems which will be encountered cannot be accurately foreseen. Consequently, the apparent international consensus not to establish fixed principles at this time seems desirable. Nonetheless, preliminary attempts to formulate the guidelines eventually to be imposed should keep pace with technological developments. Initial formulation of guiding principles in a non-binding declaration would both permit examination of them in light of developing practice and give notice to broadcasters, whether governmental or civilian, of an initial consensus within the international community regarding broadcasting standards which will harden or soften in response to the problems which are caused by initial broadcasting practices.

A third advantage of using a non-binding declaration rather than a formal convention is that it will assure receiving states of some protection against the potential for abusive programming without unduly restricting the development of direct broadcast technology. Such assurances are necessary to enable those states concerned about propaganda or other types of offensive programming to take the steps necessary to permit them to share in the benefits without excessive risk either to its investment or to national security. If a government is to invest the necessarily large sums of money to establish an effective network of receivers, it will seek assurances that on completion the receivers will pick up programming which is sufficiently beneficial to justify such a large investment.

At the same time, such assurances cannot be so restrictive as to stifle development of the technology. If the initial guidelines are sufficiently restrictive either in their form or their language to suggest to the governmental and commercial planners who are empowered to decide whether or not to develop international direct broadcasting that the investment would be wasted because of international legal restriction, development could well be diverted, with the consequence that the potential benefits of direct broadcasting would be either lost altogether, or limited to those few states able to fund their own systems.[144] A non-binding declaration could provide the necessary assurances for non-space powers without stifling the development of direct broadcasting.

Substantive Principles

After determining the form of international guidelines for the regulation of direct satellite broadcasting, the second major task in resolving the direct broadcast debate is to determine the content of those guidelines. Negotiations in the Working Group and the Legal Sub-Committee have failed thus far to reach agreement on the key questions of prior consent, program content, spillover and equal access,[145] and the resolution of these points of conflict would make possible the establishment of a consensus on a full range of general principles to guide the development of direct broadcast technology. The evolution of national positions during the fifth session of the Working Group and the fourteenth meeting of the Legal Sub-Committee suggests that agreement will be reached in the next few years on a set of principles designed to protect the interests of those states concerned with direct broadcasting's potential for abuse without imposing undue restriction on, and consequently delaying, the development and operational implementation of the technology.

The discussion below examines the points of conflict remaining after the March 1975 meeting of the Legal Sub-Committee and indicates the direction of the current trend toward consensus on each issue.

Purposes and Objectives

At the fifth session of the Working Group, the delegations agreed that direct broadcasting should have as its goals the promotion of international peace, the facilitation of global economic and social development and the furtherance of intercultural understanding.[146] The report concluded that all direct broadcasting activities should be conducted exclusively in a manner compatible with those goals.[147] However, at the fourteenth session of the Legal Sub-Committee, one group of delegates argued that the policy should be made mandatory, while others contended that the principle in question should remain a non-obligatory statement of an ideal.[148]

Since one of the main goals of direct broadcasting agreed upon by the Working Group is to bring to all participating states the benefits of improved educational opportunities, and increased flow of information, news and cultural events among nations, all for the purpose of promoting international peace, the principle should state that direct broadcasting *shall* be carried out exclusively in a manner designed to facilitate that goal. The statement of that policy in mandatory terms would constitute an important step toward allaying fears of offensive broadcast content, but would not affect adversely the expressed intentions of broadcasters.

International Cooperation

When the Legal Sub-Committee adjourned its fourteenth session, dispute remained whether direct broadcasting activities "shall be based on" or "should encourage" international cooperation.[149] Adoption of the second alternative would introduce into the declaration of principles a provision which would be repetitious of the statement made above regarding the purposes and objectives of direct broadcasting. Approval of the first alternative, however, would indicate the basic means by which the purposes and objectives are to be achieved.

Applicability of International Law

Still unresolved is the issue whether the draft principle regarding the applicability of international law should state that direct broadcasting "should be" conducted in accordance with generally recognized rules or whether such a provision should impose on states the obligation to ensure the compliance of activities within their jurisdiction.[150] In addition, disagreement remained relating to the inclusion among the principles to be applied of the Universal Declaration of Human Rights, the International Covenant on Civil and Political Rights and the Declaration on Principles of International Law Concerning Friendly Relations and Cooperation Among States.[151]

Article III of the 1967 Outer Space Treaty appears to resolve the first question by obligating states who are parties to the treaty to conduct activities in outer space in accordance with international law.[152] In addition, two policy considerations support the inclusion of mandatory language. First, the obligation of states to comply with international law would not be diminished by omission of an express statement of the obligation. Second, the expression in a declaration of principles of a duty among states to conduct space activities in accordance with traditional international legal principles would not upset the balance proposed below between sovereignty and the free flow of information.

Although the inclusion of general references to the Universal

Declaration of Human Rights, the International Covenant on Civil and Political Rights, and the Declaration of Principles of International Law Concerning Friendly Relations and Cooperation Among States could be justified as an additional step toward the establishment as a rule of customary international law of an international obligation to protect human rights, the practicalities of international negotiation in the present case seem to indicate that reference will be made only to those principles particularly relevant to the direct broadcast controversy, namely sovereignty, non-intervention, and the free flow of information.

Limited Prior Consent

The growing pressure for protection against real or imagined abuses of the technology suggests that the final declaration of principles probably will center around a provision which would permit direct broadcasting only when the receiving state has given its express consent. Nearly every proposal before the Working Group and the Legal Sub-Committee has recommended the establishment of a prior consent regime,[153] and the United States has been the only major dissenter.

Three main arguments have been raised against the adoption of a prior consent rule. First, prior consent is said to abrogate the principle of the free flow of information embodied in the Universal Declaration of Human Rights and other international instruments.[154] However, the principle, even if established as binding upon all nations, is not absolute. In the International Covenant on Civil and Political Rights, for example, Article 19(2) delineates the free flow principle. In the third paragraph of that article, however, certain restrictions are permitted, including those for the preservation of the rights and reputation of others, and the protection of the national security, the public order, and public health and morals. Also imposing limits on the free flow principle, Article 20 provides:

> 1. Any propaganda for war shall be prohibited by law.
> 2. Any advocacy of national, racial or religious hatred that constitutes incitement to discrimination, hostility or violence shall be prohibited by law.[155]

Thus, the argument that the principle of free flow of information would be improperly abrogated by a principle granting a receiving state a right of prior consent may exaggerate the scope and legal significance of the principle. A better approach would be to provide for a flexible balance with other principles.[156]

The second major argument against the prior consent principle is that any restrictive regulation is, for the near future at least, premature. The problems likely to arise with the use of direct satellite broadcasting cannot be effectively evaluated at this time, first, because the necessary technology is not yet adequately developed, and second, because no country has concrete plans to deploy an operational system capable of broadcasting directly to unaugmented receivers.[157] That argument could be allayed significantly by the decision to approve a declaration of principles rather than a binding treaty.

Another argument against prior consent is that although such a rule would dispel fears of intrusive transmissions, it could also frustrate the development of direct broadcasting technology.[158] Rejection of prior consent, however, seems equally likely to hinder rather than promote technological development.[159] The United States, for example, is interested primarily in broadcasting by commercial entities. If these entities intend to broadcast normal commercial programming based on advertising, most receiving states seem unlikely to take the steps necessary to make direct broadcasting commercially feasible, especially by encouraging production and installation of augmented receivers. If these elements are absent, direct broadcasting based on commercial programming would remain unprofitable for some time. If, on the other hand, broadcasters would provide only educational programming direct broadcasting could become profitable, but only under contract with the receiving state. In that case, however, the receiving state would undoubtedly insist on some control with respect to frequencies used, broadcasting time, and at least to some extent, over the nature of the programming.

By accepting a prior consent rule, the United States could expect to derive important benefits, including the creation of an atmosphere conducive to early widespread implementation of operational direct broadcasting. The establishment of such a rule would facilitate bilateral and multilateral exchanges leading eventually to the creation of regional organizations for satellite broadcasting.[160] In addition, the United States could expect to gain support from those countries which traditionally support the free flow of information, but which have advocated a prior consent rule to prevent the imposition of one country's values on others through direct broadcasting.[161] Finally, rapid implementation would maximize the benefits the United States expects to derive from the export of direct broadcasting hardware and technical assistance.

The acceptability of a prior consent regime to proponents of the free flow principle is also dependent upon the content of other components of the legal regime. The Soviet Union, for example, has consistently tied its prior consent proposal to principles limiting program content.[162] The Swedish-Canadian proposals have omitted any mention of program content, preferring to leave any limitations to specific agreements between the broadcasting and receiving states.[163] Since the negotiations necessary for a prior consent regime would probably give the receiving state some control over content, the Swedish-Canadian approach seems likely to prevail, because it gives adequate protection against offensive programming, while avoiding the difficult and excessively time-consuming process of negotiating a set of limits on program content which would be both effective and universally acceptable.

The Swedish-Canadian prior consent rule has, however, been criticized as giving inadequate protection to the free flow of information, because it fails to place adequate limits on the receiving state's right to deny its consent. As presently drafted, the joint proposal would apparently permit the receiving state to withhold its consent arbitrarily and without any obligation to consider the principle of free flow of information.[164] In addition, the Swedish-Canadian recommendations seem to permit the receiving state to withhold its consent on a program-by-program basis. Such an extensive right of review would permit prior restraint on free speech and would, by permitting official examination of each program, unnecessarily burden the flow of information across national borders.[165]

Two sets of limitations on a strict prior consent rule will probably result from the pressure to preserve an atmosphere conducive to technological progress. First, where the broadcast signal is not actually receivable in the receiving state with available equipment, consent is not likely to be required.[166] Second, the negative effects on the free flow of information of an unlimited consent requirement could be mitigated by tailoring the requirement closely to the optimum balance between the free flow of information and the purposes for conditioning the right to broadcast on the receiving state's consent. The 1972 UNESCO declaration distinguishes among four main categories of programming, and recommends basic principles for each type. Article V (1) declares the main objective of direct broadcasting with respect to the free flow of information to be "to ensure the widest possible dissemination among the peoples of the world, of news of all countries, developed and developing alike."[167] The second paragraph of Article V imposes no requirement on news broadcasts other than to make every effort to ensure factual accuracy and to identify the source of the news broadcast, as well as of particular new items where appropriate.[168] In the case of direct broadcast news programming, the receiving state's right to consent will be limited to the right to demand assurances of the factual accuracy and identification of news sources.

Article VI of the UNESCO declaration establishes the right of a receiving state to determine the content of educational programming broadcast via satellite to its people and, in cases where such programming is produced in conjunction with other countries, to take part in the planning and production on an equal footing.[169] The receiving state's interest in preventing propagandistic or otherwise offensive programming is strongest with respect to educational programming. In that area, receiving states will probably secure a relatively unrestrained right to deny their consent.

The interest of the receiving state is somewhat weaker in the case of cultural programs, including artistic performances and sporting events. In such cases, the UNESCO declaration called for a balance between the enrichment of all cultures through cultural exchange, while respecting the value of each culture and the right of all peoples to preserve their cultures as part of the "common heritage of mankind."[170] Debates in the Legal Sub-Committee suggest the evolution of a consensus on a provision permitting the receiving state to deny its consent to cultural programming only where it can demonstrate that substantial harm to its own culture would result from transmission of the challenged program.[171]

The final programming category delineated by the UNESCO declaration related to commercial advertising. Implicitly recognizing the potentially disruptive influence of consumer-oriented advertising originating in more advanced societies, the UNESCO declaration called upon the broadcasting state to reach a specific agreement with the receiving state prior to the transmission of commercial advertising.[172] Since advertising is one of the programming areas most threatening to less developed states,[173] and since the free exchange of advertising is less essential to values underlying the free flow of information than other types of programming,[174] the establishment of a relatively unrestricted right of the receiving state to deny its consent appears probable. The inclusion of a principle giving the receiving state the right to deny its consent – subject to the conditions described above – to direct satellite broadcasts would provide an optimum balance between legitimate interests in both the free flow of information and national political and cultural integrity.

Spillover

Another criticism of the prior consent rule is that it would interfere with direct broadcasting by giving the right to deny consent not only to the intended receiving state, but also to any neighboring state inadvertently irradiated by the satellite.[175] Initially, spillover is not likely to be a major source of friction because the first direct broadcast systems will probably be national systems in large, underdeveloped countries, followed shortly by regional systems based on regional linguistic and cultural similarities.[176]

Once spillover becomes a source of conflict, however, the undesirable effects could be limited through the exercise of control by the government of the receiving state over community receivers. That solution, however, carries several undesirable consequences. First, the cost of avoiding the effects of spillover would be borne entirely by the receiving state.[177] The costs include not only the financial cost, but also the political costs of appearing to impose censorship for the benefit of the government. Second, government control of receivers would tend to subjugate freedom of information to direct and indirect assertions of national security interests.[178]

The Legal Sub-Committee is more likely to place the burden of reducing spillover on the broadcasting state, thereby providing some protection to the spillover states, while reducing the incentive for receiving states to exert international political pressure for broader restrictions. The growing consensus is based primarily on Article 7, § 428A of the Radio Regulations adopted by the ITU at its 1971 convention. Section 428A requires the broadcasting state to reduce spillover to the maximum extent practicable unless a prior agreement has been reached between the broadcasting state and the states receiving spillover.[179] Building on that foundation, the Swedish-Canadian proposal to the fourth and fifth sessions of the Working Group provided that the right of consent shall apply in those cases:

> (a) where coverage of the territory of a foreign State entails radiation of the satellite signal beyond the limits considered technically unavoidable under the Radio Regulations of the International Telecommunication Union or

(b) where notwithstanding the technical unavoidability of spill-over to the territory of a foreign State, the satellite broadcast is aimed specifically at an audience in that State within the area of spill-over; . . .[180]

The Legal Sub-Committee could yield to pressure by the United States to extend the Swedish-Canadian proposal so that the limited prior consent rule as described above would apply in all cases *except* where:

(1) the elimination of spillover is considered technically impossible under the present state of the art, as determined in accord with the ITU Radio Regulations;
(2) the direct broadcast system is entirely domestic in character; or
(3) the broadcast, although irradiating a part of the complaining state's territory, is not actually receivable using standard or easily augmented receivers readily available in the area irradiated.

A second paragraph would restore the right to deny consent where the spillover broadcast was aimed specifically at an audience within the receiving state. A third paragraph taken from the Soviet draft declaration submitted to the fifth session of the Working Group could be added to the spillover article to ensure that international cooperation and consultation will govern the relations between broadcasting and receiving states with regard to spillover:

1. If any State has reason to believe that activities connected with direct television broadcasting planned by that State will cause potentially harmful interference to other States or will lead to unintentional radiation of their territory, it shall hold appropriate consultations before undertaking such activities.
2. If a State has reason to believe that unintentional radiation of its territory will occur as a result of direct television broadcasts by another State, it may request that appropriate consultations be held. If, as a result of such unintentional radiation, foreign programmes can be received in the territory of a State by ordinary receivers or by receivers fitted with simple additional devices, the broadcasting State shall immediately enter into consultations with the former State on its request regarding the content of the programmes received.[181]

Participation or Equal Access

A further controversial issue is the question whether receiving states should participate in the use of direct broadcast systems. The 1972 UNESCO declaration of principles for direct broadcasting set forth the right of the receiving state to participate on an equal footing with any other state in the production of educational programming destined for the receiving state.[182] The Swedish-Canadian draft declaration submitted to the fifth session of the Working Group went further, giving the receiving state not only the right to deny its consent to satellite broadcasting, but also to participate in activities related to programming broadcast into its territory.[183] It has further been proposed that all states receiving broadcasts should have the right – in law and in fact – to have access to the system on an equal footing, including the rights of access to transmitters and to sufficient international assistance to enable those states to make meaningful use of the access rights.[184]

Both the UNESCO and Swedish-Canadian participation principles are intended to enhance the receiving state's ability to influence the programming broadcast to its citizens. In Article VI (2), the UNESCO version gives the receiving state the right to participate on an equal footing in the planning and production of programming, but only as an adjunct to the provision proclaiming the right of the receiving state to determine the content of educational programming.[185] By including its participation provision in the general prior consent paragraph, the Swedish-Canadian draft declaration extends the right to participate to encompass all types of programming and all stages of programming activities.[186] The inclusion of a right of participation for the purpose of ensuring the receiving state's power to affect the content of broadcasts beamed to it would alter the balance in favor of those interests demanding that the receiving states' cultural and political integrity be protected against the intrusion of unwanted foreign broadcasting over the interests in realizing the benefits of direct broadcasting through operational use. As a result, operational application would probably be delayed substantially.

A second rationale advanced for inclusion of a principle in the proposed declaration permitting the receiving state to participate in direct broadcasting over its territory is to give effect to the principle of free flow of information.[187] On numerous occasions, potential broadcasting states, particularly the United States, have based their arguments supporting an unrestrictive regulatory scheme for direct broadcasting at least partially on the contention that a restrictive regime would inhibit the free flow of information.[188]

Sound policy considerations support the integration of the free flow principle into the structure of legal principles to govern direct broadcasting. At present, the two most important requirements for effective development of satellite communication technology for operational use are, first, the uninhibited exchange and testing of information and ideas, and second, the assurance that the value of investments in development will not be nullified by the imposition of unnecessarily restrictive regulations upon innovative systems. A legal structure designed to promote rather than inhibit the free flow of information will encourage designers and planners to explore the potential uses and benefits of recent technical advances.

Viewed pragmatically, however, the principle of free flow of information is reduced to a fiction unless it is coupled with a second principle calling upon the international community to promote development of satellites and ground facilities in such a way as to facilitate access to transmitter and program production facilities by any state willing to contribute to development and operating costs. In the absence of an equal access clause, free flow of information would probably mean a unidirectional flow from the more developed countries to the less developed. The principle of free flow opposes not only unnecessary limitations on the influx of information from abroad, but also monopolization of a medium for ideological purposes.[189] That potential imbalance is the source of the fears of cultural and economic imperialism expressed by potential receiving states, with detrimental effects for both international cooperation and technology development. The inclusion of an equal access provision, however, would both allay those fears and set in motion a search for means to achieve the goal of equal access without sacrificing the interests of the broadcasting states.

Although an equal access principle is likely to be included in a declaration of principles, the lack of certainty regarding the circumstances under which operational direct broadcasting will be conducted makes necessary a particularly careful choice of language to avoid interference with the balance of interests established in the preceding discussions of the prior consent and spillover provisions. The form of the final participation provision probably will parallel the principle presented by the United States in its draft declaration submitted to the fifth session of the Working Group. This draft entitles every state to share in the benefits of direct broadcasting and provides further that such sharing "should increasingly include, as practical difficulties are overcome, opportunities for access to the use of [direct broadcasting] technology for the purpose of sending as well as receiving broadcasts."[190] As this right of access becomes available from a practical standpoint, allocation of transponder time should be made available on a non-discriminatory basis.

Presumably, a receiving state would exercise its right to obtain transponder time on a non-discriminatory basis at least initially for the purpose of transmitting its own programming to its own citizens. Self-sufficiency in that sense is desirable, and broadcasting states should be encouraged to provide the technical assistance necessary to achieve that goal. To impose an obligation to provide such assistance is, however, unnecessary since investment in technical assistance would provide a two-fold return. First, increased interest in direct broadcasting systems would accelerate demand for the exportation of the necessary technical equipment and software expertise from the broadcasting states.[191] Second, an increasing right of participation would create a greater community of interests between broadcasting and receiving states, with the result that the latter would promote rather than inhibit the operational application of direct broadcast technology.

The Continuing Impasse

For more than twelve years members of the United Nations have debated the direct broadcast issues with little demonstrable progress. In the meantime, communication satellite technology has developed rapidly toward operational availability of direct broadcast systems. Consequently, pressures both to realize the benefits of the technology and to limit the potential abuses, even at the cost of delaying operational applications, have increased. Despite these pressures, however, an impasse has resulted. It has come about, first of all, from the failure of those concerned about abusive applications to understand the benefits to be derived as well as the technical and practical limitations which make unnecessary even long-range fears of propaganda or cultural intrusion. The second factor causing unnecessary delay in the reaching of an international consensus has been the failure of broadcasting states either to allay fears of potential abuses or to recognize the psychological need among receiving states for some protection against the perceived dangers, regardless of how unreasonable technically advanced states may consider those perceptions.

Even in the absence of an international consensus regarding guidelines for operational applications, the experimental sophistication of direct broadcast technology will continue to increase. At some point, however, the international community will bear the costs resulting either from the delay of operational benefits or from the loss of the opportunity it presently has to channel within broad limits the use of the technology.

The development of direct broadcasting promises to increase the pace of social and economic development in many countries and to facilitate mutual understanding among nations. The consequence for all nations will be the establishment of conditions under which both the implementation of needed national and international changes and the preservation of international peace can occur. In order to establish those conditions, however, the international community must strike a balance between the interest in developing the technology in a commercially feasible form and the interest of less developed states in political and cultural integrity. The principles described above give both interests sufficient recognition without causing the dysfunctional consequences which will follow from allowing either interest to overshadow the other. New initiatives based on those proposals, combined with efforts to increase understanding among the participants of both potential benefits and present technical limitations and the foreseeable circumstances under which direct broadcasting will occur, seem likely to dissolve the impasse which has until now prevented the establishment of consensus on the appropriate international legal response to advances in the technology of direct satellite broadcasting.

9

EPILOGUE

In Chapters Three and Four NASA's research in satellite communications was traced to the point of transfer of communication satellite technology to the private sector. Chapters Five, Six, and Seven discussed the institutional ramifications of the technology transfer. This final chapter picks up once more the history of NASA's research and experimentation with communications satellites from the time of Comsat's incorporation to the present. With the adoption of the Applications Technology Satellite series as its major communications effort, NASA began a second-generation research and development program. Since 1966 NASA has conducted advanced communications research, first with ATS-1, and later with ATS-3, ATS-5, and finally with ATS-6, which was launched in May 1974.

The Applications Technology Satellite Program

The legislative history of the 1964 NASA Authorization Act, mentioned in Chapter Five, is of particular importance from the perspective of its effect upon subsequent NASA programs. At that time the House Subcommittee on Applications and Tracking and Data Acquisition, after extensive examination, endorsed NASA's overall communication satellite program objectives and appropriated a total of \$ 42.2 million, enabling the space agency to continue with its communication experiments. This authorization was not without controversy, however the House subcommittee actually trimmed NASA's budget request by millions of dollars in the belief that cost of launch vehicles and space components for the Advanced Syncom project could be deferred.[1] The Senate took action to restore \$ 2.0 million to the budget but finally agreed to the \$ 42.2 million figure in return for House acceptance of the Senate's recommended provisions concerning reimbursement.[2] The budget cut in effect constituted a slowdown in the Advanced Syncom program. This cut, together with the debate over reimbursement and the persistent questioning of NASA's role in relation to Comsat, exerted pressure on NASA to reassess the aims and objectives of its communication satellite research and development. Congressional pressure therefore was a significant factor directing a change in NASA's communication program philosophy.

The Transition to ATS

One year later, when NASA submitted its budget request for fiscal year 1965, the communication satellite program underwent a substantial revision: NASA decided to stop flying communication satellites per se and instead chose to incorporate further communication experiments on multipurpose, advanced technology satellites. Accordingly, the Advanced Syncom project, designed as a synchronous communication satellite, was cancelled, and in its place NASA introduced the Advanced Technology Satellite (ATS) program. The changeover from Advanced Syncom to ATS was initially proposed by NASA's Office of Space Science and Applications during a meeting with Robert Seamans, deputy administrator of NASA, on 28 October 1963.[3] In October of the following year, the project title was changed from Advanced Technology Satellites to Applications Technology Satellites, still maintaining the acronym ATS. The name change was proposed in order to "bring the name of the project more into line with its purpose, i.e., applications technology."[4] Technological emphases were oriented toward improvements necessary not only for communication but also for other satellite applications.[5] As the ATS program evolved, new satellite applications were identified and incorporated so that by 1973, nine years after the origination of the ATS concept, NASA's communication program grew in scope to include five elements: multiple data collection, navigation and traffic control, data relay, broadcast television and information networking.[6] Since the 1974 launch of ATS-6, the application program has become oriented specifically to the needs of the communications user.

A number of factors influenced the transition from Advanced Syncom to ATS. First, the changeover was in response to the congressional pressure that had been leveled against NASA's communication program during 1964. The adoption of the ATS concept enabled the agency to split its communication satellite budget by shifting funds out of the communication satellite classification and into the ATS program. Thus the total budget for communication satellites per se dropped from the authorized $ 42.2 million to a modest $ 13.5 million.[7] However, a total of $ 18.5 million was allocated for the ATS program from funds made available through the termination of the Advanced Syncom project. In general, the shift resulted in a net reduction of $ 10.2 million between the two programs – a reduction made possible by the slower ATS schedule compared to the previous proposed Advanced Syncom schedule.[8]

A second determining factor was economy. In addition to Advanced Syncom, NASA had been planning several individual spacecraft programs involving experiments in navigation, radiation detection and meteorology; the agency was also preparing a medium-altitude satellite which was designed specifically to evaluate gravity-gradient stabilization.[9] The consolidation of these multiple experiments into a single program promised both to increase efficiency and to decrease costs.

The third and most important factor behind the change-over was NASA's decision to terminate research and development in areas which were the responsibility of the private sector. Since Comsat had already decided to develop a synchronous rather than a low-altitude operational system, NASA was concerned that the Advanced Syncom satellite, if authorized and launched, would have become a prototype for operational use; its development would have constituted an encroachment upon an area that was considered the responsibility of the industrial community.[10] The ATS program, on the other hand, was in keeping with NASA's policy to focus on technology that would not otherwise be developed by private industry. When Comsat decided to utilize synchronous satellites, NASA program planners looked to more advanced technologies which would not be within the technical parameters of Comsat's initial operational system, such as gravity-gradient stabilization, increased satellite power and mechanically despun antennas. Moreover, as stated above, the technical experiments in synchronous orbit planned for ATS would serve many uses other than communications. In essence, the creation of Comsat, the elimination of Advanced Syncom, and adoption of the multidisciplinary ATS program philosophy did not mark the end of NASA's involvement with communication satellites but rather signalled a substantial alteration in the direction of the space agency's research and development activities.

NASA's early communication satellites – Echo, Relay and Syncom – had been designed to demonstrate the technical and economic feasibility of using satellites for routine telephone, television relay, and data transmission and also to facilitate the rapid implementation of the technology for intercontinental communications. The last of these first-generation satellites, Syncom III, was launched in August 1964 and actually served as a prototype for Early Bird, the first operational commercial communication satellite.[11] The second generation of communications experimentation, the ATS series of spacecraft, focused on the development of entirely new satellite capabilities and services, such as information networking and L-band aeronautical communications. Moreover, while the ATS program originated as essentially an outgrowth of Advanced Syncom, employing its engineering design studies and program techniques, the overall program philosophy was broadened with the adoption of the multipurpose concept.

The 1964 "Project Approval Document" stated the specific objectives of the new ATS program:

> a) to investigate and flight test technology common to a number of satellite applications,
> b) to investigate and flight test technological developments useful to satellites which operate in a stationary orbit,
> c) to conduct a carefully instrumented gravity-gradient experiment directed toward providing basic design information, and
> d) to flight test applications and scientific experiments peculiar to the orbits of the various missions.[12]

During the remainder of the 1960s and into the 1970s, NASA practiced an experimentation approach, the first step of which consisted of an assessment of user requirements for new communications services. Once these requirements were identified, they were evaluated in order to determine whether they could best be met by satellites or by ground telecommunication facilities. After determining that a suggested application was appropriate to and technically feasible for transmission via satellite, NASA then developed the requisite technology to match the stated requirements of the user. Invitations to participate in the ATS program were issued to NASA research centers, the Department of Defense, and private industry.[13] This user-oriented approach had already proved successful for the solicitation of experimentation ideas involving NASA scientific satellites. The space agency also provided ongoing technical consultation to other government agencies interested in potential communication satellite applications. Actual space flight experimentation with the ATS series constituted an essential part of this assistance.

Advanced Technological Development in the ATS Series

In accordance with the technical plan, five satellites were launched at intervals from late 1966 to August 1969. All of the spacecraft were constructed by Hughes Aircraft. The five satellites of the series were referred to as ATS-A through E prior to launch, after which time the letter designations changed to numbers. The first of these, ATS-A, was designed as a gravity-gradient stabilized, medium-altitude satellite. On the other hand, ATS-B and C were geosynchronous, spin-stabilized spacecraft. They were both designed to carry an electronically or mechanically despun antenna, a communications transponder, as well as meteorological, radiation and other experiments suitable for a spinning satellite. ATS-D and E would flight test a third type of spacecraft design combining the synchronous orbit and gravity-gradient techniques. These satellites would be launched into a spinning synchronous orbit; once on-station they would despin and achieve a gravity-gradient earth orientation. Experiments requiring earth orientation would be performed on these missions.[14] For the overall program, an ad hoc group selected a total of forty-six applications and technology experiments and twenty-three purely scientific experiments.[15]

Since ATS-B was launched before ATS-A was ready, it became the first in the series to be flown. Launched by an Atlas-Agena launch vehicle on 6 December 1966, the spacecraft was maneuvered into a spin-stabilized, geostationary orbit over the Pacific Ocean and designated ATS-1. The principal objectives of the mission were "to inject the spacecraft into synchronous orbit and place it on-station; to operate the spacecraft for the first thirty days or longer, and to operate and obtain useful data from a number of applications technology and scientific experiments carried on the spacecraft."[16] Six scientific and eleven applications and technology experiments were conducted on the spacecraft. ATS-1 continued to operate after completing its primary mission and was subsequently used to conduct additional user-oriented experiments. ATS-1 demonstrated an antenna improvement which allowed for greater directivity of the satellite's power.

The primary objectives of ATS-2 (ATS-A) were "to place the spacecraft into a medium altitude orbit of approximately 6,000 nautical miles and to obtain design and operational data useful in evaluating a gravity-gradient system for spacecraft stabilization."[17] Data collection from ten scientific and applications technology experiments was a secondary objective. The spacecraft was launched from Cape Kennedy on 5 April 1967, but an ignition failure in the second stage of the Agena rocket prevented it from achieving the desired 6,000-nautical mile circular orbit, thereby precluding a meaningful evaluation of the gravity-gradient experiment. Accordingly, the mission was judged unsuccessful.[18]

The objective of ATS-3 (ATS-C), like ATS-1, was primarily to conduct experiments on a spin-stabilized spacecraft in geostationary orbit. ATS-3 was launched into near synchronous orbit on 5 November 1967 and placed on-station the following day.[19] Nine experiments were carried on the spacecraft. As of 1975, ATS-3 was still functional, and since the completion of its original technical mission it has been used for additional experimentation.

Failure of the Atlas-Centaur launch vehicle prevented the successful operation of ATS-4. All but one of the experiments on the satellite were rescheduled on another flight.[20] Finally, the ATS-5 (ATS-E) mission, like ATS-4, was designed to test flight and conduct experimentation on a gravity-gradient stabilized, synchronous satellite. Launched on 12 August 1969 by an Atlas-Centaur launch vehicle, ATS-5 failed to properly despin, preventing achievement of the primary objective—namely, the deployment and exercise of the gravity-gradient stabilization system. However, the satellite was placed in synchronous orbit over the western United States, and some of the experiments returned good results.[21]

The ATS 1-5 Technology Experiments

The Syncom program, culminating in the successful launch of the Early Bird satellite in 1965, demonstrated the technical feasibility of geosynchronous satellite communication. Although no innovation or improvement to date has come close to the initial feat of designing and launching a synchronous satellite, a number of significant advances have accompanied the ATS series. With specific reference to communications aspects (bearing in mind that ATS 1-5 tested multidimensional space applications), many state-of-the-art refinements have emerged in the areas of antenna technology, frequency levels, signal transmission power, and development of small mobile earth terminals.[22] The spacecraft of the ATS series were used to experiment with high-frequency message transmission. The objectives of experiments in the super high-frequency range were to

(1) evaluate a multiple access system having a 1200-channel capacity in voice, teletype, data, and facsimile modes of operation;
(2) evaluate wideband transmission techniques;
(3) investigate polarization and transmission phenomena; and
(4) provide a communications transmission capability in support of other applications technology satellite experiments.[23]

Experiments in the very high-frequency range tested the feasibility of using these frequenties for four types of satellite applications: (1) two-way voice communications with aircraft, (2) distribution of weather facsimile, (3) data collection from multiple small remote platforms, and (4) position location. The VHF transponders on ATS-1 and ATS-3, utilized for the aircraft communication experiments, produced promising results. When the satellite was twenty degrees above the horizon, communications were eighty percent reliable, which is considerably better than that obtainable by conventional methods of communication. The Federal Aviation Administration, the Department of Defense, and a number of airlines participated in these experiments. Other experiments demonstrated the feasibility of using spacecraft and VHF communications for relaying data between weather monitoring stations and central, data-gathering weather facilities. In one of these experiments, weather facsimile data from a U.S. meteorological center were transmitted via an ATS spacecraft to a number of automatic picture transmission weather stations. In general, this experiment demonstrated the suitability of providing near real-time facsimile data to small installations, enabling them to obtain data and to make predictions on a par with the larger, more sophisticated meteorological centers.[24]

The ATS program also investigated the feasibility of collecting data from remote or automatic data platforms and then relaying the information to central analysis facilities. A VHF data collection experiment demonstrated a great improvement over the present methods for gathering data from such platforms. Utilizing ATS, three river gauges in Arkansas, California, and Alaska were queried by the satellite, which in turn sent the data to a central analysis installation, thus allowing for quick, geographical reading of the data. Position-fixing capabilities were also demonstrated with ATS-1 and ATS-3.

For example, ATS VHF transponders possessed multiple-access capabilities permitting simultaneous position-fixing of two targets. Using two satellites concentrating on one aircraft or sea craft, locations were obtained with reasonable accuracy. ATS-1 and ATS-3 located a jet aircraft with an accuracy of about five miles.[25] Although this determination was not of sufficient accuracy to be useful for air and sea traffic control, it did indicate a great potential for fixing marine and aeronautic positions with satellites. Improvement in location accuracy to 0.1 km (about 300 feet) can be readily obtained in the L-band frequency region.

Experiments in multiple-access antenna technology and frequency utilization conducted on ATS-1, 3 and 5 made progress toward the development of capabilities for new applications. It had been recognized early in the ATS program that applications such as over-ocean air traffic control-coordination, all-weather global navigation or position-fixing aids, air-sea emergency, search and rescue aids, orbital and suborbital space vehicle tracking aids, spacecraft-to-spacecraft-to-ground communications, and direct-to-home broadcasting would depend on technological advances. These service objectives led to the development of small, mobile terminals for use on ground and sea or in aircraft under a variety of conditions.[26]This line of research also led to the development of more powerful spacecraft capable of reaching successively smaller, more inexpensive earth terminals. ATS-1 carried antenna technology with eight times the directivity as that of Syncom; thus more satellite power could be aimed at ground receiving stations. The power level of ATS-3 represented an increase to twenty-five watts, compared to twelve watts with ATS-1. One early assessment commented that "such research is of particular importance in connection with the extension of the commercial satellite system to the less developed countries where numerous small stations would be necessary to meet communications requirements."[27] NASA's technical innovation led directly to an expansion of Comsat's and other satellite entities' service possibilities. Moreover, the trend toward smaller, mobile earth terminals accompanied by a decrease in terminal costs has resulted in an expansion of the user base for satellite communications.

The ATS 1-5 Communications Experiments

The engineering and scientific experiments on ATS-1, 3 and 5 had been largely concluded by 1969 and the satellites remained operable. By that time it had become clear to NASA that technical experiments were only one side of communications experimentation; the communicators themselves could benefit from the opportunity to utilize satellites for investigation critical to their needs. In addition, NASA recognized that the user community could make important contributions to both an experimental program and to an eventual operational system. Consequently, NASA adopted the view that many potential satellite applications—including interchange of information in specialized professional areas and educational broadcasting to home or community receivers—were important areas for its research and development efforts. Since its adoption, the NASA user experimentation policy has been the cornerstone of the space agency's communication satellite programs. This policy opened the way for a number of communication user experiments on ATS-1, 3 and 5.

The Corporation for Public Broadcasting (CPB) proposed to use NASA experimental satellites for relaying educational television programming from the East to the West Coast in a demonstration designed to assess the potential of domestic satellites for public television broadcasting. NASA approved the CPB proposal in November 1969 and authorized the use of ATS-1, ATS-3 and the ground stations in Rosman, North Carolina, and Mojave, California. From January to March 1970 three hours of public television broadcasts were transmitted coast-to-coast, five days per week. Another of the ATS user investigations was an experiment in fingerprint transmission via satellite. NASA supplied the C-band transponder on ATS-1 and made a small, mobile terminal available for the experiment. The purpose of the test was to determine which satellite and ground terminal capabilities were required in order to transmit fingerprints of a quality suitable for use in identifications. The experiment demonstrated that satellites were able to transmit high quality fingerprint images.[27a] In the spring of 1971 a series of experiments was undertaken in order to determine the feasibility of using satellites for relaying communications to and from remote areas where common carrier services were severely limited. Under the direction of the Geophysical Institute, a network of twenty-six ground stations was established throughout Alaska. The terminals, which cost about three thousand dollars each, were equipped with audio-only transmit/receive capability and were interconnected via the VHF transponder on ATS-1. Three different types of experimentation occurred in Alaska using the ATS satellite: biomedical, educational and networking. The

ATS experiments enabled doctors at central medical facilities to confer on a routine basis with health aides stationed in isolated communities, provided educational services to remote villages, and allowed network radio programs to be transmitted from the contiguous United States to the Alaskan mainland.[27b]

User Experimentation with ATS-6

On 30 May 1974 the sixth satellite of the ATS series was launched aboard a Titan III-C rocket and then successfully placed in synchronous orbit. The increased capabilities of the spacecraft, designated ATS-6, have added momentum to the program of user experimentation begun during the earlier ATS projects. In order to perform the series of complex telecommunication experiments authorized for the project, the spacecraft was equipped with a number of advanced technical subsystems including a travelling wave tube amplifier, with a power output level of twenty-one watts, and a large, circular antenna, nine meters in diameter when fully deployed. Electrical power for the signal transmitters is acquired by two, semicylindrical solar panels attached to long, arm-like extensions. Advanced attitude control systems stabilize the spacecraft in three axes while each of the experiments is underway; and thus ATS-6 is able to maintain a geosynchronous orbit at a constant attitude and posture. At a height of 35,680 kilometers (22,300 statute miles), ATS-6 is able to point narrow spot beams at particular earth surface areas. The geographic region illuminated by the signal is referred to as the "footprint." The footprints are about 1,000 miles long and 300 miles wide. Utilizing multiple frequencies, ATS-6 can simultaneously direct a number of spot beams to different earth locations. The two high-powered transmitters provide signals comparable in quality to those transmitted by terrestrial television systems. Finally, the orbital weight of the spacecraft is 1402 kilograms (3090 pounds).

The ATS-6 research projects included two major demonstrations: (1) the Health/Education Telecommunications Experiments (HET) Project, designed to build on the foundation laid by the previous ATS experiments; and (2) the joint U.S.-India Satellite Instructional Television Experiment (SITE), which will both build on previous work and break important new ground. Regarding the first of these, NASA and the Department of Health, Education and Welfare in 1971 agreed to conduct a series of communication experiments with the ATS-6 satellite. Although the rural areas of the United States are not nearly so isolated as those of, for example, India, there are regions where poverty and physical isolation present obstacles to terrestrial communications systems. Appalachia, the Rocky Mountain region, the Pacific Northwestern states, and Alaska were chosen as the test areas for the Health/Education Telecommunications Experiments.[28] In general, the residents of these relatively remote areas have not received the educational and health services which are available to the majority of Americans.

HET policy planners established four major objectives in order to ascertain whether satellites like ATS-6 would be able to furnish essential social services to dispersed groups. These objectives were: (1) to furnish a technical demonstration of the feasibility of using satellite broadcast technology with low-cost community receivers; (2) to support the development of new cost-effective social service delivery systems; (3) to encourage new institutional structures which can utilize regional or even national systems to service local needs; and (4) to act as models in service areas where public commitment is evident but no developed institutional response exists.

The Rocky Mountain States' Satellite Technology Demonstration (STD) explored the effectiveness of using ATS-6 to deliver educational and community programming to communities in eight states. Like the other HET experiments, the STD project involved a large regional population. The STD experiment was directed by the Federation of Rocky Mountain States, a regional consortium of business and government leaders. Formed in 1966, the Federation's primary purpose was to coordinate cooperative attempts to solve regional problems.[29].

The STD reached a substantial number of participants in fifty-six Rocky Mountain communities. These sites were equipped with television terminals of two main types: thirty-two communities were given receive-only terminals, while the remaining twenty-four were equipped with send/receive terminals capable of transmitting audio signals back to the control center in Denver. Other sites were serviced through inter-connection with existing public television and cable networks. The programming for both types of sites consisted of four main segments. The first centered around career-development education for junior high school students. In-service training for teachers constituted the second segment of STD programming; the third comprised a series of eleven evening programs intended for the entire community. The community assembled at the local STD school on Thursday evenings to watch the broadcasts. The final STD segment was a materials distribution service which made a library of more than 500 instructional films available to users at participating sites on specific request.

The remaining HET satellite experiments emphasized two-way video consultations for specialized audiences. The Appalachian Educational Satellite Program, for example, offered advanced university courses for schoolteachers. Each participating school district placed terminals in one of its schools where all of the teachers within its district could see the programming. The Veterans Administration assumed primary responsibility for another ATS-6 experiment emphasizing medical telecommunications. Specialized medical information was made available via satellite from central locations to selected hospitals in remote rural areas. In Alaska and the Pacific Northwest three separate experimental projects were carried out using ATS-6. The three experiments provided services via satellite in medical education, health information, teacher in-service training, and public broadcasting.

With the Rocky Mountain, Appalachian, Veteran's Administration and Alaskan experiments completed, NASA moved the satellite from its original station over the Galapagos Islands to a new position above Lake Victoria in East Africa. From its new location the satellite began relaying signals for the India-United States Satellite Instructional Television Experiment in August 1975. SITE is the first major experiment in the use of communication satellites for educational television in a developing country.[30] As such it will help answer critical questions about the role of communications in economic and national development and about the usefulness of satellite television for India and other developing nations.

The ATS-6 is being used to beam educational television programs directly to about 2400 rural villages located in six geographical areas throughout India. Each village has its own antenna and receiver to take advantage of the unique direct-broadcast characteristics of the ATS-6. The programs shown via the satellite emphasize family planning and improved agricultural techniques – two crucial areas for a developing country. While NASA provided the satellite itself, the Indian government has taken full responsibility for all phases of the ground effort including manufacture of receivers, maintenance, and development of the educational programs to be shown the village audiences. Although the evaluation of the experiment has not concluded, the hardware has performed beyond expectations in delivering video images to rural areas not accessible by conventional terrestrial television broadcasting.

The most concrete progress toward carrying the user experiments through to operational systems has been the formation of a user consortium, the Public Service Satellite Consortium (PSSC). A non-profit organization, PSSC was created to coordinate distribution of educational and health programming. The consortium plans to coordinate telecommunications planning for public and private institutions and agencies dealing with social services, to organize potential satellite users and represent them in negotiating with service providers, to offer technical advice and to encourage satellite experimentation.

NASA's Phase-Out Decision

This brief review of the ATS series completes the overview of NASA's research program in communication satellites since NASA announced that, as of 1 January 1973, no further communication satellite experimentation would be undertaken. The value of continuing NASA's communication program was first questioned in late 1962, after the formation of Comsat. NASA, however, was able to convince Congress at that time of the need for publicly sponsored research and development. Since that time, a number of reasons have been raised for continuing federal research activities. It was argued during the mid-1960s, for instance, that Comsat, as a fledgling industry, needed the support of government in order to preserve the U.S. technological advantage. Later, proponents of NASA's program argued that private industry alone would not support long-range research and development, and that it would be less likely to investigate social service applications of satellite technology than would the federal government. Finally, it was considered essential for the space agency to retain a research role in order to meet its statutory responsibility to provide technical assistance to policymaking entities such as the Federal Communications Commission and the Office of Telecommunications Policy.[31]

Although a persuasive argument did exist for a continuation of NASA's communication satellite experiments, the issue was not unequivocally resolved; the private sector still stood to benefit from costly, tax-supported research and experimentation. A federal budget agency evidenced concern over this situation in 1969 when it decided to reexamine NASA's research role on the premise that "given the existence of Comsat and other potential private beneficiaries, the Administration must decide what types and how much federally funded communications research and development is in the public interest."[32] Another important consideration was that both Comsat and Intelsat had established themselves as viable commercial entities during the late 1960s and early 1970s. The FCC's multiple-entry domsat policy decision of 1972, moreover, was leading to an increase in the number of private organizations owning and operating satellite systems. In the view of those involved with the formulation of government policy, the private sector was becoming increasingly more able to assume responsibility for ongoing research and development of communication satellite technology.

As a result of these developments, NASA announced that it would "phase-out its work on communication satellites," and that "further advances in satellite communications research and development can be accomplished by industry on a commercial basis without government support."[33] The phase-out decision was part of NASA's overall program to reduce expenditures for fiscal year 1973. In congressional testimony, Charles W. Mathews, NASA's associate administrator for applications, placed the decision in its historical context. For the past fifteen years, according to Mathews, NASA had successfully sponsored the development of communication satellite technology to the point where private industry was now able to finance, develop and operate satellite systems:

> Today, intercontinental communications by satellite are sustained through existence of a privately financed, effective, and profitable international communications service which can support its own research and development efforts. Today, private industry is prepared to finance and manage domestic communications satellites to serve the United States. With these conditions established, NASA plans this calendar and fiscal year to commence to phase out its R&D activities in support of commercial communications satellites.[34]

Future progress in the development of communication satellite technology would certainly be slowed as a consequence of the phase-out decision.[35] This prospect raised considerable concern in both government and private industry. Attempting to reassure interested parties from these sectors, NASA Administrator James C. Fletcher stated in January 1974 that the space agency would continue to fulfill its basic responsibilities. Further, NASA recognized the necessity of making continued advances in the development of the technology:

It is clear that the technical and management capabilities in satellite communications that NASA has developed over the past decade must be maintained and made available as other agencies request. It is important that such capabilities continue to exist within the government. Private industry can meet short-term commercial needs. But continued NASA activity is essential to identify and meet long-term national needs.[36]

According to Fletcher, NASA would engage in advanced communications research and would provide competent technical and support services to other federal agencies. Therefore, NASA's phase-out of satellite communication research could be more aptly described as a phase-down. Nevertheless, Fletcher reiterated a crucial point of the original decision – NASA would not conduct any new communication flight projects.[37]

Somewhat unexpectedly the phase-out announcement actually intensified the debate over research and development responsibilities. On behalf of industry, the Electronic Industries Association (EIA) issued a strong position paper in which it urged NASA to reconsider the decision. The association contended that continued space flight experimentation was essential for the identification of new applications areas. The EIA stated that the phase-out, in general, would have "serious implications to the public and to U.S. industry."[38] The EIA cited a number of reasons for not relinquishing the government's research and development role:

First, private industry does not have available sufficient resources to risk in advanced development where the early financial return is so uncertain.
Second, vastly more research is required to reach even the first plateau in technology.
Third, the U.S. must not lose its technological lead over other advanced nations or our foreign and domestic markets will be imperiled.
Fourth, research is mandatory to bring into existence such new projects as direct satellite broadcasting to communities for education in the U.S. and abroad.[39]

Congress also reacted to the decision. During July 1974, the Senate Aeronautical and Space Science Committee held a series of hearings in an effort to authorize the launch of a seventh Applications Technology Satellite, ATS Prime, as a follow-on to ATS-6. The aim of the committee was to provide continuity for the user experiments then underway on ATS-6 and also to allow the user community to gain more experience in satellite applications. Although ATS Prime was already constructed, the cost of launching the spacecraft was estimated at $ 45.7 million. Both NASA and the Department of Health, Education and Welfare stated that they did not have sufficient funds to pay the launch costs.[40] Consequently the spacecraft was never launched. Despite this setback Senators Frank Moss, the Committee's chairman, and Barry Goldwater, the ranking minority member, remained supporters of a continued role for NASA. Senator Moss expressed his belief that "a properly structured NASA program in satellite communication, if proposed by the administration, would be accepted by the Congress."[41]

Not surprisingly, ATS user groups were unhappy with the phase-out decision. Without NASA-sponsored spacecraft and without a favorable federal attitude toward subsidization of experiments, their prospects for satellite demonstrations appear bleak. Use of facilities on a commercial domsat is a possibility, but it is doubtful that many private carriers will attempt to provide social service applications until a solid market has been established. Recognizing this problem, NASA has decided to reevaluate its withdrawal from further communications research and development. The space agency is especially concerned that the private sector will not be able to incorporate the direct broadcast technology developed for the ATS and CTS programs into an operational system.

According to George M. Low, deputy administrator of NASA, the government might actually reverse its phase-out decision if the carriers fail to provide social service delivery systems.[42] In addition, a study conducted by the Space Applications Board concluded that the United States "could lose important opportunities and possibly forfeit its position of technical leadership in the field" unless NASA decided to resume its research and development role.[43] The basic problem with the private sector, the report stated, is that it can develop and use technology only "at a pace dictated by its own perception of the character and size of the markets and in a manner consistent with present investments, capital resources, and the present character of the aerospace and communications common carrier industries."[44]

CONCLUSIONS

The age of satellite communications began with the dreams and speculations of science fiction writers. The first concrete step toward realization of the dream of communication via satellite was taken when the U.S. Department of Defense expressed an interest in possible military applications of the technology. The development of powerful rockets for the ICBM program along with advances in electronics combined to make the first communications satellite a reality. After the various branches of the government became aware of the vast potential of these aerospace technologies, a civilian agency, NASA, was created by congressional legislation in order to promote and manage the entrance of the United States into the space age. The first major effort of the new agency was in satellite communications. Within five years of NASA's formation, the implementation of a global communication satellite system was so imminent that a unique public/private corporation, Comsat, was established by an act of Congress in order to promote the development of a global system and to operate the U.S. portion of the system. While representatives from Comsat and the telecommunications administrations and foreign policy entities of other interested nations negotiated the arrangements leading to the creation of Intelsat and launched successive generations of satellites, NASA was continuing its research on and development of increasingly advanced models of communication satellites. Both NASA research and the early commercial success of the Intelsat system brought pressure on the U.S. government to formulate a policy regulating the use of satellites for purely domestic communications. Climaxing a long government and industry debate, the FCC's multiple-entry decision of 1972 authorized any private entity with sufficient financial and technical resources to launch and operate a domestic satellite system, subject to certain licensing and regulatory provisions. On the public international level, the question of direct satellite broadcasting has been discussed in several bodies of the United Nations throughout the past twelve years. The participants in these discussions, however, have been able neither to elaborate a treaty nor agree on the legal principles governing the use and application of this powerful new technology. Finally, the January 1973 decision of NASA to phase out its active communication satellite experimentation marks the end of a definable era, because it was the involvement and effort of the national space agency which was largely responsible for guiding the development of the technology from its rudimentary beginnings to the state of technical sophistication now utilized in the Intelsat and ATS spacecraft, the satellites of the various domsat systems, and in the Communications Technology Satellite. At this time, therefore, it appears appropriate to assess in retrospective fashion the developmental process pertaining to communication satellites.

A Space Technology Integration Model

The path from idea to application described in this volume has been neither straight nor simple. No description of the technological development of satellite communication per se can do justice to the complex processes underlying the use of satellites for communications. The case of communication satellites, nevertheless, is a paradigm for technological integration in the full sense of the term. In the Introduction technology integration or TI was defined as the *process whereby government manages the development, testing and application of new technologies such that the final result is an economically or socially useful application of the technology,* and a framework for conceptualizing the TI process was developed. Having traced the strategy of communication satellite development in the context of this book, it is now possible to integrate it into the conceptual framework of TI and to develop a descriptive model of technology integration as it relates specifically to space technology.

An Analysis of Satellite Communications with the TI Framework

The conceptual framework for TI views the process on a two-dimensional plane with the vertical axis representing the government management spectrum on a continuum from stimulation to regulation and the horizontal axis representing the implementation spectrum on a continuum from needs to concrete uses. The direction of technology flow as it progresses from the stage of requisite imaginative, scientific and technical input, through the various developmental stages of feasibility recognition, idea testing and prototype and technology development, to the stage of implementation and diffusion, is a function of the relationship of government management to the implementation process.

The progress of satellite communications to date supports the choice of employing the general framework developed in the Introduction as a standpoint from which to view the process of space technology integration. The technology flow was indeed defined by the relationship of government management to the implementation process in each of the three major areas of applications: international satellite communications, domestic satellite communications and direct broadcasting satellite applications. To describe precisely how this relationship unfolded in each case, it is necessary to analyze each area of application separately. In the process several general trends will emerge.

The First Transfer of Communication Satellite Applications

The case of the development and implementation of the international communication satellite system (Intelsat) is perhaps the most clearly defined instance of technology integration. The process of implementation began before the creation of NASA with the first recognition on the part of science fiction writers, technologists and the U.S. military establishment of the potential of earth-orbiting satellites for international communications. Two guiding ideas materially contributed to the realization of the feasibility of communication satellites: a recognition of the possibility of inserting satellite vehicles into earth orbits and a realization of the potential of satellites for communications. The former, since it is common to many space capabilities, is of little concern here, although it should be noted in this regard that realizations of technological possibilities do not always come in logical step-by-step order. The potentials of satellites for communications were being actively investigated before it was certain that there were no uncrossable obstacles to earth-orbital missions in general.

The place of science fiction writers and other cultural prognosticators in the recognition of technical feasibilities is often underestimated. Feasibility recognition is not the exclusive province of engineers and scientists who are on the leading edge of research in a given area. In fact, it is sometimes the case that those most intimately connected with a particular line of investigation do not have the wider perspective necessary for the first visionary realizations of novel applications of developing technology. After the initial steps in the recognition of feasibility, however, the consultation of technical experts is unavoidable. Satellite communication, for example, shows thid complementarity between scientific dreamers and practical engineers. It has often been suggested that every great technological innovation in the last fifty years was predicted somewhere in fantasy or science fiction; by the same token, no technological innovation could occur without those who can appropriate the necessary equipment and tools and answer the basic questions of technological and practical feasibility.

By the time NASA was established in 1958 the process of technology integration had already been set in motion. Along the implementation spectrum the stage of feasibility recognition was already reached; the military services had begun to stimulate and direct the course of idea testing and technological development in planning for the Score and Courier projects. The creation of NASA placed responsibility for developing peaceful applications of space technology in the hands of a civilian government agency. It is significant that this occurence coincided with the recognition on the part of American industry of the feasibility of satellite communications to serve its needs by providing improved international commercial communications systems. The subsequent course of communications satellite technology integration in the area of international common carrier applications was defined to a great extent by the relationship established between the private sector, which was actively interested in furthering the implementation of commercial satellite applications, and NASA, which in pursuit of its mandate to develop civilian applications of space systems assumed a lead role in influencing progress along the government management spectrum.

The complexities inherent in government management of the TI process become apparent in analyzing the difficult role NASA played in communication satellite development. On one hand, as a research and development agency charged with the responsibility of developing space-related technologies, NASA was responsible for developing the technology required to ensure implementation of an operational international communications satellite system—a function which directly served the interests of the private organizations that would eventually operate the system. On the other hand, because NASA recognized the extensive legal, social and political implications of the technology for such a system, it attempted to mitigate the possible harmful effects of uncontrolled commercial utilization. NASA's research and development role inevitably involved the agency in the web of non-technical policy decisions characteristic of the government management phase of technology integration.

As the extensive legal and political implications of the new technology began to be comprehended, alternative policy choices presented themselves in a number of areas. In retrospect these decisions can be grouped into five categories: (1) decisions regarding civil-military roles and relationships; (2) decisions regarding the roles of the public and private sectors in the development and operation of communication satellites; (3) decisions regarding interagency roles and responsibilities for policy formation; (4) decisions on the corporate form of industry ownership; and (5) decisions on the appropriate method for safeguarding the public interest and promoting international participation in a global communication satellite network. Within each of these categories various options came into focus as a national communications satellite policy took shape.

One of the first policy determinations involved delineating *civil-military roles* and their respective responsibilities for satellite communications. Since both NASA and the DOD had mandates to conduct research and development, close coordination was necessary. The original agreement was that NASA would engage in the development of passive communication satellites with its Echo project, while the Department of Defense pursued the development of active satellites. As commercial communications requirements became apparent, however, the agencies were able to coordinate their activities so as to allow NASA to enter the active satellite field with Project Relay and later Syncom. The effect was to accelerate the process of technology integration.

Determination of the appropriate role for the *government* to play in relation to *private industry* was a particularly crucial issue. In the developmental stage, the tasks involved close NASA coordination with industry to ascertain industry's interests and plans, and the design of a research and development program which both supported industry involvement in the development of communication satellites and at the same time ensured that public as well as private interests were served. To this end, NASA cooperated with industry to launch AT&T's Telstar satellite in 1962, and at the same time pursued an expansive research and development program of its own, which widened both the technical base and the extent of industry support for eventual technology transfer.

The issues and alternatives involved in determining the government's role in relation to the *institutionalization* of satellite systems were extensive. In the extremes, the options ranged from complete government ownership and operation to relatively unbridled private ownership with communication companies regulated as traditional international common carriers. Between these extremes the issues focused on the extent of government regulation, control and support. There were precedents for various degrees of government involvement, ranging from a system of regulatory control modeled after the Atomic Energy Commission, to government sponsorship modeled after the Tenessee Valley Authority, to government support in the form of subsidies such as those provided to the railroad and aviation industries; the very diversity of earlier approaches illustrated that there was no definitive standard to follow, opening the way to consideration of new approaches to public-private cooperation.

The need to coordinate *interagency roles* and responsibilities in the formation of communication satellite policy was apparent from the start. Interest in communication satellites was government-wide. NASA and the DOD shared responsibility for space research, development and applications. The FCC allocated frequencies and licensed communications carriers. The State Department had special interests in the potential of communication satellites as instruments of foreign policy. The Justice Department was concerned with the possibility of monopoly. Numerous congressional committees including the House Committee on Science and Astronautics, the Senate Committee on Aeronautical and Space Sciences, and the Commerce and Foreign Relations Committees had special interest in commercial communication satellite applications, and, ultimately, the Executive Office of the President was responsible for giving administrative direction of national policy. Lines had to be drawn between the responsibilities of each group in determining communication satellite policy; working liaisons had to be created to regulate commercial operations.

Once agreement was reached by the various agencies that industry would participate in the ownership and operation of the global satellite system, the central issue focused on *incorporation alternatives*. The general consensus favored private ownership by a joint corporation or consortium; opinions varied, however, on who should participate in the joint venture. The options ranged from exclusive ownership and operation by international common carriers to various plans for including domestic carriers, equipment manufacturers and the public at large in the ownership structure of Comsat. Other points at issue regarding the corporate structure included deciding whether the communication companies themselves or the joint corporation would own ground stations, determining whether a company's investment in the satellite corporation should be included in its rate base, and deciding how the government would maintain adequate controls over the corporation.

Finally, decisions had to be made on the appropriate methods for safeguarding the *public interest* on both a national and an international level. While commercial communication carriers were particularly interested in serving high traffic areas in the North Atlantic and North Pacific, part of the international social value of communications satellites depended upon the establishment of a global system offering services to less developed areas of the world. The public interest would best be served by encouraging extensive foreign participation in a global system. As a consequence of this fact the respective roles of government and industry in promoting international involvement and in negotiating foreign arrangements became a critical issue.

These five areas of policy decisions were key determinants in shaping the course of technology flow from the stage of feasibility recognition through the stage of prototype and technology development and into the final stage of implementation. Moreover, these policy considerations spanned the entire technology integration process, rather than paralleling any particular stage in the process. For example, the passage of the Communication Satellite Act of 1962, which culminated a policymaking process, occurred while NASA was still in the process of stimulating technology development through its Relay and Syncom experiments. In fact, although plans were formalized to test the feasibility of geosynchronous communication satellites, Syncom had not yet been launched when Congress was debating the formation of the Communication Satellite Corporation; the institutional framework for implementing an operational system was accordingly organized on the assumption that Comsat would develop a low- or medium-altitude system. Continuing NASA research and development, however, enabled Comsat to develop the more technically advanced geosynchronous satellite system. Thus, while the legislative creation of Comsat to own and operate the U.S.

segment of a global international communication satellite system exemplifies a high level of regulation on the government management spectrum, a level which would normally correspond to technology implementation and diffusion in the earlier formulation of the TI framework, the actual implementation and application of the technology was influenced by ongoing research and development as well as by regulation. This and other evidences of far-reaching policy decision at all stages of the development of communication satellites indicate a unique characteristic of space-oriented technology integration.

The Second Transfer of Communication Satellite Applications

The movement of domestic satellite applications from idea to use represents a second layer in the technology integration process. Although the development of domsats occurred in a much different political context than the earlier international transfer of satellite technology, the domsat experience can also be understood within the TI framework. Two points of divergence between the case of international communication satellites and the case of domestic communications satellites are noteworthy. The development and implementation of domestic satellite systems did not depend directly on the stimulus of new government research and development on domestic systems; the domsats were primarily an outgrowth of basic government research and development directed toward international satellite communications. This does not imply of course that the stimulatory aspect of government management was inoperative in the implementation of domestic satellite communications. On the contrary, successful government-sponsored technology development was responsible for creating an awareness of the feasibility of communication satellites for domestic use. Once that potential was recognized by the private sector, the government management role focused on policy planning and regulation. Many of the same issues that faced policy planners in the Comsat case re-emerged. For example, interagency roles and responsibilities for policy formation had to be coordinated between OTP and the FCC, and decisions had to be made regarding the structure of industry competition in the private sector.

A comparison of the cases of Comsat and the domsats also illustrates how the government management spectrum influences the timing as well as the direction of technology flow and points up the second difference between Comsat and the domsats. In the Comsat example, government regulation and technology development occurred simultaneously, whereas organizational planning for domestic satellites systems occurred after the basic technology was developed and involved lengthy deliberations which delayed the implementation of operational systems for many years. The effect of government management in the Comsat case, then, was to facilitate rapid implementation of operational applications, while in the domsat case it served to prolong the integration process.

Direct Broadcasting Satellite Applications

The use of satellites for direct broadcasting purposes is the third layer of the development to be incorporated into an STI model. Unlike the international and domestic applications of communication satellites, the potential of satellites for direct broadcast uses stands in doubt concerning its ultimate implementation. As pointed out in the Epilogue, NASA has underwritten the development of direct broadcast technology and has involved itself in the effort to find users of the technology. Nevertheless, the relationship of direct broadcast possibilities to the regulatory and management functions on both a national and an international level has served to circumvent the implementation pressures.

Some obvious parallels exist between the development of commercial communication satellites and the development of direct broadcasting satellites. Direct broadcasting satellites, of course, are a further refinement of commercial communication satellites, but they also represent further involvement in research and development. Accordingly, the actual development and testing of direct broadcast capabilities has required the stimulation of government funding. To this extent the development of direct broadcast satellites explicitly matches the definition of TI in this volume.

Where the divergence with the case of commercial communication satellites occurs in the direct broadcast situation is in the progress toward technology diffusion. The capabilities of direct broadcast satellites are so countervalent to vested interests and represent such a spectrum of controversial applications that efforts toward legal and regulatory control of direct broadcasting has outstripped the implementation of the actual hardware. The relationship between legal regulation and technical development is not direct, however, especially the case of direct broadcasting satellites: NASA continued to develop direct broadcasting capabilities and refinements in the late 60s and early 70s while the direct broadcast controversy was at its height. It remains a question, nevertheless, to what extent future applications of direct broadcast technology will be hindered by restrictive international regulations or by the threat of such regulations.

If it is correct to conclude that premature regulation had an influence, however indirect, on the timely implementation of direct broadcast technology, then it would not be too far astray from the framework of analysis to conclude that technology management strategies should take into account the need for regulation to wait upon the development of technical configurations. In retrospect it is clear that some of the early concerns about propagandizing by satellite were based upon slightly distorted ideas of the capabilities and incapabilities of direct broadcast hardware. In terms of the STI model which will be elucidated, the technological flow must not be represented as intruding too early during the implementation process into the area of regulative control.

Development of the Model

The preceding analysis of the correspondences between the development of satellite communications and the TI framework points up some areas of significant divergence between the hypothetical framework and the process of technology integration as it has historically unfolded in the development of satellite communications. These points of divergence will be noted for the purpose of developing a descriptive model of the space technology integration (STI) process.

(1) The first divergence is due to the failure of the framework to account for the institutional arrangements which provide essential links in the flow of technology from feasibility recognition to implementation. It has proved imperative, at the level of stimulation on the government management spectrum, to establish some form of government/user interface before technology development can proceed. Similarly, at the level of regulation it has been necessary to structure an organizational framework for implementing the technology on an operational base before the hardware could be utilized.

(2) The hypothetical framework views the developmental phase as a series of separate stages of idea testing, prototype development and technology development. Although this may be a logically accurate depiction of technology flow, it is not typical in the specific case of space technology integration. Both the large capital outlays needed

for space technology development and the inherent public policy implications have necessitated the consolidation of these stages into a unified research and development program under the direction and sponsorship of the federal government.

(3) The framework also does not account specifically for the central role of policy planning which accompanies government interfacing with the flow of technology development. On the STI model the various governmental interactions with the TI flow must be designated in some way to indicate the dialectic policy interchanges between government and technology development which determines the course and timing of technology implementation.

(4) Finally, some provision must be made to incorporate the feedback dynamic of the technology integration process into the model. A major conclusion of the historical analysis was that technology integration was not a linear process with a clearly definable beginning or end. The cases of international satellite communications and domestic satellite communications demonstrate that the process is repeatable and layered and that federal government research and development plays a central role in facilitating repetition. This is represented in the STI model by depicting technology flow as an ongoing cyclical process with government research and development as the central construct. The research function serves both to generate ideas for new applications in the innovative cycle and to stimulate the processes of application and diffusion within the institutional cycle.

STI Model

Incorporating the distinctives of the development of satellite communications into the TI framework allows a specific STI model to be constructed which will serve as a point of comprehension and analysis to future space applications and as a tool for retrospective technology assessment. A few of the implications of this model will be taken up in the next section. The STI model on the following page (figure 5) differs from the TI framework at the points mentioned in the preceding text. Note in particular the cycles depicted on the chart: the process of TI, given the appropriate supportive functions, is capable of stimulating its own repetition.

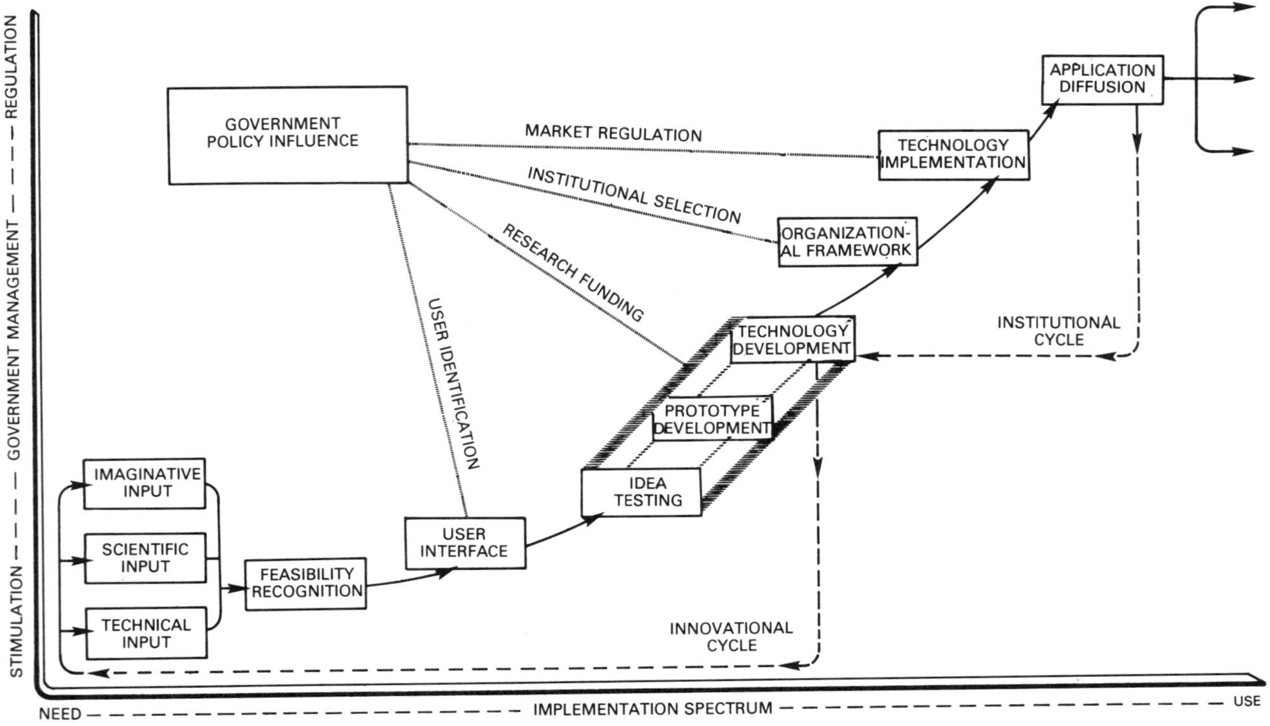

Figure # 5. Space Technology Integration Model

Implications of the STI Model

Communication Satellites

Although the STI model is basically a descriptive model, constructed from an analysis of the communication satellite experience, some implications of the model can be applied to prescriptive purposes. There is one particular aspect of the communication satellite experience about which the STI model is able to raise significant questions: NASA's decision in 1973 to withdraw from further communications satellite experimentation. The pause cued by the phase-out decision has prompted a reassessment of the role of government management in the area of communication satellite applications. NASA's 1958 charter and its subsequent interpretation confined NASA's role to one of research and prototype development. NASA has avoided intense involvement in the application of technology outside of its limited mandate, preferring to transfer its technology to the private sector of the economy as soon as circumstances permitted. While this strategy was feasible with communication satellites because of the obvious commercial applications and the active interest of large corporations, it may not be the best approach for all potential applications of communication satellite technology. Many novel applications may not be finally realized because of the lack of sufficient financial returns. As a result of these considerations, NASA has been weighing the advantages and disadvantages of renewed effort in the field of communication satellites.

The question of what NASA's future role in communication satellites will be has been partly obscured by the commercial success of the transfer of communication satellite technology to the private sector. Comsat is operating an efficient, commercial communication satellite system in a consortium with the other Intelsat signatories and is providing telephone, television and data transmission services on an international basis. The public interest has been served by the rapid development of a global communication satellite network and by legal provisions which provide for a broad base of ownership and control and ensure nondiscriminatory use and equal access to the system. Although organizational problems delayed the establishment of domestic satellite systems for many years, the controversy has now been resolved and domsat systems are also beginning to provide communication satellite services within the domestic market.

As significant as the accomplishments of satellite communications are, it is also evident that existing systems are not delivering all of the services which communications satellites are capable of providing. The emphasis throughout the development of communication satellites has been on providing a better technology for present services rather than on developing new services. Even in the early research stage the potential value of communication satellites was seen only in their ability to replace existing technologies and improve inadequate intercontinental communication links. Little thought was given to more speculative applications of the technology, and no experimentation was directed toward social service uses except within the NASA context. It is not surprising then that commercial communication satellites have been used largely as a substitute for cables and land lines to provide traditional types of common carrier services. To date, only highly profitable and clearly segmented user groups have been identified and serviced. Moreover, to the extent that private companies are already involved in profitable operations, they have little incentive to search out peripheral users. Marginally profitable areas such as social services have been virtually ignored within an operational context.

On the international level, the concept of a global village and the vision of communication satellites as a means of education and cultural exchange has amounted to little more than a subject of discussion and speculation. At the 1971 Nice Colloquium on Educational Satellites, for example, recommendations were made for experiments with satellite television, for regional research on designing programming, for literacy and vocational training using direct broadcasting, and for the linking of medical centers for diagnosis and teaching. Educators, professors, researchers, and representatives of international organizations all advocated international cooperation, international teleconferencing between universities, and international experimentation with direct broadcasting. Few of these suggestions, however, have been extended into an experimental stage, much less into operational practice.

The only tangible progress toward the development of speculative user services beyond the traditional common carrier applications has been made as a result of federal government sponsorship of user experiments in the Applications Technology Satellite program, mentioned in Chapter Nine. The full concept of user experimentation, however, was not introduced into the ATS program until 1969, and then only after ATS-1 and 3 had completed their original technical missions and after the organizational configurations for operational, commercial systems were fairly well established. Current NASA experiments are for the first time investigating many new applications of communication satellite technology. The phase-out decision, however, transfers all responsibility for further experimentation to the private sector.

The rationale for the phase-out decision was based on the assumptions that communication satellite technology integration is a *fait accompli*, and the private sector will conduct further research and development and provide services to meet future communications needs. The STI model, however, raises serious doubts as to whether the communication satellite applications development is in fact a *fait accompli*. The end product of the process of technology integration is operational utilization, and while communication satellite applications have been transferred to operational status in some instances, there are many more potential applications which are not yet operational. It must be recognized that the process of STI does not conclude at the point in time when a technology is transferred to initial operational use. The process begins long before the technology becomes operational and the application of the technology in new markets and in new manners continues long after the technology is operational. The model shows that the process of STI is multilayered and repeating: the innovative and institutional cycles can be reinstituted where needs can be identified and sufficient funding and research management is available. This fact in itself points to the need for some continuing role for the public sector in facilitating the process of technology integration in the field of satellite communications.

The second assumption – that the private sector will carry on advanced research and development and provide the services necessary to meet future needs – must also be questioned. There is little evidence to support the proposition that the private sector will be willing or able to advance research and development along the lines dictated by public interest requirements. The high-venture costs to private companies, which stem from risks ranging from technological and jurisdictional risks to uncertainty of user applicability, are often well beyond the capacity of even the largest corporations in the space telecommunications or space hardware industries. It has never been a tenet of American society that private enterprise has the responsibility for supporting research and development in areas where the financial rewards are extremely speculative and the markets as yet unsegregated. In the case of a capital-intensive industry such as satellite communications, where years of experimentation on ATS-1 and 3 and presently on ATS-6 have not provided persuasive evidence of users willing to pay for services and the narrow scope of the experiments has not provided the arena for large-scale public acceptance, it is unrealistic to expect private industry to accept the financial and social responsibility for continuing innovative research.

As the STI model indicates, government research and development is central to repeating the process of technology integration. Future STI will involve the interconnection of the services of a wide variety of industries providing carrier functions, specialized service functions, networking, and terminal equipment. Only governmental management and experiment control can bring together these divergent entities. If the public interest is to be best served it will be necessary to experiment with user groups to determine the type of services to be developed. This undertaking will require significant funding which private industry is not likely to provide. The markets are divided such that a given company may only have a narrow interest in services which would not justify large scale studies, and to the extent that there are already profitable operations there will be no obvious incentive for the involved companies to search out peripheral users for what would probably turn out to be marginally profitable services.

Space technology integration is a significant activity in that it assumes public benefit as its result. The cessation of communication satellite experimentation not only terminates further technology integration, but also severs the link between the innovational and institutional cycles represented in the STI model. This is not an optimum circumstance. It is more likely that a continued role for the federal government operating within the innovational cycle to stimulate development of new applications, accompanied by technology transfers to the institutional cycle, will best serve the public interest.

As new experimental areas are developed, private industry can initiate operational systems which can continually be altered through interchange with NASA and the other federal agencies with mandates in respective areas of STI management. The STI model clearly suggests that the future development of other communication satellite services, and the social service applications in particular, depends upon a reenactment of the technological flow described by the model. Without a continuation of government research efforts in satellite communications, little progress will be made in further technology integration.

Analogous Applications

One of the most relevant applications of the STI model is to the development of other types of satellite applications. Communication satellites have often been singled out as a prime example of the successful transfer to private operational modes of a federal research and development effort; there are several other satellite applications, however, which could benefit more by avoiding the complicated developmental path of communication satellites. The STI model can provide useful criteria for the implementation of other types of satellite applications.

Earth resource satellite applications is the most immediate area for which the STI model can serve as a prescriptive tool in directing the course of experimentation and technology utilization. NASA's current experiments in remote sensing via Landsat satellites have indicated a vast applications potential for the technology, ranging from pollution control to mineral exploration. The private sector, as well as government agencies on the federal, state and international levels, are all interested in fostering implementation of the technology on an operational basis. As the STI model suggests, actions within the spectrum of government management will ultimately determine the course of TI as it progresses along the implementation line. Many of the organizational and policy management problems that surrounded the transfer of communication satellite technology from the innovational to the institutional cycle will again arise in relation to the development of earth resources satellite systems. Decisions will have to be made regarding the respective roles of the public and private sectors in both the development and operation of these systems; interagency roles and responsibilities will have to be coordinated; decisions will have to be made concerning the organizational framework for an operational system; and appropriate structures will have to be devised to safeguard the public interest, to ensure equal access, and to provide for international participation.

As the STI model indicates, the social, economic, legal and international implications of remote sensing via satellite must be thoroughly studied and policy options must be clearly delineated. Policy management must focus initially on interagency coordination. As with communication satellites, interest in earth resources satellites is government-wide in scope: presently, NASA controls the space segment for the satellite experiments while the Department of Interior distributes the data acquired from the satellites. The State Department and USDA also share respective interests in the program. Interface between these various agencies to coordinate the formation of national policy guidelines to direct the development of an operational system is exigent.

The international implications of earth remote sensing will be a particularly sensitive issue. Since remote sensing satellites survey the entire globe without respect for national borders, there are serious international legal questions concerning national sovereignty and rights to data collected on resources and physical features located within sovereign borders. At the same time, however, an operational program could provide a focal point for international cooperation and a developmental tool for many Third World nations. Earth resources satellites will undoubtedly meet many of the same organizational and legal barriers in the international sphere which have been encountered by direct broadcast proposals.

While the STI model notes the importance of policy planning on both the international and domestic fronts, it is also apparent from the model that policy planning is only one facet of STI; federal government research and development is also central to the process. As illustrated in the case of communication satellites, the role of research and development is threefold, consisting not only of technology development but also of prototype development and basic idea experimentation. These functions are essential not only to facilitate the initial transfer of technology to operational status, but also to ensure the continual transfer and integration of new applications and to promote the widest possible distribution and diffusion of satellite services. Unless this other facet of the model is recognized, an earth resources satellite program may follow the course of communication satellite systems and service highly profitable fields, such as mineral and fossil fuel exploration, while marginally profitable services to unsegmented user groups are ignored.

One solution to this dilemma, whether we are speaking of communication saltellites or earth resource survey satellites, lies in a recognition of the critical importance of government stimulation in the innovational cycle of the STI process. As is apparent from the history of communication satellites, the role of experimentation in visibly demonstrating the service potential of the technology is a crucial factor in promoting acceptance, adoptation and utilization of technological innovation. Just as NASA's early technology-driven experiments demonstrated the practical feasibility of point-to-point satellite communications, thereby convincing industry to adopt satellite technology, so also future user-driven experiments can stimulate a demand for new user services. Thus, future experimentation within the innovational cycle should not be directed simply toward developing a better technology but also toward developing these new applications. In this regard, new technology development should be aimed at improving system links between satellites and users. The success of an earth remote-sensing satellite program, for example, will depend to a great extent on the ability of the ground segment to process and disseminate data in a usable and timely manner.

Whatever configuration is established for an operational earth resources satellite system, the STI model clearly indicates that an ongoing role for the federal government should be provided not only in future space applications technology development, but also in the investigation and identification of new applications of data acquired from space systrems. In the past, there has been an unfortunate tendency to think that the government research and development function ceases at the point when a technology is transferred to operational use. This was evident in the 1964 congressional debates over continuing NASA research and development which followed the creation of the Comsat Corporation and again in the 1973 phase-out decision which followed the initial organizational steps of the domestic satellite industry. The misconception stems from the fact that the mere transfer of technological capabilities, which is only one factor within the broad process of STI, is often seen as an ultimate goal. As suggested by the STI model, the transfer of NASA-developed technologies to initial operational use does not end the space agency's responsibility to facilitate the development of new applications by the diffusion of the technology in new channels and toward new user markets. The major implication of the STI model, however, is that the development and transfer processes are multifaceted, repeatable and layered, and that in the process of repetition there is a continuing need for federal government research and development to be re-instituted at certain critical points.

This volume has analyzed the strategy of communication satellite development and has provided a retrospective technology assessment. An effort has been made to describe accurately the developmental process and to assess objectively, insofar as is possible, the meaning of the communication satellite experience. In the area of space research, as in perhaps no other area of modern public concern, dreams and visions have shared in policy development. If this study has in some way clarified the complex interactions of visions with reality, it has not been done with the plan to minimize the visionary aspect of the movement toward useful space systems, but to lay a foundation on which succeeding visions may reach out to the future.

NOTES

Full bibliographical citations will be found in the Bibliography. Notes followed by the word *NASA* indicate that the document was found in the National Aeronautics and Space Administration Historical Archives in Washington, D.C.

NOTES TO INTRODUCTION

1. Samuel I. Doctors, *The Role of Federal Agencies in Technology Transfer*, p. 10.
2. See, for example, ibid.; Richard Rosenbloom, *Technology Transfer—Process and Policy* (Washington, D.C.: National Planning Association Special Report No. 62, July 1965); Richard Lesher and George Howick, *Assessing Technology Transfer* (Washington, D.C.: U.S. Government Printing Office, 1966); Harvey Brooks, *The Government of Science* (Cambridge, Mass.: The MIT Press, 1968).
3. Derek Medford, *Environmental Harassment or Technology Assessment?*, pp. 15-91, has a concise discussion of the legislative history of these bills.
4. Erich Jantsch, *Technological Forecasting in Perspective*, p. 15.

NOTES TO CHAPTER 1

1. Edward Everett Hale, *The Brick Moon and Other Stories,* p. i.
2. Ibid., p. 62.
3. Ibid., p. vi.
4. Arthur C. Clarke, "Extraterrestial Relays: Can Rocket Stations Give Worldwide Radio Coverage?" reprinted in Arthur C. Clarke, *Voices from the Sky,* p. 235.
5. Hermann Oberth, *Die Rakete zu den Planetenräumen* (The Rocket into Interplanetary Space), (Munich: R. Oldenbourg Pub., 1923), cited by ibid., p. 124.
6. Ibid., p. 124.
7. Ibid., p. 125.
8. U.S., Congress, Senate, Committee on Aeronautical and Space Sciences, *Soviet Space Programs 1962-65,* 89th Cong., 2nd sess., 1966, p. 226. The Russian claim was not made until after the launch of Sputnik in 1957.
9. Clarke, *Voices from the Sky,* p. 137.
10. John R. Pierce, "Don't Write—Telegraph," *Science, Art and Communications,* ed. John R. Pierce, pp. 29-30.
11. John R. Pierce, "Orbital Radio Relays," ibid., p. 51.

NOTES TO CHAPTER 2

1. Wernher von Braun, "German Reminiscences of Rocketry," in *The Coming of the Space Age,* ed. Arthur Clarke, pp. 49-50.
2. Ibid., p. 52.
3. Ibid., p. 39.
4. Eugene M. Emme, *A History of Space Flight,* p. 104.
5. William Shelton, *Soviet Space Exploration,* p. 35.
6. U.S., Congress, Senate, Special Committee on Atomic Energy, *Atomic Energy Hearings . . . Pursuant to S. Res. 179,* 79th Cong., 1st sess., 1945, Part 1, p. 179.
7. Emme, *A History of Space Flight,* p. 105.
8. Ibid., p. 108.
9. Ibid., p. 109.
10. Cited by R. Cargill Hall, "Early U.S. Satellite Proposals," *History of Rocket Technology,* ed. Eugene M. Emme, p. 86
11. Ibid.
12. Ibid.
13. Ibid., pp. 68-9.
14. Ibid., p. 69.
15. Memorandum by Harvey Hall, "Early History and Background on Earth Satellites," 29 November 1957, p. 3. (NASA)
16. Ibid., p. 4.
17. Ibid.
18. Project Rand, "Preliminary Design of an Experimental World-Circling Spaceship," pp. ii-viii.
19. R. Cargill Hall, "Early U.S. Satellite Proposals," p. 76.
20. Project Rand Report, p. 9.
21. Ibid., p. 15.
22. The Army Air Force had been reorganized as a separate service under the National Security Act on 26 July 1947.
23. Quoted in Emme, *Aeronautics & Astronautics,* p. 59.
24. R. Cargill Hall, "Early U.S. Satellite Proposals," p. 86.
25. Ibid. p. 88.
26. Rand Corporation, "Conference on Methods for Studying the Psychological Effects of Unconventional Weapons: Summer Report," p. 11.
27. Ibid., p. 12.
28. A.V. Grosse, "Report on the Present Status of the Satellite Program," 25 August 1953. (NASA) At the time the report was prepared A.V. Grosse was associated with the Research Institute of Temple University.
29. Ibid., p. 6.
30. Albert Parry, *Russia's Rockets and Missiles,* p. 208.
31. Emme, *Aeronautics & Astronautics,* p. 51.
32. J. H. DeWitt, Jr., and E.K. Stodola, "Detection of Radio Signals

Reflected from the Moon," *Proceedings of the I.R.E.*, March 1949, p. 229.

33. Emme, *Aeronautics & Astronautics*, p. 75.

34. Emme, *The History of Space Flight*, p. 110.

35. Frank Malina, "The Jet Propulsion Laboratory," in Arthur C. Clarke, *The Coming of the Space Age*, p. 65.

36. Constance Green and Milton Lomask, *Vanguard: A History*, p. 11.

37. Emme, *A History of Space Flight*, p. 118.

38. Ibid., pp. 117-19.

39. Green and Lomask, *Vanguard*, p. 36.

40. Vernon Van Dyke, *Pride and Power*, pp. 13-14.

41. U.S., Congress, Senate, Committee on Armed Services, Subcommittee on Preparedness Investigating, *Inquiry into Satellite and Missile Programs, Hearings*, 85th Cong., 1st and 2nd sess., 1958, Part I, p. 320.

42. Van Dyke, *Pride and Power*, p. 14. Van Dyke is quoting a report to a House committee.

43. Ibid.

44. *New York Times*, 5 October 1957, p. 3.

45. To the credit of the Vanguard team, it should be noted that the 6 December launch was intended only as a test, but the White House press releases had created an impression of an actual launch. Vanguard was successfully launched before the end of the I.G.Y. and received top I.G.Y. honors for its scientific accomplishments. (Emme, *The History of Space Flight*, p. 123.)

46. Statement by Wernher von Braun cited in William R. Shelton, *Man's Conquest of Space*, p. 12.

47. Van Dyke, *Pride and Power*, p. 11.

48. U.S., Congress, House, Select Committee on Astronautics and Space Exploration, *The National Space Program, H.R. No. 1758*, 85th Cong., 2nd sess., 1958, pp. 30-31.

49. "Eisenhower Speaks on Science and Security," *Bulletin of the Atomic Scientists*, December 1957, p. 359.

50. Ibid.

51. In Eugene Rabinowitch's article "After Missiles and Satellites What," *Bulletin of the Atomic Scientists*, December 1957, pp. 346-50. The author mentions such a fantasy based on a 1946 piece by Louis Ridenour called "Pilot Lights of the Apocalypse," *Fortune*, January 1946, p. 116.

52. One of the first disparaging comments concerning Sputnik was voiced by Admiral Rawson Bennett, Chief of Naval Operations, the office in charge of launching U.S. satellites, when he said anybody could launch a "hunk of iron." (*New York Times*, 5 October 1957, p. 2)

53. Van Dyke, *Pride and Power*, p. 16.

54. Ibid., pp. 16-17.

55. Emme, *The History of Space Flight*, p. 125..

1. The *New York Times* published daily time records noting when the second Russian satellite would be over specific cities.

2. U.S., Congress, Senate, Committee on Armed Services, *Hearings, Inquiry into Satellite Programs,* 85th Cong., 2nd sess., 1958, Part 1, p. 3.

3. U.S., Congress, House, Select Committee on Astronautics and Space Exploration, *Hearings, Astronautics and Space Exploration,* 85th Cong., 2nd sess., 1958.

4. *New York Times,* 27 March 1958, p. 14.

5. Letter from President Eisenhower to the U.S. Congress, 2 April 1958. See *New York Times,* 3 April 1958, pp. 1, 14.

6. Eilene Galloway, "The Problems of Congress in Formulating Outer Space Legislation," U.S., Congress, House, Select Committee on Astronautics and Space Exploration, *Hearings, Astronautics and Space Exploration,* pp. 8-10.

7. Ibid., pp. 3-5.

8. Robert C. Rosholt, *An Administrative History of NASA, 1958-1963,* p. 5.

9. Lloyd N. Berkner, "Man's Space Satellites," reprinted in U.S., Congress, House, Select Committee on Astronautics and Space Exploration, *Hearings, Astronautics and Space Exploration,* p. 1079.

10. The National Aeronautics and Space Act of 1958, Public Law 85-568, *U.S.C.A. 42 § 2451,* approved 29 July 1958, Section (b). Emphasis added.

11. U.S., Congress, House, Committee on Science and Astronautics, *Hearings, Review of the Space Program,* 86th Cong., 2nd sess., 1960, testimony of Richard Horner, p. 236.

12. *U.S.C.A. 42 § 2451,* (c).

13. Ibid., *42 § 2452(1).*

14. U.S., Congress, Senate, Committee on Aeronautical and Space Sciences, *Policy Planning for Space Telecommunications,* Staff Report, 86th Cong., 2nd sess., 1960, pp. 102-125; 191-201.

15. U.S., Congress, House, Committee on Science and Astronautics, *Hearings, Communications Satellites,* 87th Cong., 1st sess., 1961, Part 1, p. 12.

16. Ibid., 408.

17. U.S., Congress, House, Committee on Science and Astronautics, *Hearings, Satellites for World Communications,* 86th Cong., 1st. sess., 1959, p. 36.

18. Ibid., p. 38.

19. Ibid., p. 115.

20. Ibid., pp. 50-55; see also U.S., Congress, House, Committee on Science and Astronautics, *Hearings, Communications Satellites,* Part 1, p. 409.

21. Lawrence Lessing, "Launching a Communications System in Space," *The Space Industry, Fortune* editors, p. 141.

22. Letter from T. Keith Glennan of NASA to deputy secretary of

defense, Department of Defense, dated 18 August 1960, as reprinted in U.S., Congress, Senate, Committee on Aeronautical and Space Sciences, *Policy Planning Report,* p. 201.

23. Ibid., p. 113.

24. T. Keith Glennan of NASA, testimony in the U.S., Congress, House, Committee on Science and Astronautics, *Review of the Space Program,* p. 168.

25. Ibid., p. 382. Statement by Dr. Tepper of NASA.

26. U.S., Congress, House, Committee in Science and Astronautics, *Satellites for World Communications, Hearings,* 86th Cong., 1st sess., 1959, p. 15.

27. "NASA Compendium of Satellite Communications Programs," p. 2-1.

28. Ibid., p. 2-8.

29. Ibid., p. 2-2.

30. Ibid., p. 4-1.

31. Ibid., p. 4-2.

32. Pierce, *Science, Art and Communications,* pp. 40-45.

33. Midwest Research Institute, "Economic Impact of Stimulated Technological Activity: Part II – Case Study – Technological Progress and Commercialization of Communication Satellites," p. 7. See also correspondence file for John R. Pierce (NASA).

34. See Leonard Jaffe, *Communications in Space,* pp. 67-91, for a technical description of the Echo system.

35. "NASA Compendium of Satellite Communications Programs," p. 3-5.

36. U.S., Congress, House, Committee on Government Operations, *Government Operations in Space,* Thirteenth Report, 89th Cong., 1st sess., 1965, p. 124.

37. Jaffe, *Communications in Space,* p. 80.

38. Ibid.

39. U.S., Congress, Senate, Committee on Aeronautical and Space Sciences, Staff Report, *United States International Space Programs,* 89th Cong., 1st sess., 1965, p. 409 ff.

40. "NASA Compendium of Satellite Communications," p. 3-20.

41. NASA, *Sixth Semiannual Report to Congress, July 1 through December 31, 1961,* 1962, p. 38.

42. *New York Times,* 25 July 1960, pp. 1, 10.

43. *Washington (D.C.) Star,* 27 December 1958, p. 1.

44. U.S., Congress, Senate, Committee on Aeronautical and Space Sciences, *Policy Planning Report,* pp. 115, 118.

45. Ibid., p. 14.

46. U.S., Congress, House, Committee on Science and Astronautics, *Project Advent, Military Communications Satellite Program, Report,* 87th Cong., 1st sess., 1962.

47. U.S., Congress, House, Committee on Science and Astronautics, *Hearings, Project Advent – Military Communications Satellite Program,* 87th Cong., 2nd sess., 1962, p. 91.

48. Ibid.

49. U.S., Congress, House, Committee on Science and Astronautics, *Hearings, Satellites for World Communications,* p. 36.

50. Ibid.

51. C.C. Cutler, "Radio Communication by Means of Satellites," Bell Telephone Laboraties, enclosure in letter from John Pierce to Dr. Dryden, 14 June 1959, report dated 12 January 1959, pp. 1-2. (NASA)

52. *New York Times,* 18 October 1960, p. 10.

53. *Wall Street Journal,* 30 September 1960, p. 20.

54. Letter, Jerrems to Carver, 17 September 1959. (NASA)

55. Letter, Jerrems to Distribution, 9 October 1959, Hughes Aircraft Company. (NASA)

56. Letter, Lutz to Haeff, 22 October 1959. (NASA)

57. Hughes Aircraft Company, "Commercial Communication Satellite," January 1960.

58. Interview with D. P. Rogers, Washington, D.C., 19 November 1973; interview with Leonard Jaffe, Washington, D.C., 3 September 1974.

59. Notes of Interview, E. W. Morse with Leonard Jaffe, 14 August 1964. (NASA)

60. Letter, Puckett to Clark, 8 April 1960; letter, Lord to Puckett, 19 July 1960. (NASA)

1. U.S., Congress, Senate, Committee on Aeronautical and Space Sciences, *Radio Frequency Control in Space Telecommunications,* 86th cong., 2nd sess., 1960.

2. Two documents assessing U.S. frequency needs appeared during 1960: *Radio Frequency Control in Space Telecommunications* by Dr. Edward Wenk, Jr., and *Policy Planning for Space Telecommunications,* a Senate Staff Report prepared at the request of Senator Lyndon B. Johnson, Chairman of the Senate Committee on Aeronautical and Space Sciences. Both reports served to focus the importance of this country's early identification of space frequency requirements. The latter also made a point of stressing the "need for expanding the base of interest on the part of other—particularly less technologically developed—nations, in the benefits of space communications" *(Policy Planning Report,* p. 96). This was important in planning for acceptance of the U.S. position on international frequency allocation because the United States was anticipating some resistance to its frequency requests by communist nations. Additionally, the *Policy Planning Report* devoted some passages to possible operational space communications demands with respect to international traffic requirements as an attempt to indicate the commercial potential of satellite links.

3. Frutkin, *International Cooperation in Space,* p. 142.

4. Letter from William B. Macomber, Department of State, to Senator L. B. Johnson, 23 June 1960, reprinted in Appendix I of the U.S., Congress, Senate, Committee on Aeronautical and Space Sciences, *Policy Planning Report,* pp. 145-49.

5. Letter from James Gleason of NASA to Senator L. B. Johnson, 12 July 1960, reprinted in U.S., Congress, Senate, *Policy Planning Report,* pp. 127-32.

6. *New York Times,* 18 October 1960, p. 10. Also see Files of Robert Nunn, vol. 3 (NASA), for mention of AT&T's interactions with foreign governments.

7. For information concerning the 1960 level of NASA's interest, see the memorandum from Special Assistant Robert Nunn to Administrator T. K. Glennan, 1 August 1960, Nunn Files. (NASA)

8. U.S., Congress, House, Select Committee on Astronautics and Space Exploration, *The Next Ten Years in Space 1959-1969,* Staff Report, 86th Cong., 1st sess., 1959, p. 121.

9. U.S., Congress, House, Committee on Science and Astronautics, *Satellites for World Communications, Report,* p. 5.

10. Letter from General Johnson to T. K. Glennan, 12 December 1958. (NASA)

11. Another example of NASA-DOD was the formation of a new Aeronautics and Astronautics Coordinating Board. U.S., Congress, Senate, Committee on Aeronautical and Space Sciences, *Policy Planning Report,* p. 27.

12. For further information about NASA-DOD working relationships see U.S., Congress, House, Committee on Science and Astronautics, *Hearings, 1963 NASA Authorization,* 87th Cong., 2nd sess., 1962, Part 5, pp. 2226-35.

13. Enclosure in a letter from James P. Gleason to L.B. Johnson, 12 July 1960, reprinted in U.S., Congress, Senate, Committee on Aeronautical and Space Sciences, *Policy Planning Report,* Appendix A, pp. 127-32.

14. Hughes Aircraft Company, Space Systems Division, "Syncom III 100-Day Performance Summary," 1 December 1964, p. 7.

15. See Nunn Files, vol. 3, for various memoranda on these meetings. (NASA)

16. Memorandum of Robert Nunn to T. K. Glennan, 3 March 1960, Nunn Files, vol. 3. (NASA)

17. Interview with Robert Nunn, 2 October 1974.

18. This agreement was formalized by letter, Glennan to Douglas, 18 August 1960. (NASA)

19. NASA News Release No. 60-262, 15 September 1960. (NASA)

20. Memorandum, Robert Nunn to T. K. Glennan, 1 August 1960, Nunn Files, vol. 3. (NASA)

21. Memorandum, T. K. Glennan for file, 18 August 1960, Nunn Files, vol. 3. (NASA)

22. Booz-Allen and Hamilton, "Business Planning Study for a Commercial Telecommunications Satellite," prepared for Lockheed Aircraft Corporation, 31 October 1960.

23. The Rand Corporation, RM–2709–NASA, September 1960; RM–2809–NASA, June 1961; RM–2778–NASA, June 1961. See also, the House Staff Report of the Select Committee on Astronautics and Space Exploration, *Space Handbook: Astonautics and its Applications,* prepared in connection with Rand.

24. Francis S. Humphrey, "A Resumé of Worldwide Commercial Communications," 5 December 1960. (NASA)

25. Interview with Robert Nunn, 2 October 1974.

26. *Fortune* Editors, *The Space Industry,* p. 135.

27. Booz-Allen and Hamilton, "Business Planning Study," pp. 39-66.

28. *Fortune* Editors, *The Space Industry,* p. 135.

29. Ibid.

30. The National Aeronautics and Space Act of 1958, Section 102(c) (5).

31. U.S. Congress, Senate, *Policy Planning Report,* p. 117.

32. Memorandum from Robert Nunn to T.K. Glennan, 2 September 1960, Nunn Files, vol. 3. (NASA)

33. Interview with Robert Nunn, 2 October 1974.

34. T. Keith Glennan, "Space Exploration and Exploitation," presentation to the Science, Engineering and New Technologies Committee, Oregon State Department of Planning and Development, Portland, Oregon, 12 October 1960, Nunn Files, vol. 1. (NASA)

35. Ibid.

36. Senator Johnson requested a staff report on space telecommunications and also addressed a series of inquiries to various departments and agencies on space communications during 1960. Replies to these inquiries are reprinted in the Appendix A of the U.S., Congress, Senate, Committee on Aeronautical and Space Sciences, *Policy Planning Report.*

37. Memorandum for file by T. K. Glennan, 18 August 1960, Nunn Files, vol. 3. (NASA)

38. Memorandum to members of the Unmanned Spacecraft Panel from Homer Newell, 21 November 1960, Nunn Files, vol. 3. (NASA)

39. See Nunn Files, vol. 3 (NASA), for memoranda relating to October industry conferences.

40. Letter from George Best, Vice President of AT&T to T. K. Glennan, NASA, 15 September 1960, Nunn Files, vol. 3. (NASA)

41. Internal NASA memorandum on NASA – AT&T Conference, 16 September 1960, Nunn Files, vol. 3. (NASA)

42. Letter from George Best to T. K. Glennan, 15 September 1960, Nunn Files, vol. 3. (NASA)

43. Letter from E. I. Green, executive vice-president, AT&T, to T. K. Glennan, 20 October 1960, "Proposed Bell System Experiment on Active Satellite Communications," enclosed, Nunn Files, vol. 2. (NASA)

44. Letter from J. B. Fisk, president, AT&T, to T. K. Glennan, 24 October 1960, "Draft Discussion: Bell System Plans for Transoceanic Communications via Active Satellites," enclosed, Nunn Files, vol. 2. (NASA)

45. Memorandum by Robert Nunn regarding 27 October 1960 NASA meeting with AT&T, 31 October 1960, Nunn Files, vol. 2. (NASA)

46. Memorandum by Robert Nunn for T.K. Glennan, 25 October 1960, Nunn Files, vol. 3. (NASA)

47. Memorandum by Robert Nunn regarding 27 October 1960 NASA meeting with AT&T, 31 October 1960, Nunn Files, vol. 2. (NASA)

48. Interview with L. Jaffe, 3 September 1974.

49. Memorandum by Robert Nunn to file, 6 October 1960, Nunn Files, vol. 3. (NASA)

50. Interview with Robert Nunn, 2 October 1974.

51. White House Press Release, 30 December 1960. (NASA)

52. Letter from F. R. Kappel, president, AT&T, to J. Webb, administrator, NASA, 5 April 1960, Nunn Files, vol. 3. (NASA)

53. Memorandum for the record, Robert Nunn, 23 December 1960, Nunn Files, vol. 3. (NASA)

54. On 12 January 1961 George Best sent a telegram to T.K. Glennan stating that AT&T was prepared to arrange for ground stations equipment and operation overseas. On 17 January Robert Nunn replied to Best's telegram stating only that NASA would discuss the nature of AT&T participation in NASA negotiations with foreign countries. Best in turn responded in a letter dated 19 January 1961 that a misunderstanding had arisen regarding AT&T's role. He felt that AT&T should be allowed to handle

negotiations with overseas communications agencies with respect to the provisions of ground stations. Nunn Files, vol. 2. (NASA)

55. Memorandum by Robert Nunn regarding NASA—AT&T meeting, held 31 January 1961, Nunn Files, vol. 2. (NASA)

56. Memorandum of Understanding Between the Federal Communications Commission and the National Aeronautics and Space Administration, 27 February 1961, Nunn Files, vol. 1. (NASA)

57. Ibid.

58. U.S., Congress, House, Committee on Science and Astronautics, *1962 NASA Authorization Hearings,* 87th Cong., 1st sess., 1961, Part 3, p. 1039; U.S., Congres, Senate, Committee on Aeronautical and Space Sciences, *1962 NASA Authorization Hearings,* 87th Cong., 1st sess., 1961, p. 36.

59. NASA News Release No. 61-65, "Background Briefing on the Budget," 28 March 1961, Nunn Files, vol. 1. (NASA)

60. Jack Posner, "The Implementation of the Communications Satellite Act of 1962," Ph.D. dissertation, American University, 1967, p. 67.

61. NASA News Release No. 61-65, 28 March 1961, p. 3.

62. Ibid.

63. Ibid.

64. U.S., Congress, House, Committee on Science and Astronautics, *1962 NASA Authorization Hearings,* p. 192. Emphasis added.

65. Letter from Newton N. Minow, chairman, FCC, to James Webb, administrator, NASA, 26 April 1961, Nunn Files, vol. 1. (NASA)

66. NASA News Release No. 61-164, "NASA to Launch AT&T Experimental Communications Satellite," 28 July 1961, Nunn Files, vol. 1. (NASA)

67. "Report to the President-Elect of the Ad Hoc Committee on Space," reprinted in U.S., Congress, House, Committee on Science and Astronautics, *Defense Space Interests,* 87th Cong., 1st sess., 1961, pp. 22-23.

68. Ibid.

69. Letter from President John F. Kennedy to James Webb, administrator, NASA, 15 May 1961, Nunn Files, vol. 1. (NASA)

70. Ibid.

71. NASA News Release No. 61-112, statement by James E. Webb, following president's message to Congress, 25 May 1961, Nunn Files, vol. 1. (NASA)

72. Memorandum by Robert Nunn to James E. Webb, administrator, NASA, 1 May 1961, Nunn Files, vol. 3. (NASA)

73. Memorandum by Robert Nunn to Administrator James E. Webb, NASA, 11 May 1961, Nunn Files, vol. 3. (NASA)

74. U.S., President, *Public Papers of the Presidents of the United States,* John F. Kennedy, 1961, p. 472.

75. Memorandum by E.C. Welsh for the President from the National Aeronautics and Space Council, 15 July 1961, Nunn Files, vol. 1. (NASA)

76. U.S., President, *Public Papers,* Kennedy, p. 530.

77. Ibid.

78. "NASA Compendium," p. 7-1.

79. *NASA Seventh Semiannual Report to Congress,* 1963, p. 64.

80. Memorandum for the record, Robert Nunn, 19 May 1961, Nunn Files, vol. 3. (NASA)

81. Midwest Research Institute, "Economic Impact," Part II, p. 9.

82. "NASA Compendium," p. 6-1.

83. Jaffe, *Communications in Space,* p. 112.

84. U.S., Congress, Senate, Committee on Aeronautical and Space Sciences, *1962 NASA Authorization Hearings,* p. 44-49.

85. U.S., Congress, House, Committee on Science and Astronautics, *Hearings, Project Advent,* pp. 30, 98.

86. Ibid., pp. 96-102.

87. Letter, Deputy Secretary of Defense to James Webb, administrator, NASA, 28 June 1961. (NASA)

88. Notes from an Interview of Edgar Morse with Leonard Jaffe, 14 August 1964. (NASA)

89. Ibid.

90. Letter from NASA Headquarters to Goddard, 27 July 1961. (NASA)

91. "Sole Source Justification," Goddard Contract File, n.d. (NASA)

92. NASA News Release No. 61-178, "NASA Announces Project Syncom." (NASA)

93. "NASA Compendium," pp. 8-1 to 8-14.

94. "Memorandum of Understanding Between NASA and the Department of Defense Concerning the Transfer of Control and Syncom II and III to the DOD," 31 December 1964. (NASA)

95. Interview with Robert Nunn, 2 October 1974.

1. U.S., National Aeronautics and Space Administration, "Memorandum of Understanding Between the Federal Communications Commission and the National Aeronautics and Space Administration," 27 February 1961, Nunn Files, vol. 1. (NASA)

2. The 12 respondents to FCC Docket 14024 included: American Rocket Society; American Securities Corporation (for the future Western Union International, Inc.); American Telephone and Telegraph Company; General Electric Company; General Telephone and Electronics Corporation; Hawaiian Telephone Company; International Telephone and Telegraph Corporation (and American Cable & Radio Corporation); Lockheed Aircraft Corporation; Press Wireless, Inc.; Radio Corporation of America (and RCA Communications, Inc.); the Western Union Telegraph Company; and the Department of Justice (commenting only on antitrust matters). Replies to such responses were filed by American Telephone and Telegraph Company, General Electric Company, and Lockheed Aircraft Corporation. U.S., FCC, "First Report on Docket 14024," 24 May 1961, reprinted in U.S., Congress, Senate, Select Committee on Small Business, Subcommittee on Monopoly, *Hearings, Space Satellite Communications,* 87th Cong., 1st sess., 1961, p. 494.

3. Ibid.

4. Ibid.

5. *Fortune* Editors, *The Space Industry,* pp. 142-43.

6. U.S., Congress, Senate, Select Committee on Small Business, Subcommittee on Monopoly, *Hearings, Space Satellite Communications,* p. 494.

7. Ibid.

8. Ibid.

9. Ibid., p. 489.

10. The five minor international carriers included: Hawaiian Telephone Co.; Press Wireless, Inc.; South Puerto Rico Sugar Corp.; Tropical Radio Telegraph Co.; and United States-Liberia Radio Corp., ibid., p. 680.

11. Ad Hoc Carrier Committee, Report of the Ad Hoc Carrier Committee to the Federal Communications Commission, reprinted in U.S., Congress, Senate, Select Committee on Small Business, Subcommittee on Monopoly, *Hearings, Space Satellite Communications,* Part. 2, pp. 690-93.

12. "Minority Statement of the Western Union Telegraph Company, Report of the Ad Hoc Carrier Committee to the Federal Communications Commission," 12 October 1961, reprinted in ibid., Part 2, p. 726.

13. Jonathan F. Galloway, *The Politics and Technology of Satellite Communications,* p. 41.

14. U.S., Congress, Senate, Select Committee on Small Business, Subcommittee on Monopoly, *Hearings, Space Satellite Communications.* Part 2, p. 663.

15. U.S., Congress, Senate, Committee on the Judiciary, Subcommittee on

Antitrust and Monopoly, *Hearings, Antitrust Problems of the Satellite Communication System,* 87th Cong., 2nd sess., 1962, Part 1, p. 142.

16. Ibid., Part 2, p. 320.

17. Ibid., Part 2, p. 321.

18. Letter to the president from selected members of Congress, 24 August 1961, reprinted in U.S., Congress, Senate, Committee on Foreign Relations, *Hearings, Communication Satellite Act of 1962,* 87th Cong., 2nd sess., 1962, pp. 51-54.

19. Posner, "The Communications Satellite Act of 1962," p. 86.

20. Ibid., p. 86-87.

21. Interview with Robert Nunn, 2 October 1974.

22. Ibid.; also Galloway, *The Politics and Technology of Satellite Communications,* pp. 47-48.

23. Ibid., p. 48.

24. U.S., Congress, House, Committee on Interstate and Foreign Commerce, *Hearings, Communications Satellites,* 87th Cong., 2nd sess., 1962, Part 2, p. 363-64.

25. Posner, "The Communications Satellite Act of 1962," p. 93.

26. Ibid., p. 101-10.

27. Ibid., p. 107-108.

28. Ibid., p. 110-12.

29. U.S., Congress, Senate, Committee on Aeronautical and Space Sciences, *Communications Satellite Act of 1962,* 87th Cong., 2nd sess., 1962, p. 3-9; U.S., Congress, Senate, Committee on Commerce, *Hearings, Communications Satellite Legislation,* 87th Cong., 2nd sess., 1962, p. 13-16, 18-21, 24-25.

30. Posner, "The Communications Satellite Act of 1962," pp. 122-26; Galloway, *The Politics and Technology of Satellite Communications,* pp. 67-68.

31. U.S., Congress, Senate, Committee on Commerce, *Communications Satellite Act of 1962,* p. 55.

32. Posner, "The Communications Satellite Act of 1962," p. 116.

33. U.S., Congress, Senate, Committee on the Judiciary, Subcommittee on Antitrust and Monopoly, *Satellite Communications Hearings,* Part 1, p. 3.

34. U.S., Congress, Senate, Committee on Aeronautical and Space Sciences, *Hearings, Communications Satellite Legislation,* 87th Cong., 2nd sess., 1962, p. 353.

35. U.S., Congress, Senate, Committee on Commerce, *Communications Satellite Act of 1962,* p. 51.

36. Galloway, *The Politics and Technology of Satellite Communications,* p. 55.

37. U.S., Congress, Senate, Committee on Commerce, *Hearings, Communications Satellite Legislation,* p. 339.

38. U.S., Congress, Senate, Committee on Foreign Relations, *Communications Satellite Act of 1962,* p. 7.

39. Galloway, *The Politics and Technology of Satellite Communications,* p. 69; Posner, "The Communications Satellite Act of 1962", p. 127-29.
40. Communications Satellite Act of 1962, Public Law 87-624, *U.S.C.A. 47 § 731.*
41. Posner, "The Communications Satellite Act of 1962," p. 134.
42. Communications Satellite Act of 1962, *U.S.C.A. 47 § 721(a).*
43. *U.S.C.A. 47 § 721 (c).*
44. *U.S.C.A. 47 § 742.*
45. U.S., Congress, House, Committee on Government Operations, Subcommittee on Military Operations, *Satellite Communications,* 88th Cong., 2nd sess., 1964, p. 37.
46. *U.S.C.A. 47 § 721(b).*
47. U.S., Congress, House, Committee on Government Operations, Subcommittee on Military Operations, *Satellite Communications,* pp. 36-37.
48. *U.S.C.A. 47 § 735(b)(1).*
49. Interview with Leonard Jaffe, Deputy Associate Administrator for Applications, NASA Headquarters, 3 September 1974.
50. U.S., Congress, House, Committee on Government Operations, Subcommittee on Military Operations, *Satellite Communications,* p. 37.
51. Ibid.
52. U.S., Congress, Senate, Committee on Commerce, Subcommittee on Communications, *Hearings, Satellite Communications,* 88th Cong., 1st sess., 1963, pp. 158-59.
53. U.S., Congress, House, Committee on Science and Astronautics, Subcommittee on Applications and Tracking and Data Acquisition, *Hearings, 1964 NASA Authorization,* 88th Cong., 1st sess, 1963, pp. 3162-67.
54. U.S., Congress, Senate, Committee on Commerce, Subcommittee on Communications, *Satellite Communications Hearings,* p. 64.
55. U.S., Congress, House, Committee on Science and Astronautics, Subcommittee on Applications and Tracking and Data Acquisition, *Hearings 1964 NASA Authorization,* p. 3169.
56. Ibid., p. 3137.
57. Ibid, pp. 3155-70.
58. U.S., Congress, House, Committee on Government Operations, Subcommittee on Military Operations, *Satellite Communications,* p. 39.
59. Leonard Jaffe, "NASA Communication Satellite Developments," *Astronautics and Aerospace Engineering,* p. 49.
60. U.S., Congress, House, Committee on Science and Astronautics, Subcommittee on Applications and Tracking and Data Acquisition, *Hearings 1964 NASA Authorization,* pp. 3161-62.
61. Jaffe, "NASA Communication Satellite Developments," p. 49.
62. U.S., Congress, House, Committee on Science and Astronautics, Subcommittee on Applications and Tracking and Data Acquisition, *Hearings 1964 NASA Authorization,* p. 3160.
63. Ibid., p. 3164.

64. Ibid., p. 3206.
65. Ibid.
66. Ibid.
67. Ibid., p. 3155.
68. Ibid., p. 3160.
69. Ibid., p. 3167.
70. Ibid., p. 3159.
71. Ibid., p. 3205.
72. U.S., Congress, House, Committee on Government Operations, Subcommittee on Military Operations, *Satellite Communications*, p. 37.
73. Ibid., p. 39.
74. U.S., Congress, House, Committee on Science and Astronautics, Subcommittee on Applications and Tracking and Data Acquisition, *1964 NASA Authorization Hearings*, p. 3327.
75. Ibid.
76. Ibid., p. 3328.
77. Ibid.
78. U.S., Congress, House, Committee on Government Operations, Subcommittee on Military Operations, *Satellite Communications*, p. 42.
79. Ibid., emphasis added.
80. U.S., Congress, House, Committee on Science and Astronautics, *Authorizing Appropriations to the National Aeronautics and Space Administration*, 88th Cong., 2nd sess., 1964, p. 96.

1. *U.S.C.A. 42 § 2451-77.* For a description and discussion of the National Aeronautics and Space Act of 1958, see Chapter 3.
2. *U.S.C.A. 42 § 2451(c).*
3. *U.S.C.A. 42 § 2475.*
4. *U.S.C.A. 42 § 2451(b).*
5. Information from "International Programs," prepared by the Office of International Affairs of NASA, January 1975. (NASA)
6. Letter from Leonard Jaffe to Dr. Rechtin, Jet Propulsion Lab, Enclosure, Project Echo, 25 August 1959, pp. 1-2. (NASA)
7. Robert J. Mackey, Jr., memorandum entitled "Project Echo Program for Independent Experimenters," 14 March 1960. (NASA)
8. Arnold W. Frutkin, *International Cooperation in Space,* p. 5.
9. *New York Times,* 13 August 1960, p. 1.
10. Robert J. Mackey, Jr., Memorandum entitled "Project Echo, Meeting to Discuss Foreign Participation," 9 September 1960. (NASA)
11. U.S., Congress, Senate, Committee on Aeronautical and Space Sciences, *Policy Planning Report,* pp. 192-93.
12. Notes of interview of Edgar W. Morse with Leonard Jaffe on 14 August 1964, p. 4.
13. "Memorandum of Understanding Between Her Majesty's Post Office and the U.S. National Aeronautics and Space Administration," 14 February 1961, as reprinted in U.S., Congress, Senate, Committee on Aeronautical and Space Sciences, Staff Report, *United States International Space Programs,* 89th Cong., 1st sess., 1965.
14. "Memorandum of Understanding Between the National Center for Telecommunications Research (France) and the U.S. National Aeronautics and Space Administration," 27 February 1961, reprinted in U.S., Congress, Senate, Committee on Aeronautical and Space Sciences, *U.S. International Space Programs.*
15. Ibid., pp. 229-79.
16. During the early 1960s the United States attempted to initiate a program of bilateral satellite experimentation with the Soviet Union. In August 1961, one year after the launch of Echo I, NASA's Arnold Frutkin suggested to A.A. Blagonravov of the Soviet Academy of Sciences that the two nations transmit voice communications via satellite as a gesture of good will. During March of the following year, President Kennedy and Chairman Khruschev exchanged written correspondence in which they discussed the prospects for cooperation in space. Shortly thereafter, Hugh L. Dryden, then deputy administrator of NASA, negotiated the requisite arrangements with Mr. Blagonravov for joint experimentation with the Echo II spacecraft. NASA launched the satellite on 25 January 1964 and within a month radio signals transmitted from Jodrell Bank Observatory in Great Britain were

bounced off Echo II's aluminum surface and received in the Soviet Union.

Despite the success of this venture, continued bilateral experimentation did not characterize the years ahead. In fact the Soviet Union chose to develop communication satellite technology in virtual isolation. On 23 April 1965 the Soviet Union launched its first commercial communication satellite, Molniya I, into an elliptical polar orbit. The satellite reached two 24,000 mile high apogees during its twenty-four hour orbital period, one over Soviet territory and the other over the North American continent. After launching seventeen Molniya I spacecraft, the Soviet Union in 1971 introduced the improved Molniya II series of communication satellites. Like their predecessors, the Molniya II satellites utilize the eccentric polar orbit and provide long distance television, telephone and telegraph distribution services. In December 1974 the Soviet Union launched and positioned a Statsionar satellite into geosynchronous orbit.

The Molniya satellites function as the space segment of the Orbita domestic communications system. A special effort was made to extend satellite coverage throughout the Soviet Union for the fiftieth anniversary in 1967 of the Russian Revolution. In November of the anniversary year, Radio Moscow was able to report that twenty-three Orbita ground stations were supplying nearly 100 million people with modern space communications. On 5 August 1968 the Soviet Union along with Bulgaria, Cuba, Czechoslovakia, Hungary, Mongolia, Poland and Rumania announced plans for the establishment of an international satellite system, known as Intersputnik. Even though invitations were extended to the Western nations, the Intersputnik system has never constituted an economic threat to Intelsat, the total membership of which had already reached eighty-two by the time that the signatories finalized the arrangements for their system in 1971 and deposited a treaty with the United Nations. For additional information about Soviet activities with communication satellites, see Frutkin, *International Cooperation in Space;* U.S., Congress, Senate, Committee on Aeronautical and Space Sciences, *Soviet Space Programs 1962-1965: Goals, Purposes, Achievements and Plans,* 89th Cong., 2nd sess., 30 December 1966; U.S., Congress, Senate, Committee on Aeronautical and Space Sciences, *Soviet Space Programs 1966-1970,* 92nd Cong., 1st sess., 9 December 1971; Shelton, *Soviet Space Exploration: The First Decade;* and T.L. Shillinglaw, "The Soviet Union and International Satellite Communications," *Stanford Journal of International Studies* (June 1970), pp. 199-226; and S.E. Doyle, "An Analysis of the Socialist States' Proposal for Intersputnik: An International Communications Satellite System," *Villanova Law Review* 15 (Fall 1969), pp. 83-105.

17. Frutkin, *International Cooperation in Space,* p. 64.

18. Ibid.

19. U.S., Congress, Senate, Committee on Aeronautical and Space Sciences, *Policy Planning Report,* p. 3.

20. Ibid., p. 96.

21. Robert G. Nunn, Jr., memorandum for Dr. Glennan, 1 August 1960,

Files of Robert Nunn, vol. 3. (NASA)

22. Ibid.

23. U.S., President, *Public Papers of the Presidents of the United States*, Dwight Eisenhower, 1960-61, pp. 889-90.

24. "Statement of Mr. James E. Webb before the House Committee on Science and Astronautics," 10 April 1961, Nunn files, vol. 1. (NASA)

25. "Memorandum of Understanding Between the Federal Communications Commission and the National Aeronautics and Space Administration," 27 February 1961, Nunn files, vol. 1. (NASA)

26. For a full discussion and description of President Kennedy's statement on communication satellite policy, see Chapter 4.

27. Statement of Mr. James E. Webb before the House Committee on Science and Astronautics, 13 July 1961, Nunn files, vol. 1. (NASA)

28. Galloway, *The Politics and Technology of Satellite Communications*, pp. 48-49.

29. Ibid., p. 49.

30. U.S., Congress, Senate, Committee on Aeronautical and Space Sciences, *Hearings, Communications Satellite Legislation*, 87th Cong., 2nd sess., 1962, p. 159.

31. On 7 February 1962 the president's bill was introduced to the Senate as S. 12814 and in the House as H.R. 10138.

32. U.S., Congress, Senate, Committee on Aeronautical and Space Sciences, *Hearings, Communications Satellite Legislation*, p. 309.

33. Communications Satellite Act of 1962, *U.S.C.A. 47 § 742.*

34. U.S., Congress, Senate, Committee on Foreign Relations, *Hearings, Communications Satellite Act of 1962*, 87th Cong., 2nd sess., 1962, p. 199.

35. Ibid., p. 274.

36. Ibid., p. 191.

37. Ibid., p. 172, 178.

38. Ibid., p. 260.

39. Galloway, *The Politics and Technology of Satellite Communications*, pp. 93-94.

40. Ibid., p. 81.

41. Letter of Leo D. Welch to E. William Henry, chairman of FCC, 7 August 1963. Reprinted as Attachment C in U.S., Congress, House, Committee on Interstate and Foreign Commerce, *Communications Satellite Act of 1962—The First Year*, 88th Cong., 1st sess., 1963, p. 19.

42. Abram Chayes, Thomas Ehrlich, Andreas F. Lowenfeld, *International Legal Process*, p. 662

43. Ibid.

44. Richard N. Gardner, "Space Meteorology and Communications: A Challenge to Science and Diplomacy," *Department of State Bulletin*, 13 May 1963, pp. 743-45.

45. Judith Tegger Kildow, *Intelsat: Policy-Maker's Dilemma*, p. 14.

46. Galloway, *The Politics and Technology of Satellite Communications*, p. 83.

47. U.S., Congress, House, Committee on Interstate and Foreign Commerce, *Communications Satellite Act of 1962 – The First Year,* p. 29.

48. Chayes, *International Legal Process,* p. 663.

49. Kildow, *Intelsat,* p. 14.

50. Communications Satellite Corporation, "Statement Relating to Anticipated Participation by Foreign Governments or Business Entities in Such a System," reprinted in U.S., Congress, House, Committee on Interstate and Foreign Commerce, *Communications Satellite Act of 1962 – The First Year.*

51. U.S., Congress, Senate, Committee on Foreign Relations, *Hearings, Communications Satellite Act of 1962,* p. 274.

52. Statement of Mr James E. Webb before the House Committee on Science and Astronautics, 13 July 1961, Nunn files, vol. 1. (NASA)

53. Frutkin, *International Cooperation in Space,* p. 152.

54. Galloway, *The Politics and Technology of Satellite Communications,* p. 76.

55. "Report on Geneva Space Radio Communication Conference and Progress Made in Establishing Global Communication Satellite System," as printed in *U.S. Congressional Record,* House, 88th Cong., 2nd sess., 1964, p. 183.

56. Ibid.

57. Ibid.

58. Richard R. Colino, "Intelsat: Doing Business in Outer Space," *The Columbia Journal of Transnational Law,* 6 (Spring 1967): 30.

59. "Report on Geneva Space Radio Conference," *U.S. Congressional Record,* House, 1964, p. 186.

60. Ibid.

61. Ibid.

62. Ibid., p. 189.

63. Chayes, *International Legal Process,* p. 663.

64. Galloway, *The Politics and Technology of Satellite Communications,* p. 87.

65. *New York Times,* 9 February 1964, p. 1.

66. *New York Times,* 26 January 1964, p. 2.

67. Interview with Leonard Jaffe, Deputy Associate Administrator of the Office of Applications, NASA Headquarters, Washington, D.C., 3 September 1974.

68. U.S., Congress, House, Committee on Government Operations, Subcommittee on Military Operations, *Hearings on Satellite Communications – 1964,* 88th Cong., 2nd sess., 1964, p. 119.

69. *New York Times,* 26 January 1964, p. 2.

70. U.S., Congress, House, Committee on Government Operations, Subcommittee on Military Operations, *Hearings on Satellite Communications,* p. 662.

71. Ibid., pp. 663-64.

72. *New York Times,* 9 February 1964, p. 1.

73. Galloway, *The Politics and Technology of Satellite Communications*, pp. 95-96.

74. U.S., Congress, House, Committee on Government Operations, Subcommittee on Military Operations, *Hearings on Satellite Communications*, pp. 661-64.

75. Colino, "Intelsat," pp. 45-56.

76. Ibid.

77. U.S., Congress, House, Committee on Government Operations, Subcommittee on Military Operations, *Hearings on Satellite Communications*, p. 667.

78. Colino, "Intelsat," pp. 45-56.

79. "Agreement with Other Government Establishing Interim Arrangements for a Global Commercial Communications Satellite System," Art. IX(c).

80. U.S., Congress, House, Committee on Government Operations, Subcommittee on Military Operations, *Hearings on Satellite Communications*, pp. 668-69.

81. Ibid., p. 668.

82. Ibid.

83. "Agreement with Other Governments Establishing Interim Arrangements for a Global Commercial Communications Satellite System with Special Agreement," 20 August 1964, *15. U.S.T. 1705*, T.I.A.S. No. 5646.

84. U.S., Department of State, *Department of State Bulletin*, 24 August 1964.

85. Richard N. Gardner, "Space Meteorology and Communications: A Challenge to Science and Diplomacy," *Department of State Bulletin*, 13 May 1963, pp. 743-44.

86. Kildow, *Intelsat*, p. 15.

87. Postmaster General of Great Britain as quoted in U.S., Congress, House, Committee on Government Operations, Subcommittee on Military Operations, *Hearings on Satellite Communications*, Part 1, p. 28.

88. W.C. Wetmore, "U.S.-Europe Divided on Comsats," *Aviation Week and Space Technology*, 15 July 1968, pp. 39-43.

89. Kildow, *Intelsat*, p. 33.

90. The use of this approach in the European Space Research Organization and the European Launch Development Organization generated numerous management debates and was one of the reasons for the lack of significant achievement in satellite development during the 1960s.

91. Katherine Johnsen, "Intelsat IV Program Stresses International Subcontracting," *Aviation Week and Space Technology*, 1 July 1968, pp. 52-53.

92. Kildow, *Intelsat*, p. 54.

93. Spokesman for Arab—Latin American bloc as quoted in Katherine Johnson, "Arabs Hit Intelsat Subcontracting," *Aviation Week and Space Technology*, 27 January 1969, p. 23.

94. Kildow, *Intelsat*, p. 64.

95. Chayes, *International Legal Process,* p. 696.

96. Galloway, *The Politics and Technology of Satellite Communications,* pp. 130-132, 141.

97. "Europe Unifying Policy for Intelsat Talks," *Aviation Week and Space Technology,* 27 November 1967, p. 69.

98. "President's Message to Congress on Communications Policy," 14 August 1967, reprinted in U.S., Congress, House, Committee on Government Operations, *Government Use of Satellite Communications – 1967,* 90th Cong., 1st sess., 1967.

99. Ibid.

100. Quotation cited from Richard G. O'Lone, "U.S., Dominance Seen Hindering Intelsat," *Aviation Week and Space Technology,* 28 August 1967, p. 31.

101. Ibid. As of 1975 the Soviet Union has not officially joined the Intelsat organization although it has announced plans to construct a large earth terminal near Lvov in the Ukraine, which is to be operated in conjunction with the Intelsat space segment. The major objection of the Soviet Union to the Intelsat organizational structure was that ownership percentages were allocated in proportion to use of the system by each signatory.

102. "U.S. Assures Europeans of Satellite Communication Launch," *Aviation Week and Space Technology,* 8 November 1971, p. 23.

103. Statement of Erik Esping, ibid.

104. Galloway, *The Politics and Technology of Satellite Communications,* p. 156.

105. Joseph N. Pelton, *Global Communications Satellite Policy: Intelsat, Politics and Functionalism,* pp. 105-106.

106. Galloway, *The Politics and Technology of Satellite Communications,* p. 155.

107. Richard R. Colino, *The Intelsat Definitive Arrangements: Ushering in a New Era in Satellite Telecommunications,* p. 14.

108. F.G. Nixon, "Intelsat: A Progress Report on the Move Toward Definitive Agreements," *University of Toronto Law Journal* 20 (1970): 380-85; Colino, *The Intelsat Definitive Arrangements,* p. 14.

109. Art. IX(c): "The Report of the Committee shall be considered at an international conference, at which duly designated communications entities may also participate, to be convened by the Government of the United States of America for that purpose within three months following submission of the report."

110. Colino, *The Intelsat Definitive Arrangements,* p. 15.

111. "Comsat, State Department Split Over Negotiations," *Aviation Week and Space Technology,* 31 March 1969, pp. 24-25.

112. Colino, *The Intelsat Definitive Arrangements,* pp. 15-16.

113. Ibid., p. 16; Stephen E. Doyle, "Permament Arrangements for the Global Commercial Communication Satellite System of Intelsat," *The*

International Lawyer, 6 (April 1972): 271.

114. Document PC(II)/45, Second Preparatory Conference on Definitive Arrangements for the International Telecommunications Satellite Consortium, 18 September 1969, p. 1; see also Addenda 1-3 and PC(III)/33, Third Preparatory Conference, 21 November 1969. Cosponsors of the document included the delegations from Australia, Brazil, Chile, Guatemala, Italy, Malaysia, New Zealand, Panama, Peru, the Philippines, Spain, Thailand, and Venezuela. After the submission of the draft agreement to the Preparatory Committee, Denmark, Mexico, Indonesia, the Republic of China, Greece, Singapore, and Nicaragua extended their support as well.

115. Pelton, *Global Communications Satellite Policy,* pp. 112-15.

116. Document PC(III)/54, Third Preparatory Conference on Definitive Arrangements for the International Telecommunications Satellite Consortium, 24 November 1969.

117. Pelton, *Global Communications Satellite Policy,* pp. 115-18.

118. Document 93, Resumed Plenipotentiary Conference on Definitive Arrangements for the International Telecommunications Satellite Consortium, 20 March 1970.

119. Pelton, *Global Communications Satellite Policy,* pp. 118-19.

120. Document 93.

121. Cited from Katherine Johnsen, "Japan, Australia Offer Intelsat Compromise," *Aviation Week and Space Technology,* 2 March 1970, p. 20.

122. Cited from "Assembly Deadlocks Intelsat Committee," *Aviation Week and Space Technology,* 8 June 1970, p. 21.

123. "Agreement Relating to the International Telecommunications Satellite Organization 'Intelsat' with Annexes A, B, C, and D."

124. "Operating Agreement Relating to the International Telecommunications Satellite Organization 'Intelsat' with one Annex,"

125. Ibid., Art. 5(b).

126. Colino, *The Intelsat Definitive Arrangements,* p. 20; see also 1971 Plenipotentiary Conference on Definitive Arrangements for the International Telecommunications Satellite Consortium, "Summary Record of Plenary," Document SR/63 (Final), 27 May 1971.

127. "Agreement, Relating to Inselsat," Art. VII(f); Art. VIII(e).

128. Ibid., Art. X(a).

129. Ibid., Art. IX(g)(iv).

130. Ibid., Art. IX(j)(i).

131. Ibid., Art. IX(j)(ii).

132. Ibid., Art. XII(c)(d)(e).

133. Ibid., Arts. XI and XII; Annex A; Annex B; and Annex D.

134. Colino, *The Intelsat Definitive Arrangements,* p. 1.

135. John McDonald, "The Comsat Compromise Starts a Revolution," *Fortune,* October 1965, p. 128.

136. Address by Wernher von Braun, NASA Earth Resources Survey Symposium, Houston, Texas, 9 June 1975.

137. Communications Satellite Corporation, "The First Ten Years," pp. 5-6.

138. "Commercial Satellite Usage Enters Second Decade in 1975," *Communications News,* February 1975, p. 28.

139. Comsat, *The First Ten Years,* p. 66.

140. *Telecommunications Reports* 40 (8 April 1974): 35.

141. "Last Intelsat Launch Caps Global Chain," *Communications News,* July 1975, p. 41.

142. Comsat, *The First Ten Years,* p. 104.

143. Colino, *The Intelsat Definitive Arrangements,* pp. 7-8.

144. Ibid., p. 8.

145. Comsat, *The First Ten Years,* pp. 7-9.

146. "Last Intelsat Launch Caps Global Chain," *Communications News,* July 1975, p. 41.

147. "The Global Communications Satellite System," *Aviation Week and Space Technology,* 2 June 1975, p. 166.

1. Communications Satellite Act of 1962, *U.S.C.A. 47 § 701(d).*
2. C.E. Silberman, "The Little Bird that Casts a Big Shadow," *Fortune,* February 1967, p. 110.
3. Ibid.
4. For a description of the Syncom and Relay satellite programs, see Chapter 4 of this volume.
5. The United States did not establish the first operational domsat system. In 1965 the Soviet Union launched a Molniya I satellite and transmitted telephone and television signals between Moscow and Vladisvostok. The many spacecraft of the Molniya I and II series form the space segment of the Orbita domestic communication system. See also Chapter 6, note 16. Canada constructed the first domestic geosynchronous satellite system: Anik I was sent into orbit on 9 November 1972, and Anik II, on 20 April 1973. Both of the Anik *(brother* in Eskimo) spacecraft were manufactured by a U.S. contractor, Hughes Aircraft, and were launched aboard rockets leased from NASA. A number of other nations have begun either to plan or to construct domestic systems, including Algeria, Brazil, Indonesia, Iran, Japan, Malaysia, Norway, the Philippines, and Saudi Arabia.
6. "Application by American Broadcasting Companies, Inc., for a Satellite Authorization in the Auxiliary Radio Broadcast Services for Television Program Distribution Purposes," before the FCC, 21 September 1965.
7. U.S., FCC, "Notice of Inquiry, in the Matter of Establishment of Domestic Noncommon Carrier Communication Satellite Facilities by Nongovernmental Entities," *2 FCC 2nd (1966),* p. 668.
8. Ibid., p. 669.
9. American Broadcasting Co.; American Petroleum Institute; AT&T; American Trucking Association; Carnegie Commission on Educational Television; Columbia Broadcasting System; Comsat; Department of Health, Education and Welfare; Dow Jones and Company, Inc.; Ford Foundation; General Telephone and Electronics Corp.; Hawaiian Telephone Co.; ITT World Communications, Inc.; JFD Electronics Corp.; National Association of Educational Broadcasters; National Association of Manufacturers; National Broadcasting Co.; Western Union Telegraph Co.; and Western Union International.
10. Ford Foundation, "Legal Brief before the FCC in the Matter of Establishment of Domestic Noncommon Carrier Communication Satellite Facilities by Nongovernmental Entities," FCC No. 16495, 1 August 1966, pp. 19-20.
11. Loren H. Mitchell, "The Future of Domestic Satellite Communications," *Stanford Law Review* 19 (May 1967): 1081.
12. Ford Foundation, "Comments before the FCC in the Matter of Establishment of Domestic Noncommon Carrier Communication Satellite

Facilities by Nongovernmental Entities," FCC No. 16495, 1 August 1966.

13. For the text of McGeorge Bundy's letter introducing the Ford Foundation satellite proposal to Rosel H. Hyde, then chairman of the FCC, see *New York Times*, 2 August 1966, p. 18.

14. Silberman, "The Little Bird that Casts a Big Shadow," p. 110.

15. Communications Satellite Corp., "Legal Brief before the FCC in the Matter of Establishment of Domestic Noncommon Carrier Communication Satellite Facilities by Nongovernmental Entities," FCC No. 16495, 1 August 1966, pp. 11-18.

16. "Report and Order, in the Matter of Establishment of Domestic Communication Satellite Facilities by Nongovernmental Entities," FCC No. 16495, 20 March 1970, *22 FCC 2d, (1970)*, p. 112.

17. "Supplemental Notice of Inquiry, in the Matter of Establishment of Domestic Communication Satellite Facilities by Nongovernmental Entities," FCC No. 16495, 20 October 1966, *5 FCC 2d (1966)*, p. 354.

18. "Report and Order," 20 March 1970, *22 FCC 2d (1970)*, p. 114.

19. Silberman, "The Little Bird that Casts a Big Shadow," p. 111.

20. "Report and Order," 20 March 1970, *22 FCC 2d (1970)*, p. 109.

21. American Telephone and Telegraph Corporation, "Comments before the FCC in the Matter of Establishment of Domestic Communications Satellite Facilities by Nongovernmental Entities," FCC No. 16495, 15 December 1966, p. 5.

22. Ibid., p. 10.

23. Ibid., pp. 13-14.

24. Ibid., Attachment 1.

25. Letter from Lowell F. Wingert, vice prisident of AT&T, to James McCormack, chairman of the board of Comsat, 23 March 1966. Reprinted in ibid., Attachment 2.

26. Comsat was also experiencing considerable difficulty obtaining a favorable ruling from the FCC in matters relating to international communications. On 20 July 1966 the Commission issued its "Authorized User" policy statement, which prohibited Comsat from offering services directly to non-carrier users or to the U.S. government, except in special circumstances. Instead, Comsat was to operate as a "carrier's carrier" and to serve authorized international carriers only. See *4 FCC 2d (1966)*, p. 421. On 7 December 1966, the FCC overturned an earlier ruling and reduced Comsat's ownership share of Intelsat ground stations located in the contiguous states, Hawaii, Puerto Rico, and the Virgin Islands from one hundred percent to fifty percent. The remaining ownership percentage was apportioned among AT&T, ITT Worldcom, RCA Globcom, Hawaiian Telephone Co., and Western Union International. See *5 FCC 2d (1966)*, p. 812.

27. Mitchell, "The Future of Domestic Satellite Communications," pp. 1079-80.

28. "Report and Order," 20 March 1970, *22 FCC 2d (1970)*, pp. 115-16.

29. Ibid., pp. 118-119.

30. James Ridgeway, "Fourth Network," *New Republic*, 17 September 1966, p. 14.

31. See "Report and Order," 20 March 1970, *22 FCC 2d, (1970)*, p. 119.

32. AT&T preferred carrier ownership of these Intelsat earth stations. However, the FCC divided ownership among Comsat and the international carriers. AT&T was awarded 28.5% of all stations located within the continental United States.

33. See "Report and Order," 20 March 1970, *22 FCC 2d (1970)*, pp. 119-120.

34. Lyndon B. Johnson, "Message from the President of the United States: Recommendations Relative to World Communications," 14 August 1967, in U.S., President, President's Task Force on Communications Policy, *Final Report*, 7 December 1968, Appendix A.

35. Ibid., p. 18.

36. Ibid., pp. 15-16.

37. Ibid., p. 3.

38. Ibid., p. 35.

39. Ibid., pp. 30-33.

40. Ibid., pp. 33-34.

41. "White House Gets into the FCC Act," *Business Week*, 26 July 1969, p. 31.

42. Memorandum from Peter Flanigan, assistant to the president, to Dean Burch, chairman of the FCC, 23 January 1970, as reprinted in "Report and Order," 20 March 1970, *22 FCC 2d (1970)*, pp. 126-27.

43. Ibid., p. 127.

44. *New York Times*, 24 January 1970, p. 1; "Wide Open Domestic Satellite Policy Recommended," *Broadcasting*, 26 January 1970, p. 9.

45. Ibid.

46. *New York Times*, 10 February 1970, p. 25.

47. *U.S. Government Manual 1972-1973*, (1972), pp. 85-86.

48. Edwin B. Spievak, "Presidential Assault on Telecommunications," *Federal Communications Bar Journal* 23 (1969): 157; "OTP, CPB Clash Over Funding Bill," *Broadcasting*, 23 August 1971, p. 38; "Hoked Up Conspiracy," *The New Republic*, 22 July 1972, p. 23; John Paris, "The Politics of Public Broadcasting," *Commonwealth*, 24 November 1972, p. 180; Julius Duscha, "The White House Watch Over TV and the Press," *New York Times Magazine*, 20 August 1972, p. 9.

49. "Report and Order," 20 March 1970, *22 FCC 2d (1970)*, p. 93.

50. Ibid., pp. 93-94.

51. Ibid., p. 94.

52. Ibid., p. 129.

53. Hughes Aircraft Co., vol. I, "Application for a Domestic Communication Satellite System"; vol. II, "Application for Construction Permit for a Domestic Communication Satellite System Earth Terminal: San Juan, California"; vol. III, "Application for Construction Permit for a Domestic

Communication Satellite System Earth Terminal: Califon, New Jersey"; vol. IV, "Application for Construction Permit for Terrestrial Interconnects"; vol. V, "Application for Domestic Satellite Orbital Locations: 97°, 100° and 103° W. Longitude"; and vol. VI, "Application for Construction Permit for Domestic Communication System Receive-Only Earth Terminals;" before the FCC, FCC No. 16495, November 1970.

54. Western Tele-Communications, Inc., "Application for a Domestic Communication Satellite System"; vol. I, "System Description of Domestic Communications Satellite System"; vol. II, "Space Segment of Domestic Communications Satellite System"; vol. III, "Earth Segment of Domestic Communications Satellite System"; "Amendments to vols. I, II and III"; before the FCC, FCC No. 16495, March 1971.

55. MCI Lockheed Satellite Corp., "Application of MCI Lockheed Satellite Corporation for a Domestic Communications Satellite System": vol. I, "System Application"; vol. II, "Individual Applications For Space Stations and Earth Stations;" vol. III, "Individual Applications for Terrestrial Interconnecting Facilities"; and vol. IV, "Exhibits"; before the FCC, FCC No. 16495, February 1971.

56. Fairchild Hiller Corp., vol. I, "Application for a Domestic Communication Satellite System"; and vol. II, "Applications for Earth Stations for Use as Part of a Domestic Communications Satellite System"; before the FCC, FCC No. 16495, March 1971.

57. Western Union Telegraph Co., "Proposal by the Western Union Telegraph Company for a Domestic Communications Satellite System; Applications by the Western Union Telegraph Company for Authority to Construct and Operate Domestic Satellite Earth Stations in New Jersey, California, Alabama, Washington, Arkansas and Wisconsin. Applications by the Western Union Telegraph Company for Authority to Launch and Operate Geostationary Communications Satellites at 95° West Longitude, 102° West Longitude, and 116° West Longitude; Addenda; Amendment; and Applications by the Western Union Telegraph Company for Authority to Construct and Operate Receive-Only Domestic Satellite Earth Stations on the West Coast and in Hawaii"; before the FCC, FCC No. 16495, 1 July 1970.

58. RCA Global Communications, Inc., and RCA Alaska Communications, Inc., vol. I, "Application for a Domestic Communication Satellite System"; vol. II, "Applications for Geostationary Communication Satellites"; vol. III, "Applications for Satellite Earth Stations; Technical Annex to vol. I; Amendments to vol. I, II, III, and to Technical Annex"; before the FCC, FCC No. 16495, March 1971.

59. American Telephone and Telegraph Co., "Application for a Domestic Communications Satellite System", before the FCC, FCC No. 16495, March 1971.

60. Communications Satellite Corp., "Application to Construct a System of Domestic Satellite Facilities For Use by AT&T, Revised; Multi-Purpose Domestic Satellite Communications System": vol. I, "System Application";

vol. II, "Technical Data and Satellite Applications"; and vol. III, "Earth Stations Applications"; before the FCC, FCC No. 16495, March 1971. In addition to the system applicants, five organizations filed applications for earth stations only: Hawaiian Telephone Company; Twin County Trans-Video, Inc.; TelePrompTer Corp.; LVO Cable, Inc. and United Video, Inc.; and Phoenix Satellite Corp.

61. "Report and Order," 20 March 1970, *22 FCC 2d (1970)*, pp. 95-97.

62. Ibid., p. 96.

63. John McDonald, "Getting Our Communications Satellites Off the Ground," *Fortune*, July 1972, p. 122.

64. Ibid.

65. "Justice Department Slows AT&T Systems Case," *Aviation Week and Space Technology*, 23 August 1971, pp. 38-40.

66. Letter from OTP's Clay Whitehead to Dean Burch, chairman of the FCC, as quoted in "White House office Recommends Approving All U.S. Satcom Bids, "*Aviation Week and Space Technology*, 8 November 1971, p. 20.

67. Ibid.

68. "Memorandum Opinion and Order, in the Matter of Establishment of Domestic Communication Satellite Facilities by Nongovernmental Entities," FCC No. 16495, 15 March 1972, *34 FCC 2d (1972)*, p. 1; "Proposed Second Report and Order," 15 March 1972, *34 FCC 2d (1972)*, p. 9.

69. "Memorandum Opinion and Order," 15 March 1972, *34 FCC 2d (1972)*, p. 2.

70. Ibid., p. 3.

71. Ibid., pp. 3-4.

72. Proposed Second Report and Order, 15 March 1972, *34 FCC 2d (1972)*, pp. 40-41.

73. Ibid., p. 41.

74. Ibid., p. 40.

75. Ibid., pp. 38-39.

76. Cited from "White House Office Recommends Approving All U.S. Satcom Bids," *Aviation Week and Space Technology*, 8 November 1971, p. 20.

77. "Proposed Second Report and Order," 15 March 1972, *34 FCC 2d (1972)*, p. 53.

78. Ibid., p. 50.

79. Ibid., p. 45.

80. "Memorandum Opinion and Order," 15 March 1972, *34 FCC 2d (1972)*, p. 8.

81. "Whitehead Flexes OTP's Muscle," *Broadcasting*, 17 April 1972, p. 23.

82. "They're Still Far Apart on Satellites," *Broadcasting*, 24 April 1972, p. 46.

83. Ibid.

84. "Is FCC Moving to Advocacy of Open-Entry Satellite Plan?", *Broadcasting*, 8 May 1972, p. 53; McDonald, "Getting Our Communication

Satellites Off the Ground," *Fortune*, July 1972, p. 124.

85. "Second Report and Order, in the Matter of Establishment of Domestic Communication Satellite Facilities by Nongovernmental Entities," FCC No. 16495, 16 June 1972, *35 FCC 2d (1972)*, p. 844.

86. Ibid., p. 850.

87. Ibid., p. 860.

88. Ibid., p. 851.

89. Ibid., pp. 851-52.

90. Ibid., p. 852.

91. Ibid.

92. Ibid., p. 849.

93. Ibid., pp. 848-49.

94. Ibid.

95. Ibid., p. 853.

96. Ibid., p. 854.

97. Ibid.

98. Ibid.

99. Ibid., p. 855.

100. Ibid.

101. Ibid., pp. 856-57.

102. Ibid., pp. 855-56.

103. Ibid., p. 859.

104. "Dissenting Statement by Chairman Burch," ibid., p. 861.

105. Ibid., p. 862.

106. In addition to Comsat and AT&T, other interested parties filing petitions were RCA Global Communications, Inc. and RCA Alaska Communications, Inc.; Network Project; National Association of Educational Broadcasters; and Western Union International.

107. "Memorandum Opinion and Order," *38 FCC 2d (1972)*, p. 665.

108. Ibid., p. 688.

109. Ibid., pp. 680-82.

110. Ibid., p. 687.

111. Ibid., pp. 684-85.

112. *Telecommunications Reports* 40 (22 April 1974): 16.

113. "Westar Domestic Satellite Provides New Answers for Private Telephone Networks," *Communications News*, 12 (February 1975): 36.

114. Lawrence R. Kilty, "American Satellite Builds Vast Government Satellite Network," *Communications News* 12 (February 1975): 32.

115. "Satcom Bridges Continent with Commercial Satellite Services," *Communications News* 12 (February 1975): 30.

116. *Telecommunications Reports* 41 (10 November 1975): 14.

117. *Telecommunications Reports* 40 (22 April 1974): 1.

118. *Telecommunications Reports* 41 (10 February 1975): 5.

119. "Three Firms Volunteer Marisat Funds," *Aviation Week and Space Technology*, 18 June 1973, p. 77.

120. *Telecommunications Reports* 40 (9 September 1974): 24.

121. *Telecommunications Reports* 40 (22 July 1974): 24.

122. Quotation from a speech by Donald I Baker, deputy assistant attorney general in the Justice Department Antitrust Division, to the annual convention of the Federal Bar Association, cited from *Telecommunications Reports* 40 (9 September 1974): 8.

123. *Telecommunications Reports* 40 (9 September 1974): 8.

124. *Telecommunications Reports* 41 (27 January 1975): 1-3.

125. "Aetna Life to be Partner in CML Satellite System," *Aviation Week and Space Technology*, 6 October 1975, p. 22.

1. See Chapter 3.
2. See Chapter 5.
3. See Chapter 6.
4. American Society of International Law (ASIL) Panel on International Telecommunications Policy, *Direct Broadcasting from Satellites: Policies and Problems*, p. 9.
5. Galloway, *The Politics and Technology of Satellite Communications*, p. 75.
6. Ibid., pp. 76-77.
7. Ibid.
8. For a detailed description of Soviet aerospace programs, see U.S., Senate, Committee on Aeronautical and Space Sciences, *Soviet Space Programs 1962-1965*.
9. G.A. Res. 1348 (XIII) in U.N., General Assembly, U.N. Doc. A/4090 (1958), *13 U.N. GAOR Suppl. 18*, pp. 5-6.
10. G.A. Res. 1472 (XIV) in U.N., General Assembly, U.N. Doc. A/4354 (1959), *14 U.N. GAOR Suppl. 16*, pp. 5-6.
11. Ithiel de Sola Pool, "The Satellite Broadcast Controversy," p. 4.
12. *Treaty on Principles Governing the Activities of States in the Exploration and Use of Outer Space, Including the Moon and Other Celestial Bodies*, opened for signature 27 January 1967.
13. C.M. Dalfen, "Direct Satellite Broadcasting: Towards International Arrangements to Transcend and Marshall the Political Realities," *University of Toronto Law Journal* 20 (1970): 370.
14. Ibid., pp. 370-71; Comment, "The Outer Space Treaty: An Interpretation in Light of the No-Sovereignty Provision," *Harvard International Law Journal* 9 (1968): 144; Statement of Ambassador Arthur J. Goldberg, U.S., Congress, Senate, Committee on Astronautical and Space Sciences, *Soviet Space Programs 1962-1965*, p. 53.
15. Comment, "The Outer Space Treaty," p. 142.
16. Ibid., p. 143.
17. Hinchman, "Issues in Spectrum Resource Management," in Twentieth Century Fund Task Force, *The Future of Satellite Communications*, p. 55.
18. de Sola Pool, "The Satellite Broadcast Controversy," p. 5.
19. G.A. Res. 2260 (XXII) in U.N., General Assembly, U.N. Doc. A/6716, (1967), *22 U.N. GAOR Suppl. 16*, pp. 11-12.
20. G.A. Res. 2453 B (XXIII) in U.N., General Assembly, U.N. Doc. A/7218 (1968), *23 U.N. GAOR Suppl. 18*, pp. 10-11.
21. U.N. General Assembly, *Report of the Working Group on Direct Broadcast Satellites at its First Session*, para. 9 (b)-(c).
22. U.N., General Assembly, *Working Paper Submitted by France to the Second Session of the Working Group on Direct Broadcast Satellites*, p. 6.

23. U.N., General Assembly, *Working Paper Submitted by Canada and Sweden to the Second Session of the Working Group on Direct Broadcast Satellites,* p. 25.

24. Statement of Herbert Reis, U.S. representative to the Working Group on Direct Broadcast Satellites at its Second Session, 31 July 1969, as summarized in K.M. Queeney, "An Analysis of the Role of the United Nations in the Formulation of Principles Governing Direct Broadcast Satellites," Ph.D. dissertation, Ohio University, March 1975, pp. 95-96.

25. See text accompanying notes 13-14 in this chapter.

26. U.N., General Assembly, *French Working Paper to the Second Session of the Working Group,* p. 6.

27. U.N., General Assembly, *Report of the Second Session of the Working Group on Direct Broadcast Satellites,* p. 10.

28. Ibid., pp. 17-19.

29. de Sola Pool, "The Satellite Broadcast Controversy," p. 29.

30. U.N., General Assembly, *Report of the Working Group on Direct Broadcast Satellites on its Third Session,* Annex II, p. 25.

31. U.N., General Assembly, *Third Working Group Report,* Annex IV, p. 27.

32. Ibid., p. 28.

33. Ibid., Annex V, pp. 29-31.

34. Ibid., p. 31.

35. U.N., General Assembly, *Third Working Group Report,* pp. 15-16.

36. Ibid.

37. Ibid., p. 15.

38. For a complete discussion of the 1971 WARC-ST Conference, see "The World Administrative Radio Conference for Space Telecommunications," *Telecommunications Journal* 38 (October 1971): 673-82.

39. Ibid., pp. 678-79. The frequencies allocated range from 620 MHz to 86 GHz, and standard UHF television transmissions occur in the 450 MHz to 900 MHz range. A. Chayes, and L. Chazen, "Policy Problems in Direct Broadcasting from Satellites," *Stanford Journal of International Studies* 5 (1970): 10.

40. "The World Administrative Radio Conference," pp. 680-81.

41. ITU Resolution No. Spa 2-3, clause 428A quoted in ASIL, *Direct Broadcasting from Satellites,* p. 20.

42. Summary of Discussions held at the Conference on Direct Broadcasting convened by the Amercian Society of International Law and the International Broadcast Institute at Bellagio, Italy on 20 February 1974, reported in ibid., pp. 89, 93.

43. P. Laskin and A. Chayes, "A Report of the Panel on International Telecommunications Policy," in ibid., pp. 20-21.

44. U.S.S.R., "Draft Convention on Principles Governing the Use by States of Artificial Earth Satellites for Direct Television Broadcasting," reprinted in U.N., General Assembly, *Fourth Working Group Report,* Annex III.

45. U.N., General Assembly, Minister for Foreign Affairs of the U.S.S.R.,

Request for the Inclusion of a Supplementary Item in the Agenda of the Twenty-Seventh Session, 9 August 1972, pp. 1-2.

46. "Soviet Draft Convention," Art. V., in the U.N., General Assembly, *Fourth Working Group Report,* Annex III.

47. Art. III, ibid.

48. Art. IX, ibid.

49. See the text accompanying notes 31-32.

50. U.N., General Assembly, Minister for Foreign Affairs of the U.S.S.R., *Request for the Inclusion of a Supplementary Item in the Agenda,* p. 2. Ithiel de Sola Pool also reports that the Soviets had attempted to introduce language permitting the destruction of direct broadcast satellites operating in violation of the proposed limitations when UNESCO convened its Meeting of Experts, de Sola Pool, "The Satellite Broadcast Controversy," p. 15.

51. Queeney, "The Role of the United Nations," p. 195.

52. G.A. Res. 2916 (XXVII) in U.N., General Assembly, U.N. Doc. A/8730 (1972), *27 U.N. GAOR Suppl. 30,* p. 14.

53. U.N. Doc. A/AC.105/109. For a description of UNESCO action leading to the 1972 declaration, see UNESCO General Conference, Seventeenth Session, *Draft Declaration of Guiding Principles on the Use of Satellite Broadcasting for the Flow of Information, the Spread of Education and Greater Cultural Exchange,* UNESCO Doc. 17 C/76, 21 July 1972, pp. 1-2.

54. G.A. Res. 2915 in U.N., General Assembly, U.N. Doc. A/8730 (1972), *27 U.N. GAOR Suppl. 30,* pp. 12-14. In addition to the new ITU regulations, the Soviet draft convention and the UNESCO declaration, the Working Group had before it at its fourth session a draft convention on the freedom of information (U.N. Doc. A/AC.105/WG.3/L.2); the report of the United Nations panel which met in India to study the Satellite Instructional Television Experiment (U.N. Doc. A/AC.105/114); the UNESCO/WIPO draft convention against the unauthorized distribution of program-carrying signals carried by satellite; a progress report by UNESCO on its activities in the field of space communications (U.N. Doc. A/AC.105/WG.3/L.5); and a working paper submitted by the United States based on a technical presentation by its delegation, which is summarized in U.N. Doc. A/AC.105/L.71. (U.N., General Assembly, *Fourth Working Group Report,* p. 2).

55. U.N., General Assembly, *Fourth Working Group Report,* p. 9. The chairman's suggestion was contained in his opening remarks which are reprinted in Annex I, p. 4.

56. See the *Working Paper* presented by Canada and Sweden to the fourth working group, U.N. Doc. A/AC.105/WG.3/L.4, June 1973. "The Swedish-Canadian Draft Principles Governing Direct Television Broadcasting by Satellite" are reprinted in U.N., General Assembly, *Fourth Working Group Report,* Annex IV.

57. Ibid., Annex IV, Art. V.

58. Ibid., Art. VIII.

59. Compare "Soviet Draft Convention," ibid., Annex III, Art. VI, with

the "Swedish-Canadian Draft Principles," ibid., Annex IV, Art. VIII.
60. Ibid., Art. VI.
61. Ibid., Art. X.
62. U.N., General Assembly, *Fourth Working Group Report*, p. 16.
63. G.A. Res. 3182 (XXVIII) in U.N., General Assembly, U.N. Doc. A/9030 (1973), 28 *U.N. GAOR Suppl. 30*, pp. 19-21.
64. The United States of America, "Draft Principles on Direct Broadcast Satellites." U.N. Doc. A/AC.105/WG.3(V)/CRP.2, March 1974, reprinted in U.N., General Assembly, *Report of the Working Group on Direct Broadcast Satellites on the Work of its Fifth Session*, Annex IV.
65. Ibid., Arts. I and II.
66. Ibid., Arts. III and IV.
67. Ibid., Art. IV.
68. Ibid., Art. V.
69. Ibid., Arts. VI-IX.
70. Ibid., Art. X.
71. Ibid., Art. XI.
72. U.S.S.R., "Principles Governing the Use by States of Artificial Earth Satellites for Direct Television Broadcasting," reprinted in U.N., General Assembly, *Fifth Working Group Report*, Annex II.
73. The text of Article VI is reproduced in the text following footnote 46.
74. "Soviet Draft Declaration of Principles," U.N., General Assembly, *Fifth Working Group Report*, Art. VIII(2).
75. Compare Art. V of the Soviet Draft Convention, U.N., General Assembly, *Fourth Working Group Report*, Annex III, with Art. V of the "Soviet Draft Declaration of Principles," U.N., General Assembly, *Fifth Working Group Report*, Annex II.
76. See the text accompanying footnotes 48-51.
77. Soviet Draft Declaration, U.N., General Assembly, *Fifth Working Group Report*, Annex II, Art. IX(1).
78. U.N., General Assembly, *Fifth Working Group Report*, pp. 10-13.
79. Ibid., pp. 13-14.
80. Ibid., p. 13. See also the text accompanying notes 41-43.
81. Ibid., p. 14.
82. Ibid., pp. 14-15. Article 19 of the Universal Declaration of Human Rights provides:

> Everyone has the right to freedom of opinion and expression; this right includes freedom to hold opinions without interference and to seek, receive and impart information and ideas through any media and regardless of frontiers.

83. Ibid., p. 15.
84. Ibid., p. 16.
85. Ibid.
86. Ibid., p. 17.

87. Compare the listing in ibid., with Arts. IV and VI of the "Soviet Draft Convention," U.N., General Assembly, *Fourth Working Group Report*, Annex III, and with Art. IV of the "Soviet Draft Declaration of Principles," U.N., General Assembly, *Fifth Working Group Report*, Annex II.

88. U.N., General Assembly, *Fifth Working Group Report*, p. 17.

89. Ibid.

90. Ibid., p. 18.

91, Ibid.

92. See text accompanying note 63.

93. U.N. General Assembly, *Report of the Legal Sub-Committee on the Work of its Thirteenth Session*, p. 3.

94. Ibid., Annex III, p. 1.

95. U.N., General Assembly, *Report of the Legal Sub-Committee on the Work of its Fourteenth Session.*

96. U.N. General Assembly, *Thirteenth Legal Sub-Committee Report*, Annex III, pp. 1-3.

97. U.N., General Assembly, *Fifth Working Group Report*, p. 10.

98. Ibid.

99. U.N., General Assembly, *Fourteenth Legal Sub-Committee Report*, Annex II, pp. 1-2.

100. Ibid., p. 2.

101. U.N., General Assembly, *Fifth Working Group Report*, p. 11.

102. Ibid.

103. U.N., General Assembly, *Fourteenth Legal Sub-Committee Report*, Annex II, p. 2.

104. See "Model General Principles for the Use of Artificial Earth Satellites for Radio and Television Broadcasting," U.N. General Assembly, *Third Working Group Report*, Annex IV, para 5, p. 27; 1972 "Soviet Draft Convention," U.N., General Assembly, *Fourth Working Group Report*, Annex III, Art. XII; "Principles Governing the Use by States of Artificial Earth Satellites for Direct Television Broadcasting," General Assembly, *Fifth Working Group Report*, Annex II, Art. VII.

105. U.N., General Assembly, *Fourteenth Legal Sub-Committee Report*, Annex II, p. 2.

106. U.N., General Assembly, *Fifth Working Group Report*, p. 11.

107. U.N., General Assembly, *Fourteenth Legal Sub-Committee Report*, Annex II, p. 3.

108. U.N., General Assembly, *Fifth Working Group Report*, p. 13. Art. VI of the Outer Space Treaty provides:

> States Parties to the Treaty shall bear international responsibility for national activities in outer space, including the moon and other celestial bodies, whether such activities are carried on by governmental agencies or by non-governmental entities, and for assuring that national activities are carried out in conformity with the provisions set forth in the present Treaty. The activities of non-governmental entities in outer

space, including the moon and other celestial bodies, shall require authorization and continuing supervision by the State concerned. When activities are carried on in outer space, including the moon and other celestial bodies, by an international organization, responsibility for compliance with this Treaty shall be borne both by the international organization and by the States Parties to the Treaty participating in such organization.

109. Ibid., p. 13. Consensus was also reached on the need to resolve disputes through established international procedures. Ibid., p. 19.

110. U.N., General Assembly, *Fourteenth Legal Sub-Committee Report,* Annex II, p. 3.

111. Ibid.

112. U.N., General Assembly, *Fifth Working Group Report,* pp. 13-16.

113. U.N., General Assembly, *Fourteenth Legal Sub-Committee Report,* Annex II, p. 3.

114. U.N., General Assembly, *Fourth Working Group Report,* Annex IV, pp. 1-4.

115. U.N., General Assembly, *Fourteenth Legal Sub-Committee Report,* pp. 3-4.

116. Ibid., p. 4.

117. Ibid.

118. Ibid.

119. Ibid.

120. Ibid.

121. Ibid.

122. Compare ibid., pp. 4-5 with "Soviet Draft Principles," U.N., General Assembly, *Fifth Working Group Report,* Annex II, Art. VI, p. 2.

123. U.N., General Assembly, *Fourteenth Legal Sub-Committee Report,* Annex II, pp. 4-5.

124. Compare ibid., p. 5, with "Soviet Draft Principles," in U.N., General Assembly, *Fifth Working Group Report,* Annex II, Art. IX(1). Article 33 of the United Nations Charter calls upon nations to emply "negotiations, enquiry, mediation, conciliation, arbitration, judicial settlement, resort to regional agencies or arrangements, . . ." before any other.

125. See the discussions of ATS 1, 3, 5 and 6 experiments, Chapter 9.

126. For a more complete discussion of the SITE experiment see Chapter 9.

127. U.N., CPUOS, *Report of the United Nations Panel Meeting on Satellite Broadcasting Systems for Education,* Annex I, p. 3.

128. Ibid., p. 5.

129. Ibid, p. 4, and Annex I, p. 1.

130. Ibid., Annex I, pp. 1-2.

131. Ibid., pp. 9-10.

132. Galloway, *The Politics and Technology of Satellite Communications,* p. 131.

133. U.N., General Assembly, *First Working Group Report,* para. 9[a].
134. de Sola Pool, "The Satellite Broadcast Controversy," p. 26.
135. ASIL, *Direct Broadcasting from Satellites,* p. 5.
136. See the "Memorandum of Understanding Between the Department of Atomic Energy of the Government of India and the United States National Aeronautics and Space Administration," 18 September 1969, para 3.2.
137. U.N., CPUOS, *Panel Report on Satellite Broadcasting System,* p. 19.
138. Ibid.
139. Ibid., p. 20.
140. Comment of Nandasiri Jasentuliyana, in Panel Discussion, "Direct Satellite Broadcasting and the Third World," *Columbia Journal of Transnational Law* 13 (1974): 68.
141. U.N., General Assembly, *First Working Group Report,* para. 8. All estimates are based on U.S. dollars.
142. See text accompanying note 39.
143. See text accompanying notes 40-43.
144. F.S. Ruddy, "Broadcasting Satellites: An American Perspective," *Lawyer of the Americas* 3 (1971): 499, 503-504; L. Marks, "International Conflict and the Free Flow of Information," The Aspen Institute Program on Communications and Society, *Control of the Direct Broadcast Satellite: Values in Conflict,* p. 66.
145. See text accompanying notes 112-124.
146. U.N., General Assembly, *Fifth Working Group Report,* p. 10.
147. Ibid.
148. U.N., General Assembly, *Fourteenth Legal Sub-Committee Report,* Annex II, pp. 1-2.
149. Ibid., p. 3.
150. Ibid., p. 2.
151. Ibid.
152. 1967 Outer Space Treaty, Art. III.
153. See, for example, the "Soviet Draft Declaration," Art. V, in U.N., General Assembly, *Fifth Working Group Report,* Annex II; the "Soviet Draft Convention," Art. V and the "Swedish-Canadian Draft Principles," Art. V in U.N., General Assembly, *Fourth Working Group Report,* Annexes III, IV.
154. See, for example, Ruddy, "Broadcasting Satellites," p. 503.
Among the relevant instruments are the First Amendment to the Constitution of the United States; the Universal Declaration of Human Rights, G.A. Resol. 217A(III), 10 December 1948; The International Convention on the Elimination of All Forms of Racial Discrimination (articles 4 and 5) adopted by U.N. General Assembly Res. 2106A (XX) of 21 December 1965, and entering into force on 9 January 1969; The International Covenant of Civil and Political Rights (Article 19), adopted by U.N. General Assembly Res. 2200 (XXI), 16 December 1966; The European Convention of Human Rights (Article 10), signed at Rome, 9 November 1950, entered into force 3 September 1953; The

American Declaration of the Rights and Duties of Man (Article IV), Res. XXX adopted at the Ninth International Conference of American States, Bogota, Colombia, 30 March to 2 May 1948; and The American Convention on Human Rights (Article 13), signed on 22 November 1969, at the Inter-American Specialized Conference on Human Rights, San Jose, Costa Rica.

155. U.N., General Assembly, *The International Covenant of Civil and Political Rights*, Art. 20. For similar limitations on the principle of free flow in other international instruments, see T. Buergenthal, "The Right to Receive Information Across National Boundaries," Aspen Institute, *Control of the Direct Braodcast Satellite*, pp. 76-78.

156. Laskin, "Legal Strategies for Advancing Information Flow," Aspen Institute, *Control of the Direct Broadcast Satellite*, p. 62.

157. L. Marks in Aspen Institute, *Control of the Direct Broadcast Satellite*, p. 69.

158. Ruddy, "Broadcasting Satellites," pp. 503-504.

159. In agreement is Laskin, "Legal Strategies," in the Aspen Institute, *Control of the Direct Broadcast Satellite*, p. 61.

160. Ibid.

161. Ibid.

162. See, for example, the "Soviet Draft Declaration," Arts. IV and V, in the U.N., General Assembly, *Fifth Working Group Report*, Annex II; "Soviet Draft Convention," Arts. IV, V and VI, in the U.N., General Assembly, *Fourth Working Group Report*, Annex III.

163. "Swedish-Canadian Draft Principles," Art. V, in the U.N., General Assembly, *Fourth Working Group Report*, Annex IV.

164. ASIL Panel, *Direct Broadcasting from Satellites*, p. 30.

165. Ibid.

166. Proposals for the exclusion of spillover from the prior consent regime are discussed below in the text accompanying notes 174-180.

167. U.N., UNESCO, *Declaration of Guiding Principles in the Use of Satellite Broadcasting for the Free Flow of Information, the Spread of Education and Greater Cultural Exchange*, Art. V(1).

168. Ibid., Art. V(2).

169. Ibid., Art. VI(2).

170. Ibid., Art. VII(2).

171. On the doctrine of "harmful effects," see Delbert D. Smith, *International Telecommunication Control*, pp. 185-205.

172. U.N., UNESCO, *Declaration of Guiding Principles in the Use of Satellite Broadcasting*, Art. IX(2).

173. Laskin and Chayes, "A Report of the Panel on International Telecommunications Policy," in ASIL Panel, *Direct Broadcasting from Satellites*, p. 9.

174. Compare Laskin, "Legal Strategies," on the Aspen Institute, *Control of Direct Broadcasting Satellites*, p. 62.

175. Chayes and Chazen, "Policy Problems", p. 15.

176. Comment of Abram Chayes in Panel Discussion, "Direct Satellite

Broadcasting," p. 78.

177. Note, "Approaches to Controlling Propaganda and Spillover from Direct Broadcast Satellites," *Stanford Journal of International Studies* 5 (1970): 175.

178. Ibid.

179. The text of § 428A is reprinted in the text accompanying note 41.

180. U.N., General Assembly, *Fourth Working Group Report,* Annex IV, Art. VI; U.N., General Assembly, *Fifth Working Group Report,* Annex III, Art. VI.

181. U.N., General Assembly, *Fifth Working Group Report,* Annex II, Art. VIII.

182. U.N., UNESCO, *Declaration of Guiding Principles,* Art. VI (2).

183. U.N., General Assembly, *Fifth Working Group Report,* Annex III, Art. V.

184. Dalfen, "Direct Broadcasting," p. 373.

185. U.N., UNESCO, *Declaration of Guiding Principles,* Art. VI (2).

186. "Swedish-Canadian Draft Principles," U.N., General Assembly, *Fifth Working Group Report,* Annex III, Art. V.

187. See, for example, Dalfen, "Direct Broadcasting," p. 373; E. McAnany, "Reflections on the International Flow of Information," in the Aspen Institute, *Control of the Direct Broadcast Satellite,* p. 16.

188. See Ruddy, "Broadcasting Satellites," p. 503.

189. Comment, "Direct Broadcast Satellites: Implications for Less Developed Countries," *Virginia Journal of International Law* 12 (1971): 84.

190. "United States Draft Principles," in U.N., General Assembly, *Fifth Working Group Report,* Annex IV, Art. V.

191. See also Marks' article in the Aspen Institute, *Control of Direct Broadcast Satellites,* p. 66.

NOTES TO CHAPTER 9

1. U.S., Congress, House, Committee on Government Operations, Subcommittee on Military Operations, *Satellite Communications*, p. 40.
2. Ibid., p. 41.
3. Memorandum from Homer E. Newell, associate administrator, Office of Space Science and Applications, to Robert Seamans, 10 March 1964. (NASA)
4. Memorandum from Homer E. Newell, associate administrator, OSSA, 2 October 1964. (NASA)
5. NASA, Office of Space Sciences and Applications, "Prospectus 1964, Appendix A, Goals and Objectives 1965-1980."
6. U.S., Congress, House, Committee on Science and Astronautics, Subcommittee on Space Science and Applications, *1973 NASA Authorization, Hearings*, 92nd Cong., 2nd sess., Part 3, p. 302.
7. U.S., Congress, House, Committee on Science and Astronautics, Subcommittee on Space Science and Applications, *Hearings, 1965 NASA Authorization*, 88th Cong., 2nd sess., 1964, p. 1519.
8. National Aeronautics and Space Administration, "1965 Background Briefing on ATS," NASA News Release. (NASA)
9. Interview with Leonard Jaffe, deputy associate administrator for applications, NASA Headquarters, 3 September 1974.
10. Leonard Jaffe, "NASA Space Applications Program," *Astronautics and Aeronautics*, p. 3.
11. U.S., Congress, House, Committee on Government Operations, *Hearings, Government Use of Satellite Communications*, 89th Cong., 2nd sess., 1966, p. 434.
12. NASA, "Advanced Technology Satellites: Project Approval Document," 10 March 1964, p. 1. (NASA)
13. Memorandum from Homer E. Newell, associate administrator, Office of Space Science and Applications files, for distribution to NASA Centers, "Opportunities for Proposing Technical Experiments for ATS," 16 November 1964. (NASA)
14. NASA, "Advanced Technology Satellites: Project Approval Document," 10 March 1964, p. 2. (NASA)
15. NASA, Office of Space Science and Applications, "Mission Operation Report: Applications Technology Satellite E, Report No. S-630-69-05, Appendix, "29 July 1969, Tables I and II.
16. NASA, Office of Space Science and Applications, "Prelaunch Mission Operation Report: Applications Technology Satellite B." Report No. S-630-66-01, 2 December 1966, p. 4.
17. NASA, Office of Space Science and Applications, "Prelaunch Mission Operation Report: Applications Technology Satellite A," Report No. S-630-67-02, 28 March 1967, p. 4.

18. NASA, Office of Space Science and Applications, "ATS II Post Launch Report 3," Mission Operation Report No. S-630-67-02, 1 June 1967, p. 4.

19. NASA, Office of Space Science and Applications, "ATS III Post Launch Report 2," Mission Operation Report No. S-630-67-03, 27 December 1967, p. 1.

20. NASA, Office of Space Science and Applications, "ATS IV Post Launch Report 2," Mission Operation Report No. S-630-68-04, 28 October 1968, p. 2.

21. NASA, Office of Space Science and Applications, "ATS V Post Launch Report 3," Mission Operation Report No. S-630-69-05, 27 January 1970, p. 5.

22. "NASA Compendium of Satellite Communications Programs," p. 13-5. For a complete technical description of ATS accomplishments, see Chapter 13 of the Compendium.

23. Ibid., pp. 13-2 and 13-3.

24. Ibid., pp. 13-5, 13-18 to 13-25.

25. Ibid.

26. NASA, Office of Space Science and Applications, "Prospectus 1964," Appendix A, pp. 75-76.

27. Memorandum by W.A. Radius, "Study Program on Communications Satellite Policy: Progress Report," 20 May 1965, p. 3. (NASA)

27a. "Index of ATS-1, 3 and 5 User Experiments," n.d. (NASA)

27b. Heather E. Hudson and Edwin B. Parker, "Medical Communications in Alaska by Satellite," *New England Journal of Medicine* 289 (20 December 1973): 1351-56.

28. See "ATS-6 Satellite Health/Education Telecommunications Experiments," National Institute of Education (HEW).

29. *Final Report: Satellite Technology Demonstration,* done for the Federation of Rocky Mountain States, is an official study of these experiments.

30. A seminal study is Jai P. Singh and Dean T. Jamison, "The Satellite Instructional Television Experiment in India: A Case Study."

31. See the NASA Report to the Office of Management and Budget, "NASA Communications Research and Development Program," 8 September 1969. (NASA)

32. Ibid.

33. NASA Press Release No. 73-3, "NASA Program Reductions," 5 January 1973, pp. 2-4. (NASA)

34. U.S., Congress, Senate, Committee on Aeronautical and Space Sciences, *NASA Authorization on Fiscal Year 1974, Hearings,* 93rd Cong., 1st sess., 1973, Part II, pp. 759-60.

35. Ibid., p. 761.

36. James C. Fletcher, "Address to the Armed Forces Communications and Electronics Association," 3 January 1974, p. 1.

37. Ibid., p. 3. In conjunction with the 7 January 1973 decision to phase out

actual space flight experiments, NASA cancelled plans for ATS-G which was designed as a follow-on to ATS-6. (NASA Press Release No. 73-3).

38. Electronics Industries Association. "The NASA R&D Program on Satellite Communications: A Position Paper of the Satellite Telecommunications Section, Communications and Industrial Electronics Division and the Government Products Division," 25 January 1974, p. 9.

39. Ibid.

40. William A. Shumann, "NASA, HEW Oppose Backup ATS-6," *Aviation Week and Space Technology,* 29 July 1974, p. 20.

41. Statement of Senator Frank E. Moss, Chairman of the Senate Aeronautical and Space Sciences Committee, to the EASCON '73 meeting in Washington, D.C., cited from *Telecommunications Reports* 39 (24 September 1973): 17.

42. "NASA Revaluating Its Decision to Abandon Research on Satcom," *Aviation Week and Space Technology,* 3 February 1975, p. 20.

43. See *Telecommunications Reports* 41 (18 August 1975): 27.

44. Ibid.

BIBLIOGRAPHY

The National Aeronautics and Space Administration Historical Archives, Washington, D.C., proved to be a most valuable source of materials for this volume. Particularly helpful were the *Files of Robert Nunn,* former special assistant to the NASA administrator (1960-1962). These files are collected in three volumes: I. Official Papers; II. Industry Matters, III. Internal Memos; Research and Development Programs.

U.N. Documents

U.N. Committee on the Peaceful Uses of Outer Space. *Report of the United Nations Panel Meeting on Satellite Broadcasting Systems for Education.* U.N. Doc. A/AC. 105/128, 5 April 1974. Annex I.

U.N. General Assembly. *The International Covenant of Civil and Political Rights.* G.A. Res. 2200, 16 December 1966.

U.N. General Assembly. *Request for the Inclusion of a Supplementary Item in the Agenda of the Twenty-Seventh Session.* Minister for Foreign Affairs of the U.S.S.R., 9 August 1972.

U.N. General Assembly. *Report of the Legal Sub-Committee on the Work of its Thirteenth Session.* U.N. Doc. A/ AC. 105/133, 6 June 1974.

U.N. General Assembly. *Report of the Legal Sub-Committee on the Work of its Fourteenth Session.* U.N. Doc. A/AC. 105/147, 11 March 1975.

U.N. General Assembly. *Report of the Working Group on Direct Broadcast Satellites at its First Session.* U.N. Doc. A/ AC.105/51, 26 February 1969.

U.N. General Assembly. *Report of the Working Group on Direct Broadcast Satellites at its Second Session.* U.N. Doc. A/ AC. 105/66, 12 August 1969.

U.N. General Assembly. *Report of the Working Group on Direct Broadcast Satellites on its Third Session.* U.N. Doc. A/ AC. 105/83, 25 May 1970.

U.N. General Assembly. *Report of the Working Group on Direct Broadcast Satellites on the Work of its Fourth Session.* U.N. Doc. A/ AC. 105/117, 22 June 1973.

U.N. General Assembly. *Report of the Working Group on Direct Broadcasting Satellites on the Work of its Fifth Session.* U.N. Doc. A/ AC. 105/127, 2 April 1974.

U.N. General Assembly. *Report of the Working Group on Direct Broadcast Satellites: Comments Received from Governments, Specialized Agencies and Other Competent National Bodies.* U.N. Doc. A/ AC. 105/79, 7 April 1970.

U.N. General Assembly. *Working Paper Submitted by France to the Second Session of the Working Group on Direct Broadcast Satellites.* U.N. Doc. A/AC. 105/62, 30 June 1969.
U.N. General Assembly. *Working Paper Submitted by Canada and Sweden to the Second Session of the Working Group on Direct Broadcast Satellites.* U.N. Doc. A/AC. 105/59, 20 June 1969.
U.N. UNESCO. General Conference. *Draft Declaration of Guiding Principles on the Use of Satellite Broadcasting for the Flow of Information, the Spread of Education and Greater Cultural Exchange.* UNESCO Doc. 17c/76, 21 July 1972.
U.N. UNESCO. *Broadcasting From Space.* UNESCO Doc. COM170. XVII.60A. Paris, 1970.
U.N. UNESCO. *Declaration of Guiding Principles in the Use of Satellite Broadcasting for the Free Flow of Information, the Spread of Education and Greater Cultural Exchange.* U.N. Doc. A/ AC. 105/109, 12 February 1973.

Treaties

U.S. Department of State. *Treaty on Principles Governing the Activities of States in the Exploration and Use of Outer Space, Including the Moon and Other Celestial Bodies.* 18 U.S.T. 2410. T.I.A.S. No. 6347. 610 U.N.T.S. 205.

U.S. Statutes

U.S. The Communications Satellite Act of 1962. Public Law 87-624, 87th Cong., *76 Stat. 419*, 31 August 1962.
U.S. The National Aeronautics and Space Act of 1958. Public Law 85-568, 85th Cong., *72 Stat. 426*, 29 July 1958.

Government Documents

U.S. Congress. House. Committee on Government Operations. *Government Operations in Space.* Thirteenth Report, H.R. 445, Appendix D, 1965.
U.S. Congress. House. Committee on Government Operations. *Government Use of Satellite Communications – 1967.* 90th Cong., 1st sess., 1967.
U.S. Congress. House. Committee on Government Operations. *Hearings, Government Use of Satellite Communications.* 89th Cong., 2nd sess., 1966.
U.S. Congress. House. Committee on Government Operations. Subcommittee on Military Operations. *Hearings on Satellite Communications – 1964.* 88th Cong., 2nd sess., 1964. Parts 1 and 2.
U.S. Congress. House. Committee on Government Operations. Subcommittee on Military Operations. *Satellite Communications (Military-Civil Roles and Relationships).* 88th Cong., 2nd sess., 1964.
U.S. Congress. House. Committee on Interstate and Foreign Commerce.

Communications Satellite Act of 1962—The First Year. 88th Cong., 1st sess., 1963.
U.S. Congress. House. Committee on Interstate and Foreign Commerce. *Hearings, Communications Satellites*. 87th Cong., 2nd sess., 1962. Part 2.
U.S. Congress. House. Committee on Science and Astronautics. *Authorizing Appropriations to the National Aeronautics and Space Administration*. 88th Cong., 2nd sess., 1964.
U.S. Congress. House. Committee on Science and Astronautics. *Defense Space Interests*. 87th Cong., 1st sess., 1961.
U.S. Congress. House. Committee on Science and Astronautics. *Hearings, Communications Satellites*, 87th Cong., 1st sess., 1961. Part 1.
U.S. Congress. House. Committee on Science and Astronautics. *Hearings, 1963 NASA Authorization*. 87th Cong., 2nd sess., 1962.
U.S. Congress. House. Committee on Science and Astronautics. *Hearings, Project Advent—Military Communications Satellite Program*. 87th Cong., 2nd sess., 1962.
U.S. Congress. House. Committee on Science and Astronautics. *Hearings, Review of the Space Program*. 86th Cong., 2nd sess., 1960. Part 1.
U.S. Congress. House. Committee on Science and Astronautics. *Hearings, Satellites for World Communications*. 86th Cong., 1st. sess., 1959.
U.S. Congress. House. Committee on Science and Astronautics. *1962 NASA Authorization Hearings*. 87th Cong., 1st sess., 1961.
U.S. Congress. House. Committee on Science and Astronautics. *Project Advent, Military Communications Satellite Program, Report*. 87th Cong., 1st sess., 1961.
U.S. Congress. House. Committee on Science and Astronautics, *Satellites for World Communications, Report*. 86th Cong., 1st sess., 1959.
U.S. Congress. House. Committee on Science and Astronautics. Subcommittee on Applications and Tracking and Data Acquisition. *Hearings, 1964 NASA Authorization*. 88th Cong., 1st sess., 1963. Part 4.
U.S. Congress. House. Committee on Science and Astronautics. Subcommittee on Space Science and Applications. *Hearings, 1965 NASA Authorization*. 88th Cong., 2nd sess., 1964.
U.S. Congress. House. Committee on Science and Astronautics. Subcommittee on Space Science and Applications. *1973 NASA Authorization Hearings*. 92nd Cong., 2nd sess., 1970. Part. 3.
U.S. Congress. House. Select Committee on Astronautics and Space Exploration. *Hearings, Astronautics and Space Exploration*. 85th Cong., 2nd sess., 1958.
U.S. Congress. House. Select Committee on Astronautics and Space Exploration. *The National Space Program*. 85th Cong., 2nd sess., 1958.
U.S. Congress. House. Select Committee on Astronautics and Space Exploration. Staff Report. *The Next Ten Years in Space 1959-1964*. 86th Cong., 1st sess., 1959.
U.S. Congress. Senate. Committee on Aeronautical and Space Sciences.

Communications Satellite Act of 1962. 87th Cong., 2nd sess., 1962.
U.S. Congress. Senate. Committee on Aeronautical and Space Sciences. *Hearings, Communications Satellite Legislation.* 87th Cong., 2nd sess., 1962.
U.S. Congress. Senate. Committee on Aeronautical and Space Sciences. *Hearings, NASA Authorization on Fiscal Year 1974.* 93rd Cong., 1st sess., 1973. Part 2.
U.S. Congress. Senate. Committee on Aeronautical and Space Sciences. *1962 NASA Authorization Hearings.* 87th Cong., 1st sess., 1961.
U.S. Congress. Senate. Committee on Aeronautical and Space Sciences. Staff Report. *Policy Planning for Space Telecommunications.* 86th Cong., 2nd sess., 1960.
U.S. Congress. Senate. Committee on Aeronautical and Space Sciences. *Radio Frequency Control in Space Telecommunications* by E. Wenk. 86th Cong., 2nd sess., 1960.
U.S. Congress. Senate. Committee on Aeronautical and Space Sciences. *Soviet Space Programs 1962-65.* 89th Cong., 2nd sess., 1966.
U.S. Congress. Senate. Committee on Aeronautical and Space Sciences. *Soviet Space Programs 1966-1970.* 92nd Cong., 1st sess., 1971.
U.S. Congress. Senate. Committee on Aeronautical and Space Sciences. Staff Report. *United States International Space Programs.* 89th Cong., 1st sess., 1965.
U.S. Congress. Senate. Committee on Armed Services. Subcommittee on Preparedness Investigating. *Hearings, Inquiry into Satellite and Missile Programs.* 85th Cong., 1st and 2nd sess., 1958. Part 1.
U.S. Congress. Senate. Committee on Commerce. *Communications Satellite Act of 1962.* 87th Cong., 2nd sess., 1962.
U.S. Congress. Senate. Committee on Commerce. *Hearings, Communications Satellite Legislation.* 87th Cong., 2nd sess., 1962.
U.S. Congress. Senate. Committee on Commerce. Subcommittee on Communications. *Hearings, Satellite Communications.* 88th Cong., 1st sess., 1963.
U.S. Congress. Senate. Committee on Foreign Relations. *Communications Satellite Act of 1962.* 87th Cong., 2nd sess., 1962.
U.S. Congress. Senate. Committee on Foreign Relations. *Hearings, Communications Satellite Act of 1962.* 87th Cong., 2nd sess., 1962.
U.S. Congress. Senate. Committee on the Judiciary. Subcommittee on Antitrust and Monopoly. *Hearings, Antitrust Problems of the Satellite Communication System.* 87th Cong., 2nd sess., 1962. Part 1.
U.S. Congress. Senate. Special Committee on Atomic Energy. *Atomic Energy Hearings Pursuant to S. Res. 179,* 79th Cong., 1st sess., 1945. Part 1.
U.S. Congress. Senate. Select Committee on Small Business. Subcommittee on Monopoly. *Hearings, Space Satellite Communications.* 87th Cong., 1st sess., 1961. Parts 1 and 2.
U.S. Department of Commerce. Clearinghouse for Federal Scientific and

Technical Information. "Soviet Views of Communications Satellites and International Relations." Washington, D.C.: Joint Publication Service, 1968.

U.S. Federal Communications Commission. *Decisions and Reports of the Federal Communications Commission of the United States.* Second series, vols. 22 and 35. Washington, D.C. 1971.

U.S. Federal Communications Commission. *First Report on Docket 14024: An Inquiry into the Administrative and Regulatory Problems Relating to the Authorization of Commercially Operable Space Communications Systems.* 24 May 1961.

U.S. Federal Communications Commission. "Memorandum Opinion and Order, in the Matter of Establishment of Domestic Communication Satellite Facilities by Nongovernmental Entities," *34 FCC 2d 1972.* FCC Docket No. 16495, 15 March 1972.

U.S. Federal Communications Commission. "Notice of Inquiry, in the Matter of Establishment of Domestic Noncommon Carrier Communication Satellite Facilities by Nongovernmental Entities." *2 FCC 2d 1966.* FCC No. 16495, 2 March 1966.

U.S. Federal Communications Commission. "Report and Order in the Matter of Establishment of Domestic Communication Satellite Facilities by Nongovernmental Entities." *22 FCC 2d 1970.* FCC Docket No. 16495, 20 March 1970.

U.S. Federal Communications Commission. "Second Report and Order, in the Matter of Establishment of Domestic Communication Satellite Facilities by Nongovernmental Entities," *35 FCC 2d 1972.* FCC No. 16495, 16 June 1972.

U.S. General Services Administration. *Government Organizations Manual 1972-1973.* Office of the Federal Register, National Archives and Records Service. Washington, D.C., 1972.

U.S. National Aeronautics and Space Administration. *Sixth Semiannual Report to Congress, July 1 through December 31, 1961.* Washington, D.C.: NASA, 1962.

U.S. President. *President's Task Force on Communications Policy.* Final Report. Washington, D.C.: U.S. Government Printing Office, 7 December 1968.

U.S. President. *Public Papers of the Presidents of the United States.* Washington, D.C.: Office of the Federal Register, National Archives and Records Service. Dwight D. Eisenhower, 1960-1961.

U.S. President. *Public Papers of the Presidents of the United States.* Washington, D.C.: Office of the Federal Register, National Archives and Records Service. Lyndon Baines Johnson, 1967.

U.S. President. *Public Papers of the Presidents of the United States.* Washington, D.C.: Office of the Federal Register, National Archives and Records Service. John F. Kennedy, 1961.

Interviews

Interview (telephone) with John Briskman, Program Manager Domestic Systems, Comsat General. Washington, D.C., December 1974.

Interview with Albert T. Christensen, Office of User Affairs, NASA Office of Applications. Washington, D.C., 8 August 1974.

Interviews with Leonard Jaffe, Deputy Associate Administrator, NASA Office of Applications. Washington, D.C., 9 August 1974; 3-4 September 1974.

Interviews with Richard Marsten, Director of Communications Programs, NASA Office of Applications. Washington, D.C., 19 November 1973, 19 June 1974.

Interviews with Robert Nunn, former Special Assistant to the NASA Administrator. Washington, D.C., 28 August 1974; Rochester, Minnesota, 2 October 1974.

Interview with Jack Posner, Office of User Affairs, NASA Office of Applications. Washington, D.C., 18 January 1973.

Interview with Walter Radius, Technical Coordinator for Communications, NASA Office of DOD and Interagency Affairs. Washington, D.C., 7 August 1974.

Interview with D.P. Rogers, NASA Office of Applications, Washington, D.C., 19 November 1973.

Books

American Society of International Law (ASIL) Panel on International Telecommunications Policy. *Direct Broadcasting from Satellites: Policies and Problems.* Minneapolis, Minn.: West Publishing Co., 1975.

Aspen Institute Program on Communication and Society. *Control of the Direct Broadcast Satellite: Values in Conflict.* Palo Alto, Calif.: Aspen Institute, 1974.

Chayes, Abram et. al. *International Legal Process.* Vol. I. New York: Little, Brown and Co., 1968.

Clarke, Arthur C., ed. *The Coming of the Space Age.* New York: Meredith Press, 1967.

Clarke, Arthur C. *Voices from the Sky: Previews of the Coming Space Age.* New York: Harper and Row, 1965.

Colino, Richard R. *The Intelsat Definitive Arrangements: Ushering in a New Era in Satellite Telecommunications.* Geneva, Switzerland: The European Broadcasting Union, 1973.

Doctors, Samuel I. *The Role of Federal Agencies in Technology Transfer.* Cambridge, Mass.: MIT Press, 1969.

Emme, Eugene M. *Aeronautics and Astronautics.* Washington, D.C.: National Aeronautics and Space Administration, 1961.

Emme, Eugene M., ed. *History of Rocket Technology.* Detroit: Wayne State University Press, 1964.

Emme, Eugene M. *A History of Space Flight*. New York: Holt, Rinehart and Winston, 1965.
Fortune Editors. *The Space Industry: America's Newest Giant*. Englewood Cliffs, N.J.: Prentice-Hall, 1962.
Frutkin, Arnold W. *International Cooperation in Space*. Englewood Cliffs, N.J.: Prentice-Hall, 1965.
Galloway, Jonathan F. *The Politics and Technology of Satellite Communications*. Lexington, Mass.: D.C. Heath & Co., 1972.
Gruber, William H. and Marquis, Donald G., eds. *Factors in the Transfer of Technology*. Cambridge, Mass.: MIT Press, 1969.
Hale, Edward Everett. *The Brick Moon and Other Stories*. Boston: Little, Brown and Co., 1899.
Jaffe, Leonard. *Communications in Space*. New York: Holt, Rinehart and Winston, 1966.
Jantsch, Erich. *Technical Forecasting in Perspective*. Paris: Organization for Economic Cooperation and Development, 1967.
Kildow, Judith Tegger. *INTELSAT: Policy-maker's Dilemma*. Lexington, Mass.: Lexington Books, 1973.
Medford, Derek. *Environmental Harassment or Technology Assessment?* Amsterdam: Elsevier Scientific Publishing Company, 1973.
Musolf, Lloyd D., ed. *Communications Satellites in Political Orbit*. San Francisco: Chandler Publishing Co., 1968.
O'Neill, William L. *Coming Apart: An Informal History of America in the 1960's*. Chicago: Quadrangle Books, 1971.
Ordway, Adams and Sharpe. *Dividends From Space*. New York: Thomas Y. Crowell Co., 1971.
Parry, Albert. *Russia's Rockets and Missiles*. New York: Doubleday and Co., 1960.
Pelton, Joseph N. *Global Communications Satellite Policy: INTELSAT, Politics and Functionalism*. Mt. Airy, Maryland: Lomond Books, 1974.
Pierce, John R. *Science, Art and Communications*. New York: Clarkson N. Potter, Inc., 1968.
Polcyn, Kenneth A. *An Educator's Guide to Communication Satellite Technology*, Academy for Educational Development, September, 1973.
Rosholt, Robert C. *An Administrative History of NASA, 1958-1963*. Washington, D.C.: NASA, 1966.
Sagan, Carl. *The Cosmic Connection: An Extraterrestrial Perspective*. New York: Dell Publishing Co., 1975.
Shelton, William R. *Man's Conquest of Space*. Washington, D.C.: National Geographic Society, 1968.
Shelton, William. *Soviet Space Exploration: The First Decade*. New York: Washington Square Press, 1968.
Smith, Delbert D. *International Telecommunication Control*. Leyden, Netherlands: A.W. Sijthoff, 1969.
Twentieth Century Fund, Task Force on International Satellite Communica-

tions. *The Future of Satellite Communications*. New York: The Twentieth Century Fund, 1970.
Van Dyke, Vernon. *Pride and Power: Rationale of the American Space Program*. Urbana, Ill.: University of Illinois Press, 1964.

Articles

"Aetna Life to be Partner in CML Satellite System." *Aviation Week and Space Technology*, 6 October 1970.
"Assembly Deadlocks INTELSAT Committee." *Aviation Week and Space Technology*, 8 June 1970.
Bylinsky, Gene. "ERTS Puts the World Under a Microscope." *Fortune*, February 1975.
Chayes, A. and Chazen, L. "Policy Problems in Direct Broadcasting from Satellites." *Stanford Journal of International Studies* 5 (1970): 4-20.
Colino, Richard R. "INTELSAT: Doing Business in Outer Space." *The Columbia Journal of Transnational Law* 6 (Spring 1967).
Comment. "Direct Broadcast Satellites: Implications for Less Developed Countries." *Virginia Journal of International Law* 12 (1971): 66-90.
Comment. "The Outer Space Treaty: An Interpretation in the Light of the No-Sovereignty Provision." *Harvard International Law Journal* 9 (1968).
"Commercial Satellite Usage Enters Second Decade in 1975." *Communications News*, February 1975.
"Comsat Looks to Home." *Business Week*, 17 December 1966.
"Comsat, State Department Split Over Negotiations." *Aviation Week and Space Technology*, 31 March 1969.
Dalfen, C.M. "Direct Satellite Broadcasting: Towards International Arrangements to Transcend and Marshall the Political Realities." *University of Toronto Law Journal* 20 (1970): 366-74.
DeWitt, J.H., Jr., and Stodola, E.K. "Detection of Radio Signals Reflected from the Moon." *Proceedings of the I.R.E.*, March 1949.
Doyle, Stephen E. "Permanent Arrangements for the Global Commercial Communication Satellite System of INTELSAT." *The International Lawyer* 6 (April 1972): 258-89.
Duscha, Julius. "The White House Watch Over TV and the Press." *New York Times Magazine*. 20 August 1972.
"Eisenhower Speaks on Science and Security." *Bulletin of the Atomic Scientists*, December 1957.
"Europe Unifying Policy for INTELSAT Talks." *Aviation Week and Space Technology*, 27 November 1967.
"FCC Staff Splits with OTP over Satellites." *Broadcasting*, 20 March 1972.
Fink, Daniel J. "Refreshing the NASA Charter." *Astronautics and Aeronautics*, December 1973.
Gardner, Richard N. "Space Meteorology and Communications: A Challenge to Science and Diplomacy." *Department of State Bulletin*, 13 May 1963.

"Hoked Up Conspiracy." *New Republic,* 22 July 1972.
"Is FCC Moving to Advocacy of Open-Entry Satellite Plan?" *Broadcasting,* 8 May 1972.
Jaffe, Leonard. "NASA Communication Satellite Developments." *Astronautics and Aerospace Engineering,* September 1963.
Jaffe, Leonard. "NASA Space Applications Program." *Astronautics and Aeronautics,* June 1966.
Johnsen, Katherine. "Ambitious Domestic Satcom Urged." *Aviation Week and Space Technology,* 26 April 1971.
Johnsen, Katherine, "Arabs Hit INTELSAT Subcontracting." *Aviation Week and Space Technology,* 27 January 1969.
Johnsen, Katherine. "INTELSAT IV Program Stresses International Subcontracting." *Aviation Week and Space Technology,* 1 July 1968.
Johnsen, Katherine. "Japan, Australia Offer INTELSAT Compromise." *Aviation Week and Space Technology,* 2 March 1970.
Johnsen, Katherine. "Soviets Plan Major Earth Station as Link to INTELSAT Space System." *Aviation Week and Space Technology,* 8 April 1974.
Johnsen, Katherine. "U.S. Will Fight for INTELSAT Preservation." *Aviation Week and Space Technology,* 21 August 1967.
"Justice Department Slows AT&T Systems Case." *Aviation Week and Space Technology,* 23 August 1971.
Kilty, Lawrence. "American Satellite Builds Vast Government Satellite Network." *Communications News,* February 1975.
Lambeth, Edmund. "Comsat, Ma Bell and ETV." *Nation,* 23 January 1967.
Lessing, Lawrence. "Cinderella in the Sky." *Fortune,* October 1967.
Lessing, Lawrence. "Laying the Great Cable in Space." *Fortune,* July 1961.
McDonald, John. "The Comsat Compromise Starts a Revolution." *Fortune,* October 1965.
McDonald, John. "Getting Our Communication Satellites off the Ground." *Fortune,* July 1972.
Mitchell, Loren H. "The Future of Domestic Satellite Communications." *Stanford Law Review* 19 (May 1967): 1058-81.
Nixon, F.G. "INTELSAT: A Progress Report on the Move Toward Definitive Agreements." *University of Toronto Law Journal* 20 (1970).
Note, "Approaches for Controlling Propaganda and Spillover from Direct Broadcast Satellites." *Stanford Journal of International Studies* 5 (1970): 167-98.
Note, "The United Nations, 27th Session." *Harvard International Law Journal* 14 (1973): 601-11.
O'Lone, Richard G. "U.S. Dominance Seen Hindering INTELSAT." *Aviation Week and Space Technology,* 28 August 1967.
"OTP, CPB Clash Over Funding Bill." *Broadcasting,* 23 August 1971.
Panel Discussion. "Direct Satellite Broadcasting and the Third World." *Columbia Journal of Transnational Law* 13 (1974): 68-80.

Paris, John. "The Politics of Public Broadcasting." *Commonwealth,* 24 November 1972.
"Proposals for U.S. Systems Described." *Aviation Week and Space Technology,* 23 August 1971.
Rabinowitch, Eugene. "After Missiles and Satellites What?" *Bulletin of the Atomic Scientists,* December 1957.
Ridenour, Louis, "Pilot Lights of the Apocalypse." *Fortune,* January 1946.
Ridgeway, James. "Fourth Network." *New Republic,* 17 September 1966.
Ruddy, F.S. "Broadcasting Satellites: An American Perspective," *Lawyer of the Americas* 3 (1971).
"Satcom Bridges Continent with Commercial Satellite Services." *Communications News,* February 1975.
"Satellites Open Up the World of Reliable, Low-Cost Communication." *Communications News,* February 1975.
"Second Pacific INTELSAT IV Begins Commercial Service." *Communications News,* February 1975.
Silberman, C.E. "The Little Bird that Casts a Big Shadow." *Fortune,* February 1967.
Spievak, Edwin B. "Presidential Assault on Telecommunications." *Federal Communications Bar Journal* 23 (1969), part 1.
Telecommunications Reports 40-41 (1974-75), *passim.*
"They're Still Far Apart on Satellites." *Broadcasting,* 24 April 1972.
"Three Firms Volunteer Marisat Funds." *Aviation Week and Space Technology,* 18 June 1973.
"Three More INTELSAT IV-A Satellites to be Developed" *Communications News,* February 1975.
"U.S. Assures Europeans of Satellite Communication Launch." *Aviation Week and Space Technology,* 8 November 1971.
"Westar Domestic Satellite Provides New Answers for Private Telephone Networks." *Communication News,* February 1975.
Wetmore, W.C. "U.S.-Europe Divided on Comsats." *Aviation Week and Space Technology,* 15 July 1968.
"White House Gets into the FCC Act." *Business Week,* 26 July 1969.
"White House Office Recommends Approving All U.S. Satcom Bids." *Aviation Week and Space Technology,* 8 November 1971.
"Whitehead Flexes OTP's Muscle." *Broadcasting,* 17 April 1972.
"Whitehead Prods FCC on Satellites." *Broadcasting,* 1 November 1971.
"Wide-Open Domestic Satellite Policy Recommended." *Broadcasting,* 26 January 1970.
"The World Administrative Radio Conference for Space Telecommunications." *Telecommunications Journal* 38 (October 1971): 673-82.

Studies and Miscellaneous Documents

Ambrose, Mary S. "The National Space Program Phase I: Passage of the

National Aeronautics and Space Act of 1958." M.A. Thesis, American University, 1960.
American Telephone and Telegraph Company. Before the Federal Communications Commission, Docket No. 16495. "Application for a Domestic Communications Satellite System," 3 March 1971.
"ATS-6 Satellite Health/Education Telecommunications Experiments." Washington, D.C.: National Institute of Education (HEW), n.d.
Booz-Allen and Hamilton. "Business Planning Study for a Commercial Telecommuncations Satellite." Prepared for Lockheed Aircraft Corporation, 31 October 1960.
Centre National d'Etudes Spatiales. Papers presented at the International Colloquium on Educational Satellites. Nice, France, May 1971.
Communications Satellite Corporation. The First Ten Years. 1973 Report to the President and Congress. Washington, D.C.: Comsat Corp., July 1973.
Communications Satellite Corporation. "New Venture for a New Decade." Annual Report 1973. Washington, D.C.: Comsat Corp., March 1974.
Communications Satellite Corporation. "Before the Federal Communications Commission, Docket No. 16495: Multipurpose Domestic Satellite Communications System," 1 March 1971.
de Sola Pool, Ithiel. "The Satellite Broadcast Controversy." MIT: A Report for the Center for International Studies, 1974.
Electronic Industries Association. "The NASA R&D Program on Satellite Communications: A Position Paper of the Satellite Telecommunications Section, Communications and Industrial Electronics Division and the Government Products Division." 25 January 1974.
Fairchild Hiller Corporation. "Submissions Concerning Docket No. 16495," Federal Communications Commission, Washington, D.C.
Final Report: Satellite Technology Demonstration. Denver, Colorado: Federation of Rocky Mountain States, 1975.
Fletcher, James C. "Address to the Armed Forces Communications and Electronics Association," 3 January 1974.
Ford Foundation. "Before the Federal Communications Commission in the Matter of the Establishment of Domestic Communication-Satellite Facilities by Non-Governmental Entitities." Docket No. 16495, New York, 1966.
Hughes Aircraft Company. Before the Federal Communications Commission, Docket 16495. vol. 1, "Application for a Domestic Communication Satellite System"; vol. 2, "Application for a Construction Permit for a Domestic Communication Satellite Earth Terminal: San Juan, California"; vol. 3, "Application for a Construction Permit for a Domestic Communication Satellite System Earth Terminal: Califon, N.J."; vol. 4, "Application for Construction Permit for Terrestrial Interconnects." November 1970.
Hughes Aircraft Company. "Commercial Communication Satellite," January 1960.

Hughes Aircraft Company. Space Systems Division. "Syncom III 100-Day Performance Summary," 1 December 1964.

Humphrey, Francis S. "A Resume of Worldwide Commercial Communications." NASA Contract No. NASW-6, Technical Memorandum No. 33-34. Jet Propulsion Laboratory. Pasadena, California: California Institute of Technology, 5 December 1960.

Klein, B.H., Goldsen, J.M. et. al. "Communications Satellites and Public Policy: An Introductory Report." Santa Monica, Calif.: The Rand Corporation, December 1961.

MCI Lockheed Satellite Corporation. "Before the Federal Communications Commission. Docket No. 16495." February 1971.

Midwest Research Institute. "Economic Impact of Stimulated Technological Activity: Part II, Case Study, Technological Progress and Commercialization of Communication Satellites." Report prepared for NASA, 22 November 1971.

"Multidisciplinary Studies of the Social, Economic and Political Impact Resulting from Recent Advances in Satellite Meteorology." Vol. I-V. Madison, Wisconsin: Space Science and Engineering Center, 1971-73.

"NASA Compendium of Satellite Communications Programs." Greenbelt, Md.: Goddard Space Flight Center, June 1973.

NASA Memorandum. "U.S. Domestic Considerations." Washington, D.C.: Radius Files, NASA Headquarters Archive, 30 March 1965.

NASA. "NASA Communications Technology." Presentation to Office of Telecommunications Policy (Clay T. Whitehead) at NASA Headquarters, 15 August 1969.

NASA Office of Programming. "Program Review: Communication and Navigation Problems." 26 October 1965.

NASA Office of Space Science and Applications. "Communications Programs Review," 21 January 1970.

NASA Office of Space Science and Applications. "Prospectus 1964, Appendix A, Goals and Objectives 1965-1980," Washington, D.C.

NASA Office of Space Science and Applications. "Prelaunch Mission Operation Report: Applications Technology Satellite A." Report No. S-630-67-02, 28 March 1967.

NASA Office of Space Science and Applications. "Prelaunch Mission Operation Report: Applications Technology Satellite B." Report No. S-630-66-01, 2 December 1966.

NASA Office of Space Science and Applications. "ATS II Post Launch Report 3." Mission Operation Report No. S-630-67-02, 1 June 1967.

NASA Office of Space Science and Applications. "ATS III Post Launch Report 2." Mission Operation Report No. S-630-67-03, 27 December 1967.

NASA Office of Space Science and Applications. "ATS IV Post Launch Report 2." Mission Operation Report No. S-630-68-04, 28 October 1968.

NASA Office of Space Science and Applications. "Prelaunch Mission Operation Report: Applications Technology Satellite D." Report No. S-630-68-04, 15 July 1968.

NASA Office of Space Science and Applications. "ATS V Post Launch Report 3." Mission Operation Report No. S-630-69-05, 27 January 1970.

NASA Office of Space Science and Applications. "Mission Operation Report: Applications Technology Satellite E." Report No. S-630-69-05, 29 July 1969.

National Academy of Sciences. "Useful Application of Earth Oriented Satellites: Point to Point Communications," Summer Study on Space Applications, Washington, D.C., 1969.

Posner, Jack. "The Implementation of the Communications Satellite Act of 1962." Ph. D. dissertation, American University, 1967.

Project Rand. "Preliminary Design of an Experimental World Circling Spaceship." Report no. SM 11827. Santa Monica, Calif.: Douglas Aircraft Co., 2 May 1946.

Queeney, K.M. "An Analysis of the Role of the United Nations in the Formulation of Principles Governing Direct Broadcast Satellites." Ph.D. dissertation, Ohio University, March 1975.

Radius, W.A. "Study Program on Communications Satellite Policy: Progress Report," 20 May 1965. Washington, D.C.: Radius Files, NASA Headquarters Archives.

Rand Corporation. "Conference on Methods for Studying the Psychological Effects of Unconventional Weapons: Summary Report." Santa Monica, Calif., 21 February 1949.

RCA Global Communications, Inc., and RCA Alaska Communications, Inc. Before the Federal Communications Commission, Docket No. 16495. Vol. 1, "Application for a Domestic Communications Satellite System"; vol. 2, "Applications for Geostationary Communication Satellites"; vol. 3, "Applications for Satellite Earth Stations," 11 March 1971.

Schwartz, Murray L. and Goldsen, Joseph M. "Foreign Participation in Communications Satellite Systems: Implications of the Communications Satellite Act of 1962." Santa Monica, Calif.: The Rand Corporation, February 1963.

Singh, Jai P. and Jamison, Dean T. "The Satellite Instructional Television Experiment: A Case Study." Academy for Educational Development, Report No. 5.

Western Tele-Communications, "Inc. Before the Federal Communications Commission, Docket 16495. Application for a Domestic Communication Satellite System": vol. 1, "System Description of Domestic Communications Satellite System"; vol. 2, "Space Segment of Domestic Communications Satellite System"; vol. 3, "Earth Segment of Domestic Communications Satellite System," 15 March 1971.

Western Union Telegraph Company. "Proposal for a Domestic Communications Satellite System. Before the Federal Communications Commission, Docket 16495." n.d.

INDEX